A Vindication of Judaism
The Polemics of the Hertz *Pentateuch*

This book has been published with the generous support of the Kazis Family Publication Fund

A Vindication of Judaism
The Polemics of the Hertz *Pentateuch*

by

Harvey Warren Meirovich

Foreword by Ismar Schorsch

THE JEWISH THEOLOGICAL SEMINARY OF AMERICA
NEW YORK AND JERUSALEM
1998

Copyright ©1998
The Jewish Theological Seminary of America

Library of Congress Cataloging-in-Publication Data

Meirovich, Harvey W.
    The vindication of Judaism : the polemics of the Hertz Pentateuch / by Harvey Warren Meirovich.
    p. cm. — (The Moreshet series ; v. 14)
    Includes bibliographical references and index.
    ISBN 0-87334-073-6
    1. Hertz, Joseph H. (Joseph Herman), 1872–1946—Contributions in intrepreting the Pentateuch. 2. Bible. O.T. Pentateuch—Criticism, Interpretation, etc., Jewish—History—20th century. 3. Orthodox Judaism—Apologetic works. I. Title. II. Series.
BS1225.H45M45   1997
222'.106'0942—dc21   96–49370
                                                                      CIP

Manufactured in the United States of America

I feel privileged to dedicate this book to my wife, Cheryl, who personifies the definition of love uttered by the medieval Sufi mystic, Jalal ed-Din Rumi: "For when true love awakens, dies the self, that despot, dark and vain." Truly, it was the marvelous integration of her quiet strength and selflessness, along with her abiding friendship and belief in me, which empowered me to bring this labor of love to completion.

September 13, 1996
Erev Rosh Hashana, 5757

Contents

Foreword	ix
Acknowledgments	xiii
Introduction	xv
Chapter 1: Intellectual Roots, Theological Objectives	1
Chapter 2: Inspiration and Perspiration	19
Chapter 3: Biblical Criticism	49
Chapter 4: Hebraism and Hellenism	81
Chapter 5: Aspects of a Jewish Theology	123
Chapter 6: Achievement and Impact	167
Appendix	187
Notes	191
Bibliography	237
Index of Biblical and Rabbinic Citations	255
Index of Names and Subjects	263

Foreword

History swarms with surprises. In November 1938, on the night of Kristallnacht, my father, the last rabbi of the Jewish community in Hanover, was dragged off to Buchenwald. The Nazis could not release him until my mother could produce a visa to England. Forced emigration was still the policy. The visa had been gotten for our family of four by relatives in England through the good offices of the Chief Rabbi of the British Empire, Joseph Herman Hertz. The government had favored him with the token power of securing visas for rabbis from Germany. We arrived in London safely and penniless in December, on the first day of Hanukkah. Thus it would not be an overstatement to say that the first rabbi to graduate from the Jewish Theological Seminary of America on June 14, 1894, saved the life of the three-year-old refugee who would eventually become its sixth chancellor in 1986.

My personal edition of the "Hertz Humash," the celebrated commentary on *The Pentateuch and Haftorahs* by the Chief Rabbi is a two-volume set published in the United States in 1941 (the first American edition). I never replaced it with the more compact one-volume edition which became standard later, because like many youngsters I had received it at the time of my bar mitzva.

The work accompanied me through the ferment of my adolescent years as a sympathetic teacher of Torah. I was drawn to Hertz's vigorous prose, his Jewish pride unthreatened by worldliness and his strong views. I admired his courage to attack what he disdained—the teachings of Charles Darwin and Julius Welhausen, for example—without excessive dogmatism, and his determination to verify the historicity of the Torah. Above all, he gave me a glimpse of a literary corpus still beyond my ken: the world of rabbinic Judaism. Many a conversation on Shabbat with my father was triggered or informed by his commentary.

I suspect Hertz has played a similar role in the lives of many other Jews, young and old alike, over the last two generations. In the millennial history of biblical exegesis never has a Torah commentary been so widely disseminated so quickly. The "Hertz Humash" is part of the history of Judaism in the 20th century. Nor is that achievement due solely to its remarkable degree of elegance, coherence and balance. It appeared in a decade of ominous foreboding. Hertz completed his vast project exactly three years after the Nazis came to power. The ensuing destruction of European Jewry shifted the center of gravity in Jewish life to the English speaking world. Ever mindful of the community for which he wrote, Hertz had forged in advance for the Jews of England and America a tool to sustain their fortitude and faith. As in other dark times, a sudden new Bible commentary (Rashi, Ramban and Abravanel) appeared to offer a fount of consolation to endure a spiritual crisis.

With this masterful study of the "Hertz Humash" by Dr. Harvey Meirovich, I have finally repaid my debts to the Chief Rabbi. Many years ago, when Dr. Meirovich was my doctoral student at the Seminary, I suggested to him to write on the commentary as a cultural monument, a unique summary of Jewish religious thought after a century of stormy exposure to Western science, scholarship and philosophy. Long after the dissertation, Dr. Meirovich stayed with the subject, hopelessly hooked, to enlarge the scope of his biographical research and enrich his analysis of the influences that animated the work. The laudable result is a mature and polished book which should go a long way to shattering the prevailing contempt engendered by over-exposure.

What emerges surprisingly, but beyond a shadow of a doubt, is the Conservative patrimony and coloration of Hertz's commentary. The formidable Protestant scholarship on the Hebrew Bible in the 19th century had driven Sabato Morais and Solomon Schechter, the founders of the Seminary, to grope for an adequate Jewish response. The challenge could not go unmet. Samuel David Luzzatto of Padua had shown the way with his unmatched knowledge of the Hebrew language and highly original biblical commentaries, and Morais, born in Livorno, drew inspiration from Luzzatto. The vision of all three men came to fruition in Hertz's undertaking, as did their common conception of Judaism. The early Seminary owes as much to Padua as it does to Breslau, and the "Hertz Humash" now looms as the fullest and finest statement of its religious position in its formative years.

Ismar Schorsch, Chancellor
Jewish Theological Seminary

Acknowledgments

This book is a major revision and expansion of my doctoral research written under the mentorship of Professor Ismar Schorsch, prior to his appointment as Chancellor of the Jewish Theological Seminary of America. Under his exacting standards of scholarship, I learned the craft of expounding intellectual history. His encouragement, coupled with a Seminary grant, enabled me to prepare my dissertation for presentation to a wider reading public. I thank him for his patience and endurance. Each page of this *oeuvre* bears the weight of his imprint. I am proud and privileged to walk in his footsteps.

I pursued most of my research while a post-rabbinic fellow at the Shalom Hartman Institute, Jerusalem. The intensive study of talmudic texts proved to be a healthy recipe for my task as an historian engaged in the art of conceptualization. My thanks to the Institute's founder and director, Professor David Hartman, and to the fellows of the Institute for their collegiality.

I am indebted to the hard-working library staff of the Judaica Reading Room at the National Library of the Hebrew University, Jerusalem. Their amiability and assistance helped immeasurably to ease the burden of loneliness which sometimes accompanies intensive scholarship.

The archival research so necessary for unravelling the *Sitz im Leben* of the period under review was facilitated by the doyen of *Wissenschaft* rabbinic learning in England, Rabbi Dr. Louis Jacobs. I am also grateful for courtesies extended to me by Dr. Hyam Maccoby of Leo Baeck College, London who gave me unfettered access to the papers of Chief Rabbi Hertz, and allowed me to lock the library doors at night at the close of a day's research.

I express deep appreciation to Ann David Blaff, Toronto, who transplanted my scissors-and-paste research—initially typed on a twenty-five dollar Underwood typewriter—to a computer. Subsequently, it passed the scrutiny of two talented copyeditors, Rabbi Hayim Meyerson, Jerusalem, and Janice Meyerson, New York. I stand in particular awe of Janice's uncanny ability to so completely digest the contents of the manuscript that she knew them as well as I. Dr. Bella Weinberg of St. John's University exerted considerable effort in preparing the indexes, checking references, and enhancing the accuracy of the book. The manuscript was read carefully by a dear friend and colleague, Rabbi Hillel Millgram. I also thank Professor Menahem Schmelzer, Provost of the Jewish Theological Seminary of America, for facilitating and guiding the manuscript through to publication.

I also take pleasure in acknowledging the assistance of my uncle, Toby Meirovich, Regina, Saskatchewan, whose financial backing was instrumental in my three years of relaxed study in Jerusalem, and who responded graciously to another call for help as this work neared completion.

During some trying and dark days in my life, I was the fortunate recipient of professional guidance. My heartfelt gratitude goes out to Dr. Samuel Birenbaum and Tannis Silverstein, Toronto, and to Dr. Aaron Auerbach and David Levinstein, Jerusalem. Several other cherished friends motivated me to persevere in the face of what, at times, seemed to be insurmountable stumbling blocks. Stan and Ritasue Fisher, Janice and Irving Goldfein, Gershon Kekst, my brother Hazzan Moshe Meirovich and my dear parents, Louis and Sally Meirovich, are embodiments of Abraham Joshua Heschel's godly insight: "The mother of medicine is not human curiosity but human compassion."

Aharon, aharon haviv! I am blessed with four wonderful and amazing children: Danya, Ari, Elina, and Batya. They, no less than myself, are witnesses to the birth of this book and the "labor pains" associated with it. They are an ever-present source of joy, inspiration, and renewal for me. I thank them for acting as effective goads, reminding me to balance the passion of scholarship with my need to be their abba.

Introduction

The Hertz *Pentateuch* commentary on the Torah, which was edited in England by Rabbi Dr. Joseph Herman Hertz (1872–1946)—with the assistance of Anglo-Jewish colleagues Joshua Abelson (1873–1940) of Leeds, Abraham Cohen (1887–1957) of Birmingham, Samuel Frampton (1862–1943) of Liverpool, and Gerald Friedlander (1871–1923) and Isidore Epstein (1894–1962) of London—and published between 1929 and 1936, marked the first English commentary on the Pentateuch that was written exclusively by Jews.

Hertz lamented the fact that Judaism was threatened by the Wellhausenian reconstruction of history, which characterized Jewish law (halakhah) as anachronistic as compared with Christianity's relevant emphasis on faith and morality. He was equally vexed by the mounting self-confidence of Liberal or Reform Judaism, particularly the pronouncements of Claude Goldsmid Montefiore (1858–1938), who, in criticizing specific aspects of rabbinic Judaism, believed that Judaism would evolve into a more refined and ethically noble religion by integrating into its ethos specific Christian and Hellenistic teachings. The Hertz *Pentateuch* may thus be read as a defense and glorification of biblical and Jewish civilization and specifically as editor Hertz's personal reaction to the challenge that he perceived Judaism was confronted with from "within" (i.e., the perceived threat of Liberal Judaism) and from "without" (i.e., the Wellhausenian brand of biblical criticism).

In an effort to preserve the integrity of biblical law, the Commentary sought to uphold the contention—using selected evidence from the field of archaeology and philology—that Moses had authored the Pentateuch under divine inspiration and that rabbinic Judaism had evolved legitimately from its biblical roots.

Judaism's legal and ritual system underwent change and modification at the hands of scholars who took account of changing economic and social factors and ethical sensibilities. The Commentary portrayed Judaism as a religion deeply aware of man's need for moral growth, and its overall perception of religion had much in common with the rational, medieval perceptions of Maimonides. Thus, Hertz claimed that cultic sacrifices, miracles, and the Darwinian notion of evolution meshed well with a rationally oriented approach to religion.

In response to Western thinkers who wrote disparagingly of Judaism's morality and who propped up the moral integrity of Greco-Roman civilization and of Christendom, Hertz retaliated polemically by depicting Hellenism and Christianity, and hence Western civilization, as morally deficient. Consequently, specific Jewish humanitarian values as transmitted by God's chosen agents, the Jewish people, were necessary for the spiritual salvation of mankind. It was, therefore, critical that the Jewish people preserve its allegiance to rabbinic law, which functioned as a cementing agent in humanizing and shaping its character, and that the Jewish people nurture a separatistic "ghetto" consciousness in order to protect itself from the spiritual pollutants emitted from Western society. In a secular world heavily infiltrated with pagan value concepts, the Jewish people—aligned with Rabbinism—was a living model of moral sanity. Fortunately, the Western ethos had integrated some of Judaism's ethical insights and would continue to benefit from Judaism's spiritual outlook insofar as it recognized the right and duty of the Jewish people to preserve its religious integrity.

Chapter 1: Intellectual Roots, Theological Objectives

The Enemy from "Without" and "Within"

Cambridge University afforded Solomon Schechter (1847–1915) a fine vantage point from which to evaluate the social and religious matrix of English Jewry. From his chair in rabbinics, he reflected on the internal condition of its religious life and rendered judgment on the attitude of Christian savants toward the biblical and rabbinic heritages. In 1901—one year before his relocation to New York City, where he assumed academic command of the reorganized Jewish Theological Seminary of America—Schechter's verdict appeared in the pages of the *Jewish Chronicle*. He lamented the failure of British Jewry to anchor its youth in an adequate religious commitment. Looking outward toward the general community, he noted the fixation of gentile scholars who propped up the long-reigning charge of Judaism's inferiority and illegitimacy vis-à-vis Christianity:

> It must be clear to everybody ... that the new century does not open under very favourable auspices for Judaism. ... [O]ur Scriptures are the constant object of attack, our history is questioned, and its morality is declared to be an inferior sort. Worst of all is that attitude of the younger generation, who if not directly hostile, are by dint of mere ignorance sadly indifferent to everything Jewish, and incapable of taking the place of their parents in the Synagogue. ... [T]hey are bound to end in that cold critical attitude toward Judaism terminating in drifting away from it altogether.[1]

Schechter pointed to the appalling gap that separated the self-hating twentieth-century Western assimilating Jew from his Eastern European brother; the latter, like the prophets of Israel, envisioned a world that was Judaized.[2]

It was Schechter's considered opinion that an English commentary to the Bible written under Jewish auspices would serve the twofold purpose of countering the external gentile critique of Judaism as well as fortifying a positive Anglo-Jewish allegiance to Jewish sources:

> it is . . . of supreme importance that we repossess ourselves of our Scriptures. . . . I am not unmindful of the profit which the Biblical student may derive from the works of such men as Ewald, Dillmann, Kuenen, and many others of the same schools. But it must not be forgotten that there is such a thing as Christian bias.[3]

It was in reaction to this crisis, and with the hope that Jewish Scriptures might again become an object of edification and study, that Schechter urged the writing of a Jewish commentary to the entire Bible.

Schechter's plea, which he repeated after his move to New York, did not go unheeded. Some years later, it became central in the thinking of Rabbi Joseph Herman Hertz, first graduate of the recently established Jewish Theological Seminary of America. Hertz was born in 1872 in Rebrin (now Zemplinska Siroka, near Michalovce), Slovakia, and grew up on New York City's Lower East Side. He attended The City College in New York and was awarded a doctorate from Columbia University in 1894, the year of his rabbinic ordination. After serving congregations in Syracuse, New York (1894–98), Johannesburg (1898–1911), and New York City (1912), he was appointed chief rabbi of the United Hebrew Congregations of the British Empire in 1913, a position he was to hold until his death in 1946.

Since his demise, Hertz is unquestionably best remembered for the Torah commentary that bears his name, the Hertz *Pentateuch*. The Hertz Commentary[4] may well lay claim to the distinction of having almost single-handedly given shape to the way in which English-speaking Jewish laymen the world over have understood their Judaism over the course of the past two generations.

Officially, Joseph Hertz embarked on the gargantuan enterprise of designing his Torah commentary in 1920. Not until 1929, however, did the first volume—on Genesis—roll off the press, and the final tractate on Deuteronomy did not appear until 1936. During an extremely active and stormy communal career as chief rabbi, Hertz often toiled well into the early hours of the morning, crafting for popular consumption a particular vision of Judaism that was

Chapter 1: Intellectual Roots, Theological Objectives

ideological and edifying. His *oeuvre* bristles with a determination to touch the minds and hearts of his people with a broad-based perception of Judaism that wed halakhic-religious obligation to an ethical base. The sixteen years that he devoted to the project testify to his perseverance and stamina in the face of a voluminous workload as chief rabbi. At the same time, his years of investment define his labor as a mission of sacred love.

After an initial period of failure in launching the project, Hertz succeeded in bringing together a small cadre of research associates (Rev. Joshua Abelson, Rev. Abraham Cohen, and Rev. Gerald Friedlander), all of whom, it turned out, had two qualifications in common—extensive experience as pulpit teachers, and a keen knowledge of and appreciation for Maimonides' rationalist orientation to religion. A fourth collaborator who joined Hertz's research team was Samuel Frampton, chief minister of the Liverpool Old Hebrew Congregation. Periodically, these men submitted drafts on the books of the Torah and Haftarot to Hertz, which he then recast in his own distinctive and honed prose style. In the process, Rabbi Hertz also crafted a sophisticated polemic—vociferously anti-Christian in tone—that unashamedly underscored the halakhic and moral integrity of Judaism as an evolving religious civilization.

The Intellectual Roots of the Hertz *Pentateuch*

It is fair to say that the Hertz *Pentateuch* may be likened to a palimpsest, through which the astute reader can detect the imprint of Hertz's mentors. Their intellectual and theological opinions mesh with remarkable exactitude and neatness with the leitmotifs of the work. The chief rabbi wove choice elements of his teachers' thought patterns with considerable dexterity into the warp and woof of his magnum opus. In retrospect, it should hardly come as a surprise to find echoes of his teachers' doctrines reverberating throughout the pages of the Torah commentary. Three years before his death, the ailing chief rabbi acknowledged that his religious worldview had been substantially shaped by his Seminary teachers, who hailed from the worlds of Sephardic and German-American scholarship.[5]

It is relatively easy to pinpoint whom Hertz had in mind. In the course of the seven years (1887–94) he spent as a Seminary student, two of his most outstanding exemplars were Sabato Morais (1823–97) and Alexander Kohut (1842–94). On the day of his ordination, he singled them both out for special citation, calling the former his "revered patriarch" and the genius who had inspired him, while naming the latter the "giant intellect" who had opened up to him the "vast ocean of talmudic lore," revealing to him the way to become a Jewish scholar.[6] Several years later, Hertz had occasion to repeat these encomiums, noting that he had "the exceptional honor of belonging to the company of Sabato Morais and an Alexander Kohut." So deep ran Hertz's adulation of Morais that he designated him as the "the most potent religious influence in my life."[7]

For purposes of exposition, the principal ideas of these two mentors may be grouped under several headings: defending the Mosaic authorship of the Torah; decoding the Jewish past through the prism of history; recognizing the theme of organic growth as an essential component of rabbinic thinking; and using the tools of rationalism to analyze Judaism.

Hertz and Wellhausen

Because Hertz clearly appreciated the indispensable role of historical scholarship in decoding the Jewish past (see below), it is difficult at first to understand why he stubbornly refused to recognize the legitimacy of this very same discipline when applied by Protestant Bible critics in their efforts at unraveling the historiography of the Pentateuch. Yet he was hardly alone! To a man, his teachers felt only scorn for the main lines of the documentary hypothesis concerning the formation of the biblical text. The main proponents of this hypothesis were German Protestant scholar Julius Wellhausen (1844–1918) and his predecessors, Karl Heinrich Graf (1815–69) and Abraham Kuenen (1828–91).

Conceptually, Wellhausen's reconstruction of Israelite religion rested on the Darwinian axiom of natural evolutionary development, which presupposed an ineluctable movement from simple to complex forms. As applied to biblical history, this meant for Wellhausen that the early Israelites were not strict monotheists, but rather henotheists. The initial period of their sojourn in the desert under Moses was punctuated by a spirit of *joie de vivre* and a worship style suffused with spontaneity. This joyful air was gradually supplanted in the prophetic era by an increasing sense of foreboding and fixation on complex cultic rituals. This process of prescribed religious exercises reached its unfortunate—and artificial—denouement under the scribe Ezra, the actual founder of a lugubrious and legalistic Judaism.

Chapter 1: Intellectual Roots, Theological Objectives

Wellhausen's revisionist historiography amounted to more than merely transplanting the origins of the Pentateuch from the preexilic age of Moses to the postexilic period of the Second Commonwealth. Wellhausen came to his research with a predetermined agenda—the construction of a Christological edifice, at the expense of Jewish behavioral norms that he believed were artificial and divorced from reality. Thus, in Wellhausen's estimation it took the birth of Christianity, with its supreme faith quotient, to restore ultimate sanity to the religious enterprise while transcending the morality of the prophets.[8]

When Hertz proclaimed in the preface to his *Pentateuch* that Wellhausen's perceptions were a perversion of Jewish history, he was repeating the sentiments of both his teachers, Morais and Kohut. In a debate with the leading Reform theologian of the era, Kaufmann Kohler (1843–1926), several months prior to the establishment of the Seminary, Morais declared that he read his Bible without the spectacles of Wellhausen.[9] Several years later, Kohut concurred:

> The sooner we turn away from the Kuenen, Wellhausen hypercritical absurdities, the better we will be off in an unbiased investigation of Holy Scriptures. . . . To us the Pentateuch is a *noli me tangere*! Hands off! We disclaim all honor of handling *sakina harifa mipaska kerai* (*Bava Batra* 111b) "the sharp knife which cuts the Bible into a thousand pieces."[10]

Morais made a point of keeping abreast of the growth of Wellhausen's impact upon the English-speaking public. In an 1881 essay, he dismissed as fallacious the judgment rendered by Wellhausen-inspired, pioneer anthropologist William Robertson Smith (1846–94) that "the Pentateuch was a post-Mosaic invention of an interested priesthood."[11] Years later, when Claude Goldsmid Montefiore, leader of Liberal Judaism in England, sought to make Wellhausen's name an honorable household word among Jewish laymen, Morais sallied forth with a blistering critique, panning Montefiore's polemic, *The Bible for Home Reading*, as offensive to the Jewish spirit. He claimed that the author's Wellhausenian bent desecrated the thrust of Jewish religious life that had been sanctified by the combined Jewish wisdom of the ages.[12] So pervasive was Wellhausen's threat that Morais felt compelled to speak out on January 2, 1887, the day the Seminary officially began classes. The founding father of the Seminary declared that the theological tone of the fledgling institution would remain hostile to the icy-cold criticism and Christian overtones of German-Dutch scholarship: "Never will we suffer an exegesis, as un-Jewish as it is insidious, aye, murderous to our creed, to convert our trained defenders into conspiring foes, and to make the synagogue pulpit bristle with arms ready to fire upon the holy Law."[13]

Mosaic Authorship of the Torah

One of the most striking features of the Hertz Commentary was its tenacious defense of the Mosaic authorship of the Torah and the corollary belief in the historicity of the revelation at Sinai. A prima facie case may be made that this stance automatically identified the chief rabbi as an ideological adherent of Orthodoxy.[14] However, such a conclusion is unwarranted when we consider that an array of non-Orthodox Jewish theologians and historians, whom Hertz held in high esteem, also upheld this belief. *Jüdische Wissenschaft* researchers such as Zacharias Frankel (1801–75), Alexander Kohut, Heinrich Graetz (1817–91), and Sabato Morais[15] all proclaimed public allegiance to the Torah as a divine document transmitted in completed form to Moses.

Alexander Kohut, whose rejection of biblical criticism has already been mentioned, inherited the posture from his mentor, Zacharias Frankel, shaper of European Conservatism.[16] Heinrich Graetz, the national historian of *Jüdische Wissenschaft*, also aligned himself with those who insisted on the unity and preexilic origin of the Pentateuch. Paradoxically, however, Graetz did not hesitate to wield the sharp scalpel of the Bible critics to decipher the ruminations of the prophets and the Hagiographa.[17]

The Prism of History

At the same time, contrary to Orthodox dogma, these same scholars were perfectly willing to promote the notion of historical positivism in reconstructing the history of the oral tradition. It was their unanimous judgment that the explanatory notes and details of biblical legislation that later formed the corpus of the Talmud were not given at Sinai. On the other hand, both Samson Raphael Hirsch (1808–88) and Esriel Hildesheimer (1820–99), deans of German neo-Orthodoxy, built their theological edifices around the very different axiom that God absolutely transmitted and clarified the entire talmudic tradition to Moses atop Sinai.[18]

Morais, like Zacharias Frankel before him, took strong exception to such an ahistorical reading of the Jewish past. It was a "monstrous assertion" to claim that Mount Sinai was the birthplace of the Talmud: "The minds of its most zealous followers never conceived that idea. It is too preposterous to be entertained even by unreasoning fanatics."[19] Morais—and for that matter, Kohut as well—had clearly inherited the operative principle of *Wissenschaft*, that the plain meaning of the Talmud could only be elicited by introducing the category of time. The context of history was decisive in a text's evolutionary journey.

Hertz advanced his teachers' claims one step further. The quest to arrive at the *peshat* (i.e., the actual meaning of the biblical verse in its historical context, in contrast to its later rabbinic interpretation) was greatly facilitated by gathering evidence from the burgeoning fields of Semitic philology and archaeology. These disciplines confirmed that the Israelites had never lived in a cultural vacuum; they had always maintained direct contact with the surrounding pagan civilizations of the ancient Near East. Biblical society had not remained immune to the dominant linguistic and cultural influences of neighboring pagan societies.[20]

Joseph Hertz used philological and archaeological data to support his two major programmatic claims that were opposed to the conclusions of Wellhausenian criticism: 1) Torahitic laws were preexilic,[21] and 2) there were substantive differences in psychology and spirit between Israel and her pagan neighbors. Despite the surface literary resemblances between Israelite and pagan law codes, the moral theology of Israel was *sui generis* and represented a superior spiritual civilization.[22] Rather than perceiving the study of history to be a threat to faith, Hertz co-opted it as an ally in legitimizing Judaism. Hertz had acquired this methodology from instructors such as Cyrus Adler (1863–1940), who taught biblical archaeology at Morais' seminary from 1887 to 1902.[23]

For all the support that the historical method gave him, the chief rabbi held back from drawing the logical conclusion that one ought to distinguish between the divine and human elements that went into the formation of the Torah. Logically, the light cast by archaeology and linguistics upon the *peshat* of the Torah testified, or at least pointed strongly to, direct human input in the composition of the Pentateuch. Yet Hertz resisted drawing this conclusion, deciding instead to resort to the convenient talmudic theological axiom *dibrah torah kilshon bene adam*—God had chosen those forms of literary expression that would be most effective with the hearers to whom they were addressed.[24]

This raises an intriguing historiographical question. What factors compelled scholars like Morais, Kohut, and Hertz to compartmentalize their thinking—on the one hand, denying the presence of a human element in the formation of the Pentateuch while, on the other, insisting on an undogmatic reading of postpentateuchal tracts? What propelled them when interpreting just the Five Books of Moses to sacrifice their cherished scientific methodology on the altar of a simple supernatural faith? What appears at first to reflect a divided intellect becomes more coherent when measured by their compulsive drive to rehabilitate Jewish self-esteem by reconstructing the foundations of faith and the integrity of the halakhah.

This mandate brought into sharp focus the need to thwart the well-disguised—though undeniable—conspiracy against Judaism launched by European Protestant Old Testament scholars. By these scholars' designation of Mosaic legalism as a postexilic fabrication of Ezra and his Pharisaic scribes, the historiography of Graf-Wellhausen meant to deal a death blow to the legitimacy of rabbinic Judaism. Within this context, Hertz's defense of Mosaic authorship of the Torah takes on all the coloration of a polemical response. His teachers' cause became his own. Some two years before Hertz's ordination, Sabato Morais and Alexander Kohut pleaded the case for rescuing the Pentateuch from the onslaught of the "hypercritics."[25] By the time he left the Seminary as a neophyte rabbi, Joseph Hertz was imbued with the need to regain Jewish possession of the Bible![26]

Sabato Morais was motivated by yet another consideration in refusing to grant a dispassionate hearing to the case of the Bible critics: he feared the Seminary might turn out religious skeptics! He took pains to point this out in his 1887 inaugural address to the student body and faculty.[27] His misgivings were shared by the head of American Reform, Isaac Mayer Wise, who, despite his aversion to rabbinic law, held no sympathy for the claims of Wellhausen and his compatriots.[28] Even Wise's eventual successor at the Hebrew Union College, Kaufmann Kohler (who introduced source criticism into the rabbinical school curriculum of HUC), candidly admitted that inherent in the scientific study of Judaism was a marked tendency to produce students who would internalize skepticism, agnosticism, and religious indifference.[29]

This potential danger was not lost on Chief Rabbi Hertz. So zealous was he in his perception of the harm that modern biblical criticism would bring upon the religious consciousness of Jews that he took steps to prevent Zevi Perez Chajes, chief rabbi of Vienna (a proponent of the critical approach to the Bible), from receiving the coveted inaugural lectureship at the Hebrew University.[30] Clearly, Hertz's overall educational blueprint summoned nominal Jews to return to Jewish life. Wellhausen's reconstruction of the biblical past with its underlying Christian ethos constituted, in his estimation, an obvious obstruction. He felt he had little choice but to embark on a public campaign of rebuttal.

Hertz stood at a different point in time from that of the father of *Wissenschaft* learning, Leopold Zunz (1794–1886), who had concealed his support of biblical source criticism from the Jewish community by refusing to publish his research in any Jewish journal.[31] Clearly, hiding this kind of information was no longer possible by the 1920s. The views of the Bible critics were slowly seeping into the consciousness of the Jewish public, most notably in England through the efforts of Claude Goldsmid Montefiore, spiritual expositor of Liberal Judaism. Montefiore touted Wellhausen's reconstruction as the epitome of religious truth. In Hertz's estimation, therefore, the only course of action was to counter the antinomian nihilism of both Wellhausen and Montefiore publicly. The pages of the *Pentateuch* constituted his clarion call to war.

Joseph Hertz's categorical support for the Mosaic authorship of the Torah may thus be best understood not in terms of his presumed Orthodoxy, but as an allegiance to the conservative or traditional wing of *Wissenschaft* scholarship. Following the lead of his mentors, he, too, committed himself to erecting an intellectual barrier that would stem the tide of a biased Protestant historiography while responding to a growing internal specter of Jewish religious skepticism. From a Hertzian perspective, both of these issues—one external, the other internal—necessitated making the case for preserving the moral and halakhic integrity of Judaism.

Tradition and Change

Another leitmotif of the Commentary was the presentation of Judaism as an organic entity displaying legal growth and flexibility.[32] Here, too, Joseph Hertz was indebted to his Seminary teachers. Both Morais and Kohut held that the Jewish legal tradition functioned as an evolving organism. This position led, of course, to their denying the final authority of the *Shulhan Arukh*. Both scholars argued, for example, that there was a pressing need to formulate a modern code of Jewish practice that would factor in the changing sociological reality of American life. Morais spoke to the point in 1875: "we of the present century absolutely need a code where the [ritual] rules . . . are laid down unequivocally, with clearness and brevity, and likewise with due regard to our changed condition."[33]

He returned to the theme a decade later:

> The rabbis, too, were reformers . . . when the liberal applications of the Torah conflicted with the best social interests of the commonwealth, the leading minds in Israel sought, and effectively applied the spirit of Mosaism. No design to conciliate Gentilism in its chameleon-like changes, actuated our sainted preceptors. The alterations which they agreed upon were inspired by an eager wish to maintain the faith, and through their marvelous foresight have we remained imperishable.[34]

Nowhere does Morais' stance of cloaking the tradition in new garb come through more clearly than in his unabashed antipathy toward restoration of the sacrificial cult in a rebuilt temple. Though his personal piety required that he pray for the dawning of such a day, he personally found the notion morally repugnant, a posture that brought down upon him the ire of Judah David Eisenstein, a prominent Orthodox spokesman in New York, who labeled the Seminary president a Conservative Jew.[35]

Alexander Kohut asserted in similar fashion that Judaism responded creatively to the dilemmas posed by each new age:

> The teaching of the ancients we must make our starting point, but we must not lose sight of what is needed in every generation. . . . If the power to make changes was granted to the elders, is not that power given equally to us? "But they were giants," we are told, "and, we, compared with them, are mere pigmies." Perhaps so; let us not forget, however, that a pigmy on a giant's shoulder can see farther than the giant himself.[36]

Morais and Kohut were also of one mind concerning who was ultimately empowered to institute changes in the halakhic tradition. Unlike their left-wing progressive colleagues, Benjamin Szold of Baltimore and Marcus Jastrow of Philadelphia, who entrusted this power to the individual rabbi based exclusively on his personal interpretation of the sources,[37] Kohut and Morais insisted

Chapter 1: Intellectual Roots, Theological Objectives

that legal vitality emanated from the collective judgment of recognized religious authorities.[38]

Chief Rabbi Hertz followed suit. In 1925, he lauded the efforts of the grand rabbi of France, who appealed to the spiritual heads of Eastern European Orthodoxy to relieve the plight of the *agunah* by enacting modifications to the law. Hertz castigated the European rabbinate for failing to take advantage of the inherent flexibility of Jewish religious law, arguing that the rabbinate's intransigence had resulted in the law's "arrested development." Almost in anticipation of its reluctance to act decisively, Hertz favored transferring authority from the European sector to the Jerusalem rabbinate, which, in his estimation, appreciated Jewish law as an "ever-flowing river" and was, therefore, strategically placed to grapple in a bold way with the many problems that baffled the rabbinate in the West. Not surprisingly, this plea found its way into the pages of the *Pentateuch*.[39] Indeed, a major premise of the Commentary was the recognition that changing social realities subjected biblical laws to evolutionary development, modification, and even cancellation by the rabbis.[40]

At the same time, Joseph Hertz was a confirmed traditionalist, committed to preserving the integrity of halakhic observance. Halakhah embodied the will of God no less than did the Israelite experience in the desert. The Pentateuch regularly highlighted the edifying and therapeutic value of the commandments and their power to transform the life of the Jew.[41] Here, too, the chief rabbi had removed a leaf from the notebooks of his mentors, Morais and Kohut. Both scholars held that the canon of history served the dual purpose of legitimizing innovation, flexibility, and development, while—paradoxically—confirming the sacredness of rituals sanctified by centuries of use. Having internalized this lesson from his own teacher, Zacharias Frankel, Alexander Kohut drew attention to the point in his public censure of American Reform, shortly after his arrival upon American shores from Hungary: "That which still has hold upon the hearts of men and women, which still retains vitality should be preserved as sacred. . . . Development does not mean destruction. Recasting is a very different process from casting aside."[42]

A year before the establishment of the Seminary, Sabato Morais pressed home the notion that the process of change was not to be construed as a license for arbitrary innovation. Change carried an inherent caveat: ancient rituals could be cast aside only if there was certainty that what replaced the old was of superior fitness and sterling worth.⁴³

The Rational Orientation of the *Pentateuch*

The glorification of rationalism was another important strand woven into the texture of the Hertz *Pentateuch*. It was also a keystone in the thinking of Sabato Morais. As Morais' diligent disciple, Hertz learned to hold the kabbalah and nonrational approaches to Judaism in contempt. Morais, for example, applauded the devastating blow leveled against mysticism by his own Italian mentor and countryman, Samuel David Luzzatto, who claimed that kabbalah and Judaism were mutually antagonistic because of mysticism's asceticism and "total abstraction from the world."⁴⁴ Morais often railed from the pulpit against nonrational elements that had crept into Judaism. In fact, the very last sermon of his life was a diatribe against religious acts that thwarted reason, specifically the use of *gematria* (assigning numerical values to the letters of the Hebrew alphabet) and the belief in amulets.⁴⁵

Initially, Hertz took up his teacher's hostile posture. In a 1914 sermon, he echoed Morais' critique, equating the kabbalists, the Essenes, and the medieval Karaites with modern Liberal Jews. In his judgment, they were all deviant, schismatic groups who, like Nadab and Abihu, had offered strange fire to the Lord.⁴⁶ However, in 1916, Hertz did an about-face, tendering a more sympathetic appraisal of Jewish mysticism. Its sources, he argued, were authentically rooted in Jewish antiquity—having developed according to their own inner laws—and ran parallel to, and in constant interaction with the other currents of Jewish life.⁴⁷

On two separate occasions in 1924, as he began to devote serious time to writing his Torah commentary, the chief rabbi drew attention to the distinctive contribution of mysticism to the nurturing of the human spirit, likening religion without mysticism to a rose bereft of perfume. At the same time, he took note of the mystical belief in "breaking of the vessels," homiletically applying its notion of chaos and confusion to the tragedy of moral confusion playing itself out on the field of Jewish religious education. He admitted in all candor that it was the antimystical thrust of nineteenth-century *Wissenschaft* historiography that was responsible for the bad press mystical thought had received at the hands of otherwise eminent Jewish scholars. The hour called for rectifying this unfortunate and unwarranted bias by broadening the legitimate religious horizons of Jewish theology.⁴⁸

Nevertheless, as editor of the Commentary, the chief rabbi chose to ignore his own advice. He refrained assiduously from integrating mystical insights into the homiletical framework of the *Pentateuch*. His rejection of the mystical tradition came out, for example, in his categorical claim that only "a few of the Rabbis occasionally lament Eve's share in the poisoning of the human race by the serpent." A reviewer of the commentary to the Book of Genesis was quick to point out, however, that this notion lay at the heart of kabbalistic theology.⁴⁹

The intriguing question, therefore, was why Hertz gave short shrift to mystical doctrines, instead clothing the Commentary in rationalist garb. Hints of an answer can be gleaned from his otherwise generally sympathetic 1916 appraisal of mystic currents in Jewish thought. There he leveled pointed criticisms against what he termed a litany of "degenerate" features within the mystical tradition that were "sad aberration[s] of the human mind." These included the focus on dreams, demons, magic, *notarikon* (the letters of a word being shorthand notes of an ampler statement), and *gematria*. These doctrines provided grist for the mills of both Christian and Karaite detractors of rabbinic Judaism. He was equally disturbed by a sometimes defiant antinomian and antitalmudic tone within mystical sources that at times burst into open revolt.⁵⁰ From the perspective of the twentieth century, these were precisely the kinds of notions that played into the hands of both Christians and Reform Jews seeking to validate their own religious worth at the expense of traditional Judaism.

Hence, it may be argued that Hertz would not have wished to supply his ideological foes with material that could then be used to indict Judaism's authenticity. At the same time, the chief rabbi believed passionately in the axiom that "the best defense is a powerful offense." As a counterpoint to his Christian and Reform detractors, the Commentary unashamedly put forward Judaism's best face to the gentile world by highlighting the impact of Mosaic and rabbinic values on the evolution of Western civilization.⁵¹

Hertz's Affiliation as a Conservative Jew

Another of Joseph Hertz's teachers was Bernard Drachman (1861–1952), who, like Kohut, was an alumnus of the Breslau seminary.

Under Morais, Drachman served on the Seminary faculty in New York as instructor in Bible, Hebrew grammar, and composition. On the occasion of Drachman's celebration of fifty years in the rabbinate, Hertz referred to him as a "beloved and revered teacher." When Schechter arrived at the Seminary in 1902, there was a gradual falling out between him and Drachman, for reasons not entirely known. Drachman's autobiography, however, contains a notation by his son about his father's bitter lament and disillusionment that the Seminary, under Schechter, had departed from its original character as an Orthodox institution.[52] Solomon Schechter, on the other hand, claimed in his presidential inaugural address in 1902 that the reorganized Seminary carried forward the religious spirit and academic integrity of Sabato Morais and Alexander Kohut.[53] Dr. Cyrus Adler, who assumed Schechter's mantle, echoed the same sentiment when he stressed that the mission of the "new Seminary" was "strengthening the Seminary as it was founded."[54]

Which perception was closer to reality, the one expressed by Drachman or the one by Schechter and Adler? By allowing Joseph Hertz to step into this breach and speak, we gain access to the personal evaluation of an alumnus, as to the connection between the original and revamped Seminary, as well as to how he perceived his own relationship with his alma mater.

It can be said unequivocally that Joseph Hertz, as chief rabbi of the British Empire, not only did not sever his relationship with the reorganized Seminary, but continued to identify with its religious ideology under Schechter's leadership and of his successors, Cyrus Adler and Louis Finkelstein (1895–1991). He noted for the public record that the Seminary under Schechter continued the legacy bequeathed by Morais, and that he personally looked upon Schechter as "the Master" ideologue.[55] Moreover, Hertz envisioned the Conservative religious platform of the United Synagogue of America established by Schechter in 1913 as a working model for the Anglo-Jewish rabbinate.[56] He had, in fact, delivered the invocation at the founding meeting of the United Synagogue just prior to his departure for England as chief rabbi-elect.[57]

Hertz's pride in his alma mater took the form of his referring fondly to Jews' College as the sister institution of the Jewish Theological Seminary of America.[58] This identification clearly reflected his deep philosophical affinity with the Seminary. Toward the end of his life, on two separate occasions, Hertz encapsulated his religious philosophy and that of Jews' College as a commitment to "positive historical Judaism,"[59] the phrase formulated by Zacharias Frankel, and later synonymous with the tenets of Conservative Judaism. At a 1925 conference of Anglo-Jewish preachers, he went so far as to equate his brand of Orthodoxy with that of positive historical Judaism.[60] Not only was he aware that this term embodied the religious posture of Zacharias Frankel's Jewish Theological Seminary of Breslau, but he considered the establishment of the Breslau school as "nothing less than epoch-making in modern Jewish spiritual history."[61] Hertz's ideological affinity with Breslau is also mirrored in his felicitous reference to Jews' College as the Jewish Theological Seminary of the British Empire.[62] Hertz's stance stood in sharp contrast, for example, to that of Rabbi Esriel Hildesheimer, the head of the Orthodox Berlin Rabbinerseminar, who personally branded Frankel a heretic whose teachings inevitably produced "hypocrites and worse."[63]

The chief rabbi's spiritual allegiance to Zacharias Frankel and Solomon Schechter was punctuated by labeling his brand of Judaism as "progressive conservatism." By this, he meant "religious advance without loss of traditional Jewish values and without estrangement from the collective consciousness of the House of Israel."[64] Hertz was clearly calling here for a triple fusion: preservation of tradition, validation of historical change and development, and—to invoke the term coined by Solomon Schechter—a reverence for the collective consciousness of "Catholic Israel." In his 1913 inaugural address as chief rabbi, Hertz incorporated the twin Conservative notions of tradition and change transmitted to him personally by Morais and Kohut and, indirectly, through the writings of Solomon Schechter. He noted the authentic tension between adherence to tradition and evolutionary development: "There is no inherent, sacramental virtue in change as change. The new is not always the true.... [At the same time] 'new occasions teach new duties,' and new conditions require new methods."[65]

Thanks to a number of letters that have survived from correspondence between Rabbi Hertz and members of the Seminary administration spanning three decades, it is clear that he retained a staunch identification with the reorganized Seminary. In 1919, the Seminary awarded its first alumnus an honorary doctorate upon his completion of a quarter of a century of rabbinic service. In agreeing to accept the honor, Hertz wrote: "I am gratified more than words can express that my [reward for] twenty-five years [of] striving fearlessly to uphold the ideals of Sabato Morais and Solomon Schechter is to receive such signal recognition at the hands of the Faculty and Directors of my Alma Mater."[66]

Over the next two decades and into the early 1940s, Hertz sustained a warm and collegial correspondence with Cyrus Adler and Louis Finkelstein. As an expression of the pride and admiration he felt toward the Seminary, he was eager to comply with Adler's request—in connection with the Seminary's jubilee celebration—that he place all his publications on deposit at the Seminary library.[67]

The Seminary administration continuously sought out opportunities to highlight its first graduate's spiritual affinity to his alma mater. On at least two occasions in the 1930s, the chief rabbi was invited to deliver the commencement address and charge to the Seminary's graduating rabbis and teachers,[68] and on the occasion of the twenty-fifth anniversary of his appointment as chief rabbi, the Seminary organized a radio tribute to him.[69]

In what may be considered a most eloquent testimony to Joseph Hertz's ideological alignment with the tenets of Conservative Judaism as espoused by Morais, Kohut, and Schechter, Louis Finkelstein was prompted, at the urging of the Seminary faculty, to invite Hertz to visit America for the purpose of delivering four addresses on behalf of the Seminary in the cities of New York, Chicago, Philadelphia, and Boston. The invitation was tendered one month before the outbreak of World War II, and the chief rabbi's "tentative promise" to assist the Seminary came to naught.[70]

Unquestionably, the *pièce de résistance* of Hertz's abiding loyalty and linkage to the reorganized Seminary was conveyed in a remarkably frank letter he composed to Solomon Schechter in 1909 while serving as a congregational rabbi in Johannesburg. He put forward his candidacy to fill the vacant chair of homiletics following the death of its holder, Reverend Joseph Mayor Asher, who had been a protégé of Schechter's at Cambridge.[71] Hertz was even prepared, in principle, to earn less money than a pulpit rabbi, after factoring in what he considered to be "the ideal advantages of a scholar's life." Hertz was quite candid about his qualifications:

> I can write and preach a Jewish sermon. But in addition to Homiletics I could also render good service in other directions. As no man on the Seminary faculty, I know from personal experience the practi-

cal difficulties of the beginner in pulpit, pastoral or communal work. And then should it not be some gratification to a theological institution to have the first graduate occupy its chair of Homiletics, "Pastoral Theology" and—let us say—Apologetics?[72]

Though Schechter's reply is not extant, history recorded that he eventually offered the post to a more recent Seminary graduate, Mordecai Kaplan (1881–1983)! Nevertheless, some four years later, Schechter came to Hertz's defense when, in the final stages of the selection process for chief rabbi of the British Empire, Hertz came under attack from a small but vocal group of local ministers and laymen who questioned his scholarship and his orthodoxy.[73] Word came to Hertz in New York that doubts were being cast on his qualifications, and that an endorsement from Schechter would aid his candidacy. When Schechter was approached, he laughed, being reminded

> of the Hasid who was asked to have *a glezele bronfn* [a nip of whiskey] immediately after the morning service. "It's the wrong time of day," the Hasid replied, *"ahuts dem hob ich shoyn getrunken a gloz bronfn"* [besides, I've had a whole glass of whiskey already]. I've already sent London an all-round recommendation.[74]

In a timely, hard-hitting letter published in the pages of the *Jewish Chronicle* and subsequently read before the selection committee, Schechter wrote a glowing recommendation of Hertz's qualifications:

> Dr. Hertz is a fine Hebrew scholar, even in rabbinics, a great preacher, and an accomplished student in many respects. He must also have had a large experience in pastoral work, to which his long activity in a British colony, composed of most heterogeneous elements, has given him ample opportunity. . . . He is, moreover, a very industrious student, an omnivorous reader, and endowed with a fine philosophic mind, and will, I am sure, constantly grow both in learning and in practical work. I believe that, unless you have a man of his oratory, able to present the ideas and ideals of ancient Judaism in an intelligent and lucid manner, and even to enlist modernity itself in the defense of conservatism, Traditional Judaism will soon be a matter of the past. It is not a question of denouncing Radicalism, which is out of date, but of giving Conservative Judaism a fair chance by explaining and interpreting it in such a manner as to awaken the sympathies and arouse the loyalty and devotion of the congregation to our great heritage. And I thoroughly believe that Dr. Hertz is the man able to accomplish this great task.[75]

Schechter's readiness to lend the considerable weight of his scholarship and piety in backing Hertz was not lost on the Seminary's first graduate. When he, as chief rabbi-elect, and his wife were feted at a Seminary-sponsored banquet a few weeks later, on the eve of their departure for London, Joseph Hertz used the occasion to refer to Schechter as "his best friend on earth" while, at the same time, proclaiming his abiding allegiance to his alma mater: "I want to tell you that I shall always consider myself a post-graduate of the Theological Seminary because its ideals and teachings shall always be mine."[76]

Destiny paved a unique road for Joseph Hertz to travel, one that ultimately transformed him into a major spokesman for Judaism's legitimacy before a doubting Christian world. Simultaneously, he projected to his own people the vibrancy of Jewish life as an evolving religious civilization. Until the end of his life, he was resolute about the rabbinic prerequisites for disseminating Jewish religious teaching and culture. The first two requirements were possession of "wide general culture" and "wide Jewish knowledge." But infinitely more crucial than these was the rabbi's character:

> I have never been oblivious of the fact that it is not knowledge, but conviction, that moves the world . . . I shall mention only one [conviction] which has dominated my life's activities; viz. that the mission of the Jew is, first of all, to be a Jew. Therefore, no compromise with any breaking away from *positive, historical Judaism*.[77]

Chapter 2:
Inspiration and Perspiration

In 1913, Joseph Hertz, the recently appointed chief rabbi of the United Hebrew Congregations of the British Empire, echoed Solomon Schechter's sentiments: only a new generation of qualified teachers could alleviate the state of siege under which committed Jews labored. Hertz saw Judaism as embattled on two fronts:

> Israel is challenged from *without* and *within*, and it is for us a question of life and death to succeed in raising up interpreters—men who will truly and worthily interpret Judaism to its children and thus bridge the chasm between the past and the future; who will justify and vindicate our faith when misunderstood or misrepresented by ignorance or malice, who will make Jews live up to the best of Judaism and, at the same time, bring Judaism—in its institutional and communal aspects—up to the level of the best Jews.[1]

Whom the chief rabbi had in mind when he spoke of the challenge from "without" and "within" may be reasonably ascertained from an analysis of the completed edition of his Commentary to the Pentateuch, published between 1929 and 1936.[2] The phrase "from without" may be taken to refer to the harsh critique of Judaism propagated by the school of higher biblical criticism generally associated with Julius Wellhausen and his disciples.

For more than fifty years, spanning the close of the nineteenth and the beginning of the twentieth centuries, prestigious Bible scholars had systematically and severely called the authenticity and legitimacy of rabbinic Judaism into question. Specifically, their disapproval of Judaism manifested itself in the leveling of two serious charges, the first being that Mosaic religion's professed allegiance to institutional forms of ceremony, cult, and law as described in the Pentateuch was at best nothing more than a "theological fairy tale" and at worst, a fraudulent lie.³ As articulated by the Wellhausenians, the core of ancient Israel's impulse lay, rather, in simple and spontaneous modes of worship and devotion. Lamentably, the founders of Rabbinism had created, *de novo*, both the institutional framework and the ponderous legalisms of the Five Books of Moses. Their zealousness for an institutionally oriented religion prompted them to authorize a deliberate campaign of rewriting and editing of earlier biblical sources. Consequently, Wellhausen and his disciples cast Moses in the role of a proto-rabbi and not as the Sinaitic scribal author of the Torah.

The higher critics' second allegation focused on Rabbinism's inherent moral deficiencies vis-à-vis Christianity. In deed and speech, Jesus provided ample testimony that his teaching had superseded all rabbinic notions of morality. In him, the rabbinic word had become flesh. The unmediated spiritual presence of the founder of Christianity surpassed talmudic exegesis. Conventional Christian theologians claimed that though Rabbinism had deviated tragically from the path leading to the moral treasure, the early Church had successfully mined the spiritual jewels embedded in prophetic faith.

Rabbi Hertz was disturbed by the general affinity shown to both of these theories from "within" the Anglo-Jewish community by the non-Orthodox constituency of Liberal Jews presided over doctrinally by Claude Goldsmid Montefiore.⁴ Hertz maintained that Christians and Jewish Liberals were both bent on minimizing the integrity of the Mosaic code.⁵ At the same time, it was patently clear that the chief rabbi did not regard Montefiore's radical religious posture as malicious. On at least two occasions, Hertz attended receptions tendered by Montefiore.⁶ Furthermore, Hertz and Montefiore corresponded with each other over the years. Each man dissented in an ever respectful manner from the theological views held by the other. Rabbi Hertz, for example, appreciated that Montefiore sent him a copy of his work *Rabbinic Literature and Gospel Teachings*. Hertz complimented the Liberal leader on his "splendid sifting of 'comparative' material," the interpretation of which was "bound to dispense prejudice."⁷ As a token of personal esteem in which he held the Liberal leader, the chief rabbi cabled personal congratulations on Montefiore's eightieth birthday.⁸

Personal fondness and scholarly respect aside, however, the chief rabbi held Montefiore's theology in contempt. In his estimation, it harbored affinities to the anti-Semitic postures of Friedrich Delitzsch (1850–1922) and Julius Wellhausen; moreover, it was insidious.[9] Left unchallenged, Montefiore's religious outlook was potentially life-threatening to traditional[10] Judaism, defined by Hertz in 1923 as "progressive conservatism—the synthesis of the best citizenship and broadest humanitarianism, with the warmth and colour, the depth and discipline of the olden Jewish life in the eyes of our people."[11]

A year after donning the mantle of chief rabbi, Dr. Hertz confidently classified Liberal Jews as a novel, yet isolated schismatic fringe element that posed no immediate danger to the religious and intellectual stability of Anglo-Jewish life.[12] His confidence at that time was obviously not shaken by Montefiore's radical theology and persistent pleading for a spiritual rapprochement with Christianity.[13]

Hertz's perception of Liberalism, however, subsequently underwent a marked metamorphosis. His posture, which was tantamount to neutrality and benign neglect, turned into an almost uncontrollable rage against the Liberals in the mid-twenties; this change of heart was triggered to a considerable degree by pressure brought to bear upon him by rabbinic representatives of Eastern European extraction who had in recent years emigrated to England. They were particularly repulsed by what they perceived as the charlatan "Anglican" image of the English rabbinate personified so graphically by the Victorian rabbinates of Hertz's predecessors, Marcus Adler and Hermann Adler, and they were peeved by the aura of legitimacy accorded Liberal Judaism by a majority of Anglo-Jewry's lay leaders. Overall, this cadre of European-trained rabbis, whose ranks included Hakham Moses Gaster and the future chief rabbi of Israel, Isaac Herzog of Dublin, gravitated to a more insular brand of religious civilization, one with broad ideological sympathy for the religious outlook of Germany's Samson Raphael Hirsch.[14]

By the mid-1920s, Hertz no longer identified Liberalism as a novel and isolated phenomenon possessing "charm," but as a "ruthless radicalism" on a par with American Reform.[15] In 1926, and again the following year, the chief rabbi excoriated the Liberal movement in a series of homiletical tirades delivered from a number of prominent London pulpits. These sermons—virtual diatribes—were reproduced first in the pages of the *Jewish Chronicle*, and subsequently published under the titles *The New Paths:*

Whither Do They Lead? (1926) and *Affirmations of Judaism* (1927). In Hertz's estimation, Liberal Judaism was spiritually sterile and antinomian; its adherents were religious nihilists who had overthrown the historic foundations of Judaism by estranging themselves "from the collective consciousness of the Jewish People." They had willfully gone astray by waging "war against forms and symbols," flirting with the doctrine of the Trinity, adopting an attitude of undiscriminating adulation toward the founder of Christianity, and elevating the Gospels to a level of sanctity. Hertz maintained that their stated intent of holding on "for the present" to rites like circumcision, the shofar, and the Passover seder for "reasons of expediency" were blatantly deceptive.[16] The chief rabbi took umbrage at their aggressive missionary posture in the form of "public propaganda meetings, private canvassing for membership . . . and the adoption of Christian conversionist devices to lure Orthodox Jewish children to their fold." These tactics, Hertz noted, were in violation of a gentlemen's agreement not to interfere with those who found spiritual succor within the traditionalist camp.[17]

In general, Jewish readers were kept abreast, in summary fashion, of Claude Montefiore's theology through the pages of the *Jewish Chronicle*. For example, the newspaper recorded a debate in 1928 on whether Liberalism was an alternative to Orthodoxy, as Montefiore contended, or nearer to being its antithesis.[18] Hertz found particularly inappropriate and indelicate the Liberals' decision to broaden their base of contempt for what they regarded as antiquated Judaism, by bringing their case before non-Jewish readers. When a spate of newspaper articles and interviews appeared signed by Liberals, Hertz dubbed them "sensational." They pointed, in his opinion, to Liberalism's new accommodation with Christianity and, hence, the specter of a growing split within the ranks of British Jewry. One press headline entitled "Liberal Judaism and the Modern State" cast aspersions on the loyalty of Orthodox Jews to king and country.

A 1921 essay penned by Montefiore, which appeared in the monthly review *The Nineteenth Century*, particularly infuriated the chief rabbi, prompting him to deride it as "notorious."[19] Montefiore, who, it is worth noting, was a former student of Solomon Schechter's, claimed before a general audience that the Old Testament, and the Pentateuch in particular, did not enshrine religious and moral perfection. The Hebrew Scriptures were imperfect theological documents; the men who composed them were limited in

Chapter 2: Inspiration and Perspiration

fathoming God's nature. Hence, he argued, there was a categorical need for Liberal Jewish thinkers, and for Christian pathfinders as well, to supplement Old Testament theology.[20]

It was during these years, too, that Hertz became the personal butt of insults leveled at him when the respected newspaper *Jewish Guardian* saw fit to open its pages to pronouncements of Liberal ministers. In fact, one of the most prominent lay leaders of the era, Robert Waley Cohen, notwithstanding his personal sympathies for the Liberal platform, was chagrined over the obvious fact that the *Jewish Guardian* had revealed itself to be a "definite organ of Liberal Judaism" through its "rather intemperate and unpleasant references" to traditional Judaism.[21] In a confession to an intended lay financial backer about a year before the commentary to Genesis was published in 1929, the chief rabbi admitted that he had become utterly compulsive in waging war against Liberal Judaism:

> The cause which occupied my entire time during the last two and a half years has been the defense of Traditional Judaism against the Liberal onslaught without and within the United Synagogue. The series of sermons called The New Paths followed by Affirmations of Judaism took up all my energy. In my opinion, this duty took precedence over all other tasks, and in this matter I alone am judge.[22]

An early confrontation with Liberal Judaism occurred in 1915. It revolved around the personal theology of a promising though brash young minister, Dr. Joseph Hockman, who had been appointed to a prestigious post at the New West End Synagogue, succeeding the late Reverend Simeon Singer. Hockman used the pulpit to call for a liberalization of time-honored Jewish traditions as a means of drawing young people back to the synagogue. His platform, which he classified as Conservative, was, in fact, in alignment with many tenets of Liberal teaching: permission to ride to synagogue on the Sabbath, mixed seating, equality of women in synagogue life, permission to eat nonkosher food, replacement of Hebrew with greater use of English in the worship service, cancellation of the second day of festivals, and reading the Torah using a triennial cycle. His subsequent resignation in the summer of 1915, which, as one perceptive reader realized, was really an expulsion, forestalled an expected broadside from Hertz. Incensed, Hockman saw fit to belittle the Jewish community by dragging his religious premises into the general press, a move for which he was roundly denounced by the editor of the *Jewish Chronicle*.[23] The chief rabbi adopted a posture of not responding directly to Hockman in the Jewish press. A defense of tradition, however, was facilitated through the intervention of others, among whom were friendly colleagues of the ousted rabbi.[24] The Hockman incident showed that the chief rabbi, in not yielding any ground to his junior colleague, had effectively implemented a policy of religious uniformity among United Synagogue spiritual leaders as the preferred way of preserving communal unity.

A particular discomfort for Hertz and like-minded traditionalists, which probably deepened and intensified over time, was Claude Montefiore's publishing feats. The lay expositor of Liberalism published *Liberal Judaism and Hellenism* (1918) and *Old Testament and After* (1923), two extensive works spelling out his revolutionary theology. He also revised and updated two earlier publishing triumphs, *Outlines of Liberal Judaism* (1923), originally written in 1912, and *The Synoptic Gospels* (1927), first penned in 1909. One may add to this collection a short, yet cogently argued 1918 pamphlet, "The English Jew and His Religion," coauthored with Basil L. Q. Henriques. In a nonthreatening, delicate, and congenial style, the coauthors set up two competing theological models of Judaism: the one traditional or Orthodox, the other Reform or Liberal. In gentlemanly fashion, they urged readers to opt for the latter perception of Judaism.

Montefiore had mastered the art of writing popular religious philosophy with a journalistic flair. He brought to his craft a talent for laying out complex and intricate concepts in a straightforward yet compelling fashion. A contemporary critic observed of his literary prowess that he was "earnest to the point of enthusiasm," remarkably able to translate his thoughts "without any kind of reservation," and wrote "with a simple eloquence, the charm of which is that it is always natural and never in any sense forced."[25] It was obvious that anyone prepared to duel with him through the written word—and having the general reader in mind—would have to match his felicity and lucidity for transforming a dull dialectic into a dramatic and entertaining confrontation of ideas. His major books were marketed under the imprimatur of Macmillan, an indication that his writing, though of scholarly bent, was attractive to laymen.

Initial Reactions to Montefiore and Liberal Judaism

An earnest—though in retrospect, immature—effort at challenging and confronting Montefiore's theology was made by Dr. Isidore Epstein, lecturer in Semitic languages at Jews' College. In 1931, Epstein managed to string together inside one book cover several disparate monographs penned mostly between the years 1927 and 1930. The book bore the eye-catching title *Judaism of Tradition*. His purpose was to "lay bare the fundamental error of Liberalism," which had rejected biblical and rabbinic authority. In his prefatory remarks to these essays, Hertz was keen to inform the reader that Epstein was following in the spirit of previous Anglo-Jewish scholars who reached laymen in language they could understand by combining "research and religious thought with a style notable for both lucidity and brilliance."[26]

The chief rabbi's encomium may be appreciated against the literary backdrop of Montefiore's persuasive talents as a popular essayist. *Judaism of Tradition* reflected the same fundamental fears echoed earlier by Hertz in his *The New Paths* and *Affirmations of Judaism*. Thus, Epstein's collected addresses can be read as a companion volume that complemented and reinforced Hertz's traditional posture. At the same time, it was obvious that stylistically, neither Hertz's nor Epstein's anthologies matched the magnetism and eloquence of Montefiore's written word; nor had either traditionalist offered a complete and cogent response to the Liberal leader's religious philosophy. The fashioning of a superlative defense of traditional Judaism was still a dream awaiting realization.

A concrete illustration of the Liberals' coming of age was their pressing for *de jure* recognition as a legitimate religious alternative to mainline Orthodoxy. While Hertz was abroad on an eleven-month pastoral tour of the dominions in 1920, his forceful lay leader, Robert Waley Cohen, conceived a plan calling for the formation of a Liberal rabbinic college to operate in conjunction with Jews' College. The proposal called for both institutions to be governed by a common council. By the time Hertz returned home in the late summer of 1921, the blueprint of the proposed Academy of Jewish Learning was shorn of any rabbinical pretensions and depicted instead a neutral academic institution offering courses in "all presentations of Jewish religion."[27] It was at least as audacious an idea as that conceived back in 1895 by Claude Montefiore when he called for the physical relocation of Jews' College to within proximity of Oxford University. In keeping with his healthy respect for religious pluralism and the sharing of ideas, he encouraged the college to engage in a dialogue and "friendly rivalry with Mansfield and Manchester colleges of the Congregationalists and the Unitarians."[28] Hertz and the principal of Jews' College, Adolph Buechler (1867–1939), vigorously rejected the concept of the Academy being connected in any way to Jews' College. They insisted that if the Academy opened its doors, it had to be governed by its own administration, its own teachers, and housed separately from the College. So adamant was Hertz that it was rumored in the Jewish press that he was prepared to resign rather than succumb to Cohen's pressure.[29] Notwithstanding the eventual demise of the scheme, the move to create a nondenominational academy of learning was in itself testimony to Liberal Jewry's feelings of credibility as a religious movement. From its beginning twenty years earlier, Liberal Judaism was emerging as a viable religious alternative to Hertz's brand of traditional Judaism.

Implementing the Dream of a Jewish Bible Commentary

The notion of an enduring defense of Judaism's integrity and credibility had been crystallizing in Hertz's thinking for some years. It entailed the composition of an adequate popular English Bible commentary suited for synagogue use. The design would have an obvious advantage over the ephemeral impact of the spoken Sabbath and festival sermon on the listening public. As early as 1915, the year of Solomon Schechter's demise, the chief rabbi had charged the Union of Jewish Literary Societies "[not to] shrink from the task of a complete vindication by word and pen and life of our place in the sun. First and foremost comes the Jewish interpretation of the Bible. A Jewish commentary on the Bible is one of the crying needs of Anglo-Jewry."[30]

This theme, repeated frequently in his correspondence (from 1917 to the end of the 1920s), was a way of reinforcing another of his contentions: delegating non-Jews to teach Jewish theology was tantamount to having a stranger write one's love letters.[31] In a 1919 address entitled "Jewish Translation of the Bible in English," Hertz chided gentile Bible exegetes not only for not availing themselves of Jewish contributions to Bible study but, what was worse, for belittling and deprecating Israel's teachings:

> As a result, general Bible versions ... are as a rule, either marred by ignorance of the Hebrew language and the Jewish tradition; by theological prejudice which distorts scores of prophetic passages for Christological purposes; or, in recent decades, by flippancy and

meanness. It is as if a version of Shakespeare were made into Spanish by a Spaniard who had but an imperfect acquaintance with English, and who was, therefore, compelled to use a French translation to help him, and who, at the same time, was filled with hatred and contempt for the British character and the entire British people.[32]

Hence, as he had articulated in his installation sermon back in 1913, the hour demanded the "raising up [of] interpreters . . . who will justify and vindicate our faith when misunderstood or misrepresented by ignorance or malice, who will make Jews live up to the best of Judaism."[33]

In retrospect, it hardly appears accidental that the chief rabbi chose to render his interpretation of Judaism through the instrumentality of a Bible commentary. To be sure, there was the obvious pragmatic consideration of packaging his reading of Judaism together with the weekly cycle of Torah and Haftarah readings, thereby enabling him to touch the minds and hearts of Jews who attended the synagogue. There were, however, two other major considerations that probably affected his decision to adopt the commentary format. At the turn of the century, Solomon Schechter, whom Hertz held in high esteem, had passionately argued the need to compose a distinctly Jewish Bible commentary. In Schechter's estimation, the hour demanded a staunch defense of rabbinic Judaism's legitimacy before the eyes of a Jewish world that all too often concurred with the denigrating gentile critique of Judaism. In his 1899 inaugural address as professor of Hebrew at University College, London, Schechter cut to the core of this Christian verdict, labeling it grossly tendentious:

> The arguments for setting the dates of the documents [of the Bible] cannot possibly have been evolved on merely philological lines. Theological considerations . . . and, above all, the question as to the compatibility of a real living faith with a hearty devotion to the ceremonial law, play at least an equal part therein.[34]

Schechter left no room for doubt concerning the implications of his declaration: it was high time to proclaim publicly the vibrance and glory of Jewish religious civilization, and to restore a full measure of pride among an English-speaking Jewish laity whose Jewish knowledge and practice were far weaker than those of their immigrant parents. He was convinced that only by creating great literature would Jews recover the Bible for themselves and reclaim it, as God had intended, as the pedigree of their nobility.[35]

In May 1913, one month after assuming the mantle of chief rabbi of the British Empire, Joseph Hertz gave public notice of his allegiance to Schechter's vision. In 1915, when Schechter died, Hertz again pointed to the crying need for issuing a biblical commentary that would validate Judaism's legitimacy.[36]

Although Schechter's legacy inspired and gently goaded Hertz to defend the glory of Judaism, the chief rabbi was guided by a long-standing historical rationale: writing Bible commentaries was a time-honored Jewish vocation with a venerable pedigree, particularly when said commentary was packaged in a midrashic casing. The midrashic mode had functioned uniquely through Jewish history as a facilitator, bringing the canonical text into a relationship with the present needs of the community. Thus, it was the genre of midrash, with its compelling quest for meaning, that ultimately licensed Hertz to lay biblical verses bare in the service of a mission he undertook with stoic resolve: uplifting and edifying the spirit of the modern Jew by emancipating him from feelings of self-contempt. The first step in accomplishing this feat required that the emancipated Jew rediscover for himself the infinite wealth and worth of Jewish thought enshrined in the Jewish past. This, it was hoped, would lead in turn to the Jew's reaffirming his faith in the integrity and perennial modernity of Jewish civilization.[37]

In deciding to edit a lay-oriented English Bible commentary, Hertz resolved to enlist the cooperation of gifted researchers with a flair for writing homiletics who were committed to vindicating the spiritual authenticity of Judaism. Notwithstanding his personal passion for Jewish learning, which helped guide and give intellectual substance to his rabbinate, it was obvious that the administrative duties of his office precluded his completing the task unaided.[38] In the first edition of his commentary to Genesis (1929), Hertz outlined his expectation: "An exposition of the plain meaning and ethical values of the Torah would transmit a message of spiritual sustenance in the life of Israel and Humanity";[39] hence, non-Jews were to be included within the orbit of his concerns. Hertz accented this last point to a correspondent: "This undertaking is not merely of denominational interest. The world of non-Jewish scholarship as well must welcome a commentary of the Scriptures from the traditional point of view of the people who have produced these Scriptures."[40] Even more so, there was a pressing mandate to make Jews respect Judaism: "This is . . . Israel's spiritual tragedy today. The very men who should show

Chapter 2: Inspiration and Perspiration

forth to the world its truth and beauty are often in rebellion against Jewish teaching and the whole Jewish life."[41]

Though Hertz's intention to offer a popular biblical commentary can be traced to the years around World War I,[42] October 7, 1920, can be officially declared as the day he launched the project. On that momentous afternoon, a day before his departure on his worldwide pastoral visitation tour of the dominions, Hertz convened a meeting in London of his proposed staff of rabbinic researchers. As subsequently reported in the *Jewish Chronicle*, the chief rabbi enlisted at that time the cooperation of nineteen congregational ministers, several of whom were from the provinces. All agreed to participate in the composition of a popular commentary to the weekly Torah portions, the Haftarot, and the Megillot.[43]

The chief rabbi had a definite format in mind. The Commentary was to be "brief, popular, and homiletic in the highest sense, yet instructive and interesting." He hoped the publisher would be the Oxford University Press and that the layout would be similar to that of the Gaster Mahzor: text printed on one side, translation on the other, with commentary on the lower half, or third, of the page.[44] Each contributor was allotted a specific research assignment. Initially, Hertz assigned the task of editing to himself and to Adolph Buechler (1867–1939), principal of Jews' College. The chief rabbi suggested that the contributors consult as a working model Salomon Herxheimer's German commentary (1841–48), which elucidated the biblical text by inserting pithy notes below the parallel Hebrew text and German translation.[45] Although archaeological and historical data were to be incorporated, focus lay on ensuring that the work have a marked tone of edification: "embody[ing] everything of lasting appeal in Rashi and the Jewish commentators, as well as to utilise modern scholarship, fully to bring out the moral and spiritual teaching of the text."[46]

Precisely for this reason, Hertz in 1923 cautioned one of his early collaborators, Dr. Salis Daiches (1880–1945) of Edinburgh, not to insert complicated philological notations and detailed rabbinic references but to concentrate instead on devotional insights. The chief rabbi informed the Scottish minister, who had graduated from the Hildesheimer seminary in Berlin, that the Commentary was to be stylistically "more in the manner of Rashi than Ibn Ezra [and] less of the halakhic and more of the haggadic in the wider sense of the latter term."[47]

Early Disappointments

Upon Hertz's return to England from his around-the-world pastoral tour, very few of the initial group of ministers had made significant progress with their respective assignments. He had originally expected them to pursue their research, gratis, as a labor of love for Torah. Several of them, however, complained that either their congregational workloads or the need to earn supplementary income had prevented them from devoting the requisite time to the project.[48] In fact, one of the eventual annotators, Reverend Gerald Friedlander, who would die in the summer of 1923, had initially turned down Hertz's research invitation. He based his estimated research time at two to three hours daily, time he could ill afford to devote while serving his congregation and supplementing his salary with private lessons. He alone had earlier warned the chief rabbi: "You will find that unless you pay your collaborators, the work will not be done to time. If it be worth doing, at all, let it be done properly and if you ask for the money for this great venture you will easily get all you require."[49]

By the late fall of 1922, the idea of composing notes to the Megillot had been dropped, and it was around this time that Hertz decided to focus exclusively on a pentateuchal commentary supplemented by notes to the weekly prophetic reading. Furthermore, most of the original nineteen contributors who had met at Hertz's home in the autumn of 1920 had either bowed out of the project voluntarily or, it seems, been requested to do so by Hertz himself. The number of researchers had been reduced to five: Dr. Joshua Abelson of Leeds, Dr. Abraham Cohen of Birmingham, Dr. Salis Daiches of Edinburgh, and Rev. Morris Rosenbaum (1871–1947) and Rev. Gerald Friedlander, both of London. Hertz and Buechler proceeded to engage Friedlander as a subeditor with the understanding that he would "practically devote his entire time to the work."

Friedlander's participation, along with the other coadjutors, was facilitated by the financial backing of Aaron Blashki, a wealthy entrepreneur who had residences in Sydney, Australia, and in London. Hertz received his commitment for support in the spring of 1921 while on his pastoral tour. Blashki and his brother were keen on funding (2,000 pounds sterling to cover publishing) the volumes of the Commentary in tribute to their parents' memories. To this end, they forwarded the chief rabbi an initial sum of 500

Chapter 2: Inspiration and Perspiration

pounds one year later. With this money, the chief rabbi offered a modest honorarium to each of his colleagues, totaling 12 pounds 10 shillings per month's labor, computed on the basis of seventy-two monthly hours of research estimated at three working hours per day.[50]

By June 1923, Morris Rosenbaum had resigned from the project, having devoted half a year in preliminary reading for the Book of Numbers. Within a month, Salis Daiches also departed, feeling disenchanted over the chief rabbi's editorial policy of extensively rewriting and revising the installments submitted to him by the various annotators. In particular, Daiches took strong exception to Hertz's decision to relegate acknowledgment of the name of each commentator to the preface of each volume. Hertz had established at the 1920 inaugural meeting of the collaborators that only the editors' names would appear on the book cover; nevertheless, Daiches had taken for granted that each respective contributor would bear responsibility for his own work and would be given a comparatively free hand in the treatment of his topic.[51]

Originally, Hertz had high hopes of receiving the first draft of the entire *Pentateuch* by the early months of 1923.[52] It was not until the middle of 1924, however, that he had in hand an unedited copy of the complete Torah Commentary.[53] This did not include the submission to him of Haftarah specimens by the Reverend Samuel Frampton of Liverpool. Under the original plan, the Liverpool minister's input was confined to a segment of the Haftarot. His responsibility for researching all the Haftarot was clearly a function of his other colleagues who had failed to fulfill their initial agreements with the chief rabbi. Although Frampton was slow in taking up Hertz's research invitation, primarily for reasons of heavy pulpit responsibilities and a bout of poor health, he turned out to be a most reliable and prodigious researcher. By 1928, his contributions were crossing Hertz's desk in regular—though piecemeal—fashion. In fact, his completed notations on the Haftarot of Genesis did not reach Hertz until three months before the first volume of the Commentary rolled off the press in the late spring of 1929.[54]

Hertz was of the opinion that the manuscripts submitted to him required extensive rewriting. This task became substantially his solo performance. To his regret, his fear that the task of revision would require a great deal of time proved to be prophetic. By 1925, he had "slightly revised" the manuscript of his coadjutors but had not entered into a joint final revision with his editor, who, at the time, was Adolph Buechler.[55] It is patently clear that Buechler's commitment as coeditor never materialized. Within nine months of the publication of the Genesis volume in 1929, he had resigned from the project.[56]

Furthermore, it seems most improbable that the chief rabbi took into account the counsel and input of his research staff when giving ideological shape to the Commentary. This conclusion is substantiated by the fact that joint meetings among the contributors did not occur on a regular basis. For example, in 1923, one year before Hertz had in hand the completed *Pentateuch* in unrevised form, Salis Daiches asked him to call a planning meeting of the respective researchers: "I wonder how the other commentators are getting on? Would it not be advisable to have a meeting of the commentators during the week in which the Preacher's Conference will take place?"[57] In an earlier communiqué of that same year, the chief rabbi informed the Edinburgh minister that he and his coeditor, Adolph Buechler, possessed an "absolute free hand to edit and *harmonize* the various contributions."[58]

A further glimpse of the extent to which Hertz executed his editorial prerogative is revealed in a 1928 draft letter in which the chief rabbi confirmed his and Buechler's "absolute editorial control to amend, condense, amplify or transform any MSS submitted" to them.[59] At the end of January 1928, Hertz received a pointed letter from Wilfred Samuel, lawyer and son-in-law of Aaron Blashki, who at the time was still financing publication of the *Pentateuch*. Samuel observed that Abraham Cohen of Birmingham had tried, at Hertz's request, to revise and rewrite the manuscripts. Yet even after they were settled by Cohen, they remained a disappointment to the chief rabbi. Consequently, in Samuel's opinion, this left Hertz with one of two alternatives: either handing work back to Cohen or applying his own editorial hand to the project. If Hertz chose the latter option, then "it must involve much compression, much revision and rewriting, and the impregnation of the whole Commentary with your own literary style."[60]

The chief rabbi gave evidence of his editorial touch in a letter dispatched a few days later to Rabbi Leo Jung in New York. Hertz noted that the segment of the revised commentary that Jung was receiving on Genesis was "quite different from the MSS" forwarded to him from London some three years earlier.[61] The chief rabbi's use of editorial license is further indicated in a critical

Chapter 2: Inspiration and Perspiration

exchange of letters passed between himself and his three surviving contributors immediately following the publication of Genesis at summer's beginning in 1929. In a joint communiqué, Abelson, Cohen, and Frampton protested that the chief rabbi had repressed proper acknowledgment of their individual efforts by relegating their names to the preface instead of printing them alongside his own name on the book cover. In response, Hertz reminded them that their "contributions [had] been recast and often altogether rewritten by" himself.[62] A few years later, he reiterated this very point to Frampton: the revision work was "an incredible amount of labor, easily ten times the amount of my collaborators."[63]

Almost nine years had separated the official launching of the Torah Commentary in the autumn of 1920 and the appearance in the late spring of 1929 of the first of five scheduled volumes. The actual editorial revision time for the complete project came to twelve years (the chief rabbi possessed an unrevised draft of the Commentary in 1924). The final volume on Deuteronomy did not reach the public until 1936. Aside from the ponderous workload that fell upon him as the spiritual head of Anglo-Jewry, an additional delay, as he himself admitted, was caused by his preoccupation with the "sacred cause" of defending traditional Judaism against the Liberal menace.[64]

The failure to manufacture the five-volume Commentary by the end of 1928 had exhausted the patience of Hertz's sole financial backer, Aaron Blashki, whose support of the venture went back to 1921. It was undeniable that the chief rabbi had not kept his sole benefactor fully informed over the years of the names of his collaborators (with the exception of Gerald Friedlander), of the assignments allocated to them, or of the monies that had been paid out. Nor was Blashki acquainted with the critical fact known to Hertz as early as 1923 that, in addition to Blashki's pledge of 2,000 pounds, at least an additional 2,200 pounds was required in order to market the book at a popular price.[65] Under pressure from Blashki and Wilfred Samuel to bring the project to completion, Hertz committed himself and Buechler in the late fall of 1928 to completing the project according to the following timetable: Genesis by January 1929, Exodus by March 1929, Leviticus by May 1929, Numbers by July 1929, and Deuteronomy by January 1930. The chief rabbi protected his credibility by stipulating that these dates were provisional. As a sign of serious intent, Hertz informed his lay backers that he was "putting in from two to eight hours a day on the revision and rewriting of the Commentary; and, all being well, I intend to do so until the work is finished."⁶⁶

Blashki's forbearance finally snapped when he realized that the original estimate of 2,000 pounds to underwrite the production of 3,000 to 5,000 copies of the *Pentateuch* had more than doubled to 4,200 pounds. He was most agitated at the prospect posed to him by Hertz of having to endow one or two volumes at the outset and then waiting for sales to pay for the publication of the remaining books. Utterly disheartened that Hertz would ever succeed in bringing the task to a successful completion, Blashki suddenly removed his financial backing. He had, to cite his own words, "come to the end of my tether." Ignorant of the fact that the chief rabbi had allocated Blashki's initial down payment of 500 pounds to pay his researchers, Blashki lamented his having to face the prospect of writing off the 500 pounds he had paid to Hertz on account back in 1922.⁶⁷

In reply, Hertz drafted a dignified, but extremely firm rejoinder. He informed his resigning patron that the initial sum of 500 pounds had been well spent "on preliminary work." Over the previous six years, Gerald Friedlander had received payment for investing almost sixteen "weeks" of work; Abraham Cohen, for his fourteen "weeks"; Joshua Abelson, for roughly eleven "weeks"; and Salis Daiches, for his three "weeks." The chief rabbi then underscored for businessman Blashki a basic distinction between mechanical and literary engineering, a point he had brought to Blashki's attention on an earlier occasion: "The law of mental production is unlike the law of mechanical production. A mechanic, if he is sufficiently industrious and skillful, can turn out some useful product every day. But thought cannot be thus manufactured. All cooperative literary undertakings require a long period of time."⁶⁸ Not to be denied his moment of explanation, the chief rabbi acquainted Blashki with other parallel instances of lengthy delays between the launching and completion of a scholar's assignment: the Jewish Publication Society's Bible translation, which was begun in 1892, was not concluded until 1916; and its projected series of Bible commentaries announced in 1918 had yet to see the light of day. In 1904, Bishop Ryle initiated a commentary on Genesis for the Cambridge Bible for Schools; it was not completed until 1914 because the burden of Ryle's daily schedule left him only the leisure summer months to pursue consecutive literary work. Finally, there was the case of Dr. Israel Abrahams, who had every

Chapter 2: Inspiration and Perspiration

intention within a year's time of publishing a series of additional notes to Claude Montefiore's 1909 commentary, *The Synoptic Gospels*. Yet it took Abrahams seven years to complete half of those notes and an additional seven to complete the project. Hertz closed his brief on a note of pride:

> To my still deeper regret, you qualify [your] withdrawal with the remark, I suppose I shall have to write off the 500 pounds which I paid you on account in 1922. To this qualification of your withdrawal I could never consent. At tremendous sacrifice to myself and my family, I herewith refund you the 500 pounds which you advanced to pay for the preliminary work on the commentary. . . . You will thus not be called upon to "write off" anything in connection with an enterprise which was an old cherished dream of mine long before I mentioned it to you in Sydney. . . . I cannot close without thanking you for the encouragement you then gave me as well as for the patience with which during many years you faced our mutual disappointments. The work will continue to engage my best powers until, with the help of God, I shall have published a Chumash with a commentary worthy of Judaism and Jewry in the English-speaking world.[69]

When Blashki received Hertz's letter of explanation accounting for the expenditure, he requested of Hertz to take back the money. Hertz refused because Blashki remained firm in his original critique of Hertz's handling of the entire matter over the previous eight years.[70]

The Qualifications of Hertz's Research Associates

It was obvious from Hertz's original list of nineteen ministers who agreed to contribute to the writing of an English biblical commentary that he was not predisposed to engaging full-time academics on his research team. He gravitated instead to congregational preachers who not only had first-hand knowledge of teaching Torah to laymen but were engaged in the enterprise of imparting to laymen ethical insights colored and molded by Jewish sources. Indeed, three of Hertz's primary collaborators—Abraham Cohen, Joshua Abelson, and Gerald Friedlander—were seasoned rabbinic educators who had been tried and tested in the crucible of pulpit life. Moreover, each had demonstrated an eagerness to pursue research alongside his pastoral duties.

In particular, they showed a marked attraction for the halakhic disquisitions and religious perceptions of Maimonides. The attraction to the medieval philosopher was natural. For example, Abraham Cohen in his *The Teachings of Maimonides* (1927) lauded Maimonides' rational perception of religion in which the supremacy of reason and an emphasis on knowledge were critical for religious comprehension. Core doctrines like revelation, the sacrificial cult, and miracles were presented in the *Pentateuch* as intrinsically compatible with reason. Moreover, as would become apparent in the pages of the Commentary, there was an appreciation for the rabbinic dictum, supported in turn by Maimonides, that expressions of moral truth were to be found outside of strictly Jewish sources.[71]

The full-blown implication of Maimonides' claim, however, was severely circumscribed by Hertz and his colleagues; for, unlike Maimonides, who seriously grappled with and tried to integrate into Jewish theology the radical perceptions and otherness of Aristotle and Plato, Hertz restricted the use of non-Jewish sources in the Commentary to those that confirmed and validated longstanding Jewish perceptions. In one respect, however, this Hertzian approach of culling non-Jewish sources was in itself an innovation, for it deviated conceptually from the approach adopted in the earlier German Torah commentary of Samson Raphael Hirsch. The doyen of modern German Orthodoxy shared with Hertz an antipathy for Reform, but unlike the chief rabbi, he saw no need to validate and verify Jewish truth-claims by marshaling evidence from non-Jewish savants.

As agreed on in principle at the meeting that launched the Commentary in 1920, Hertz recorded the names of his collaborators in the preface to the *Pentateuch*. They were, principally, as previously mentioned: Joshua Abelson, Abraham Cohen, Gerald Friedlander, and Samuel Frampton.

Joshua Abelson, an alumnus of Jews' College, occupied his first pulpits in Cardiff and Bristol, served as principal of Aria College, Portsmouth, and finally settled in Leeds. He wrote two pioneering studies in 1912 and 1913, respectively, that sought to unravel the dynamics of Jewish mysticism. One view that must have endeared him to the chief rabbi, in light of the Hertz *Pentateuch*'s critique of Christianity,[72] was his delegitimization of the conventional distinction between Rabbinism's "outwardness" contrasted with the Christian faith's "inwardness" of heart. Christian theologians, the Leeds minister claimed, were at fault for letting their senti-

Chapter 2: Inspiration and Perspiration

ments block what was an authentic spiritual happening for the rabbinic-minded Jew. Crediting the theological spadework of both Montefiore and Schechter, Abelson asserted with confidence:

> Rabbinic Judaism certainly has a good deal of the outward yoke about it. But it lays quite as much emphasis upon, and ascribes quite as much beauty to the necessity of the inward call. . . . Every outward ceremonial observance which his religion bade him perform was merely the index or symbol of an inward mystical communion with Him.[73]

Abelson also explored Maimonidean issues. At the age of thirty-three, he translated Maimonides' introduction to *Perek Helek* into English, demonstrating not only his command of Hebrew, but his grasp of Arabic. His knowledge of Maimonidean thought can be particularly gleaned from a 1915 thematic overview of Maimonides' teachings in the *Encyclopaedia of Religion and Ethics* and from a 1922 *Jewish Chronicle* piece on Maimonides as a philosopher.[74] In the preparation of the Hertz *Pentateuch*, Abelson contributed manuscripts on Genesis 1–11, Numbers, and the last half of Deuteronomy.

Abraham Cohen, for more than thirty years a dynamic pulpit rabbi in Birmingham, was unquestionably the most prolific of Hertz's colleagues to submit drafts for inclusion in the *Pentateuch*. Hertz relied on him for interpretations to block sections of Genesis, Exodus, Deuteronomy, and the complete book of Leviticus.[75] According to Hertz's system of calculating research time on the basis of two to three hours per day, Cohen had devoted three and a half months to the annotation of Exodus and some five and a half months labor in the composition of Leviticus. In Hertz's estimation, Leviticus was far more difficult to present in a popular way to the lay reader than either Genesis or Exodus.[76] Cohen concurred with this perception, writing that the endeavor was "frightfully difficult" and that it remained to be seen if he could do better than the earlier attempt by Salis Daiches.[77] It should come as little surprise that after the chief rabbi reviewed Cohen's manuscript, submitted in April 1924, he sought further suggestions and annotations from his colleague Morris Rosenbaum in London and from Leo Jung in New York.[78]

A graduate of Jews' College, Cohen regarded his Torah lessons from the pulpit as the central duty of his ministry. In a series of lectures to students at the College on the craftsmanship of homiletics, he called to mind Henry Ward Beecher's distinction between the preacher and teacher: "A preacher is a teacher; but he is more. . . . He looks beyond mere knowledge to the character which that knowledge is to form. It is not enough that men shall *know.* They must *be.* . . . Preaching is the art of moving men from a lower to a higher life."[79]

In co-opting Cohen to his staff of researchers, the chief rabbi had not only engaged an outstanding preacher but an accomplished scholar who had, incidentally, echoed the frustrations of both Schechter and Hertz on the tendentious Christian denigration of the Talmud.[80] Moreover, his pointed defense of Mosaic authorship of the Torah, delivered as a lecture to colleagues at the 1923 Anglo-Jewish Preachers' Conference,[81] was in strict accord with Hertz's published sentiments. Furthermore, like Hertz, he viewed Liberal Judaism as an anarchic movement with nothing positive to contribute to Judaism's welfare.[82] During his illustrious career as a spiritual leader in Birmingham, Abraham Cohen successfully translated several key works of rabbinic literature into English: the tractate of *Berakhot* in 1921, the first ever undertaken; half of *Avodah Zarah* in 1935; and the *Midrash Rabbah* texts of Lamentations and Ecclesiastes in 1939. His 1927 *Teachings of Maimonides,* a thematically arranged anthology of various Maimonidean tracts, showed him to be no mere dilettante, but a diligent student of the medieval philosopher, as did his articles stressing the parallels and contrasts between Maimonides and Aristotle as reflected in the former's *Eight Chapters* and the latter's *Nicomachean Ethics.*[83]

Another Jews' College alumnus who contributed to the Hertz *Pentateuch* was the Reverend Gerald Friedlander, minister for almost a quarter of a century at the Western Synagogue in London. His claim to literary fame rested on his pioneering research in the field of comparative theology, specifically, his tracing of Jewish sources bearing on the Sermon on the Mount. Friedlander was also well-versed in the contents of Claude Montefiore's seminal study, *The Synoptic Gospels,* a book that he regarded as dangerous reading without proper tutorial guidance. He also impugned the integrity of Montefiore's study *Liberal Judaism and Hellenism.*[84] In fact, Friedlander's *The Jewish Sources of the Sermon on the Mount,* published in 1911, challenged Montefiore's adulation of Jesus in his *The Synoptic Gospels.*

Eulogized in the pages of the *Jewish Chronicle* on his death in

1923 as a "sworn foe" of Liberalism and by the chief rabbi as an apologist who defended the originality of Judaism, Friedlander found most disturbing Montefiore's "enthusiastic appreciation of Jesus" and "his unfeigned contempt for the Rabbis." The United Synagogue minister took strong exception to the Liberal leader's designation of talmudic literature as "third- and fourth-rate material," and to his unbalanced obsession to canonize Jesus as a prophet because he was more gifted with genius than the Hebrew prophets and the Rabbis.[85]

Unlike Montefiore, Friedlander perceived nothing novel in Jesus' message that was not already featured prominently in contemporary Jewish sources: "the Jew believes that all the good things which he can find in the Gospels, or in other books of the New Testament, are to be found either in the Old Testament, or else in Jewish, or rabbinic literature."[86]

Friedlander's message to his coreligionists was one of religious triumphalism, an approach echoed in the pages of the Hertz Commentary and one to which Claude Montefiore took strong exception to, particularly in his treatises *Liberal Judaism and Hellenism* and *Old Testament and After*. Gerald Friedlander was equally vigorous in justifying the legitimacy of the yoke of Jewish law incumbent on the Jew. In his estimation, gospel teaching was an easier religious system to abide by than that entrusted by the Rabbis to the Jewish people. Bearing this in mind, the London minister reckoned, as had Maimonides, that Jesus' teachings had their "part to play in the religious training of the world."[87]

Friedlander's works demonstrated a vast erudition of classical Jewish sources, which he peppered generously with Maimonidean citations. As early as 1911, he asked when Anglo-Jewry would print books defending Judaism against the misrepresentations of Christianity. He himself took up this battle in *The Jewish Sources of the Sermon on the Mount*.[88] His writing style was reminiscent of Philo, whom he once described as an "apologist" and "theologian who defended Judaism against atheism, polytheism, or the skeptic of the day."[89] Thus, Hertz had discovered in Friedlander a passionate lover and defender of Rabbinism.

In 1912, Friedlander published *Hellenism and Christianity*. The work was the first ever composed by a Jew to try to lay bare the penetration of Greco-Roman cults and creeds into New Testament Christology.[90] In Friedlander's opinion, this penetration was sufficient ground for a Jew adhering to the faith of his fathers. His less than flattering perception of the roots of Christian theology would be echoed loudly in the pages of the Hertz *Pentateuch*, though in considerably altered form. Whereas Friedlander had merely traced back to various Hellenistic cults the Christian notion of a dying God that came to life again, editor Hertz in his Commentary would have a veritable field day implying that church teachers had consistently allied themselves with the most barbaric features of Hellenistic civilization.[91]

Rounding out Hertz's official team of researchers was Samuel Frampton (originally Friedeberg). His contribution of notes formed the basis for the commentary on the Haftarot to the *Pentateuch*. Frampton served for forty-one years as minister of the Liverpool Old Hebrew Congregation. He received his rabbinic training at Aria College, Portsmouth, and earned an undergraduate degree from London University. He held a lectureship in Hebrew for several years at Liverpool University, and he wrote an annotated Hebrew text on the Book of Joshua.

Early in his tenure, Frampton concurred with Hermann Adler, who was then chief rabbi, that Zionism was an egregious blunder. Under Frampton's spiritual leadership, the Liverpool synagogue had supported the colonization and acquisition of land and farming settlements in Palestine (under the rubric of *Hovevei Zion*) while being known as a hotbed of anti-Zionism. Clearly, the members were troubled by the national aspirations of the Zionist movement, fearing that it might call into question their commitment as British citizens.

Hertz, meanwhile, had labored tirelessly behind the scenes on behalf of the promulgation of the Balfour Declaration, calling for the establishment of a national home for the Jewish people in Palestine. The chief rabbi lost no time in labeling British Jews like Frampton "trembling Israelites." Only in 1917, with the enactment of the Balfour Declaration, did Frampton's congregation reluctantly relinquish its fight against political Zionism. Frampton himself immediately embraced the declaration, which was enormously significant to the Jewish people.[92]

An unacclaimed contributor to the Hertz *Pentateuch* was Jews' College professor Isidore Epstein, whom Hertz acknowledged for his "helpful criticisms" in the production of the Commentary. In fact, Rabbi Epstein's contribution was somewhat more substantive. The composition of a number of the additional notes appended to each book of the *Pentateuch* bore the impress of Epstein's hand, a

Chapter 2: Inspiration and Perspiration

point that Hertz failed to make absolutely clear. He hinted that another hand had assisted him in writing the excursuses in the first editions (1929 and 1930) to Genesis and Exodus: he had written "*nearly* all the additional notes" and had embodied "several useful suggestions by Professor I. Epstein." This, however, contradicted his subsequent claim made in the one-volume 1938 edition of the *Pentateuch* that he was the sole author of these longer notations, a position he fully maintained when they were collected together in his *Sermons, Addresses and Studies*.[93] Though it is certain that, in the main, the excursuses were penned by Hertz himself from previously delivered sermons and addresses, it is equally evident that some of them must be credited directly to Professor Epstein.

Hertz's personal input, for example, was evident in the following Commentary passages: his treatment of the alleged Christological references first appeared in a 1919 lecture, "Jewish Translations of the Bible";[94] the reference in the *Pentateuch* to Professor Sellin, the German exegete and excavator, was first cited by Hertz in a May 22, 1926, sermon;[95] the notes on the Decalogue corresponded to a 1930 address;[96] the complete excursus comparing the Code of Hammurabi with Mosaic civil law was a précis of a March 27, 1928, paper read before the Society for Jewish Jurisprudence and subsequently printed later that year in *The Journal of Comparative Legislation*;[97] the citation of Robert Travers Herford, the English Unitarian theologian, was first quoted in a January 22, 1927, homily;[98] the reference to English philosopher John Stuart Mill was pulled by Hertz from a 1932 sermon;[99] the evaluation of the soul-saving power of the *Shema* was excerpted from a March 30, 1926, sermon;[100] Hertz's defense of God's unity, his denunciation of heathenism's deification of the emperor, his optimistic view of the ultimate triumph of righteousness under the kingdom of God, his critique of the moral chaos of our time, and his praise of little children as the Messiahs of mankind were first published in a 1930 essay entitled "Fundamental Ideals and Proclamations of Judaism";[101] his comments on Jewish education as well as his quotation from Anglo-Jewish folklorist Joseph Jacobs were excerpted from remarks he made at a 1924 education conference in Leeds;[102] the reference to Zunz in the *Pentateuch* was first noted in a December 4, 1926, sermon;[103] his interpretation of the position of women in Judaism appeared first as part of an October 16, 1926, homily;[104] and his severe judgment of Greek civilization was based on a 1932 address delivered at the University of London.[105]

Isidore Epstein's involvement in the composition of the Hertz *Pentateuch* can be confirmed by two illustrations. The first instance relates to editor Hertz's lengthy digression called "Jewish Attitude Towards Evolution," which contained direct quotations from an Epstein essay entitled "Judaism and Modern Knowledge," first published in the *Jewish Chronicle Supplement*[106] and later reprinted in Epstein's *Judaism of Tradition* (1930). For purposes of comparison, the relevant passages from each essay are juxtaposed:

[E]volution is conceivable only as the expression of a creative mind purposing by means of His physical and biological laws that wonderful organism which has reached its climax in Man as we know him today, endowed with rational and intellectual power and energy, capable of appreciating the higher values of life, and the highest ethical and spiritual achievements; in other words a Supreme Universal Intelligence that planned out far back in the recesses of time the great ultimate goal of the works of the beginning.[107]

[E]volution is conceivable only as the activity of a creative Mind purposing by means of physical and biological laws, that wonderful organic development which has reached its climax in a being endowed with rational and moral faculties and capable of high ethical and spiritual achievement; in other words, as the activity of a supreme, directing intelligence that has planned out, far back in the recesses of time, the ultimate goal of creation "last in production, first in thought."[107]

The essential point and truth of the message that man bears the image of God is not affected by the substitution of the dust of the earth, out of which, we are told, the Lord had formed man. Cf. Midrash Gen. Rab., VII, 7.[108]

Whence that dust was taken is not, and cannot be, of fundamental importance. Science holds that man was formed from the lower animals; are they not too 'the dust of the ground'? "And God said, Let the earth bring forth the living creature"—this command, says the Midrash, includes Adam as well.[108]

Its [the Bible's] object is not to teach the human race scientific facts, but the ways of God and the knowledge of the Lord. . . . Its object . . . is not to disclose the knowledge of natural phenomena and natural processes which man is capable of discovering for himself, but rather to convey in a sublime picture language understood by all men of all ages a heavenly message concerning God and Man.[109]

Chapter 2: Inspiration and Perspiration

> Its [the Creation chapter's] object is not to teach scientific facts; but to proclaim highest religious truths respecting God, Man and the Universe.[109]

A second prooftext testifying to Epstein's input can be gleaned from the chief rabbi's brief essay "The Sacrificial Cult," included in the notations to Leviticus. It had all the markings of an early version of Epstein's later 1948 article, "The Conception of Sacrifices in Rabbinic Teaching," which appeared in the Soncino Press English translation of the Babylonian Talmud. In view of the confirming testimony by one of Epstein's former students, Dr. Nahum Sarna, to whom he indicated privately that he had written the scholarly portions of the appendices to the *Pentateuch*,[110] there seems little reason to suspect that Epstein's 1948 article was an enlargement of one that was originally composed by Hertz; rather, the reverse would seem to hold true. By setting the relevant passages from each article side by side, a comparison can be made:

> According to Bible and Talmud, the institution of sacrifice is as old as the human race. The study of primitive man, likewise, traces its origins back to the very beginnings of human society, and declares sacrificial worship to be both an elementary and a universal fact in the history of Religion.... Apart from various unconvincing theories as to the rise of sacrifice, ... [t]he existence of animal sacrifice as a virtually universal custom of mankind from times immemorial proves that the expression of religious feeling in this form is an element of man's nature and, therefore, implanted in him by his Creator. To spiritualize this form of worship, free it from cruel practices and unholy associations, and so regulate the sacrificial cult that it makes for a life of righteousness and holiness, was the task of monotheism.[111]

> The origin of sacrifices is wrapped in obscurity. Many widely differing theories have been propounded in explanation, but all are highly conjectural. All that can be said with certainty is that sacrifices are found to have formed a universal element of worship from the earliest times, and that there are traces among the precursors of Israel of sacrificial practices anterior to those instituted in the Torah.... [T]he universality and antiquity of sacrifices only serve to testify to a deep-rooted sacrificial instinct in the human heart which seeks to respond to the claims of God upon men, and which, like all other instincts, needs correcting, purifying and directing.... It was ... essential to transform the crude ideas and desires concerning man's approach to God by filling them with a spiritual-ethical con-

tent; and it was for securing this end that the sacrifices instituted in the Torah were designed as a most effective means.[111]

Rabbinical Judaism accepted the law of sacrifices without presuming to find a satisfactory explanation of its details. "The sacrificial institutions were an integral part of revealed religion, and had the obligation of statutory law. It was of no practical concern to inquire why the divine Lawgiver had ordained thus and not otherwise. It was enough that he had enjoined upon Israel the observance of them" (Moore).[112]

Essentially rabbinic is the idea of the statutory character of obligatory sacrifices. "The sacrificial institutions," writes Moore, "were an integral part of revealed religion and had the obligation of statutory law. It was not for the interpreters of the law to narrow their scope or subtract from their authority. Nor was it of any practical concern to enquire why the divine lawgiver had ordained thus and not otherwise or indeed ordained them at all. It was enough that he had enjoined upon Israel the observance of them."[112]

Alongside the symbolic interpretation of sacrifice is the so-called juridical. It is advocated by Ibn Ezra and to some extent by Nachmanides. Its essence is: As a sinner, the offender's life is forfeit to God; but by a gracious provision he is permitted to substitute a faultless victim, to which his guilt is, as it were, transferred by the imposition of hands.[113]

Nachmanides . . . prefers to see in sacrifices a moral symbolism founded on a psychological analysis of conduct.[113]

Quite otherwise is the rationalist view of sacrifice held by Maimonides and Abarbanel. Maimonides declares that the sacrificial cult was ordained as an accommodation to the conceptions of a primitive people, and for the purpose of weaning them away from the debased religious rites of their idolatrous neighbours. (See on Lev. XVII, 7). Hence the restriction of the sacrifices to one locality, by which means God kept this particular kind of service within bounds. By a circuitous road, Israel was thus to be led slowly and gradually up to a perception of the highest kind of service, which is spiritual. Abarbanel finds support for Maimonides' view in a striking parable of Rabbi Levi recorded in the Midrash. "A king noticed that his son was wont to eat of the meat of animals that had died of themselves, or that had been torn by beasts. So the king said, 'Let him eat constantly at my table, and he will rid himself of that gross habit.'" So it was with the Israelites, who were sunk in Egyptian idolatry, and were wont to offer their sacrifices on the high places to the demons, and punishment used to come upon them. Thereupon the Holy One, blessed be He, said, "Let them at all times offer their sacrifices before Me in the Tabernacle, and they will be weaned from idolatry, and thus be saved."[114]

Likewise rabbinic in origin is the theory as to the idolatrous associations of voluntary sacrifices, being found in a Midrash which, as already mentioned, Abarbanel cites in his [Maimonides'] support.... R. Phinehas in the name of R. Levi says: The matter may be compared to the case of a king's son who thought he could do what he liked and habitually ate the flesh of *nebeloth* and *terefoth*. Said the king: "I will have him always at my own table, and he will automatically be hedged round" Similarly, because Israel were passionate followers after idolatry in Egypt and used to bring their sacrifices to the satyrs, the Holy One, blessed be He, said: "Let them offer their sacrifice at all times in the Tent of Meeting and they will be separated from idolatry."[114]

Notwithstanding these views, the Rabbis and such thinkers as Maimonides and Abarbanel did not cease to look forward to a restoration of the sacrificial cult in Messianic times.[115]

The view of the sacrifices outlined above has much bearing on the question of their restoration in the future—a restoration which Maimonides in his *Mishneh Torah* includes among the tenets of traditional Judaism.[115]

Isidore Epstein was an obvious asset to Rabbi Hertz. Professor Epstein, who was an alumnus of Jews' College, had practical experience in teaching laymen, having occupied the pulpit of the Middlesborough Hebrew Congregation, London, for seven years prior to his faculty appointment at his alma mater in 1928. Another attractive feature about Rabbi Epstein was his groundbreaking research on the theological implications of Maimonides' legal writings. In 1935, he edited Anglo-Jewish papers written in connection with the eighth centenary of Maimonides' birth, and contributed the essay "Maimonides' Conception of the Law and the Ethical Trend of his Halachah."[116]

The *Pentateuch*:
A Glorification and Defense of Traditional Judaism

The intellectual climate in England was ripe for the launching of a popular work emphasizing the integrity of traditional Judaism. Writing in 1928 of feeling overwhelmed by the truth-claims of

Wellhausenism, a Jewish Bible student begged for "a detailed conservative estimate of Early Hebrew Law. . . . [T]he time is surely ripe for constructive work; the coordination of the results of sound Higher Criticism."[117]

The writer was obviously unaware that within a year's time, a traditional lectionary would appear under Dr. Hertz's signature. Otherwise, the student would not have entered this frustrating plea:

> Will there never be a "Jewish Bible" to oust the International Critical Commentary, the Cambridge Bible, the Centenary Bible and the like? Has the Jewish student always to remain content with drinking from strange fountains? Are the heirs of the biblical treasures to remain content forever to leave their inheritance in the hands of strangers? Too long have we allowed strangers to guard our vineyards without a murmur. It was a crime to wait so long; to delay further is fatal. Is it too much to ask the many adherents of sane views on the Old Testament to consolidate their ranks, and to give a waiting world the *results* of their labour?[118]

The often passionate, exhortative sermons, essays, and monographs of Hertz and his associates testify that Anglo-Jewry was not bereft of pulpit teachers dedicated to fulfilling the aspirations of what has been termed the "conservative bloc" of the *Wissenschaft* movement. Like the German historian Heinrich Graetz, the contributors to the *Pentateuch* envisioned a glorious future for the Jewish people, one replete with a collective sense of dignity and self-worth.[119]

The Hertz *Pentateuch*, appearing more than half a century after Graetz's magnum opus, *The History of the Jews*, echoed the German historian's conviction that Jewish viability was grounded in a reverence for the past: "The Jew is what he is by the history of his fathers, and he would be losing his better self were he to lose hold of his past history."[120]

In a major address celebrating the seventy-fifth anniversary of Jews' College in 1931, Hertz had occasion to sum up his praise of those Jewish scholars who fortified traditional Jewish loyalties:

> They brought to light unsuspected treasures of Jewish aspirations and thoughts; they opened new horizons of Jewish spiritual endeavour and historic achievement; and they revealed to Jews and non-Jews alike the infinite worth and wealth of thought and ideals enshrined in the Jewish past. . . . They taught the Jewish masses that

Chapter 2: Inspiration and Perspiration

Judaism is more than a creed or a theology; greater than a denomination or a church; that it is a religious civilisation.[121]

Hertz was inspired to compose a biblical commentary by Schechter's dream of emancipating Judaism from the critique of gentile detractors. For Hertz, this took the form of defending the unity of the Pentateuch as the revealed will of God and demonstrating that the notion of law was constitutive of Israel's life from her earliest days on into the rabbinic period. Thus, in Hertz's opinion, it was imperative to neutralize Wellhausen's scholarship and thereby demonstrate that the German theologian's reconstruction of Jewish sources was nothing short of "a perversion of history and a desecration of religion."[122] Chapter 3 analyzes Hertz's efforts in this direction.

Equally vexing to Hertz and his colleagues was the specter of religious Liberalism. As the Bible critics were a goad to Hertz and his colleagues, so were reformers like Claude Montefiore and Israel Mattuck (1883–1954). Mattuck, the spiritual leader of London's Liberal synagogue, was noted throughout his career as an arch adversary of Hertz's brand of religion.[123] The chief rabbi was especially irked by the Liberal Jews' praise of many aspects of Christian theology and their urging of spiritual union between what they regarded as the best elements in Judaism and Christianity. Chapter 4 focuses on Hertz's retort to those Gentiles and Jews and, in particular, to Montefiore, who awarded Hellenism and Christianity excellent marks for religious integrity.

Hertz's proud posture as a rabbinic Jew aroused in him a vehement distaste for the higher biblical critics of his day and their intense hostility toward Talmudism. It was also responsible for his deep-seated fear of Montefiore and the Liberals—a fear that intensified as his tenure in office lengthened. He felt he could not ignore a mounting sense of self-confidence within the ranks of Liberal Judaism, nor could he afford to disregard a sustained needling from a Hirschian brand of Orthodoxy to his right.

Hertz was not an innovator but rather an anthologist who, through his wide reading of Jewish and general classics, marshaled the sources of the past to demonstrate the relevance of Judaism for the benefit of English-speaking Jews, the offspring of European immigrants. As editor-in-chief, Hertz was determined to shape his commentary, as he put it, more in the mode of Rashi's homiletical style than the *peshat* orientation of Ibn Ezra. From early on, he set a midrashic mandate before his comrades-in-arms. The finished work, he envisioned, would render a bouquet that was more aggadic than halakhic. At the same time, he welcomed the critical insights of *Wissenschaft* scholarship because it would help punctuate more fully "the moral and spiritual teaching of the text."[124] In other words, unbiased critical research, per se, was not his goal. In fact, he cautioned his associates to steer away from the shoals of pure *Wissenschaft* exercises, which paid painstaking attention to philological notations and detailed rabbinic references. The fruits of scientific inquiry were certainly to be embraced, but only insofar as they proved to be handmaidens in the service of quickening Jewish pride and allegiance to Jewish life and learning.

Hertz did not arrive at this didactic method *de novo*. He had appropriated an insight eloquently articulated almost seventy-five years earlier by Zacharias Frankel, *Wissenschaft* scholar in Germany and intellectual architect of the positive-historical vision of Judaism, the precursor of Conservative Judaism.[125] More to the point, the chief rabbi's perception of how best to exploit "the New Jewish Learning," as he called it, was one of a cluster of notions that intersected directly with teachings transmitted to him by his Seminary instructors. These approached *Wissenschaft des Judentums* not as an end in itself but rather, as a utilitarian tool that could rescue rabbinic tradition and piety from poisoned barbs hurled by an unsympathetic Reform movement on the one hand, and by a hostile Christian, revisionist rewriting of Israelite religion aimed at undermining the legitimacy of rabbinic Judaism, on the other.

Through the pages of his Torah commentary, Chief Rabbi Hertz sought to defend Judaism's legitimacy, all the while glorifying the ethical accomplishments of Jewish civilization. By intentionally choosing a midrashic mode of interpretation, he hoped to demonstrate to the lay reader that biblical-rabbinic texts, properly mined, yielded insights that were edifying and inspiring. Very near to his editorial consciousness was a triumphalist message of the kind uttered in a 1922 address: "The old Jew never claimed equality; he claimed superiority."[126]

Chapter 3:
Biblical Criticism

Judaism's Immaturity and Illegitimacy: View of the Higher Critics

There were many reputable scholars who did not appreciate Hertz's pride in Jewish civilization. There was a broad consensus, particularly among gentile scholars, that rabbinic Judaism was an illegitimate offspring of biblical religion and that it bore little respectability beside the spiritual accomplishments of Christianity.

The claim of Judaism's illegitimacy was as old as the Church itself. However, the theological arguments advanced in the Middle Ages were altered radically at the outset of the modern era. Without the reverent overlay of ancient and medieval Jewish commentary, Baruch de Spinoza[1] had argued that Judaism was a cursed deviation from the path of authentic religion as reflected in the Bible. Christianity, he claimed, was the organic successor to the religion of the Hebrews under the guiding inspiration of Jesus.[2] By the late nineteenth century, Spinoza's proposition, which he argued within a philosophical matrix, was powerfully substantiated and reinforced by two German theologians, Karl Heinrich Graf and Julius Wellhausen. Both scholars were versed in the method of historical literary criticism, a discipline that had gained increasing respect in the two centuries following Spinoza's death.[3]

Julius Wellhausen's historical reconstruction of biblical religion became the property of the broad English-speaking publics in England and in America under the English title *Prolegomena to the History of Ancient Israel* (1885). His research confirmed Spinoza's proposition: Christianity was the valid spiritual heir to the religion of biblical Israel. Pharisaic or rabbinic Judaism, on the other hand, was portrayed as a deviant expression of a healthy religion, especially when compared with the dominant moral thrust so evident in the teachings of Israel's prophets. Unlike Spinoza, whose assault was launched on the Pentateuch in its final redacted form, Wellhausen tested his thesis by availing himself of the documentary hypothesis of higher biblical criticism. The central argument supporting the theory was that Moses was not the scribal author of the Pentateuch, which was, rather, "a composite work, the product of many hands and periods." Four major pentateuchal documents were discernible: J (Yahwist), E (Elohist), D (Deuteronomy), and P (Priestly). Whereas the three preexilic sources—J, E, and D—reflected "the life of a natural people," the fourth source, P, was a postexilic creation that embodied the religious perceptions of guilt and gloom associated with proto-Pharisaism. The Priestly Code constituted the building block for the rabbinic theocracy of the Second Jewish Commonwealth.[4]

According to Wellhausen, the authentic stimulus of biblical religion emanated from the heart; religious spontaneity and thanksgiving were the hallmarks of preexilic life. Israel's leading lights, the prophets, spoke not about legalism, institutionalized ritualism, and sin offerings, which were the prime concerns of P, but of morality and the joy of worship.[5] Thus, Wellhausen concluded that the formation of the desert theocracy attributed to Moses was a clever creation of the Pharisaic scribes of the Second Temple period, who projected backward in time the thoughts and institutions of their own day.[6] Hence, "Judaism is an irregular product of history. . . . [I]t had an entirely different physiognomy from that of Hebrew antiquity, so much so that it is hard to catch a likeness. . . . [I]t commands and blocks up the access to heaven. As far as it can, it takes the soul out of religion and spoils morality."[7]

Conceptually, the school of Graf-Wellhausen claimed that it was necessary to superimpose an evolutionary mode of interpretation on the biblical text in order to decipher the religious life of ancient Israel. Historically, this meant Israel's religion had grown gradually from the simple to the complex. The cogency of the theory was predicated on the transposition of the Priestly Code, with its elaborate cultic-ritual regulations from a preexilic to a postexilic setting.[8] Wellhausen's view was corroborated by William Robertson Smith, the Cambridge University Arabist who made his mark in the virgin field of cultural anthropology. Smith maintained that early

Chapter 3: Biblical Criticism

Hebrew worship, like all civilized nature religions of antiquity, was a pleasurable affair untrammeled by a sense of trespass:

> In a religion of this kind there is no room for an abiding sense of sin and unworthiness. . . . [T]he nations of Palestine in the seventh century B.C. afforded an excellent illustration of the development of a gloomier type of worship under the pressure of accumulated political disasters.[9]

Wellhausen and Smith concurred that Israel had advanced unilinearly from a primitive belief in monolatry to the ultimate religious plateau of ethical monotheism under the inspiration and guidance of Israel's prophets. Only through gross error of judgment—ascribed to Ezekiel and Ezra—had the threads of prophetic monotheism become entangled in a hierocratic web. The feeling of national guilt, which had its beginnings in the reign of Manasseh in the seventh century, became all-pervasive with the demise of the First Commonwealth. It was this tone of despair that was incorporated into the Second Temple cult by the proto-rabbinic authors of the Priestly Code.[10]

The brilliant Oxford Bible scholar and theologian Samuel Rolles Driver (1846–1914), placed his seal of approval on Wellhausen. From his church pulpit, he spoke of an unbridgeable chasm between spirituality and law:

> The Old Testament must always share with the New Testament the position of forming a standard of pure and spiritual religion, in contradistinction to all formalism. . . . The parts of the Old Testament which . . . in the late period of Jewish history did lend themselves to exaggeration or perversion, in the direction of outward ceremonialism, are just those which were abrogated by the coming of Christ. . . . Viewed humanly, Christianity . . . took the form of a reaction against the paralyzing influences of Rabbinism, a reaction resting primarily upon a return to the more spiritual religion of the prophets.[11]

A significant reaction to this interpretation of Judaism came from Solomon Schechter. In his 1899 inaugural lecture as professor of Hebrew at University College, London, Schechter contended that many higher Bible critics were motivated by theological and not purely philological concerns. Their conclusions were tendentious: "The arguments for setting the dates of the various documents cannot possibly have been evolved on merely philological lines. Theological considerations . . . and, above all, the question as to the compatibility of a real living faith with a hearty devotion to the ceremonial law, play at least an equal part therein."[12] Schechter was reconfirming an observation he had noted several years earlier. At that time, he observed sarcastically how professors of higher criticism were deluding themselves in comparing Jewish law to a crushing weight, for the living witness of millions of observant Jews testified otherwise.[13]

Schechter must have also been troubled by Smith's *Lectures on the Religion of the Semites,* delivered publicly in 1889, one year before Schechter's arrival at Cambridge as lecturer in Talmudics.[14] Smith was one of the scholars most responsible for transplanting Wellhausen's reputation to Great Britain. He had firsthand familiarity with Wellhausen's views, not only having composed the preface to Wellhausen's *Prolegomena* but having invited the German theologian from Greifswald to break away from his academic responsibilities and holiday with him on the English coast.[15]

Smith's innovation as a cultural anthropologist was his cloaking the idea of Judaism as "root" and Christianity as "flower" in an anthropological garb. In other words, he contended that the level of Hebrew morality never rose to that articulated in the Gospels. In fact, certain aspects of Hebrew religion were inferior to the heathen practices of her neighbors. Israel's legislation on slavery, treatment of the enemy, blood revenge, and polygamy were the sentiments of a hard-hearted people.[16] Wellhausen's dictum of religions moving from lower to higher forms became Smith's paradigm for comprehending how the primitive Hebraic ideas of redemption, atonement, and purification attained ultimate perfection under Christian teaching:

> [I]n primitive life, all spiritual and ethical ideas are still wrapped up in the husk of a material embodiment. To free the spiritual truth from the husk was the great task that lay before the ancient religions. . . . That some progress in this direction was made, especially in Israel, appears from our examination. But on the whole it is manifest that none of the ritual systems of antiquity was able by mere natural development to shake itself free from the congenital defect inherent in every attempt to embody spiritual truth in material forms.[17]

Smith's discovery that Christianity had consummated the idea of the holy was a boon for the Sunday preacher. Within a year of the appearance of Smith's Lectures, S. R. Driver preached a homily that reflected the spirit of Smith's anthropological interpretation of how religions grew. Driver claimed that Israel's cumbersome sacrificial system was the way God intentionally trained His people until they were able to dispense with the ordinances of the Law and assimilate the noble teachings of Jesus. Hence, the New Testament was the invincible record of man's spiritual victory over materialism.[18]

Solomon Schechter believed the negative appraisal of Judaism by Christian theologians such as Wellhausen, Smith, and Driver to be biased. These scholars, he contended, had converted their higher criticism into a venomous brand of anti-Semitism. Thus, the hour had clearly dawned for Jews to defend Judaism's legitimacy:

> The Bible is our patent of nobility granted to us by the Almighty God, and if we disown the Bible, leaving it to the tender mercies of a Wellhausen, Stade, and Duhm, and other beautiful souls working away at diminishing the "nimbus of the Chosen People," the world will disown us. . . . [T]his intellectual persecution can only be fought by intellectual weapons, and unless we make an effort to recover our Bible and to think out our theology for ourselves, we are irrevocably lost from both worlds. A mere protest in the pulpit or a vigorous editorial in a paper, or an amateur essay in a monthly, or even a special monograph will not help us. We have to create a really living great literature, and do the same for the subjects of theology and the Bible that Europe has done for Jewish history and philosophy. . . . [W]e must gather our forces and fight the enemy.[19]

The intellectual persecution of Judaism, which so bothered traditional Jews like Schechter, continued unabated over the next quarter century. This was a period marked by an increased acceptance of Wellhausenism.[20] The impact of the comparative approach to Israel's past, pioneered by William Robertson Smith and carried forward by his friend and colleague, Sir James Frazer, gave added credibility to Wellhausen's conclusions. As discussed below, both Smith and Frazer modified Wellhausen's reconstruction of Hebrew origins and beliefs, yet concurred with his overall assessment that the Pharisees had sidetracked the natural evolution of Israelite religion.

As a cultural anthropologist, Smith applied the comparative method to religious institutions. He claimed to have unearthed a significant correlation between the primitive structure of Semitic religion and early Hebrew religion. This Cambridge scholar, who died in 1894 at the age of forty-eight, sought to demonstrate that the matrix of Semitic culture cast a penetrating light on the sources of biblical religion. He operated from an assumption held in common by anthropologists of the period that there was a psychic unity common among men and that cultural evolution was a uniform process that went through the same stages everywhere.[21] All societies were subject to similar principles of development.

Smith had limited his research to the most primitive forms of nomadic Arab religion.[22] James Frazer, who followed him, broadened the base of the theory by looking for "parallels to the ideas and institutions of the Old Testament" outside the perimeter of the Semitic world.[23] Thus, in a 1918 study, Frazer asserted that the comparative method revealed a level of barbarism within the pages of the Bible:

> Despite the high moral and religious development of the ancient Hebrews, there is no reason to suppose that they formed an exception to this general law. They, too, had probably passed through a stage of barbarism and even of savagery, and this probability, based on the analogy of other races, is confirmed by an examination of their literature, which contains many references to beliefs and practices that can hardly be explained except on the supposition that they are rudimentary survivals from a lower level of culture.[24]

A few years later, Frazer recapitulated his views, declaring that far from being a romantic or divinely inspired people, the Hebrews had evolved slowly and by natural selection, like all other nations, from a "condition of ignorance and savagery." Later Pharisaic religion, in his estimation, was not much of an improvement, having "little to say of morality, but much to say of ritual."[25]

The archaeological studies of Germany's Hugo Winckler brought to a peak the search for phenomena parallel to Israelite religion. His "pan-Babylonian" theory posited that the nations of the ancient Near East, which included Palestine, were parts of one unified cultural organism. Hence, not only did Old Testament history mirror the impact of primitive Semitic religion, as Smith and Frazer contended; it was also heavily indebted to and influenced by the cultural and religious civilization of the ancient Babylonian empire. Winckler's hypothesis was disseminated in more popular form to students of Bible by both German Bible scholar Herman Gunkel and S. R. Driver.[26] The latest conclusions documenting Israel's religious immaturity were also popularized as

Chapter 3: Biblical Criticism

well in sermonic form. For example, A. F. Kirkpatrick, one of Britain's leading clergymen, observed in 1902 to his Sunday parishioners:

> The researches of archaeology and a comparative study of religion show that the religion of Israel derived many elements from the primitive religion of the Semites, possessed much in common with the religions of surrounding nations, and was largely influenced in its development by the faith with which it came into contact in the course of its history.[27]

Conservative Christian Reactions

Jewish traditionalists like Schechter and Hertz were supported in their distrust of higher criticism by conservative Christian theologians who interpreted both Hebrew and Christian Scriptures as the definitive expression of God's word. From the perspective of these Christians, Wellhausen's output potentially undermined faith. First, by challenging, as Wellhausen did, the Mosaic authorship of the Pentateuch, one necessarily questioned the absolute truth of God's revelation to Moses. Revelation, of course, was a theological axiom essential to the New Testament image of Jesus as the consummation of the *Heilsgeschichte* of the Old Testament. Second, conservative Christians realized that the Documentary Hypothesis, which cast aspersion upon the authenticity of the revelations to Moses, could challenge the historical integrity of the New Testament as well. Were this to happen, it would result in Jesus' superhuman role being designated as myth.

A *cause célèbre* among conservative Christian theologians was the heresy case brought against William Robertson Smith by the Free Church of Scotland in 1881. The verdict that was rendered against him specified that his teachings undermined faith among believing Christians, who were ill equipped to evaluate the scholarly and technical issues raised by biblical criticism.[28] Similar concerns were voiced on both sides of the Atlantic. For example, the principal of King's College, who served as chaplain to the archbishop of Canterbury, was most anxious because the higher critical theory "involved grave questions respecting the limits of our Lord's authority and knowledge."[29] A veteran conservative Bible scholar and admirer of Judaism, Franz Delitzsch (1813–1890) of Leipzig, concurred: "Certainly . . . if his [Wellhausen's] conclusions be true, the Old Testament cannot in any distinctive sense be the Word of God."³⁰ At Drew Theological Seminary in America, a professor of Church history agreed that the new criticism could brew a storm with potentially grave consequences for preserving belief:

> The supreme issue is not faith in the historic Man of Galilee, but in the superhuman Christ. The Life is not denied ... but the Life plus its miraculous beginning is subtly dealt with, disparaged, and rejected.... [T]he Virgin Birth, the Atonement, and the Resurrection are not to be permitted to retain the place given them by revelation and history in the glorious gospel of the blessed God.³¹

Hertz and his collaborators were far removed from these exclusively Christian concerns. Nevertheless, as previously noted, they did share with Christian conservatives an uneasiness over the impact of the Graf-Wellhausen theory upon secularly educated members of their flock and the possible negative fallout such exposure would have on religious commitment.

There were gentile academicians of a more liberal bent who were annoyed at a Christian theological triumphalism that negated the legitimacy of Jewish Law. One was Robert Travers Herford (1860–1950); another was the American Presbyterian minister and Harvard scholar George Foot Moore (1851–1931). In his 1912 study, *Pharisaism, Its Aim and Its Method,* Herford validated talmudic legislation as a legitimate continuation of prophetic religion. Only Christian prejudice blinded scholars from recognizing this truth:

> in our day ... there is still the inveterate habit of regarding Rabbinical Judaism as a means of exalting Christianity; there is nearly always the criticism of Judaism from the Christian point of view, and judgment given upon premises which it never recognized. There is scarcely any attempt to learn what it really meant to those who held it as their religion, who lived by it, and who died by it, and have done so for two thousand years.³²

Moore, writing several years later, confirmed Herford's conclusions. Indeed, there was a Christian bias against Judaism:

> Christian interest in Jewish literature has always been apologetic or polemic rather than historical.... The aim of such apologies has been ... the emancipation of Christian from Mosaic Law, or the annulment of the dispensation of law altogether, or the substitution of the new law of Christ; the repudiation of the Jewish people by God for their rejection of Christ, and the succession of the church, the true Israel, the people of God, to all the prerogatives and promises once given to the Jews.³³

Chapter 3: Biblical Criticism

The American scholar criticized the underlying anti-Judaic bias of the Graf-Wellhausenians for having interpreted the Law as an inferior expression of the religious life. They had committed a gross error in judgment by claiming that Israel's older preexilic prophetic brand of religion was the direct ancestor of Christianity. Christian tendentiousness lay behind their verdict that Pharisaism had gradually petrified the prophetic kernel of religion.[34] Moore was moved to echo one of the central claims in the Hertz *Pentateuch*: "I wish to emphasize the fact that, whatever critics may opine about the literary history of Levitical law, it did not create a new kind of religion. Judaism is a normal development of the old religion of Israel in new circumstances and adapted to new conditions."[35]

Moore's exertions represented for American academia a pioneering drive to counter the negative image of Judaism that had been nurtured by a cadre of Wellhausenian disciples.[36] Moore mounted two bold points aimed at assaulting the Wellhausenian fortress: 1) anthropological and philological studies demonstrated that cultic-ritual rites were an integral part of pagan civilizations that were contemporary with biblical Israel, a point previously acknowledged even by William Robertson Smith;[37] and 2) one had to distinguish between the transmission of a rule or rite in a postexilic compilation and the possibility that it was formulated in a much earlier period.[38] This latter point had been argued as early as 1893 by canon Archibald Henry Sayce, the Oxford philologist and archaeologist: "The Book of Genesis in its present form may have undergone that revision and editing to which Jewish tradition points . . . but the documents of which it consists, the materials which it contains, are of far earlier date than the closing date of the Jewish monarchy."[39] Several years later, the American Christian theologian Lyman Abbot restated Sayce's proposition:

> It is . . . a great mistake to suppose that the authority of the law dates from the promulgation of the code. The code is generally the last step in the growth of the natural law. It is not authoritative because it is promulgated; it promulgates what is already authoritative. In general, the codification of a system of laws marks the end, not the beginnings, of its growth.[40]

Moore, Sayce, and Abbot were all cited in a positive context by editor Hertz in the *Pentateuch*.[41] Hertz was so enamored by Sayce's critique of Wellhausen that he sent the Oxford scholar his two completed volumes on Genesis and Exodus in 1931. After reviewing them, Sayce wrote back praising the Commentary and especially, the additional notes, as needed tools "in restoring confidence in the historical character of the Pentateuch and throwing light on its significance."[42]

The research of Herford in England and of Moore in America, especially the latter's two-volume study, *Judaism* (1927), represented serious gentile bids to characterize rabbinic Judaism favorably. The debut of the Hertz *Pentateuch* in 1929 signaled the beginning of a parallel thrust within the domain of English-speaking Jews.

Unity and Antiquity of the Torah

Hertz and his associates understood fully the implications inherent in the Graf-Wellhausen literary-historical model and in the comparative anthropological blueprint designed by William Robertson Smith, James Frazer, and Hugo Winckler. The higher critics generally repudiated two primary building blocks of rabbinic Judaism: 1) the Mosaic authorship of the Pentateuch and 2) the accuracy of the Pentateuch's description of cultic-ritual law as an accurate expression of life in the preexilic age. The cultural anthropologists who inherited the broad outline of this critique further undermined the uniqueness of Hebrew ethnicity and religion. In editing his commentary, Hertz was clearly conscious of a need to respond cogently to what he, and Schechter before him, perceived as the intentional defamation of Mosaism: "the avowed object of many of the critics has for a long time been to 'deprive Israel of its halo,' and to degrade its saints and heroes."[43] The editorial viewpoint of a traditionalist like Hertz was in line with the bold claim of Israel Abrahams, one of the intellectual spokesmen of Liberal Judaism in England. Though Abrahams was respectful of the methods of biblical criticism and regarded the Torah solely as the product of human genius, he was nevertheless as repulsed as his more conservative Jewish colleague by what he termed Wellhausen's "pellets of ridicule." He accurately reflected the sentiments of the chief rabbi when he noted that

> "Jewish" criticism makes the Law equally with Prophecy a factor in religious progress. The conventional treatment of the Law as a stage of degeneration from Prophecy stimulates "Jewish" opposition. . . . An excessive antinomian proclivity in certain sections of "Chris-

tian" exegesis thus provokes a defensive pronomian excess in a new "Jewish" exegesis.[44]

Hertz was passionately committed to demonstrating the organic relationship between biblical and postbiblical legal legislation. He would contend in his Torah Commentary that the transaction of religious life documented in the Talmud and related rabbinic texts was the natural outgrowth of spiritual seeds that had been sown, fertilized, and cultivated in the soil of biblical Israel. As editor, he tendered three counterarguments to the Bible critics: 1) contrary to the source-critical theory, Moses was the scribe who wrote down the Torah "as dictated" by God; 2) institutional ritualism was an intrinsic aspect of Israel's *Sitz im Leben* from her beginnings and not a postexilic creation; and 3) the political and cultural exchanges between Israel and her neighbors did not preclude the uniqueness and singularity of her religious civilization.

Wellhausen's belief in the historicity of the Sinai revelation was shattered once he was convinced that the early rabbis had intentionally tampered with the authentic religious traditions of biblical Israel to the point of distorting the "prophetic" form of the Pentateuch.[45] By way of contrast, Hertz affirmed unequivocally the "historic actuality" of God's divine revelation at Sinai and the supernatural disclosure to Israel of religious, civil, physical, and spiritual laws that treated "every phase of human and national life." Indeed, from the perspective of Jewish tradition, there was "no strong line of demarcation between the Decalogue and the civil laws."[46] Summoning a classical proof from the archives of medieval Jewish thought, the editor maintained that the credibility of the Sinaitic revelation rested on its having happened in the presence of an entire people.[47] Though the assembled community had received the Ten Commandments alone, Moses was given "additional instructions for the guidance of the Israelites throughout all time" during his forty-day retreat on the mountain. The very combination of cultic-civil legislation and moral law constituted a blessing for Israel. Law was a constitutive feature of being free.[48]

The chief rabbi sought to substantiate his claim by taking issue with two a priori assumptions of the higher critics: the first, that religions progressed as if by mathematical calculation from the simple and spontaneous to more intricate institutionalized forms of worship; and second, that cultic-ceremonial legalism, a late feature in the life span of a given religion, stood in opposition to the prophetic tradition.[49] In his considered opinion, there was a fundamental flaw in the house built by the critics; the ebb and flood tides of history did not support their simplistic view that mankind progressed ineluctably in a straight line:

> the whole idea of evolution *does not apply to a field of human history like the institution of sacrifices*. In the realm of language, for example, it is not true to say that, on the one hand, the more simple the language, the more primitive it is; nor, on the other hand, the more complex it is, the later is its appearance in the life of any ethnic group. Thus, Anglo-Saxon, with its five cases and eight declensions of the noun, is immeasurably more complicated than its direct lineal descendant, modern English; even as Latin is far more complex than Italian. The same holds true in the development of ritual laws. Besides, the statement that Leviticus must be the latest sacrificial legislation, because its ritual laws are the most elaborate, is quite against the evidence of primitive cultures. "It does not appear that very simple systems of law and observance do belong to very primitive societies, but rather the contrary" (Rawlinson).[50]

The quotation was extracted from *Lex Mosaica*, the 1894 Christian theological anthology that dismissed, peremptorily, Wellhausen's reconstruction of biblical history. The author of the quotation was the Reverend George Rawlinson, who had been canon of Canterbury and professor of ancient history at Oxford.[51] It was his kind of conservatism that fortified Hertz in his contention that the set formula of praying three times daily went back to Israel's earliest days, as did the articulate art form of poetry writing and the fixed character of the Sabbath day.[52]

A supporting column in the house of the higher critics was the postexilic dating of Deuteronomy's cultic centralization. This was based on a perception that centralized worship, initiated by vested priestly interests, had obviously strangulated the natural spontaneous piety of the layman for a more regulated and controlled form of religion. In the editor's judgment, this theory was myopic, for it failed to account for the fact unearthed by the archaeologist's spade that sacred institutionalized structures of worship were an integral aspect of paganism in antiquity.[53] Another prop used by Bible critics to dismiss a Mosaic time frame for centralization of the cult in Deuteronomy was based on the supposed early date ascribed to Exod. 20.21, which seemed to sanction a decentralized form of worship. By invoking the paradigm of "simple to complex," decentralization matched the outlook of primitive early religion, and centralization mirrored the attitudes of a more polished professional priesthood. Hertz maintained that the verse in Exodus itself supported an early date for cultic centralization, provided one were in touch with the finer nuances of biblical Hebrew. The problematic phrase *be-khol ha-makom* in Exod. 20:21 did not mean, as the critics contended, "in every place" but rather "in whatever place." This latter interpretation sanctioned centralization of the cult, that is, the erection of an altar "in any place sanctified by a special revelation of God."[54] Hence, the chief rabbi concluded that even in early Israel, "there was no freedom of *indiscriminate* altar-building."[55]

In contending that ritual was an early feature of Israelite religion, Hertz was echoing the sentiments of respected Christian academics who held Julius Wellhausen in high esteem. For example, though William Robertson Smith was of one mind with Wellhausen that one could disregard the rich cuneiform materials from Mesopotamia in seeking to discover the nature of Old Testament religion,[56] he parted company with Wellhausen by claiming that prescribed, disciplined social behavior was a ubiquitous aspect of the nomadic life of the Ur-Semite:

> Religion in primitive terms . . . was a body of fixed traditional practices, to which every member of society conformed as a matter of course. . . . [P]ractice preceded doctrinal theory. . . . To us moderns, religion is above all a matter of individual conviction and reasoned belief, but to the ancients it was a part of the citizen's public life, reduced to fixed forms. . . . [A]s long as the prescribed forms were duly observed, a man was recognized as truly pious.[57]

However, having acknowledged the legitimacy of ritual as a feature of Semitic life, Smith retreated back to Wellhausen's corner by specifically denuding Hebrew ritual of a spiritual tone: "An interest in correct ritual is found in the least spiritual religions, and there is ample proof that it was not lacking in Israel."[58]

It was Smith's protégé, Sir James Frazer, who corroborated the great antiquity of Israel's ceremonial institutions. It was apparent to him that although the Priestly Code was written down either during or following the Babylonian captivity, it enforced traditions harking back to Israel's preexilic era.[59]

There were other theologians and historians, particularly of German extraction, who, though respectful of literary source analysis, held that the legal portions of the Torah identified with P were preexilic in origin. Foremost among these, as cited by the editor, were

Eduard August Riehm, Franz Delitzsch, August Dillmann, and Rudolf Kittel. All had stood their ground against the radical reconstruction of Israel's history detailed in the *Prolegomena*.[60] Even S. R. Driver, England's foremost biblical scholar at the turn of the century and a Wellhausenian, acknowledged in 1891 that recent archaeological finds confirmed that some of the pentateuchal legal writings composed within a priestly milieu mirrored a *Sitz im Leben* prior to the destruction of the First Temple: "It is thus apparent that at least one collection of Priestly Toroth, which now forms part of P was in existence when Deuteronomy was written, and the presumption at once arises that others were."[61]

Hertz himself, however, rejected out of hand any theory that sliced up the Torah into composite documents. He was absolutely opposed even to the view of as outspoken an admirer of rabbinic Judaism as G. F. Moore, who felt at ease with the notion that pentateuchal laws that crystallized in Ezra's day were but a reworking of an earlier preexilic draft.[62]

By insisting on the unity of the Torah text, Hertz parted company with Jewish scholars whom he himself held in high regard. For example, he lauded Leopold Zunz as the "illustrious . . . founder of the new Jewish learning." Yet Zunz's verdict, that Leviticus was written after the era of the prophet Ezekiel, actually made him a "Grafian before Graf."[63] The chief rabbi's stance was more conservative even than the speculative, though temperate, tones of Solomon Schechter. A year before the turn of the new century, Schechter granted legitimacy in principle to biblical criticism. What he lamented was the certainty with which the lower and higher critics presented their views without so much as

> a note of interrogation. . . . I may premise that I am in no way opposed to criticism. . . . Nor, I trust, have I ever given way to anybody in my respect for most of the leaders of the various schools of Bible criticism, Lower as well as Higher. The attempt at an analysis of the Bible into component elements, whether one agrees with the results or assumes a sceptical attitude toward them, is one of the finest intellectual feats of this century. . . . But, as somebody has remarked, if tradition is not infallible, neither are any of its critics. . . . [N]either hypothesis of the rise of the Canon—that given by tradition and that afforded by the new school—is quite free from difficulties and improbable assumptions.[64]

Hertz's rigidity also set him apart from one of his research associates, Joshua Abelson of Leeds, who gravitated to many of the critics' findings, feeling they would not have an adverse effect on faith and commitment to Jewish tradition.[65] Thus, Hertz's adamancy in defending Mosaic authorship of the Torah identified him as standing squarely within the conservative tradition of modern biblical scholarship,[66] a posture that complemented his allegiance to the conservative block of *Wissenschaft* essayists who zealously enshrined the worth of the Jewish past.

Mosaic Authorship: Internal Literary Evidence

Hertz marshaled considerable literary testimony in his effort to defend the accuracy of Scripture and undermine the Documentary Hypothesis. He drafted into his corner the views of Harold M. Wiener, a British Jewish lawyer, who wrote as if he were personally embroiled in a vendetta against the school of Graf-Wellhausen. Wiener argued that the historical integrity of the Torah was reflected in its admission of Israel's shortcomings and frailties as a nation. Thus, the frankness with which the Torah recorded the crushing defeat sustained by the Israelites at Hormah, for instance, bore "the hallmark of truth," as the tendency of nations was to minimize, not maximize, defeats.[67] The chief rabbi reinforced Wiener's observation: the realistic reporting of the biblical record contrasted with the false transmission of information found in Near Eastern archives that specialized in glossing over mention of national catastrophes: "The Biblical writers alone, among all Oriental chroniclers, describe defeats of their king and armies; nay more, they arraign ruler and people alike whensoever these are unfaithful to the aims and ideals of the nation. This is one of the reasons why, of all Oriental chronicles, it is only the Biblical annals that deserve the name of history."[68]

Among the evidence higher critics marshaled to substantiate the Documentary Hypothesis were the many internal contradictions in the Pentateuch. Editor Hertz sought to harmonize them through force of logic. For example, Bible critics maintained that the discrepancy in the Joseph narrative over the role played by the Ishmaelite and Midianite traders in the sale of Joseph as a slave was blatant evidence of an interweaving of different literary strands.[69] The chief rabbi mustered the following argument, which upheld the unity of the story to his satisfaction. Originally, Joseph's brothers had intended to sell him to a caravan of Ishmaelites heading down to Egypt. However, while the brothers were at their meal, Midianite merchants, casually passing by and hearing human cries from the pit near the roadside, carried off Joseph and sold him to the caravan of Ishmaelites going to Egypt. Thus, when the Torah text stated unequivocally (Gen. 37:36) that it was the Midianites who ultimately sold him in Egypt to Potiphar, logic necessitated that they had done so through the Ishmaelite caravan.[70]

Another internal contradiction was the regulation relating to animal firstlings set down in Deut. 15:19–23 and Num. 18:17–19. A simple reading of the Deuteronomy passage made it clear that the *owner* consumed the animal at the central shrine. This conflicted, however, with the law in Numbers granting the *priests* exclusive rights to the firstlings. The contradiction was resolved in the editor's estimation by the German neo-Orthodox biblical scholar David Zevi Hoffmann's interpretation:

> The words "Thou shalt eat it before the Lord," in this section [Deut. 15:20] refer to the person who is entitled to eat it; i.e., the priest, as is prescribed in Numbers. As Deut. is a continuation of the preceding Books of the Pentateuch, it was obvious to Moses' hearers who it was that were to eat the firstlings, since it had already been ordained and well understood.[71]

Hertz also incorporated Hoffmann's rationale for discrepancies in details of what were otherwise parallel versions of the same incident. Such inconsistencies were most glaring when comparing the contents of Moses' sermons in Deuteronomy with parallel accounts appearing in the other four books of the Torah. Hoffmann's answer was that there was nothing illogical in Moses' having omitted reference to a particular circumstance in his capacity as historian, yet subsequently choosing to highlight a fact prior to his death, for emphasis, in his role as orator.[72]

A most problematic phrase to decipher was *be-ever ha-yarden* (Deut. 1:1). It became a significant weapon in the arsenal of literary analysts bent on denying the Mosaic composition of the Pentateuch. Ibn Ezra, the medieval commentator, and Baruch de Spinoza in the seventeenth century had both used it for this purpose. In England, S. R. Driver confirmed their verdict:

> That Dt. is of later origin than the age of Moses may be inferred. . . . The use of the phrase "beyond Jordan" . . . for the country *East* of Jordan shows that the author was a resident in *Western* Palestine. It is indeed sometimes alleged that the expression had a *fixed geographical* sense . . . and was used as a standing designation of

the trans-Jordanic territory; irrespectively of the actual position of the speaker or writer; but Dt. 3:20, 25, 11:30 and Jos. 5:1, 9:1, 12:7 . . . show that this assumption is incorrect.[73]

Hertz retorted by validating precisely that claim that Driver had dismissed as incorrect:

> Some commentators see in the words *ever ha-yarden* (lit., Transjordania) a *fixed* geographical name of the Moabite side of the Jordan, even for the inhabitants of that land. Along with this went a local usage, determined by the position of the speaker.[74]

> All difficulties disappear when we remember that to Moses and the Israelites in the land of Moab, the words "beyond Jordan" meant *west* of Jordan. This phrase therefore is another incidental confirmation of the Mosaic authorship of Genesis.[75]

Other tough discrepancies tackled in the Commentary were the parallel passages of Exod. 12:8f. and Deut. 16:7. The contradiction involved the roasting (*tzeli*) of the paschal lamb ordained in Exodus with a specific prohibition against boiling (*bishul*) the animal, and the standing order in Deuteronomy to boil it. A harmonization of the passages required that *bishul* meant "to roast." This was accomplished by incorporating the eye-catching interpretation of the English Bible commentator Marcus Kalisch: only when *bishul* was accompanied by the word "water" (*mayim*) did it mean "to boil." At all other times, *bishul* yielded the meaning of "to roast." Hence, "the expression *uvishalta* in Deut., xvi, 7 in regard to the paschal lamb receives its proper explanation by II Chronicles, xxxv, 13 where it is said that they *roasted* (*vayevashlu*) the paschal lamb in fire."[76]

This clever rendering presented by Hertz in the 1930 edition of the Commentary was subsequently deleted in the one-volume edition (1938). It would appear that the chief rabbi felt that the explanation was not airtight. Although Kalisch's interpretation was supported after a fashion in Deut. 14:21, where *bishul* was juxtaposed with *halav* (milk), i.e., a liquid, the theory ran aground when set against the backdrop of 1 Sam. 2:13, 15 where the verb *bishul* unaccompanied by the word "water" could only have the meaning of "to boil." Furthermore, the use of the Chronicle's passage to fortify the unity of Exodus and Deuteronomy was particularly suspect. An unorthodox reader might well have suspected that it was the Chronicler himself who, having recognized the discrepancy between the two Torah verses, harmonized the passages through conflation.

Mosaic Authorship: The Evidence from Archaeology

From Hertz's perspective, it would take more than the laceration of the "simple to complex" argument to wreak severe structural damage to the Graf-Wellhausen school. Additional weapons in his campaign arrived from extrabiblical sources. Archaeological and philological data, he maintained, could rescue the Pentateuch from the routine scissors-and-paste method in use among critics. For Hertz, outside archaeological and linguistic testimony fortified both the tenability of Mosaic authorship and the authenticity of fixed law as an intrinsic aspect of early Israelite religion. His decision to integrate the findings of archaeology into the pages of the Commentary was a radical gesture, boldly distinguishing his approach from that chosen a generation earlier by Samson Raphael Hirsch. As doyen of German neo-Orthodoxy, Hirsch had refrained in principle in his Torah commentary from using comparative Semitic philology to shed light on the Hebrew language. He believed that Hebrew was not only the language in which God created the world; it was also the original language of mankind.[77] Thus, he implied that Hebrew religion was *sui generis*; its origins owed absolutely nothing to the cultural-linguistic patterns of its pagan neighbors. Hence, from a Hirschian perspective, comparisons between Israelite and ancient Near Eastern societies were an exercise in futility.

The editor's intellectual openness was akin to the perception of German Bible scholar Hugo Winckler, that "he who would read the Old Testament must know Hebrew; but he who would understand the Old Testament must know 'Oriental.'"[78] To be sure, Hertz was not a pan-Babylonianist like Winckler, who claimed, following the hypothesis of Friedrich Delitzsch,[79] that the Bible was deeply rooted in a single common culture that was dominated by the Babylonians. He was repulsed by Winckler's hypothesis that Palestine was a backwater of Babylonia and that practically every Hebrew belief, rite, custom, and law was under the intellectual and religious dominance of Babylonian heathendom. Hertz did subscribe, however, to the premise that Hebrew society had not remained immune to the powerful cultural-linguistic influences of neighboring pagan civilizations. What was critical to Hertz was pagan civilization's capacity to cast light on the social and cultural life of the patriarchs and of Moses. It was this kind of indirect testimony that would support his editorial claim that the Torah mirrored historical reality. His decision to use archaeological-linguistic data was in concert with the viewpoint of a contemporary gentile scholar:

> When we came to look more closely at the details of archaeological testimony, the historical setting thus afforded for the events of the Bible narrative is seen to be exactly in harmony with the narrative.... The recent testimony of archaeology to the Scriptures, like all such testimony that has gone before, is definitely and uniformly favorable to the Scriptures at their face value, and not to the Scriptures as reconstructed by criticism.[80]

Hertz could point to one senior gentile scholar who verified his claim that archaeology provided supportive evidence of Mosaic authorship of the Pentateuch—the Reverend Archibald Henry Sayce. Sayce naturally came in for praise by the chief rabbi. Canon Sayce concluded that "wherever archaeology has been able to test the negative conclusions of criticism, they have dissolved like a bubble in the air." This stance was most heartwarming to the chief rabbi, for in a span of seventeen years the philologist-turned-archaeologist had done an about-face, having retreated from an acceptance of the Documentary Hypothesis, predicated on a preexilic dating of P, to a complete rejection of the validity of source analysis.[81]

The study of the languages of the ancient Near East—an offshoot of archaeology—proved to be of inestimable value in Hertz's defense of the Mosaicity of the Torah. He pointed out, for example, that linguistics affirmed the antiquity of the Book of Leviticus. The technical terms of the sacrificial cult were "derived from ancient Arabic and Minean"; and the book itself was devoid of "neo-Babylonian or Persian loan words that would reflect the age of the Exile." Furthermore, the existence of a parallel to the admonition of Leviticus 26 in the ancient Code of Hammurabi pointed to that chapter's preexilic origin, and this was evidence against the argument of the critics that the chapter must have been written during the Babylonian captivity, when the punishments "foreshadowed" in it came to pass.[82] Deuteronomy's antiquity was similarly confirmed by evidence of ancient Semitic codes. Old Hittite law paralleled the Mosaic stipulation (Deut. 24:16) that a child was not to be punished for the crimes of his parents. A reverence for this tradition was reflected in King Amaziah's day, when he refrained from punishing the families associated with the actual courtiers who had assassinated his father (2 Kings 14:6). Furthermore, Deuteronomy's regulations concerning the rape of a betrothed or married woman were strikingly similar to regulations of the Babylonian, Hittite, and Assyrian codes.[83]

The editor was quite at ease in admitting that loan words from surrounding civilizations had seeped into the biblical text through cultural cross-fertilization. Thus, the word *kelev* in Deut. 23:19 was a Semitic term designating a cultic male prostitute,[84] and the word *hai* in Gen. 3:20 was "the primitive Semitic [i.e., Arabic word] for 'clan'; [Thus,] Eve was the mother of every human clan, the mother of mankind."[85] This translation was confirmed by W. Robertson Smith, who had, as a strict Wellhausenian, rejected the antiquity of Deuteronomy. Yet here was the same man proclaiming that a narrative portion of the Pentateuch had emerged within an ancient historical cast.[86] Arabic influence was possibly to be detected in the theological name *Shaddai* (dispenser of benefits) and, hence, derived from a word meaning "to heap benefits."[87] The expression in Gen. 15:16, "fourth generation" (*dor revi'i*) pointing to the four hundred years of slavery to be endured in Egypt, was elucidated by the Arabic word *dahr,* which conveyed a time span of at least a century. Also, the Torah's explanation of Abram's change of name to *Abraham,* designating him as the father of a multitude of nations, was attested by the Arabic word *raham,* meaning "multitude."[88]

As a person inclined toward accepting the historicity of the Israelite sojourn in Egypt, Hertz found it quite in order to see linguistic affinities between the Hebrew and Egyptian languages. For example, the etymology of the word *shaatnez* in Deut. 22:11 was possibly of Egyptian origin, as was the name of Aaron's grandson, Phinehas.[89] The editor relied on the academic credibility of the well-known Egyptologist Abraham Solomon Yahuda, who believed that the Pentateuch originated about the time of the Exodus but before the conquest of Canaan. He interpreted the word "Moses" as a Hebraized reproduction of an Egyptian word that probably meant "child of the Nile."[90] Another Hebrew word, *hamushim,* meaning "armed," was probably derived, according to Yahuda, from the Egyptian word for "lance."[91] According to the chief rabbi, the presence of Hebrew words traceable to Egyptian as well as "a thorough familiarity with Egyptian life," as reflected in the Joseph story, pointed to "the remarkable historical exactness of the . . . narrative."[92] Moreover, the desert wanderings assumed lifelike proportion through the possible Egyptian origin of the Hebrew word *man* (Exod. 16:15).[93]

The strongest argument that Hertz used in his quest to authenticate the historicity of the Pentateuch was the cumulative weight of archaeological data. He spared no space in familiarizing the reader with relevant information. The spadework of Archibald H. Sayce had verified that the lowlands of Palestine (a word synonymous with Canaan) were settled by Canaanites prior to Abraham's day. Moreover, Hertz noted, the Canaanites "formed part of the population down to the days of the later Kings." Hence, the difficulty posed by the problematic verse "and the Canaanite was then in the land" (Gen. 12:6) fell away. There was no need to adopt the conventional critics' interpretation that "the Canaanites were *at that time* in the land, but were no longer so at the time when Genesis was written."[94]

The discovery of a painting in the tomb of Prince Khnumhotep III at Bene Hassein (= Beni Hasan), in Middle Egypt, dating from c. 1890 B.C.E., which coincided with the Patriarchal Age (c. 2200–1550 B.C.E.), cast precious light on the nature of jealousy that Joseph aroused among his brothers when he wore the coat of many colors. Semitic chiefs of that era

> wore coats of many colours as insignia of rulership. . . . Jacob [had] . . . marked [Joseph] *for the chieftainship of the tribes at his . . . death.* This sign of rulership and royalty was still in use in the household of King David, as is seen from II Sam. XIII, 18, though the chronicler must explain this strange fashion in dress. The fact that in the Joseph story no such explanatory gloss is given is proof of the antiquity of the narrative. When it was first written, its implications were perfectly intelligible.[95]

A further faithful reflection of Egyptian mores in Joseph's age was the Torah's description of why he ended up in prison, an episode that had an interesting parallel in Egyptian Wisdom literature. Hertz's purpose in mentioning this literary parallel may have been to contrast the treatment of the adulterous wife who was slain forthrightly by her husband in the Egyptian tale with the more realistic portrayal described of Potiphar's wife in the Torah, who retained her honor and integrity. Indeed, Hertz was quick to point out that a midrash sensed the cruel but pragmatic aspect surrounding Potiphar's behavior. He incarcerated Joseph instead of killing him outright because he doubted the truth of his wife's accusation against his most trusted servant. But practical considerations requiring him to uphold his wife's respectability and preserve his own honor led him to condemn Joseph instead of exonerate him.[96] The perceptive reader, however, could assess for himself which of the two sources, the Egyptian or the Hebrew, reflected a dimension that was more true to life. Another authentic detail woven into the Joseph narrative was his death at the age of 110, a time span depicted "as an ideal lifetime" in Egyptian literature.[97]

The editor also took note of the Tel El Amarna correspondence, unquestionably the most impressive bulk archaeological find of the nineteenth century. This Egyptian archive, discovered in 1887, authenticated the social and cultural backdrop of the patriarchal and Mosaic periods. Holding these writings in focus, the chief rabbi found it highly probable that the Hebrews who departed Egypt and who subsequently invaded "Palestine in the fourteenth pre-Christian century" could be identified with the nomadic Habiri mentioned so prominently in the El Amarna letters.[98] Hertz was equally convinced that the El Amarna tablets removed "every reasonable doubt concerning the authenticity of the account of Melchizedek" mentioned in Gen. 14:18–20.[99]

There was one archaeological find that threatened to undermine the accuracy of the Torah's narrative—the discovery of the Inscription of Pharaoh Merneptah (c. 1220 B.C.E.). According to the schematic overview of Genesis, all of the known families of Israel's (Jacob's) household went down to Egypt, where they were eventually enslaved. Yet the inscription outlining the Pharaoh's victories in Canaan boasted that "Ysiraal is desolated, its seed is not." On the assumption that the reference to "Ysiraal" was to the people Israel living in Canaan (and not the district of Jezreel), whom did Merneptah engage in battle? If, as the higher critics claimed, he engaged some Israelites in Palestine who never made the trek south to Egypt, then doubt was cast on the accuracy of the description in Genesis. Hertz outflanked this argument with a counterproposal: prior to the years of Israelite slavery, a group of Israelites from Egypt managed to find their way back home to southern Palestine. It was this contingent that Merneptah claimed to have defeated.[100]

Hertz contended that the archaeologist's shovel had unearthed a

Chapter 3: Biblical Criticism

volume of data pointing to the accuracy of the biblical narrative. Thus, the ceremonial form in which God established the covenant with Abraham was an authentic derivation from the "ancient" world, as was the image of Judah's hegemony symbolized in Gen. 49:10 by the ruler's staff between his feet. The chief rabbi noted that this particular monarchical configuration was engraved on the monuments of Assyrian and Persian kings.[101] Moreover, he posited that the art of goldsmithing, engraving, and precious jewelry associated with Ur and the tomb of Tutankhamen lent a measure of credibility to the biblical command to engrave the two stones on the shoulder pieces of the ephod (Exod. 28:11–12).[102]

Hertz shared with his reader the possible identification of the fourth Egyptian plague with a swarm of beetles. Archaeological data had identified the beetle or scarab with the Egyptian "emblem of the sun-god." How appropriate then, the editor implied, that God chose to demonstrate His awesome power by commanding the beetle to do His bidding. Archaeology also brought into sharp focus the intent of the ninth plague, darkness. By forcing blackness to descend on Egypt by fiat, God had dramatically undermined the religion of "the Egyptians, whose chief object of worship was Ra, the sun-god."[103] Another illuminating use of archaeological testimony was the identification of the word "hornet" (in Deut. 7:20) with the Egyptian Pharaoh Thothmes III and his successors. It so happened that the badge of these rulers was the hornet. Thus, the Deuteronomic verse "the Lord thy God will send the hornet among them [the Canaanites]," could legitimately be read as "a veiled reference to the systematic series of invasions and conquests in Palestine undertaken by that Pharaoh," invasions that weakened the resistance of the Canaanites."[104]

The Limitations of Archaeological Data

Despite the harmony of biblical traditions and ancient Near Eastern practices and ideas, Hertz refrained from asserting categorically that extrabiblical sources proved the absolute veracity of the Pentateuch. He realized that the testimony of philology and archaeology established only the verisimilitude and not the actual occurrence of biblical traditions. The foreground of the Torah could not be validated by reference to its background. Accurate comparisons did not prove historicity. The authentication of a historical setting was one thing; confirming the historical details of that setting was an undertaking of quite another order. One had to distinguish probability from actuality.

Plausible conjecture was not the same as positive proof. Archaeology merely demonstrated the possibility or high probability that a biblical event took place, but not that it actually happened.

An illustration of Hertz's caution appears in his attempt to demonstrate the reasonableness of the notion that Moses engraved the entire Torah on twelve stones (Deut. 27:2). After pointing to the actuality of the eight thousand words of the Code of Hammurabi being etched on one block of diorite, Hertz could claim no more than "that the laws of Deuteronomy, or even the whole Torah *could have been* written on twelve stones. . . . [T]here is, therefore, *no reasonable doubt* that, as Saadyah and Ibn Ezra hold, the 613 Precepts of the Torah were inscribed on those great stones."[105]

He displayed a similar reservation by only implying that the Torah's accurate description of topography and geographical distances testified to its historicity. For example, he pointed to Orientalist Edward Robinson's retracing of the journey on a camel from Mount Sinai to Kadesh-Barnea. The trek lasted "exactly eleven days," which coincided with the information recorded in the Torah.[106] Though the chief rabbi clearly intimated that this evidence contributed to authenticating the Torah's historicity, he left the reader to draw this conclusion. His editorial restraint reflected a respect for the verdict of George Adam Smith, whose observations on the geography of the Holy Land were peppered throughout the Commentary.[107] Smith rejected flatly the use of the Torah's accurate geographical notations for purposes of validating its historical accuracy:

> That a story accurately reflects geography does not necessarily mean that it is a real transcript of history, else were the Book of Judith the truest man ever wrote, instead of being what it is, a pretty piece of fiction. Many legends are wonderful photographs of scenery. . . . [A]ll that is proved is that the narrative was written in the land by someone who knew the land. . . . All that geography can do is to show whether or not the situations were possible at the time to which they were assigned, and even this is a task often beyond her resources.[108]

S. R. Driver, who was cited more times than any other Christian scholar in the Commentary, had openly declared the limitations of the archaeological enterprise as a means of authenticating the accuracy of Scripture: "this is the whole change archaeology has wrought; it has given us a background and an atmosphere for the stories in Genesis; it is unable to recall or certify their heroes."[109] Driver was joined in his assessment by researcher Stanley Arthur Cook, who, unlike Hertz (who had so much riding on the evidence of archaeology), contended that comparative documentation was incapable of bolstering even the antiquity, much less the actual reality, of the Torah. Nevertheless, the chief rabbi held Cook in high regard for his otherwise warm applause of Israel's unparalleled benevolence in protecting strangers. So respectful was Hertz of Cook's books and articles that, despite his reasonable disagreement with some of Cook's conclusions, he was pleased to forward to the Oxford scholar his Commentary on Genesis and Exodus.[110]

Uniqueness of Mosaic Law

The benefit that Hertz hoped would accrue by using analogies and resemblances from Israel's neighbors to support his claim of the Mosaicity of the entire Torah was offset by a counterclaim: Israelite beliefs and practices were hardly unique, but reflected religious conditions that prevailed over the vast geographic area of the ancient Near East.[111] James Frazer's posture of an Israel that possessed no spiritual genius or ontological uniqueness has already been mentioned.[112] Yet he was preempted by the earlier judgment of S. R. Driver:

> The general result of the archaeological and anthropological researches of the past half-century has been to take the Hebrews out of the isolated position which, as a nation, they seemed previously to hold, and to demonstrate their affinities with, and often their dependence upon, the civilizations by which they were surrounded. ... [T]heir beliefs, ... their social usages, their code of civil and criminal law, their religious institutions, can no longer be viewed, as was once possible, as differing in kind from those of other nations, and determined in every feature by direct revelation from Heaven; all, it is now known, have substantial analogies among other peoples.[113]

In light of this verdict common to higher Bible critics, one can detect a conscious effort on Hertz's part to delineate the legitimate parameters of the comparative study of religions, as well as the inherent limitations. He began with the premise that biblical society had not arisen within a historical vacuum: Hebrew society drew some of its impulses from a common sociocultural matrix.[114]

Israel had certainly been subject to external stimuli, yet it was equally valid that striking similarities between the Mosaic and pagan codes did not prove direct relations between them. Resemblances merely reflected a common usage of phraseology familiar to residents of the area. In his capacity as editor, he pointed out that his interpretation was in accord with "the best authoritative opinion."[115] Hertz was referring to the sentiment expressed by S. R. Driver, who described the relationship between the Code of Hammurabi and the Mosaic code this way:

> Probably the most satisfactory explanation will be found to be that, while direct borrowing on the part of the Hebrew legislator is not probable, the two codes do stand in some indirect relation toward each other: *codifications of an old, customary Semitic usage, common to the ancestors of both the Babylonians and the Hebrews.*[116]

It can be ascertained that Hertz had Driver in mind by comparing Driver's phraseology in the above quotation (italicized) with the following italicized comments by the chief rabbi in the *Pentateuch*:

> these two systems are independent *codifications of ancient Semitic Common Law*. The resemblances in the two codes are due to the *common usage of the Semitic ancestors of both Babylonians and Hebrews*.[117]

Hertz was obviously judicious in selecting comparative examples that had had impact on the shaping of the Torah's content. He maintained that similarities in language, in technical terms, and in stories between Israel and her neighbors illustrated the principle that Scripture chose "those forms of literary expression that would be most effective with the hearers to whom they [were] addressed." Hence, the mere duplication of a specific Hebrew law with that of a neighboring country was testimony "that common laws [were] often due to common human experience, which [was] much the same everywhere." What was truly remarkable and exceptional in the formulation of Torah law, according to the chief rabbi, was the Mosaic code's glaring ideological divergence from pagan legislative models. Not the surface contact, but the differences between Israelite and pagan religion were so fundamental as to be unbridgeable. Hertz's primary claim, repeated incessantly throughout the *Pentateuch*, was that Israel had borrowed absolutely nothing from her neighbors in the realm of moral theology. In fact, there was no way for resemblances between biblical and

Chapter 3: Biblical Criticism

pagan law to cast a penetrating light on the source of the Pentateuch's moral integrity. This could be accounted for only by introducing the variable of divine Providence.

In other words, to contend that the Torah's legal framework was derived substantially from the rites of idolatrous nations was to overlook the possibility that biblical law bore the direct impress of the Almighty. The validity of such a posture, of course, lay outside the realm of reason. This was precisely the editor's point: there were dimensions of the human experience that were not subject to logical explanation. The dynamic force that gave form to the Hebraic religious consciousness lay beyond the pale of rational-empirical epistemology.[118] Introducing the factor of God's input into the discussion gave Hertz considerable maneuverability. It legitimized his pleading with social historians and cultural anthropologists alike to recognize the limitations inherent in applying "universal" mathematical formulas as a way of accounting for human behavior. The empirical methods of historical positivism, though legitimate, were not universally applicable. There was room in the religious enterprise for the specific nonrational variable of mystery that surrounded the promulgation of the Law at Sinai. To support his case, Hertz drew upon the comment of the celebrated French historian Ernest Renan. Although Renan was a positivist and a freethinker, he had acknowledged, in the words of the Commentary, that the Ten Commandments "will be, during all centuries, the commandments of God."[119]

A central claim of the chief rabbi was that the high valuation and heightened stress placed on the worth of human life in Mosaic legislation set Hebrew society apart from idol-worshiping nations. The organizing principle of pagan civilization was harmony, not humanism. Consequently, pragmatic considerations alone determined the structure of its social order, and this bred inequality among men, which was fundamentally at odds with the Hebraic spirit.[120] Hence, to appreciate the divergence in law between Israel and her pagan neighbors, it was necessary to take account of *a difference in underlying principles.*[121] In this connection, Hertz highlighted a basic clash in values between Mosaic civil law and the Code of Hammurabi:

> Society in ancient Babylonia consisted of certain definite castes; king, court and priests, men of gentle birth (aristocrats and officers), commoners and slaves. The differences between the social grades can be seen by various regulations. . . . The value placed on human

life in this Code is slight.... There is not a trace of the Biblical ideal of personal holiness in the Babylonian Code, or of the beneficence and consideration for the poor and needy, which is so characteristic of the Mosaic legislation.... It is not the *protection of property*, but the *protection of humanity*, that is the aim of the Mosaic Code.[122]

At stake was what each civilization perceived as a priority. For example, though Israelite and Hammurabi law decreed the death penalty for the kidnapper who turned his victim into a slave, they did so for two qualitatively different reasons. The sin of the kidnapper in Babylonia was his having tampered with the property rights of another; in Israel, it was his infliction of "both loss of liberty and spiritual death" on his victim.[123] Similarly, concern for the humanity of the slave explained why runaway slaves in Israel were not to be restored to their masters. This regulation contrasted starkly with the stipulation in "the law of Hammurabi, which condemned to death anyone who sheltered a runaway slave!"[124]

Hertz contended that a fundamental cleavage in what constituted a moral judgment accounted for the different way homicide was treated inside and outside Israel's borders: "In Israel, murder [was] not only a crime committed against a fellow man, but also a sin against God, in whose image man was made."[125] Therefore, in contrast to ancient pagan custom, it was unthinkable in Israel that "loss of life could be compensated by the death of any member of the manslayer's family."[126]

Furthermore, unlike the practice of Arab tribesmen, biblical law had no provision for the atonement of murder by payment of a monetary fine.[127] The Mosaic code curbed another Bedouin provision: the power of redress in the case of the murder of a family member lay not with the murdered victim's family, but with an impartial tribunal.[128] Hertz's posture was a direct refutation of the theory of Julius Wellhausen and William Robertson Smith, both of whom insisted that Israelite law had evolved in a direct line from Arab Bedouin sources.[129] The respective applications of the *lex talionis* rounded out for Hertz the "immeasurable moral differences" between biblical and pagan perceptions of morality. Hammurabi law, unlike the Mosaic code, decreed that if a negligent jerry-builder inadvertently caused a home to collapse, killing the child of the owner, then his own child was executed.[130]

By highlighting the ideological differences between biblical and pagan law, the chief rabbi begged to differ conceptually from those cultural anthropologists like Smith, Frazer, Wellhausen, and

Winckler, among others, who believed in the homogeneity of social behavior and the uniformity of group experience. Hertz built his religious anthropology on a different premise: man's cultural evolution was not a uniform process. Hence, analogies between societies only proved common background; they could not disqualify the particularistic nuances of a specific community. Mutual resemblances in *form* between neighboring societies did not preclude substantive differences in *spirit* and psychology.

Hertz could take considerable comfort that he was not alone in his judgment; he was supported by a cadre of scholars. Among them was Stanley Arthur Cook, with whose writings, as previously mentioned, Hertz was thoroughly familiar. Cook had observed that though the comparative method was "highly stimulating," it was essential to appreciate the differences, especially in "the world of beliefs" between one civilization and another.[131] Some years before the publication of the Hertz *Pentateuch*, the French sociologist Emile Durkheim had drawn attention independently to the abuses of the comparative method: "Social facts . . . are functions of the social system of which they are a part; therefore they cannot be understood when they are detached. For this reason, two facts which come from two different societies cannot be fruitfully compared merely because they seem to resemble one another."[132]

Ernest Sellin, whom Hertz held in high esteem, concurred that biblical law had been "sifted and transmuted" in such a way as to make it utterly unique. Several years before the turn of the century, he made the declaration that no part of the Bible was directly traceable to Mesopotamia. The religion of the Hebrews was qualitatively different from other religions. Under its spirit, laws, hymns, and myths were radically transformed and re-created into something entirely new.[133] In England, Sellin's views were corroborated by another spiritual ally of Hertz, Archibald Sayce. In a scathing critique of William Robertson Smith's *Lectures on the Religion of the Semites*, Sayce charged Smith with gross intellectual misconduct. Smith had committed a major methodological error in assuming that the reaction of the human mind to natural phenomena was uniform:

> I must enter a protest against the assumption that what holds good of Kaffirs or Australians held good also for the primitive Semite. The students of language have at last learnt that what is applicable

to one family of speech is not necessarily applicable to another, and it would be well if the anthropologist would learn the same lesson.[134]

It was in this revisionist spirit that Hertz took obvious delight in pointing out, even using a small detail, how both Wellhausen and S. R. Driver acknowledged that Israel's cult was to some extent unique and did not fit into a homogeneous mold:

> Even Wellhausen admits that of this abomination [of sacrificing the human firstborn] there is no trace in the religion of Israel. Driver writes: "The instances of child-sacrifice [practiced by heathen Semites] which occur are either altogether abnormal or, as in the reigns of Ahaz and Manasseh, due to the importation of Phoenician customs into Judah."[135]

In similar fashion, the chief rabbi took delight in recording William Robertson Smith's finding that in Israel (Deut. 4:17), unlike in the northern Semitic neighboring lands, it was forbidden to represent God in animal form.[136] Another Wellhausenian quoted by Hertz as certifying the unique religious ethos of the ancient Hebrews was Karl Heinrich Cornill, professor of Old Testament theology at the University of Koenigsberg and, later, Breslau: "If Israel had been merely a race like others it would have never survived this fearful catastrophe and would have disappeared in the Babylonian exile."[137] Paradoxically, it was Samuel Rolles Driver, a Wellhausenian by temperament and discipline, who in a sermon preached back in 1892 eloquently summarized Hertz's claim: "The more minutely Israelitish institutions and ideas are compared with those of their neighbours, the more conspicuous, among much that is similar, are the diversities, and the more plainly do we perceive that purer light which shone in their midst."[138]

Summation

Joseph Herman Hertz's conviction was that Moses composed the Torah under the direct inspiration of God,[139] a verdict that was fundamentally at odds with the view of many higher critics who, aligned with Wellhausen, delegitimized the Mosaic code and rabbinic Judaism's positive appreciation of legalism. Both the radical higher critics and cultural anthropologists related to archaeology as a grand weapon with which to flay the integrity of Mosaism. They highlighted the similarities in culture and religion between Israel and her pagan neighbors, particularly emphasizing the pure and simple, or primitive composition of early Semitic religions. Thus, in what may be regarded as a *tour de force*, editor Hertz sought to render this thesis null and void through the judicious sifting of archaeological evidence. In effect, Hertz chose to "fight fire with fire." In doing so, he put before his readers a bold thesis: the influences of cultural cross-fertilization had absolutely no bearing on the shaping of biblical Israel's religious anthropology; not harmony, but humanity, was her watchword from the beginning.

Chapter 4:
Hebraism and Hellenism

Higher biblical criticism was one significant way the gentile world sought to discredit the legitimacy of rabbinic Judaism. Another was to pit the Jewish ethos against the moral contributions to humanity of "Hebraism," generally understood by gentile savants as a code word for the dynamic and positive spiritual impact of *Christianity* on Western society.

Hebraism was perceived as one of two dominant impulses that had shaped human culture in the West. The other was "Hellenism," a catch-all term that referred mainly to the intellectual, political, and aesthetic components of Western civilization traceable to Greco-Roman culture. According to conventional wisdom, mankind's progress could be accurately measured by monitoring the integrated pulse of these two great forces. Together, Hebraism and Hellenism were responsible for mankind's marvelous march forward toward perfection.[1] The dialogue that emerged over Hebraism was not always unequivocal in granting Christianity exclusive marks for spiritual excellence. There was also a tendency to bestow a religious halo upon Hellenism; it, too, contained a verifiable ethical component.[2] At the same time, many gentile men of letters, such as the English Victorian poet Matthew Arnold, refused to incorporate a Jewish factor into the Hebraism-Hellenism equation.[3] They dismissed as fanciful the notion that Jewish civilization had anything further to contribute to the moral progress of mankind. Judaism's relationship to Christianity was likened to that of a withered trunk beside a fertile branch.

Hence, it was not surprising that Jewish thinkers were drawn into this discussion, committed as they were to Judaism's legitimate perpetuation as a religious civilization. Their first point of departure was to define Hebraism as a Jewish spiritual category and not as the logical extension of the Christian ethos. The spirit of Hebraism was, in their estimation, an amalgamation of the superior humanistic values embedded in the writings of the prophets and the Rabbis.[4] Some Jewish teachers drew a severe line of demarcation between the primary concerns of the two worlds. Hebraism, which for them connoted the integrity of Judaism, emphasized proper conduct and ethical behavior. Hellenism, on the other hand, was synonymous with right thinking and aesthetics. Hebraism was primarily a moral and spiritual force expressing itself in the domain of justice. Hellenism was the incarnation of pure intellectual power exemplified in reason. Hellenism preoccupied itself with the question of man's knowledge. Its approach to life was conceptual, rational, and analytic—truth being a function of reasoned argument. By contrast, Judaism was passionately committed to unraveling the mystery of man's behavior.[5] While some Jewish thinkers proclaimed the absolute Jewish genius for morality and spirituality,[6] one Anglo-Jewish preacher, the Reverend Morris Joseph, advocated first nurturing man's quest for ethical nobility before focusing on his passion for intellectual brilliance. Proper conduct and obedience necessarily preceded man's drive for knowledge.[7] Joseph was articulating a position wholly in keeping with that of Maimonides.[8]

Another English rabbinic educator—and Hertz's collaborator—Abraham Cohen of Birmingham, chose to stress the complementary aspects of Hebraic and Hellenistic cultures in the formation of human character. Cohen claimed in a 1925 sermon that it was highly desirable that Jews incorporate into their *Weltanschauung* the intellectual fruits of other peoples' writings, especially the Greeks:

> there can be no turning back. For good or ill, the intellectual ghetto is a thing of the past. We dare not advise our inquiring young men and women to seclude themselves from the world of thought, to keep away from the currents of modern learning. . . . The truer wiser and safer course is to let the words of Japheth dwell in the tents of Shem, at the same time exhorting our youth to remember that in the tents of Shem must be their spiritual house.[9]

Rounding out the dialogue were Jewish spokesmen who detected a definite religious hue within the spirit of Hellenism. One such thinker was Asher Hirsch Ginsberg (Ahad Ha'am). Gins-

Chapter 4: Hebraism and Hellenism

berg claimed that although the Hebraic impulse was essentially distinct and lofty, finding no replicas

> among the cultured nations of antiquity prior to their coming into contact with Judaism, . . . intellectuals are mistaken if they see . . . an inherent distinction rooted in the nature of the two peoples; [it] is a fundamental error to claim that] from the outset the "ethical feeling" was given exclusively to Israel . . . while the Greeks were missing this feeling and were ill-suited to see and to understand the world in this manner. Whoever wants to know the truth . . . must recognize the Greek ethic as it arises from its sacred literature. This means not looking at the ethical wisdom of the Greek philosophers, but rather at the ethics of the masses. . . . [T]hen it will become apparent that this great nation, too, felt in its soul the reality of a moral universe. . . . However, [there is no denying] that its polytheistic structure hindered the spiritual sweep of its vision and prevented it from rising to the same exalted level which the ethical impulse attained in Israel.[10]

Ahad Ha'am was joined in his perception of the spiritual integrity of Hellenism by Reform scholar David Neumark[11] and Professor Joseph Klausner of the Hebrew University. Klausner was particularly insistent in claiming that the conventional notion that divided Judaism and Hellenism into polar opposites was nothing less than a crude distortion of reality. He argued instead that the spiritual integrity of the Greeks was an acknowledged fact in Jewish sources. For example, the *Pesikta de-Rab Kahana* referred to the kingdom of Greece as "unblemished," and the Zohar confirmed that "the Greeks were near the true faith." In other words, an ethical-religious flow coursed through the arteries of the Hellenistic world. Greco-Roman civilization was as concerned as Israel was with the moral questions of good and righteousness. Both civilizations were propelled by humanistic drives. In their thrust toward moral virtue, they represented a difference in degree and not in kind: "Greece and Judah are, thus, not real opposites. Greece sought after the good, the upright and justice to a considerable degree, even though it didn't achieve the wholeness in this area attained by Judah. Similarly, Judah loved beauty and harmony to a considerable degree, although not in the complete form achieved by Greece."[12]

By far, the foremost exponent of this thrust was Claude Goldsmid Montefiore, who was quick to award excellent grades in morality to Hellenistic civilization. Montefiore went one step further, however, and it was this step that brought him into direct confrontation with Joseph Hertz. Montefiore not only attributed a religious sensibility to Greco-Roman civilization; he claimed that some Hellenistic modes of thinking were superior to those found in the Jewish heritage. Logic dictated that these modes of thinking be absorbed by Judaism, which stood to be enriched by them and to gain a new orientation. Underlying Montefiore's call for a synthesis between Jewish and Greek ways of thinking was an appreciation that Greece had been and would continue to be a beneficiary of Jewish religious insights. There were, however, specific doctrines that Israel could learn from Greece. The viability of a creative Judaism required Jews to appropriate something of the Hellenistic spirit:

> Greece has not only taught the world how to think, but it has given it many an element in noble life. . . . Greece . . . as well as Israel, made its contribution towards religion. Israel gave more, but Greece gave something: and if Greece has more to learn from Israel, Israel has something to learn from Greece.[13]
>
> [B]oth Greek and Hebrew spirituality are immortal, yet neither can exist with fullest potency without the other.

The incorporation of certain Greek elements would fashion Judaism into a new and superior spiritual creation.[14] Montefiore's revolutionary call for the absorption of Hellenistic elements into Judaism was matched by his equally provocative definition of Hebraism. Unlike Jewish and Christian triumphalists, who each identified Hebraism as their exclusive preserve, Montefiore perceived Hebraism as embodying both Jewish and Christian elements. Montefiore did not stop at supplanting the lingering, medieval enmity between Judaism and Christianity with mutual feelings of trust and goodwill. His innovation lay in his specific call for Jews and Christians to appreciate the innate energizing qualities within each other's religious traditions.[15] He explicitly encouraged Jews to discard past prejudices, justifiable as they were, and to look afresh at the insights of the founder of Christianity.[16] In some respects, Gospel teaching deepened, refined, and amplified Old Testament teachings.[17]

Montefiore wrote vigorously of the need for Old and New Testament thinkers alike to correct each other's theology. Judaism and Christianity could, in a broad sense, complement each other. The moral and spiritual goals of Judaism and Christianity were compatible. Notwithstanding the fact that the great mass of New Testament concepts were obviously emotionally hard to accept within a synagogue setting, it behooved Judaism to wed itself to the most noble notions of its eldest religious offspring.[18]

A new era of reconciliation would be inaugurated by overcoming fright, hostility, and prejudice:

> Let us not then persist in keeping to a poorer Judaism than we need. Why should we not make our religion as rich as we can? Jesus and Paul can help us as well as Hillel and Akiba. Let them do so. What is good in them came also from God.[19]

> [I]f Rabbinic ethics carry forward and supplement Old Testament doctrine in one way, the ethics of Jesus do so in another.... We may value both. The fire and passion of Jesus may be as warmly appreciated as the delicacy and detail of the Rabbis.[20]

The premise of Montefiore's bold theology was a respect for ideational pluralism coupled with a developmental perception of truth. Truths, being the formulations of mortal men, could never be absolute or static, unyielding, and unresponsive to change. They were, rather, relative virtues that arose out of particularistic social and religious environments. Religious truths, in particular, were never the sole property of one group; they were broader than any individual or group's narrow conception. Most certainly, the sublime doctrines of religion were never delivered to a single people in a perfect state at a specific moment. The values of a specific group were not of eternal significance; rather, they were to be understood as provisional and relative. They were conditioned by an in-bred view of history that could lay no claim to finality: "no one religion, and no one stage of that religion, are in possession of perfect truth in all its fullness and completion.... Neither Hebrew Bible nor Rabbinic Talmud is immaculate or complete in doctrine or institution, in morality or in religion." [21]

Unquestionably, there were also imperfections in the literary heritage of both Hellenism and Christianity, just as there were manifestations of wisdom. In Montefiore's estimation, conventional Christian thought and an aggressive polemical mindset made Christians think that the defects of the Hebrew Scriptures had been corrected by the New Testament. Christianity, he maintained, could not claim sponsorship of *the* redemptive model of salvation. At the same time, he dismissed out of hand the claim made by Jewish theologians of the self-sufficient superiority of Jewish wisdom over the teachings of the Gospels. Rather, it was incumbent on the modern Jew to admit that certain aspects of biblical and rabbinic thought were cumbersome, primitive, unethical, and hence, erroneous, obsolete, and anachronistic. These elements needed to be expunged from the realm of Jewish thought. The only enduring features in Judaism were those that at least equaled in their nobility the parallel virtues found in Christianity and in Hellenism.[22]

The pages of the *Pentateuch* document Hertz's participation in the Hebraism-Hellenism dialogue, specifically in his defining and evaluating—as editor—the merits and demerits of both civilizations. As a traditional Jew, the chief rabbi defined Hebraism exclusively as a Jewish spiritual category. The Rabbis of the Talmud were the natural and legitimate successors to the religious enterprise set in motion by Moses and carried forward by the prophets. Ritual and moral laws were intrinsic to the life of early Israel, and to later rabbinic Judaism. Consequently, the claim that the ethical thrust in Western civilization emanated solely from Christian teaching rang hollow. At the same time, it was highly questionable whether Christian civilization had earned the moral accolades conventionally bestowed on her by gentile thinkers. In the chief rabbi's estimation, Christianity had not offered humanity a life-renewing religious transfusion.

As editor of the Commentary, Hertz also condemned the so-called merits of Hellenistic culture. Hence, his portrait of religious integrity was antithetical to that of scholars who recognized a vigorous ethical thrust and cogent spiritual ambience in Hellenism. Particularly offensive to him was Montefiore's strident claim that Judaism would be enriched by incorporating onto its trunk specific Hellenistic and Christian teachings.

Montefiore brought impressive credentials to his work of theological reconstruction. To begin with, he spoke as a highly educated Jew conversant with both biblical and rabbinic tradition, despite the fact that he played down his qualifications as a talmudist.[23] His family name conjured up immediate respect among Anglo-Jews. Like his venerable great-uncle, Moses Montefiore, Claude also pursued a tradition of philanthropy. To immigrant Jews, he embodied the English Jew who believed completely in the emancipation credo of social and religious assimilation. Yet he was

Chapter 4: Hebraism and Hellenism

also a man who took the religious enterprise seriously through his mentorship and participation in the fortunes of the fledgling Liberal Judaism movement, and also through his stalwart advocacy of communication between Jew and Christian. Montefiore's essays outlining his religious philosophy were exemplary models of a lucid, fluid, and relaxed style that appealed to schooled laymen. Finally, his reputation as a scholar of rank was ensured through his essays and books on Jewish and Christian theology.

The radical tenets of his religious philosophy were bound to rankle a traditional conservative like Hertz, who adhered to a more classical interpretation of Jewish theology. The chief rabbi held Montefiore's negative critique of Judaism to be as life-threatening as that of Graf-Wellhausen.[24] The chief rabbi classified Montefiore's perceptions of Israelite-rabbinic religion on a par with those radical Bible exegetes whom Solomon Schechter had judiciously labeled as anti-Semites. In fact, as editor of the *Pentateuch*, Hertz blacklisted Montefiore by name, alongside two other critics of Judaism—Julius Wellhausen and William Robertson Smith. The significance of singling out these three scholars cannot be minimized, for Hertz's standard practice in the Commentary was to mention by name only those who concurred with a particular proposition or opinion advanced by the editor. Admittedly, Montefiore's estimate of biblical-rabbinic religion did not coincide on all counts with Wellhausen's or with Smith's portrait of Mosaism and Rabbinism as absolute retrogressions from the path of authentic spirituality. Nor did Montefiore agree with Smith's and Wellhausen's designation of Christianity as the religious successor to Judaism. But he did promote one of Wellhausen's bottom-line judgments: the incompatibility of prophetic religion with a rigid devotion to cultic-ceremonialist formalism. This alone, however, did not induce Hertz to place him in company with Wellhausen and Smith. The capstone was, in all probability, Montefiore's insistence that Judaism remodel itself extensively in the images of both Hellenism and Christianity.[25]

In the widest sense, the barbs hurled at Hellenism and Christianity in the pages of the Hertz *Pentateuch* may be understood first as an explosive reaction to the views of Jewish and gentile scholars who, to greater or lesser degrees, awarded points to Hellenism and/or Christendom for religious integrity, and second, as a reaction to Claude Montefiore's liberal approach to Judaism.

The Commentary on Deuteronomy depicted Liberalism as having run afoul of the injunction: "thou shalt not add thereto, nor diminish from it" (Deut. 13:1):

> The various attempts made by revolutionary religious leaders to "accommodate" Judaism to present-day conditions have all suffered spiritual ship-wreck. . . . On the one hand, some attempted "to diminish Judaism" by such vital things as the Sabbath, the Hebrew language, and the love of Zion. And on the other hand, there are those who, besides, are prepared "to add" to the Jewish Heritage things that constitute a serious weakening of the Unity of God, and a radical departure from other fundamental principles of the Jewish Faith.[26]

Several years earlier, in the first edition to the Commentary on the Book of Exodus, Hertz had alluded more directly to the Reformers:

> The Temple rose silently and peacefully . . . [A] Temple of the Lord cannot be where there is discord, violence or revolt; its ramparts must arise without a noise of axe or hammer. This unfailing test of a true House of Worship is not met by so many so-called Jewish "Temples," whose walls too often resound with loud wielding of axe and hammer against the ideals and institutions vital to Judaism.[27]

Far from giving credit to Hellenism and Christianity, Hertz presented an alternate paradigm of mankind's quest for ethical nobility. Woven masterfully into the texture of the Commentary, it can be reduced conceptually to a syllogism:

A. The barbarism practiced by paganism and Greek religion effectively prevented the evolution of a moral code mandating righteous behavior among all sectors of society.

B. Christianity, though indebted outwardly to Judaism, evolved its primary ethical structure under the impact of a pagan and Hellenistic *Weltanschauung*.

C. Therefore, Christianity, like Hellenism, was effectively hindered in its attempt to sustain a pragmatic scheme of ethical behavior in the Western world.

Fortunately, these pagan-Christian shortcomings, the editor claimed, were offset historically by the moral genius of the Jewish people, whose members were taught humanism from Hebrew Scriptures and the vast corpus of rabbinic literature.

Hertz: The Ideological Architect of the Commentary

A strong argument can be made that the positive assessment of Judaism vis-à-vis Hellenism and Christianity was formulated primarily, if not entirely, by Joseph Herman Hertz without the collaboration of his research team. The evidence strongly supports the presumption that it was the chief rabbi who was responsible for the Commentary's consistent and relentless critique of paganism and the attempt to show the historic link between the values of paganism and Greco-Roman civilization and Christianity. In a 1923 communiqué, one year prior to the completion of the *Pentateuch* in unrevised manuscript form, the Reverend Salis Daiches of Edinburgh specifically requested of Hertz that a meeting to coordinate strategy take place among the collaborators.[28] Apparently, this did not occur, at least not on an ongoing basis. A short time earlier, Hertz had informed his junior colleague from Scotland that he and Professor Adolph Buechler, as coeditors, were solely responsible for harmonizing the texts submitted by the various contributors.[29] Added to this was Hertz's candid conclusion that even after Abraham Cohen of Birmingham had tried his hand at editing,[30] Hertz was dissatisfied with the quality of the manuscripts submitted to him. In this vein, Hertz's daughter, Josephine, recalled her father's complaining that if he wanted the project completed properly, he would have to undertake the task of editing himself.[31]

Further proof of the chief rabbi's dominant editorial input in shaping the Commentary's ideological thrust can be gleaned from a letter he composed to his three remaining contributors in the summer of 1929. The letter reminds them that their manuscripts had been "recast," and often altogether rewritten by himself.[32] In May 1936, with the publication of the final volume of the *Pentateuch*, Samuel Frampton of Liverpool, the researcher of the notes to the Haftarot, insisted, as he had several years earlier, that Hertz had not adequately acknowledged the full extent of his pivotal contribution in the composition of the Haftarah commentary. The chief rabbi countered, noting that depending on the particular book of the Torah, only one-tenth to one-third of the Haftarot annotations could be ascribed fairly to the Liverpool minister: "It is very rarely that any sentence of yours remains unchanged or, untransformed. You may not know that the comments you sent me on each Haftorah, were often recast or rewritten as [many] as 6 or 7 times."[33]

Further evidence pointing to Hertz as the primary architect of the Commentary's scathing polemic against the moral integrity of paganism and Christianity can be ascertained from two articles reflecting his decidedly anti-pagan and anti-Christian bias. Excerpts from these monographs were inserted, in turn, into the text of the *Pentateuch*. In a March 1928 public lecture before the Society for Jewish Jurisprudence (subsequently published in the autumn of that year), the chief rabbi, citing President Woodrow Wilson, argued for the direct positive influence of Babylonian law on later Greco-Roman legislation. Yet in the first edition of his 1930 Commentary to the Book of Exodus, Hertz negated the contribution of the Babylonian code on later ages[34] by altering the wording of this significant citation. The change of form can be explained by the editor's zealousness to play down a constructive aspect of paganism; this then allowed him to maximize the impact of Judaism's spirit on Western governments associated with Christendom.

The chief rabbi had also acknowledged in his 1928 paper several exemplary moral aspects of the Code of Hammurabi. The implication of his illustrations was that in some respects, the Code of Hammurabi was certainly on par with—or even superior to—specific norms found in Mosaism. For example, a Babylonian slave could hold property and acquire wealth with the permission of his master, and in this way eventually gain his manumission. A Babylonian wife could initiate divorce proceedings in cases of proven cruelty, and desertion by a husband automatically dissolved the marriage. When a husband chose to divorce his wife, he was required to pay her double dowry. The Code of Hammurabi also protected the landowner in need of capital. Moneylenders were forbidden to speculate in futures. When a natural disaster struck, a moratorium on interest payments was declared for that year. In capital suits, perjured witnesses were executed, and in civil trials they paid damages. Furthermore, the later biblical notion of blood revenge was totally suppressed in Hammurabi's days by a strong centralized government. As editor, Hertz did not incorporate any of these ethical illustrations into his Commentary, yet saw fit to denigrate Babylonian civilization's obsession, by contrast to biblical society, with the interests of property over humanity.[35]

In 1930, Hertz capped off his broadside attack against pagan and Christian civilization in his essay "Fundamental Ideals and Proclamations of Judaism." The arguments presented were subsequently incorporated verbatim into the pages of the Commentary. In paying tribute to Israel's distinctive moral genius, the chief rabbi outlined the salient differences between Jewish religious civilization and the religious outlooks of polytheism and Christianity. So critical were these distinctions that they amounted to Judaism's waging spiritual war against polytheism, Greco-Roman society, and Christendom. Worlds apart from other religious systems was Jewish civilization's perception of ethical monotheism, its conception of morality as law, and its weaving of holiness into the fabric of home life and ritual. Jewish teachers alone had clung both to the idea of God's unity and its necessary corollary—the moral unity and brotherhood of man. This was a fundamental principle that polytheism had desecrated. Judaism, on the other hand, had saved the honor of the human race by categorically rejecting heathenism's deification of the reigning monarch, insisting instead that God hallowed all human life equally.[36] Contrary to a contemporary vibrant strain of the pagan spirit that abolished all moral inhibitions in favor of inclination and instinct, Judaism stood squarely by its conviction that moral law originated with God and not man. Consequently, for modern man to extricate himself from "the moral chaos of our own age," he had to deem himself accountable to a divine law outside himself.[37] Human nearness to God was actualized through the doctrine of *imitatio Dei*.[38] Where Greek ethics leaned heavily on the category of beauty, Jewish ethics revolved around the standard of holiness. Acted out daily, the sublimity of holiness meant several things: an appreciation for the life-sustaining joy of disciplined ritual behavior; a commitment to parental and filial affection; a concrete reverence and respect for women; and a passionate concern for the health and welfare of the stranger.[39] The last three considerations were sorely missing, in whole or in part, from the civilizations of Babylonia, Greece, and Rome, the most enlightened nations of their time.

Further confirmation of Hertz's responsibility in giving ideological shape to the Commentary can be found in his penned interpolations on the extant manuscripts submitted to him by Samuel Frampton and Abraham Cohen. These interpolations were inserted into the final first edition of the Commentary. Significantly, the available extant manuscripts of both Frampton and Cohen harbored no pointed anti-Christian bias. To Frampton's manuscript[40] of the Haftarah to the weekly reading of *Aharei Mot*, the chief rabbi added the sentences damning the human ferocity and lack of pity and justice of Greece and Rome, compared with the moral vitality and relevance of Israel's prophets.[41] Pursuing this line further, it was Hertz's pen that characterized a pagan's marrying his father's wife as "a heinous crime."[42] In the prophetic reading of *Emor*, it was not Frampton but Hertz who made the historical connection between the large private real estate holdings of Babylonia's priests and Christendom's medieval abbeys;[43] and in the introduction to the Haftarah of *Korah*, it was Hertz who altered Frampton's manuscript in order to distinguish sharply between an Israelite and pagan perception of the monarchy.[44] Finally, galleys to the Book of Deuteronomy documented the chief rabbi's efforts to undermine the moral integrity of heathenism, pagan Hellenism, and Christianity. From his pen flowed the distinction between Greek and Jewish conceptions of justice, and it was he who publicized the Church's cruelty, and especially, the notoriety of the Inquisition in turning a profit from the punishment of idolators.

The Commentary's Critique of Paganism and Hellenism

Hertz identified paganism's often passionate subversion of decent and humane relationships among people in favor of the acquisition of material goods as the hallmark of godlessness.[45] This was reflected, for example, in the rabbinic comment that the heathen builders of the Tower of Babel were heartbroken over the loss of a brick that dropped from the heights, but paid no heed if a construction worker accidentally fell to his death.[46] In the Commentary's estimation, the priority of property over humanitarian concerns graphically summed up the inadequacy of heathen civilization, both ancient and modern. "Polytheism could never rise to the idea of Humanity; heathen society 'was vitiated by failure to recognize the moral obligation involved in our common humanity.'"[47]

The Commentary highlighted pagan and Greek barbarism by offsetting it against Israelite notions of morality. For example, the cries that rose heavenward from Sodom mirrored in rabbinic theology the "atrocious wickedness" of a heathen community:

> [l]egend graphically describes [the Sodomites'] hatred of all strangers and their fiendish punishment of all who departed from their ways. A girl, overcome by pity, supplied food to a poor stranger. On detection, she was stripped, bound, daubed with honey and placed on the roof under the burning sun to be devoured by the bees.[48]

A particular deficiency of Egyptian society steeped in paganism was its disgust for strangers. This manifested itself blatantly in Pharaoh's directive to the midwives to act barbarously toward "aliens."[49] Scripture, on the other hand, promulgated "the precept to love" or at the very least "not to oppress" the alien, no fewer than thirty-six times.[50] The Commentary also contrasted the notorious sexual immorality of the Egyptians with the behavior of Joseph, who, by resisting the wiles of Potiphar's wife, rose above the lustful temptation of having an extramarital affair.[51] Egypt's "barbarous custom" of allowing the decapitated body of a malefactor to hang exposed to public view as well as to serve as prey of birds also came in for censure; it violated Israelite norms (Deut. 21:23).[52] The pitilessness of the pagan Code of Hammurabi was equally apparent. It made provision to penalize a master who destroyed "the tooth or eye of *another* man's slave," but the injured slave himself had no recourse to a court of law to settle his grievance. Equally unnerving was the Code's decree of death for one harboring a runaway slave.[53] This repulsive disregard for the human personality of the slave became a regular feature of pagan life in medieval times: "Thus, William of Malmesbury, speaking of days before the Norman Conquest, complains of the horrible custom of Saxon Masters, who, after associating with the maid servants on their estates, sold them to a life of shame or into foreign slavery."[54]

The pagan perception of inequality among men accorded with the "deification of reckless and irresponsible power" in the hands of a despot king. This allowed the monarch to exploit his subjects with impunity. In Israel, however, such behavior was deemed an outrage against reason and human decency. Basing himself on the prophetic cry against social inequality, the editor concluded that Israel's kings, in the main, ruled with equity: "While to every other ancient monarch the subject was a slave, to the Israelite king he was a *brother*."[55]

Through a comparison with Israel's standards, the Commentary focused intensively on repudiating Greece's low-grade morality. This was in keeping with Hertz's oft-repeated opinion, particularly during the Hanukkah season, that Hellenism had to be leavened by Judaism. A contemporary recollected that Hertz, in one Hanukkah address delivered at Cambridge in the mid-thirties, proclaimed—overtly or between the lines—that it was Hellenistic civilization that had produced an Adolf Hitler.[56]

The ethical watchwords of Hebraism, in both its biblical and rabbinic manifestations, were justice, righteousness, and holiness.[57] Theologically, these virtues owed much to the notions of fear and love of God. While fear served as a powerful deterrent from evil, love was the highest incentive to living in accordance with the divine will;[58] both were in direct accord with Maimonides' description of fear and love as the two decisive ways man served God.[59]

From the biblical perspective (Ps. 89:15), justice was "the main pillar of God's Throne" on earth; it constituted the primary building block for man in his continuous struggle to fashion a lawful community.[60] Justice was the awe-inspired respect for the personality of others, and their inalienable right to life, honor, and the fruit of their toils. Being created in God's image, man could never be reduced to the level of a thing or chattel.[61] Justice manifested itself not only in charitable and philanthropic deeds, but in an insistence on strict impartiality in the courtroom.[62] The Commentary reinforced this sentiment with a rabbinic prooftext:

> The Babylonian teacher Samuel was passing over a plank laid across a stream when a stranger drew nigh and offered his hand to conduct him with safety over the frail bridge. Samuel, on inquiring who he was, learned that he was a suitor who desired him to adjudicate upon his cause. "Friend, thou hast disqualified me by thy eager courtesy. I am no longer able to judge the case with impartiality."[63]

In Hertz's estimation, justice was not the highest ethical virtue; yet it was a lofty standard capable of ordering man's lives fairly: "That which is above justice must be based on justice and include justice and be reached through justice."[64] Justice meant judging men on the scale of merit and avoiding the temptation of condemnation by appearance.[65] A higher form of justice, associated with equity, bid man to be true to something more than the mere letter of his bond.[66]

One of Matthew Arnold's and Claude Montefiore's complaints against the Jewish religion was its fixation on the external deed. In Arnold's estimation, it was to the world's good fortune that Jesus attended to "that inward world of feelings and dispositions which Judaism had too much neglected."[67] Montefiore, in turn, applauded the Christian Bible's concept of love as more venturous, more self-sacrificing, more eager, more giving than the Hebrew notion of righteousness.[68] In a categorical rejection of this outlook, the editor proclaimed that Judaism's notion of justice left ample

Chapter 4: Hebraism and Hellenism

room for acts of mercy motivated by love. Identified also with a striving after righteousness and holiness,[69] this higher manifestation of justice approximated the prophet Micah's maximal ideal of religion. These concepts appealed to man's sense of altruism. Thus, righteousness for Amos was the masterword of existence because God is righteousness.[70] In the broadest sense, the vision of human society based on righteousness constituted the messianic goal of history.[71]

Holiness, too, was an ideal concept achieved through cooperation "with others in the service of a great Cause or Ideal, as a member of a Community, Society, or 'Kingdom.'"[72] It was not attainable by flight from the world nor by monklike renunciation of human relationships.[73] Appraised by the editor to be the vintage of suffering and sorrow,[74] holiness entailed man's effort to incorporate into his life God's moral attributes of grace, love, patience, and forgiveness. These qualities were "one of the most advanced triumphs of Religion."[75] The Commentary concluded that Hebraism held that ethical values were exclusively the only values of eternal worth:[76]

> Israel's faith is a religion . . . that declares man's humanity to man as the most acceptable form of adoration of the one God.[77]

> The Prophet has taught the higher law; he has rooted all human duty, both to God and man, in love of God.[78]

> The highest manifestation[s] of the Divine . . . are God's ways manifest in the hearts and souls of men, in the home life of those who do justice, love mercy and walk humbly with their God.[79]

The touchstone of morality was the deed: "I call heaven and earth to witness that, whether it be Jew or heathen, man or woman, freeman or bondman—only according to their acts does the Divine spirit rest upon them."[80]

The *Pentateuch*'s claim that God is righteousness and not that God is love may be interpreted as a subtle rejoinder to the views of Claude Montefiore and like-minded Christian essayists who subordinated God's attribute of righteousness—a moral virtue emulated by man—to the Christian accent on God's love.[81]

Concurring with Amos' verdict, the chief rabbi declared the cardinal sin to be man's inhumanity to man.[82] The source of this evil was traceable to the ancient world of paganism and, in particular, to the doorstep of Greece. The latter's grasp of justice, especially, was akin not to holiness but to harmony. Harmony implied the construction of a social system propelled by pragmatism and a passion for orderliness: "Plato's *Republic* . . . implies a harmonious arrangement of society, by which every human peg is put into its appropriate hole, so that those who perform humble functions shall be content to perform them in due subservience to their superiors. *It stresses the inequalities of human nature.*"[83]

Hertz maintained that Greece was doomed forever in its attempts to construct "a high and consistent ethical system" because the source of its ethical mold did not begin with God, but with finite man, who assigned his own baser impulses to the gods. The tragedy of paganism was its deification of man. Paganism dethroned God and assaulted morality: "According to the oldest Hellenic idea, the murderer violated only the family sphere. Mosaism, however, by virtue of its conception of the human being as of Divine image, recognized in murder above all a sin against the Holy God."[84]

It was Greece's misfortune that it was never touched by the divine proclamation of the Decalogue, which confirmed morality.[85] In what was tantamount to a categorical rejection of the Kantian notion of moral autonomy, the editor asserted that

> no interpretation . . . is valid or in consonance with the Jewish Theistic position, which makes human reason or the human personality the *source* of . . . revelation. . . . There can be no such thing as a purely natural revelation. . . . No view of God that grew up "of itself" in the human mind, owing nothing to God's self-disclosing action, could have any value.[86]

In contrast to Hertz, Montefiore had sought to discredit the dominant biblical perception of God in his presentation of Greek theology. The Liberal theologian distinguished the wholly good and unemotional Greek god from the passionate, volatile outbursts of God depicted in Scripture.[87] In doing so, he conveniently overlooked the vulgar anthropomorphic personality traits of the Greek pantheon, preferring instead to highlight the "monotheistic" tone of several Greek philosophers. The chief rabbi argued the reverse! Normative Greek religion was inexplicable without reference to the pantheon. The human foibles and failings of the gods constituted the popular motif of Greek theology. This contrasted sharply with the Torah's exalted image of God as pure, merciful, and gracious.

Chapter 4: Hebraism and Hellenism

Consequently, the editor preferred to de-emphasize the sullen and willful image of God's nature:

> Dr. Schechter has pointed out that the Imitation of God is confined by the Rabbis to His attributes of mercy and graciousness. "The whole Rabbinic literature might be searched in vain for a single instance of the sterner Biblical attributes of God being set up as a model for a man to copy."[88]

In effect, two alternate models of God were presented in the Commentary. The popular one concurred with the perception that God exhibited emotion:

> Heb. idiom often attributes to God the feelings or emotions of man. God is thus said to "repent," when in consequence of a change in the character and conduct of men, He makes a corresponding change in the purpose toward them which He had previously announced.[89]

> The God adored by Judaism is not an impersonal Force, an It, whether spoken of as "Nature" or "World-Reason." The God of Israel is the Source not only of power and life, but of consciousness, personality, moral purpose and ethical action.[90]

At the same time, lest the reader be left with the erroneous impression that God actually possessed human emotions, the Commentary acquainted the reader in numerous places with the fundamental rabbinic concept of anthropomorphism.[91]

For those more familiar with the nuances of Jewish theology or who were perhaps familiar with Montefiore's praise of the Greeks for having contributed to the world an unemotional depiction of God, Hertz offered a similar paradigm. However, unlike Montefiore's exclusive reliance on Greek sources, the Commentary took note of a "Greek" portrait of God within the Talmud itself: "Whatever change has to be wrought must be in the heart of the sinner, not in the nature of the Deity. He is the same after man has sinned as He was before a man has sinned."[92]

It is fair to say that the Hertz *Pentateuch*'s analysis of Greek morality was culled from a wider range of Greek sources than those submitted by Montefiore. Hertz spared no ink in painting a black, malevolent portrait of Greek ethics. Admittedly, Greek civilization pursued a love of beauty and a respect for the mind. Yet in the final analysis, the Greeks "remained *barbarians* religiously and morally."[93]

Simply put, Hebraism and Hellenism conceived of the structuring of society in dramatically opposite ways. The Commentary was adamant, for example, that the marvelous contribution of free government was directly traceable to the Bible. Whereas Claude Montefiore argued that the classical Greek writers had imparted "the value of ordered freedom" and "liberty of obedience" to mankind, the editor disagreed: it was a "radical misconception" to turn to Greece for democratic inspiration.[94] Unlike Israel's unique constitutional monarchy, which accented the beneficent duties of the ruler rather than his privileges toward his people, Greece's political model was erected through its city-states, which underscored economic and social class struggle. This resulted in politics being imbued with fanaticism, which invariably led either to the massacre or exile of political opponents. Hence, the editor concurred with Nietzsche's verdict: the Greeks were the political fools of ancient history.[95]

The Commentary abounded with illustrations aimed at conclusively proving the inferior status of Greek morality. Here the editor had gone far beyond Kaufmann Kohler's gentle and mild critique of Greek culture. The American Reform theologian believed that through its prophetic strains, Judaism was destined to regenerate the moral life of humanity far more deeply than Greek culture could ever do.[96] Far more chiding was the chief rabbi's evaluation that the Greeks bred intolerance by adopting inequality as a social standard. Hertz put no credence in the partisan notion of "advanced non-Jewish writers" and "liberal Christian theologians" that tolerance was a by-product of a polytheistic worldview:

> [E]nlightened Greek polytheism permitted three of the greatest thinkers of the Periclean age—Socrates, Protagoras, and Anaxagoras—to be put to death on religious grounds. . . . [N]either Antiochus Epiphanes, who attempted to drown Judaism in the blood of its faithful children, nor Apion, the frenzied spokesman of the anti-Semites in Alexandria, displayed particular tolerance.[97]

Worse yet, the Greek mind did not estimate morality by reference to its effect upon the mass of men. Inequality, therefore, became the norm spawning a caste system that specialized in barbarism. Hellenism, for example, made no effort to ameliorate the cruel conditions of slavery. In the commentator's estimation, the Greek and Roman mentalities were geared to investments in property, rather than humanity. In contrast, the Jewish Commonwealth's passion for the rights of humanity above those of property was an entirely new idea, having no roots in the civilizations of Egypt, Greece, or Rome.[98] There was nothing comparable in Greco-Roman law to match the equity of the biblical Jubilee (Lev. 25:10, 13), which proclaimed the return of Israelites to their ancestral lands and to their families.[99] A particularly loathsome aspect of Roman and other ancient law was the definition of a slave as chattel whose existence was totally at the mercy of his master. According to Aristotle,

> a slave was deemed "an animated tool," and he could claim no more rights in his relationship to his master than a beast of burden. Agricultural labourers were chained. If at any time it was thought that there were too many slaves, they were exterminated, as wild beasts would be. Athens was an important slave market, and the State profited from it by a tax on sales. So much for "the glory that was Greece." The "grandeur that was Rome" was even more detestable.
>
> The slave was denied all human rights, and sentenced to horrible mutilation and even crucifixion at the whim of his master.... Worlds asunder from these inhumanities and *barbarities* was the treatment accorded to the Hebrew slave.[100]

Only the Mosaic code envisioned the slave as entitled to civil rights. Biblical law was especially decisive in passing the sentence of death on a master who took the life of his slave; and cruelty by a master resulting in bodily injury to his healthy slave effected the slave's immediate emancipation.[101] The brutal and despicable nature of Greek ethics was vividly illustrated in the Stoic debate over whether in a shipwreck one should sacrifice a valuable horse to save a slave.[102] Hertz obviously was not sympathetic to Claude Montefiore's elevation of Stoicism as a spiritual model that encouraged fortitude, endurance, calm, and a contempt for pain.[103]

Separating Jewish and Greco-Roman civilization, in Hertz's estimate, were their respective evaluations of the worth of human life. In ancient Greece and Rome, for example, murderers obtained asylum at the religious altar. Pagan shrines became "nurseries of criminals. In the time of Tiberius, the swarms of desperadoes had become so dangerous that the right was limited to a few cities." Worlds apart was Israel's posture: asylum was granted only to unpremeditated homicides. A willful culprit was denied refuge as well as the privilege of substituting a monetary payment to the kinsman of his victim in lieu of a court sentence. Even clergy were not exempt from prosecution.[104]

Symbolic of Israel's placing a high premium on life was the specification that the altar be constructed without the use of an iron tool. This act made the community conscious that:

> a Temple of the Lord cannot be where there is discord, violence or revolt; its ramparts must arise without noise of axe or hammer.[105]

> The purpose of the Altar is to promote peace between Israel and his Father in Heaven. Let it not, therefore, be polluted by the touch of an iron tool, the symbol of division and destruction.[106]

In Greece, the denial of the sanctity of human life manifested itself hideously in deeds of child-murder. Among the Romans, parents could abandon their children with impunity, and a father possessed the legal right to put his son to death:[107] "Tacitus deemed it a contemptible prejudice of the Jews that 'it is a crime among them to kill any child.'"[108] Far removed was the spirit of Jewish tradition:

> The child is the highest of human treasures. . . . In little children . . . God gives humanity a chance to make good its mistakes. They are "the Messiahs of mankind"—the perennial regenerative force in humanity.[109]

> [T]he children of a nation are the builders of its future. And every Jewish child must be reared to become such a builder of his People's better future; every Jewish child must be fortified by a knowledge of Judaism and trained for a life of beneficence for Israel and humanity.[110]

> None realized more clearly than the Rabbis the spiritual power that comes from the mouth of babes and sucklings (Psalm VIII, 3). "The moral universe rests upon the breath of schoolchildren," is one of their deep sayings.[111]

The disregard for the right to life also surfaced in the repulsive institution of human sacrifice. It operated "in all periods of the independent Greek states" and "in the Roman Empire" until "the fourth century of our present era."[112] Another aspect of irreverence for human life in the ancient world was illustrated dramatically by the pagan practice of publicly exposing the corpses of executed criminals, a notion that Scripture and Rabbinism interpreted as an affront to human dignity.[113]

Chapter 4: Hebraism and Hellenism 101

This diminishing of the worth of man spilled over into acts of cruelty toward the animal world: "the terrible scenes in the Roman arena [of cruelty toward animals] are only too clear an indication of the inhumanity which prevailed in the civilized world during the Talmudic period."[114] Far different was the Torahitic-Judaic spirit. The Mosaic code explicitly outlawed the "barbarous practice common among primitive races" of severing the limb of a live animal.[115] The editor reasoned that the prohibition against eating blood (Lev. 17:10–14) served as a powerful catalyst conditioning an impulse toward humaneness:

> The purpose may be to tame man's instincts of violence by weaning him from blood, and implanting within him a horror of all bloodshed.... These injunctions have undoubtedly contributed to render the Israelites a humane people. Consider the one circumstance that no Jewish mother ever killed a chicken with her own hand, and you will understand why homicide is rarer among Jews than among any other human group.[116]

Although the eating of meat was permitted by both biblical and rabbinic teachers, legislation effectively prohibited cruelty toward animals. But refraining from cruelty alone did not exhaust the profundity of the biblical-rabbinic frames of reference. Also expected was a cultivation of outright kindness to the animal world:[117] "It is one of the glories of Judaism that, thousands of years before anyone else, it so fully recognized our duties to the dumb friends and helpers of man."[118] In this vein, the Commentary implied—based on readings from Ps. 36:6, Gen. 8:1, and Jer. 21:6—that "morally speaking, there is no complete break of continuity in the scale of sentient life.... [T]he domesticated animals are in fact regarded as part of the human community."[119]

Hertz concluded that the so-called cultured nations of antiquity—Egypt, Persia, Greece, and Rome—failed to make the grade morally. All of them, for example, gave their blessings to incestuous promiscuity among near relations. Not so biblical law, which prohibited such behavior as "repellent to the finer feelings of man," or as "tainting the natural affection between near relations."[120] It was this spirit of seeking proper unions that accounted for the Torah's denunciation of homosexuality as an "unnatural vice which was prevalent in Greece and Rome."[121]

Jewish educational circles were probably disturbed by Claude Montefiore's categorical declaration that Stoic inspiration alone among the ancient teachings—biblical, rabbinic, and Aristotelian—had proclaimed unequivocally the principles of universalism and the brotherhood of man. Montefiore adamantly dismissed Ben Azzai's talmudic principle of universalism (based on Gen. 5:1) as unrepresentative of mainline rabbinic teaching, which articulated a doctrine of intolerance toward outsiders:

> The Rabbinic literature contains almost every conceivable variety of opinion. One has to ask: what is the *usual* opinion, what is the . . . predominating note? Jewish apologists . . . can collect a number of sayings by which to prove that the Rabbinical literature teaches toleration and universalism. These sayings have been collected in various elegant extracts, and they have done duty in many a sermon and controversy. But the truth is that the Rabbis were no more tolerant than Athanasius, and they peopled Gehenna with their enemies as thickly as ever Dante peopled Inferno with his.[122]

> [T]he Rabbis were intolerant, particularistic, and narrow, where the gentile and the nations were concerned. . . . Thus God is not usually made less partial in Rabbinic literature than He is in the Old Testament. He is usually more partial. He hates the enemies of Israel with an even deeper hatred.[123]

Montefiore observed that it was left to Stoic preachers to transform universalism into a full-blown religious ideal via their belief that the divine being had no special relation to any particular race.[124] Hertz considered a stand like Montefiore's as absurd: "It was impossible for polytheism to reach the conception of One Humanity. . . . Through Hebrew monotheism alone was it possible to teach the Brotherhood of Man."[125] In fact, Hellenism had learned of brotherhood and the unity of mankind directly "through the Septuagint version of the Hebrew Scriptures."[126] Through the midrashic mode, the Commentary conveyed Hebraism's commitment to perpetuating the idea of universal brotherhood:

> "From which part of the earth's great surface did God gather the dust?" ask the Rabbis. Rabbi Meir answered, "From every part of the habitable earth was the dust taken for the formation of Adam." In a word, men of all lands and climes are brothers.[127]

> Rabbi Meir used to say, "Whence do we know that even a heathen, if he obeys the law of God, will thereby attain to the same spiritual communion with God as the High Priest?" Scripture says, "which if

a *man* do, he shall live by them"—not priest, Levite or Israelite, but *man* (Talmud).[128]

The *Pentateuch* affirmed that the notion of brotherhood was even embodied in the decree to spare the condemned criminal needless suffering and in the attitude taken toward corporal punishment: "The Rabbis point out that . . . previous to receiving his punishment, the wrongdoer is termed the *wicked man*, but that after being punished he is designated *thy* brother."[129]

Mankind's moral unity was a central feature of prophetic theology,[130] receiving particularly bold expression in two Torahitic verses: Lev. 19:18, 34, which were subsequently highlighted down through the ages in a variety of Jewish aphorisms. A further indicator of Judaism's universal thrust was the classification of heathen worship—barring its immoral behavior—as a legitimate attempt to honor God's Name and as a genuine expression of man's religious reflex.[131]

The editor reminded the reader that while the Greeks "coined the infamous term 'barbarian' for all non-Greeks," biblical society extended the application of brotherhood to include decent treatment of the stranger and a "practical love" of one's enemy:[132]

> The alien was to be protected, although he was not a member of one's family, clan, religious community, or people; simply *because he was a human being*. In the alien, therefore, man discovered the idea of humanity.[133]

> Because your neighbour has done you an injury, so that you entertain a grievance against him, it is not right for you to allow it to influence your action when your duty toward him is clear. He has not ceased to be your fellowman, because he violates the law of neighbourly love toward you.[134]

The editor captured Hebraism's concern for the rights of the outsider through a Hasidic parable:

> The wife of a Hasidic rabbi, having quarreled with her maid, was setting out to the magistrate to lodge her complaint. Noticing that her husband was about to accompany her, she asked him whither he was bound. "To the magistrate," he said. His wife declared that it was beneath his dignity to take any part in a quarrel with a servant. She could deal with the matter herself. The Zaddik replied: "That may be, but I intend to represent your maid, who, when accused by you, will find no one willing to take her part."[135]

Converting one's enemy into a friend was a most sublime gesture in dealing with an adversary.[136] Esau and Joseph were paradigms of this virtue, having transformed their hate into love: Esau graciously welcomed back his estranged brother Jacob, and Joseph demonstrated magnanimity toward his brothers by burying thoughts of revenge for their having sold him into servitude. These praiseworthy actions contrasted sharply with Simeon and Levi's "martial" mentality and "blind cruelty" brought to bear against the citizens of Shechem and with the callous hatred shown Joseph by his jealous brothers.[137]

The sentiment of compassion, stimulating man to deeds of charity and kindness, embodied Judaism's understanding of *rahmanut*:

> If a Jew . . . shows himself lacking in consideration for a *fellowman* in distress or suffering, we may well doubt the purity of his Jewish descent. . . . Only Israel, the Justice-intoxicated people, in time became *rahmanim bene rahmanim*, "merciful children of merciful ancestors."[138]

The paradigm of virtue in this connection was Father Abraham. He vigorously rejected the human tendency to glorify brute force in favor of a call for pity and sympathy, which he so vigorously demonstrated on behalf of the wicked residents of Sodom.[139] Jacob, too, through the eyes of rabbinic lore, displayed genuine brotherly compassion, fearing that he might have to slay his elder brother Esau.[140]

Viewed as an anthropological category, mercy was intrinsically linked to civility. This was an idea that had a theological spin-off: God, as well, tempered His strict judgment of men with pity.[141] Montefiore himself, the *Pentateuch* noted, agreed that *rahmanut* was the most characteristic ethical quality of rabbinic Judaism.[142] The Commentary reinforced this teaching with a poignant talmudic anecdote:

> Rabbi Jose said, All my days I grieved at my not being able to explain this verse [Deut. 28:29]; for what difference can it be to the blind man, whether he gropeth in the light or in the dark? Until one night I was walking in the road, and met a blind man with a lighted torch in his hand. "Son," said I, "why dost thou carry that torch? Thou canst not see its light." "Friend," replied the blind man, "true it is I cannot see, but as long as I carry this torch in my hand, the sons of men see me, take *pity* on me, and save me from pitfalls, from thorns and briers."[143]

Greece's Legacy Transferred to Rome

The chief rabbi confirmed the earlier judgment of Rabbi Samson Raphael Hirsch[144] that the Romans were the students of Greek culture and, eventually, the heirs to Greek values. Specifically, Hertz argued that the Bible's effective neutralization of the divine right of kings must have sounded absurd to the Roman ear:

> No Jewish ruler would ever have dared to claim Divine honours, and, like the Egyptian and Roman emperors, order sacrifices to be offered to him.... It is interesting to compare this incident [i.e., the fraudulent confiscation of Naboth's property and his subsequent illegal death on orders from Jezebel] ... with the conduct of the later Roman Emperor Diocletian. It was his habit to charge with treason any of his subjects whose estates he desired; to have the owner executed; and then confiscate those estates. Of course, there was no Elijah to raise his voice against the Imperial procedure. The Diocletian incident is typical of Roman rule in the Provinces of the Empire. It was unbelievably merciless.... "Roman administration sucked the lifeblood out of its Eastern subjects, and diminished their will to live." ... In the matter of human government, Rome has as little to teach us as has Greece.[145]

In some cases, the Romans bested their mentors by finding new ways to inflict suffering. Not only were they unable to fathom the humane treatment that slaves received under the religious legislation of the Second Temple, but the Romans specialized in imposing unusually "gruesome punishments" on slaves.[146] Particularly loathsome, when compared with the practical love of one's neighbor described in the Torah, was ancient Rome's treatment of the impoverished debtor:

> The creditor could imprison him in his own private dungeon, chain him to a block, sell him into slavery, or even put him to death. If the debtor had several creditors, the Roman Law of the Twelve Tables ordained that they could hew him in pieces; and although one of them took a part of his body larger in proportion than his claim, the other creditors had no redress![147]

> Virgil praises one of his heroes because he never felt any sympathy with sufferers through want; Seneca thinks it natural to recoil in horror from a poor man; and Plautus declares feeding the hungry to be cruelty, because it merely prolongs a life of misery.[148]

Another feature of Greco-Roman civilization was xenophobia. Originally, the Romans had only one word, *hostis*, which defined both stranger and enemy.[149]

Greece and Rome's Impact on Western Life

In short, from Hertz's viewpoint, the West's misfortune was its inheritance of an array of sins from heathendom in general and Hellenism in particular. The editor collated considerable circumstantial evidence to substantiate his claim. Jewish morality, which began with justice, also demanded strict impartiality from the bench. Yet this tenet, already mentioned, was unfortunately absent from pagan and Hellenistic life. Lamentably, "judicial venality" was also a feature of contemporary life in the West. Hence, the editor implied ever so subtly that modern forms of judicial corruption and bribery were values transmitted organically from Greco-Roman civilization.[150] Similar attention was paid to monarchical privileges taking precedence over the application of justice in the ancient world, the only exception being scriptural legislation. The editor then left it to the reader to infer that modern totalitrian regimes had derived their irreverence for justice from antiquity:

> It is noteworthy that [in] the Biblical regulations . . . justice is to be above the monarchy. This is certainly without a parallel in ancient times. . . . Even in our own day, there have been and are great European states which openly and deliberately destroy the independence of their Courts of Law, and turn them into instruments of State policy.[151]

The chief rabbi pursued his negative appraisal of Western notions of morality by focusing on the slight value placed on human life in the Code of Hammurabi. By then directing the reader's eye immediately to the "exceedingly cruel modes of execution in European countries down to quite modern times"—including the English death penalty for pocket-picking and sheep-stealing—the editor implied a causal connection between pagan barbarism and Western practices.[152] Similarly, under the impact of heathendom and Hellenism, the inhumanity of slavery had become a pernicious feature of Western life. Unfortunately, nations had paid little heed historically to the humanization process of the institution, reflected in biblical and rabbinic texts:

Chapter 4: Hebraism and Hellenism

> Slavery as permitted by the Torah was quite different from Greek and Roman slavery, or even the cruel system in some modern countries down to our own times. In Hebrew law, the slave was not a thing, but a human being; he was not the chattel of a master who had unlimited power over him. . . . Brutal treatment of any slave, whether Hebrew or heathen, secured his immediate liberty.[153]

> The system of slavery which is tolerated by the Torah was fundamentally different from the cruel systems of the *ancient world*, and even of *Western countries* down to the middle of the last century.[154]

The annotator's references to the ancient world and Western countries can be understood as euphemisms for a wide spectrum of legislation ranging from Babylonian to Greco-Roman to Church-inspired jurisprudence.

In this vein, the editor recorded that the eighteenth-century practice of medieval German feudal princes selling their subjects as mercenaries in foreign wars[155] was more dishonorable than the lucrative biblical traffic in horses by several of Israel's kings. The Commentary implied that the United States, in particular, had inherited the ancient world's perception of the slave as chattel, a notion fundamentally at odds with the humanitarian thrust of biblical society:

> A strict fugitive slave law was in operation [in Hammurabi's day], which in some respects was as harsh as the American fugitive slave law of "Uncle Tom" days.[156]

> [T]he law of Hammurabi . . . condemned to death anyone who sheltered a runaway slave. . . . Among Greeks and Romans the runaway bondman was, on recapture, branded with a *red-hot iron*. Readers of *Uncle Tom's Cabin* will remember that, as late as the middle of the last century, fugitive slaves were tracked and pursued by bloodhounds.[157]

This repulsive procedure was, however, not parallel to the drilling of an ear of a biblical slave who had decided by his own will to remain in servitude.[158]

A Hellenistic mindset was also instrumental in shaping Western attitudes toward labor. Both Athens and Rome successfully transmitted to Europe a pejorative evaluation of the work ethic. Hence, the Jewish model acclaiming the dignity of labor had been benched:

This slowness in recognizing the needs of labour is no doubt due to the fact that, till quite recent times, classical literature monopolized the education of the governing classes of the European peoples. As with the Greeks and Romans, idleness became the mark of nobility; and it was deemed to be beneath the man of gentle birth to worry over the condition of serfs or toilers.[159]

Hertz felt justified in holding Rome ultimately culpable, also, for the Western tradition of civil and political inequity between aliens and their host majority. Unlike Judaism's reliance on "one of the great texts of Scripture" proclaiming one standard for stranger and citizen alike (Lev. 24:22), Roman law originally classified "every *alien* . . . as an enemy, and, therefore, devoid of any rights."[160] Such depraved behavior was evident in many contemporary nations:

In western countries, the old Bible command, *love ye the stranger* (Deut. x, 19), is honoured more in the breach than in the observance. The vulgar, high and low, deem it "patriotic" to despise *aliens*.[161]

Love of the *alien* is something unknown in ancient times. . . . The love of *alien* is still universally unheeded in modern times.[162]

Hitler's xenophobia reflected this heathen tradition: "In Nazi Germany . . . [the] prohibition [against *shehitah*] was enacted not so much out of sympathy with the beast, as out of a desire to inflict pain on human beings: 'they that sacrifice men kiss calves' (Hosea xiii, 2)."[163]

The ongoing question of Judaism's mode of slaughtering animals might have led one to suspect that paganism and Christian thought had evolved an ethic of kindness toward animals. Not only was this not the case, but a marked tradition of cruelty to animals prevailed in Western life down to the middle of the nineteenth century.[164]

Hertz's singling out the moral vices of paganism and Hellenism for close scrutiny was a calculated move. Greece and Rome were, of course, acute metaphors for Western cultures. Conventional wisdom held that modernity was eternally in debt to both civilizations for having bequeathed a constructive legacy. Hertz, however, was convinced of the need to qualify this widespread claim. While there was an acknowledgment in the Commentary that Hellenism (conceived broadly as Greco-Roman teaching) along with Hebraism (biblical and rabbinic religion) were the two dominant animating forces that had shaped the ethos of the Western world, there

Chapter 4: Hebraism and Hellenism

was an equal insistence that Greece's contribution to humanity lay strictly in the cultural sphere. The chief rabbi most certainly did not count himself among those previously mentioned who invested Hellenism with a religious hue; nor was he aligned with those men of letters who longed for an eventual fusion of the two civilizations. Above all, he was not at all predisposed to accommodate Claude Montefiore's yearning for Judaism to appropriate certain modes of Greek thought on the grounds of their ethical superiority. Hertz, in fact, countered with an alternate proposition: what the world needed was a major infusion of Hebraic, not Hellenistic, virtues. In the moral sphere, Judaism had no common ground with Hellenism. In its early pages, the Commentary passed quick sentence on the submoral standard of Hellenistic teaching: "Since their [the Rabbis'] day, serious-minded men have looked forward to a Hellenism moralised by Hebraic righteousness and holiness."[165]

Christianity: Offspring of Greco-Roman Civilization

Linking up Hertz's critique of paganism and Hellenism to part B of the previously noted syllogism[166] brings out the full import of the chief rabbi's censure of Western society. In other words, Christianity—primarily through the institution of the Church—was the direct inheritor and bearer of the moral turpitude bequeathed by paganism and Greco-Roman civilization. Specifically, the Church passed these vices on as an integral part of its spiritual wares, usually through canon law or English common law. Consequently, Christianity owed a far heavier debt to Hellenism for the formation of its spiritual values than it did to biblical and rabbinic thought.

Hertz was pressing a claim that was not entirely novel. It had the independent backing of distinguished Jewish scholars. In the thirteenth century, Maimonides linked the Roman Catholic Church with paganism.[167] A generation later, Nachmanides gave testimony at the Disputation of Barcelona to Christendom's historical record of violence, injustice, and its penchant for shedding blood.[168] In the mid-nineteenth century, the Italian biblicist Samuel David Luzzatto asserted that Christianity had evolved in its historical development into a pagan mutation:

> Even though Jesus and his disciples arose and proclaimed God's Torah and the prophets among the nations, all this is of no value.

For those nations were unable to strip from themselves the soiled garments, the ways of Greece and Rome. From there have come, and continue to come to this very day, the evil ways which dominate in the world and which I call Atticism.[169]

Human culture is made up of two aspects: Atticism and Judaism. That which is evil in our midst comes from the former, that which is good (and I speak here of the moral good) comes from the latter.[170]

In the early years of this century, Professor Isaac Husik corroborated Luzzatto's thinking, writing that "Christianity is the result of an impure Judaism modified by Hellenism."[171] Furthermore, Hertz's English colleague, Gerald Friedlander, and the American Reform theologian Kaufmann Kohler both argued that Christianity had constructed a value system that was heavily indebted to heathen thought-forms. The German-Jewish historian Heinrich Graetz had also given hints in this direction.[172]

Significantly, Hertz's interpretation of Christianity as a transmutation of Hellenism was confirmed within England by one of the ranking divines of the period, Dean William Ralph Inge of Saint Paul's, who had analyzed the impact of Hellenism on the evolution of the Christian spirit. Inge was certainly known personally to Hertz. The chief rabbi mailed him a complimentary copy of the Commentary to Deuteronomy, to which Inge replied with thanks.[173] Inge's reflections on marriage and family life were incorporated by the editor into the Commentary.[174]

In a 1921 essay, Inge began with the following positive evaluation of the impact of Greek philosophy on Catholicism:

[I]f we had to choose one man as the founder of Catholicism as a theocratic system, we should have to name neither Augustine nor St. Paul, still less Jesus Christ, but Plato, who in the Laws sketches out with wonderful prescience the conditions for such a polity. . . . Justin Martyr said that the teachings of Plato are not alien to those of Christ.[175]

To this, he added several neutral comments relating to the impact of Hellenistic thought on Western life.[176] Then, midway through the monograph, Dean Inge launched a blistering attack, identifying Christianity as an ill-fated derivative of Hellenism:

But some developments of religion which our Hellenists particularly dislike, and are therefore anxious to disclaim as alien to Greek

Chapter 4: Hebraism and Hellenism

thought and practice, such as asceticism, sacramental magic, religious persecution, and timid reliance on authority, are maladies of the Greek spirit, and came into the Church from Hellenistic and not from Jewish sources. *Christianity is the least Oriental of the great religions. . . . Outwardly the continuity with Judaism seems to be unbroken, that with paganism to be broken. In reality, the opposite is the fact. . . . The clerical profession, in nearly all its activities, is directly descended from the Hellenistic philosophers. . . .* Those who have observed the actual state of Christianity in Mediterranean countries cannot lay much stress on the difference between Christian monotheism and pagan polytheism. . . . [T]he worship of the masses in Roman Catholic countries is far more pagan than the service-books. In the imagination of many simple Catholics, Jesus, Mary, and Joseph are the chief potentates in their Olympus.[177]

Another scholar harshly critical of Christian teaching was nonconformist Anglo-Unitarian theologian Robert Travers Herford. Lecturing before students in 1923 at Jews' College, of which the chief rabbi was president, Herford took gentle yet direct aim at paganism's infiltration of Christianity:

Now it is evident that this [Christianity's expansion into the Greek world] was an extremely dangerous operation. . . . The danger came from contact with and possible corruption by a religion and morality of a lower order than itself. The danger was a very real one and by no means entirely without effect. . . . [I]t cannot be denied that the Jewish inheritance which the Church took over has been of immense importance in guarding Christianity from the peril of its immersion in the gentile world.[178]

If it can be said of Inge and Herford that they stood with Hertz in one corner of the ring in seeing Christendom as an offspring of Hellenism, then opposing them in the other corner were two other representative English opponents: Claude Montefiore and R. W. Livingstone, president of Corpus Christi College at Oxford. As if anticipating the kind of critique articulated by theologians such as Hertz, Inge, and Herford, Montefiore claimed that, their faults notwithstanding, Hellenistic-Christian civilization had advanced the West's spiritual development:

Admittedly, Christianity conquered the world partly because it underwent a considerable infiltration from Hellenism. It assimilated a certain amount of Greek thought and Greek teaching. It would be a cheap mistake to suppose that this infiltration and assimilation merely tended to paganise, that it merely weakened pure, monotheistic wine with muddy, heathen, polytheistic water.[179]

Over a twenty-five year period, Livingstone added his own peculiar nuance to the discussion:

> modern civilization is in a line of direct descent from the former [Greece] and not from the latter [Hebraic spirit]. . . . [180]

> Judaism and Christianity are very different religions. Both indeed, and especially Christianity, have black pages in their history, but these pages were not copied from their fundamental principles, the teaching of the prophets or of Jesus Christ. Both have had periods of lethargy, but they have had the power to wake from sleep.[181]

Judaism and Christianity: Moral Adversaries

The Hertz *Pentateuch*'s glorification and defense of Judaism can be understood as an intellectual response to several adversaries: to a Montefiore and a Livingstone, who invested Hellenism and Christianity with virtue; to the spirit of a prominent English poet-philosopher like Percy Bysshe Shelley, who praised Christianity for having erased the many imperfections of Athenian society;[182] and to those Christian and secular gentile writers, ranging from Julius Wellhausen to William Robertson Smith, Matthew Arnold, and Ernest Renan, who taught not only that Christianity was the more attractive development of Judaism but that Judaism had in effect conquered the world through Christianity. From a Hertzian perspective, it was preposterous to claim that the Hebraic spirit had achieved its ultimate triumph through Christianity. The Hebraic impulse was an exclusive Jewish preserve, not a Christian one.

The editor mounted inferential evidence to support his eye-catching thesis that Christianity was to be held culpable for the desuetude of morality in the Western world. For example, Hellenism's subordination of human rights to property rights, as noted above, was strictly adhered to by most Christian European countries well into the nineteenth century. This posture was reflected in the death penalty being meted out for property offenses, a procedure fundamentally at odds with biblical law.[183] Furthermore, the medieval Christian code of Justinian reinforced paganism's legislative neglect of the poor—this, notwithstanding the ephemeral attempt by Emperor Constantine in the fourth century C.E. to introduce a true Hebraic spirit.[184] The Church fortified another odious

Chapter 4: Hebraism and Hellenism

Greco-Roman practice: the granting of asylum to murderers.[185] The medieval Church was ultimately to blame as well for petrifying "into a hard and fast rule of terrible cruelty" true talionic punishment, which had originated among, what the editor termed, "primitive" and "ancient peoples." This flew in the face of Israel's humane, monetary substitution of the law of taliation. The church father Augustine accorded legitimacy to the *lex talionis* as an equitable form of justice.[186]

Hertz was deeply perturbed over the spiritual intolerance of Christian civilization, similar to that of Greece and Rome, toward those in its midst whom it branded as foes. Although there was no Torahitic source to substantiate the Gospel of Matthew's insinuation (5:43) that "to hate thine enemy" was consistent with Old Testament theology, according to Hertz, the doctrine did concisely summarize Christian behavior down through the ages. Frank confirmation came from no less an admirer of the Christian spirit than Claude Montefiore. Yet even he could not in candor deny that a major immoral impediment was embedded in the Christian ethos:

> The adherents of no religion have hated their enemies more than Christians. The atrocities which they have committed in the name of religion, both inside and outside their own pale, are unexampled in the world's history. And even today it cannot be said that the various sects of Christians love one another, while anti-Semitism is a proof that they do not love those who are not Christians.[187]

The editor identified a general lust for drawing blood through mutilation and torture within the judicial systems of Christian lands, a lust that could be traced through the millennia and into the present: the practice was utterly repugnant to the Jewish spirit.[188]

This norm of inflicting bodily pain particularly manifested itself within Christian home life, where wife-beating and wife-selling were viewed as the husband's prerogatives. While neither was tolerated in one of the classic codes of Jewish law, the *Shulhan Arukh*,[189] both were practiced in the Western world under the direct rule of canon law and common law. Hence, in the Middle Ages:

> "to chastise one's wife was not only customary, . . . but even formally granted by the Canon Law." Even in our own country, as late as the fifteenth century, "wife-beating was a recognized right of

man, and was practised without shame by high as well as low." In the reign of Charles II, this recognized right of man began to be doubted; "yet the lower ranks of the people, who were always fond of the Common Law, still claim and exert their ancient privilege." ... Even more strange was the public sale of wives that was not unknown among the very poor.... Some years ago, *The Times* (January 4, 8, 11, 17, 1924) traced a number of these sales throughout the nineteenth century; and Prof. A. R. Wright has shown that folk custom to have survived in various parts of England into the twentieth century.[190]

The chief rabbi had occasion to cite most of these sources prior to their appearance in the *Pentateuch*'s edition of the Book of Deuteronomy. He took issue with the dogmatic claim of Anglo-Jewish scholar Herbert Loewe that "wife-beating was an exceptional vice among Jews and Christians alike. . . . [I]t must clearly not be assumed that wife-beating was a test of differentiation between Jewish and Christian chivalry." Basing himself on pertinent Jewish sources, Hertz arrived at the opposite conclusion: "It is nothing less than libel on Judaism to place Jews and Christians on the same level in regard to wife-beating."[191] Admittedly, there was no way to ignore in the Commentary one Torahitic illustration of physical torture of women: the ordeal of jealousy arising from suspected instances of adultery by a wife (Numbers 5). The editor proudly noted that though later rabbinic jurisdiction effectively abolished the law in the first century of the Common Era, it nevertheless became a regular institutional feature of life in medieval Christian Europe.[192]

Hertz noted that the inferior status of women reflected a Greek, not a Jewish, posture. It was embodied in the *Odyssey*, the great epic poem of ancient Greece: Odysseus' son, Telemachus, was able to reprimand his own mother with impunity, an act virtually unthinkable for Jewish sensibilities. Interestingly, Hertz presented a uniform, monolithic, and idyllic model of the Jewish woman, rather than recording that Jewish sources depicted a variety of views over the ages.[193] Once again, his uncompromising glorification of Judaism is illuminated against the Liberal perception of Claude Montefiore:

> When we come to the wife and her position, we enter controversial ground. No amount of modern Jewish apologetic, endlessly poured forth, can alter the fact that the Rabbinic attitude toward women was very different from our own. No amount of apologetics can get

Chapter 4: Hebraism and Hellenism 115

over the implications of the daily blessing which orthodox Judaism has still lacked the courage to remove from its official prayer book. "Blessed art thou, O Lord our God, who has not made me a woman."[194]

Despite certain halakhic disabilities,[195] the editor argued, the position of women in Judaism was hallowed. Testimony to this effect began with the patriarchs, who regarded their wives as their equals.[196] Rabbinic Judaism reaffirmed this attitude by referring to the wife as the husband's "house." It was this spirit of equality that prompted the Rabbis to rule that a woman could not legally be given away in marriage without her consent. Furthermore, unlike the medieval courts of love and secular culture's enamoredness with romantic passion prior to marriage, the Jewish view preferred to sustain "life-long devotion and affection after marriage."[197] Jewish sayings reflected this reverence and respect: "Love your wife as yourself, and honour her more than yourself. Be careful not to cause a woman to weep, for God counts her tears. Israel was redeemed from Egypt on account of the virtue of its women. He who weds a good woman, it is as if he had fulfilled all the precepts of the Torah."[198]

Held up for derision was the Church decision that broadened the initial biblical and rabbinic prohibited degrees of marriage, which were "based on instinctive abhorrence and natural decorum." In the chief rabbi's opinion, this wider application by Christianity, resulted in unwarranted privation and suffering. He was absolutely certain wherein lay the blame for the Church's faulty judgment: "various Christian Churches, largely under the influence of Roman law, greatly extended these [biblical and rabbinic] prohibitions."[199] It was equally obvious to Hertz that Judaism and Christianity had radically different views of chastity. Jewish chivalry was both circumspect and not given over to fanfare. Non-Jewish chivalry, on the other hand, went hand in hand with "courts of love and chivalric tournaments."[200]

As noted previously, the pagan proclivity for drawing blood and inflicting bodily pain was embodied in its extreme form in the institution of human sacrifice.[201] In the *Pentateuch*, the editor implied that under Christian instigation the ritual blood libel offered Gentiles a vicarious way of engaging in the hideous aberration of sacrificing humans. This very point was stated unequivocally by the chief rabbi in a lead article in *The Times* of May 11, 1934. The newspaper published Hertz's protest against what it termed "ritual murder, or in other words, human sacrifice."[202] The Commentary did not stop at merely depicting Christians as bloodthirsty, but drew a subtle and demeaning inference: Christianity sublimated man's impulse and craving for blood. Being unable to sanction human bloodletting officially, the Church instead steered this primal bestial drive toward the Jews, who became legitimate targets of hate. This perception was conveyed ever so subtly in recounting the infamous persecution of heretics during the Crusades:

> Some Rabbis declare . . . [that] the case here described, viz. the destruction of a city tainted with idolatry, never occurred, nor was likely to occur. . . . This view was not shared by the Church. *Deut. xiii*, 13–19 *was embodied in the Canon Law: and ghastly records of medieval persecution [by the Crusaders] show that it was not construed as a mere warning against idolatry.*[203]

In the midst of such ghoulish ventures, the Jewish spirit soared to its most sublime height. The editor contrasted Christian inhumanity with the pietistic outpouring of Jewish purity via martyrdom:

> During every persecution and massacre, from the time of the Crusades to the wholesale slaughter of the Jewish population in the Ukraine in the years 1919 to 1921, *Shema Yisroel* has been the last sound on the lips of the victims. . . . The reading of the *Shema* . . . endowed the Jew with the double-edged sword of the spirit against the unutterable terrors of his long night of suffering and exile.[204]

At the same time, cruelty went beyond physical anguish. Backed by the Church, European nations generated their own peculiar brand of psychic pain. For example, in the Middle Ages, Jews were forcibly displaced from the domain of agriculture to the commercial realm,[205] and in modern times, Jewish residents of Christian states were burdened with severe divorce regulations. The editor specifically singled out the Catholic Church's categorical refusal to recognize the legitimacy of divorce and the Anglican Church's equally demeaning precondition of divorce—the commission of adultery. The chief rabbi dismissed out of hand the New Testament posture, supported vigorously by Claude Montefiore, accepting adultery as the sole grounds for divorce. This shameful Christian requirement, according to Hertz, was compounded by the provision that allowed an adulterous couple to marry each other.

Hertz did admit to a vexing hardship within Jewish legal tradition concerning divorce proceedings: the burden faced by a woman wanting to obtain a divorce from a recalcitrant husband and, equally tragic, the ongoing technical marriage of a woman with her husband who had disappeared. On the whole, though, the chief rabbi affirmed that Judaism was still spiritual leagues ahead of other faiths in its humane handling of divorce.

Judaism's broad, flexible principle of mutual consent as the basis for divorce stood in blatant contrast to the generally recognized fact that the real motivation in the Gospels was to prohibit divorce altogether. Equally disturbing was the founder of Christianity's perception of the remarried divorced person as an adulterer.[206]

From a Hertzian perspective, the combination of all these illustrations conveyed a subtle, yet unequivocal message: the Christian ethos was peppered with an affinity for crimes ranging from physical and mental acts of cruelty to outright barbarity. Thus, the notion of a Judeo-Christian heritage was dubious; and there was no validity to the conventional Christian belief in the ethical superiority of the Gospels over the Torah.[207]

Hertz was relentless in marshaling evidence that undermined the spiritual integrity of the Christian faith. He took note of what he perceived to be unqualified blemishes within the religious matrix of Judaism's eldest daughter religion. These had scarred both the moral and theological canvas of Western civilization. Conceptually, these flaws were manifestations of excess, deviations from the norms of moderation and balance.

For example, Hertz contended that in the realm of theology the Trinitarian creed violated pure monotheism:

> The belief that God is made up of several personalities, such as the Christian belief in the Trinity, is a departure from the pure conception of the Unity of God.[208]

> [T]he *Shema* excludes *the trinity* of the Christian creed as a violation of the Unity of God. Trinitarianism has at times been indistinguishable from tritheism, i.e., the belief in three separate gods.[209]

In calling Christianity to task for tritheism, Hertz was validating a criticism recorded by his theological nemesis, Montefiore.[210] In a 1926 letter forwarded to the *Jewish Guardian*, the chief rabbi agreed with the Liberal leader's logic that the Trinity doctrine was frequently in danger of degenerating into tritheism. Consequently, Hertz saw no reason to accept Montefiore's invitation that Jews seriously reexamine "how far the doctrine of the Trinity is or is not in accordance with the Jewish views of the Unity!"[211]

Hertz did not mince words in the Commentary; he went straight for the Christian jugular! Under Christianity's impact, some non-Jewish writers and liberal Christian theologians were but hesitant witnesses to monotheism. Lamentably, Israel's monotheistic sky was darkened by

> a novel doctrine of God's "sonship"; by identifying a man, born of woman, with God; and by advocating the doctrine of a Trinity. Said a Palestinian Rabbi of the fourth century: "Strange are those men who believe that God has a son and suffered him to die. The God who could not bear to see Abraham about to sacrifice his son, but exclaimed 'Lay not thine hand upon the lad,' would He have looked on calmly while His son was being slain, and not have reduced the whole world to chaos!"[212]

The notion of the Trinity, in the editor's judgment, had tampered with a seminal element of Judaism's monotheistic faith: each man stood before God alone, thus making it unnecessary for him to rely on an intercessor, as in Christianity:

> Israel's religion is unique because of the nearness of man to his Maker that it teaches. It proclaims, *No intermediary of any sort is required for the worshipper to approach his God in prayer.* "The Lord is nigh unto all them that call upon Him, to all that call upon Him in truth."[213]

Even more pointedly, the chief rabbi suggested that Christianity's incarnation concept was linked among the masses to what was tantamount to veneration of idols: "throughout fourteen centuries after the rise of Christianity, the prohibition of image-worship was deliberately ignored by the entire Christian Church down to the Reformation, and is still treated as null and void by the major portion of Christendom."[214]

The Christian penchant for excess also spilled over into the sexual realm, specifically in pronouncements on original sin, celibacy, and bigamy. Original sin, based on the theological axiom that "in Adam's fall, we sinned all," was a guilt-inducing concept. It dampened man's natural quest for ethical nobility, making him feel handicapped in his "ability to do right in the eyes of God." In rejecting the doctrine of man's fall, Jewish theology offered in its place a more balanced and temperate posture: "Judaism preaches the Rise of man; and instead of Original Sin, it stresses Original

Virtue (*zekhut avot*), the beneficent hereditary influence of righteous ancestors upon their descendants. . . . [E]ach age is capable of realizing the highest potentialities of the moral and spiritual life."[215]

The antipodal models of celibacy and bigamy were also contrary to man's nature; they confronted Judaism's balanced paradigm of monogamy:

> a man shall cleave "to his *wife*," not to his wives. . . . [I]t is part of the scheme of Creation.[216]

> [O]nly through married life does human personality reach its highest fulfillment. . . . The celibate life is the unblessed life: Judaism requires its saints to show their sanctity in the world, and amid the ties and obligations of family life. "He who has no wife abides without good, help, joy, blessing or atonement. He who has no wife cannot be considered a whole man."[217]

Joining the chief rabbi in his condemnation of celibacy and bigamy was Kaufmann Kohler. Kohler decried Christianity's oscillation "between austere asceticism (demanding virginity and eunuchism) on the one side and licentiousness on the other," as being an authentic reflection of paganism's perception of holiness.[218]

Hertz's unrelenting offensive against Christianity was integral to his objective of dramatizing the deleterious impact of Hellenistic-Christian values in the shaping of Western life. This aim may be further gleaned from a significant omission in the Commentary of a passage originally spoken by the chief rabbi. In 1932, Rabbi Hertz highlighted the mutual acceptance by Jews and Anglo-Saxons of the biblical injunction: "thou shalt not take vengeance" (Lev. 19:18). Though he subsequently recorded his remarks verbatim in the pages of the *Pentateuch*, he conveniently omitted the following pertinent claim:

> Now this Jewish attitude toward vengeance is also, we are happy to say, that of the English people. John Henry Newman expressed the Englishman's view when, in giving his well-known definition of the gentleman, he said, "The gentleman is too indolent for vengeance"; and recently we have been told "Inability to hate is the Englishman's strong suit in the game of life."[219]

Censoring this passage obviously tallied well with his attempt to undermine Christian civilization's claim to ethical integrity. The editor had depicted a Judaism and a Christianity destined to live in confrontation; the Church's dogma as well as its morality gave off an air of paganism and hence, was repugnant to Israel's austere monotheism.[220]

Jewish Contributions to Civilization

Discrediting Hellenistic-Christian notions of morality paved the way for Hertz to make a sweeping claim that constituted a logical and climactic corollary to his antipagan and anti-Christian syllogism: the impact of Mosaic and rabbinic values had bequeathed a modicum of moral sanity to Western civilization. In this spirit, he applauded Woodrow Wilson's contention that "the potent leaven of Judaic thought" was evident in the legislations of the Western peoples throughout the Christian era.[221] To back up the proposition, the chief rabbi put forward illustrations almost all derived from inferential reasoning.

For example, Israel's sages alone had etched the idea of *Heilsgeschichte* upon man's consciousness:

> [T]he universe to the Greeks was not the creation of one supreme mind, but the confused interplay of blind natural forces going on forever in a vain, endless recurrence, leading nowhither. Hence, they could not see any higher meaning in the story of man. . . . Not so the Teachers in Israel. They conceived of God as a Moral Power, and saw Him at work in the world. They traced the line of Divine action in the lives of men and nations. They saw in history a continuous revelation of Divine thought and purpose across the abyss of time. In clarion tones they proclaimed that Right was irresistible; and *that what ought to be must be, and will be.* They taught men to see the vision of "the kingdom of God"—human society based on righteousness—as the Messianic goal of history.[222]

Among the seminal forces of "what ought to be must be," was the democratic impulse. Unhesitatingly, the editor traced this inclination back to prophetic inspiration and to the biblical National Council, or *am ha-aretz*. This rendering of the term allowed Hertz to imply, following Judge Mayer Sulzberger's 1910 thesis, that the Hebrews were the precursors and inspiration behind the modern parliamentary system.[223] Equally significant was the Torah as a direct source of inspiration behind England's juridical system, which, like biblical society, was not tied to the monarchy. Inasmuch as this idea was unknown in ancient times, except in Israel, the chief rabbi implied that England, in its recent attainment of applying strict impartial justice to all, was eternally indebted to the pragmatism of biblical Hebraism.[224] Another significant Jewish contribution to Western life lay in the Torah's encasement of penal legislation in a moral framework. Declaring that this "wonderful spirit of humanity . . . is quite absent from the codes of ancient and even *relatively* modern times," Hertz let the reader draw the obvious conclusion that the Torah was the only other logical source that could account for the compassionate spirit of modern punitive codes.[225]

There was an insinuation in the Commentary that other aspects of modern humanitarian legislation were also adapted from Torahitic models. These included the universal right to education,[226] labor laws,[227] relief for the poor,[228] equality of civil rights for both native and alien,[229] the refugee status of runaway slaves,[230] and kindness to animals.[231]

Other critical areas of modern society that reflected Jewish contributions to the humanization of man were contained in provisions outlawing acts of sexual perversion and provisions safeguarding the sane application of marriage and divorce laws.[232] Once more, the editor either hinted at or openly declared the discernible impact of Torahitic-rabbinic legislation.

Summation

Joseph Herman Hertz shaped his anti-pagan and anti-Christian polemic in the interwar years. During this period, the civilized world witnessed the rise of fascism and communism, two different brands of totalitarianism that repudiated the ethics of Judaism. There was thus considerable merit from the chief rabbi's perspective in the argument that mankind was in paramount need of a Jewishly defined form of Hebraism that would serve as a worldwide moral beacon. Christendom, he claimed, had shown itself incapable and ineffective as an institutional mechanism for earthly salvation. Western nations were prone to intoxication from a "powerful Paganism" bent on desecrating the sanctity of man. Hertz's critique led him to lament "the moral chaos of our times." Arrayed against this malevolent specter stood the Jewish people and its religion, ready to affirm by deed the validity of the Jewish spirit. At the core of this worldview was a passionate resolve to establish a human society predicated on justice and righteousness.[233] Despite their faults as members of a mortal, religious community "the Jews remained a chosen race . . . redeemed at least from the grosser vices—a little human islet won from the waters of animalism by the genius of ancient engineers."[234]

The chief rabbi denied legitimacy to those—particularly Montefiore and his ilk—who were critical of, or dismissed, the sacred achievements of Jewish civilization. It was Hertz's conviction that the truest expression of humanity's ultimate needs belonged almost exclusively to Israel.[235] The Jewish people was fortunate in having teachers of religion whose religious anthropology was simply dumbfounded at human ferocity.

The construction of a colossal human pyramid dedicated to holiness had begun under Moses.[236] His genius for the life of the spirit subsequently became the heritage of the Jewish people:

> "The Jew is that sacred being," says Tolstoy, "who has brought down from heaven the everlasting fire, and has illumined with it the entire world. He is the religious source, spring, and fountain out of which all of the rest of the peoples have drawn their beliefs and their religions."[237]

Chapter 5:
Aspects of a Jewish Theology

Superiority of Biblical Rabbinic Morality

In his defense and glorification of Jewish civilization, Joseph Herman Hertz chose to expose his readers to the deleterious impact of pagan values on both medieval and modern Western culture. From a Hertzian perspective, it was the Church—not Rabbinism—that stood indicted for its inexcusable failure over the centuries to implant a modicum of ethical virtue among those who had come under its sway. The Commentary concurred with Dean Inge's stinging and sweeping judgment, mentioned above, that institutional Christianity had failed to check mankind's propensity for barbarism. The verdict of the chief rabbi was telling, in view of the plaudits accorded Christianity, particularly by Claude Montefiore within the Jewish community and by gentile men of letters who negated any relevance to Judaism.

Through his critique of gentile morality, the editor had, by a process of elimination, effectively classified the Hebraic-Jewish code of morality as *sui generis*. The validity of this claim, however, lay open to counterattack. A scrupulous reading of Scripture pointed to blatant immoral behavior by some biblical heroes. Furthermore, its pages were rife with displays of cruelty and lack of compassion perpetrated against outsiders and aliens as well as against those who violated the prescribed religious norms of the community— all this countenanced by Torahitic command. How tenable, then, was the Hertz *Pentateuch*'s sweeping claim that a controlling moralizing spirit was at work within the biblical community?

Cognizant of these problematic passages and the apparent character defects of major biblical personalities, the editor offered several resolutions: he tempered their severity, pointed to extenuating circumstances, or outright justified them. Tendentious as this exercise was, it synchronized with the Commentary's overarching purpose of buttressing the moral integrity of biblical-rabbinic civilization.

In general, the Hertz *Pentateuch* preserved the moral reputation of various biblical actors by adopting a pragmatic formula: biblical man was finite; hence, he was prone to sin. He stumbled and, at times, even fell:

> It is the glory of the Bible that it shows no partiality towards its heroes; they are not superhuman, sinless beings. And when they err—for "there is no man on earth who doeth good always and sinneth never"—Scripture does not gloss over their faults.[1]

Yet many of these same biblical figures remained conscious of having fallen below the moral ideal. Victory became theirs when, through struggle and conflict of conscience, they returned to "the one true way—and [rose] again."[2]

Even Abraham, an otherwise "majestic soul," was not above stumbling into sin. Fearing for his own life in Egypt, where "the husband of a beautiful wife was in danger of being murdered," he passed off his wife, Sarai, as his sister. He thereby compromised her honor by allowing her to be ushered into Pharaoh's harem. At the same time, the annotator partially exonerated Abraham's behavior by suggesting that the primary onus of guilt lay with Pharaoh. After all, it was his despicable policy that had provoked Abraham into lying.[3]

Deciphered, as well, was Rebekah's connivance in tricking Isaac to bestow his blessing on Jacob over Esau. Her action, in the estimate of the commentator, was based on what was tantamount to a theological justification: by gaining the advantage for Jacob, Rebekah was merely helping to implement the prophecy bestowed on her, indicating that "the elder shall serve the younger."[4] In equally forceful language, the Commentary defended Jacob's acquiring the birthright that lawfully belonged to his elder brother, Esau:

> At first sight, Jacob's conduct appears indeed reprehensible. On closer examination, however, we learn that the privileges of the birthright so coveted by Jacob were purely spiritual. . . . Esau's general behaviour hardly accorded with what was due from one who was to serve the supreme God; and Jacob suspected that his brother did not value the dignity and privilege of being the first born as they should be valued.[5]

Jacob was a remarkable specimen of man's moral integrity lying dormant. He was surely no saint, having committed his quota of moral sins. At the same time, when buffeted by crisis, he possessed a capacity for extracting good from the experience. Thus, his soul was forged "on the anvil of affliction."[6]

The paradigm of growing spiritually through adversity and failure was a stock theme employed by the Commentary. It preserved the esteem and virtue of many biblical heroes. Judah, for example, gave evidence of his capacity for moral reform when he stood pleading before the viceroy of Egypt on behalf of his beleaguered youngest brother, Benjamin. In the end, it was his being "true at heart" that earned him his father's blessing of future rulership.[7] In rabbinic tradition, Joseph was perceived as "the innocent victim of hatred and slander." In spite of his hurt, he was able to display a caring attitude toward his brothers who had dealt so callously with him. His chastity in handling the advances by his Egyptian master's wife naturally came in for favorable review. The Commentary labeled his invitation to his brothers to settle in Egypt as a show of "simple nobility of character rarely equalled in the past or present."[8]

The editor sustained Joseph's unblemished image by ignoring a cardinal failing: the intermarriage to an Egyptian woman. At first glance, this forgiving spirit may seem somewhat odd, in view of Hertz's passionate conviction that intermarriage posed a grave risk to Israel's continued existence. Had not Joseph's uncle, Esau, brought grief to his parents by marrying alien wives?[9] Yet the annotator chose to disregard the same sin of intermarriage when it was committed by Joseph, son of Jacob. This singling out of Esau for condemnation while guarding his nephew Joseph's virtue may be deciphered as a calculated move by editor Hertz. By denigrating Esau's intermarriage and conveniently turning a blind eye to Joseph's, the editor consolidated his contrasting models of Jewish humanism (Joseph) and Hellenistic-Christian barbarism (Esau). According to the *Pentateuch,* it was Esau's undisciplined sensual spirit and his instinct for shedding blood that set him apart from the more ethically sensitive characters of Jacob and his descendants. The Commentary contended that it was Esau's turbulent and impulsive hunting temperament that became such a pronounced cultural trait among the nations (Edom and Rome) and civilization (the Christian West) that subsequently sprang from his loins:

The difference [between] the two nations descended from Jacob and Esau is due to the difference in the character and life of these nations. The Edomites were a fierce and cruel people . . . rushing to battle as if going to a feast. . . . In the Rabbinical writings, Edom became the name, the veiled name, for tyrannous Imperial Rome, and in later times for the persecuting Christian Church.[10]

In his homiletical insight into the prophet Obadiah's condemnation of the nation of Edom, Hertz followed through on the historical paradigm, connecting Christianity to the unbecoming values of Edom. This was done subtly, by directing the reader's attention to what he referred to as Obadiah's "indictment of the 'gospel of hate' wherever held, whether by nations or individuals."[11]

The nobility of Jacob's family was sustained further by the *Pentateuch*'s interpretation of Judah's seeming intermarriage to a Canaanite woman (Gen. 38:2). The annotator tried to salvage Judah's reputation by suggesting an alternative translation of the word "Canaanite" (based on the reading of Zech. 14:21) as "merchant."[12] Similarly, the commentator sought to preserve Rachel's honor in part, following her theft of the *teraphim* from her father Laban, by accepting the midrashic rationale that she was preventing him from worshiping idols.[13] At the same time, in the first edition to the Genesis Commentary (1929), the editor did not preclude the possibility that Rachel was still within the spiritual orbit of paganism and hoped through her theft of the idols "to secure the continuation of prosperity to her husband in his new place of abode." Significantly, Hertz censored this practical motive from his final one-volume edition (1938), thereby safeguarding Rachel's untarnished matriarchal image. The one-volume *Pentateuch* similarly omitted the original 1929 notation to Gen. 35:2 explaining Jacob's order to remove strange gods from the household as a reference to Rachel, who stole the *teraphim*, and to the handmaidens who were accustomed to worshiping them.[14]

Another vexing episode requiring clarification was King David's death charge to his son Solomon to exact vengeance against two men: one (Shimei, the son of Gera) who had cursed him; and the other (Joab) who had shed blood needlessly in time of peace. After acknowledging the ethical difficulties posed by David's order, the annotator, via extenuation, promptly redeemed David's "otherwise magnanimous character." Never formally tried for his crime, Joab's treacherous deed—and presumably Shimei's, too—potentially undermined the government's responsibility to

Chapter 5: Aspects of a Jewish Theology

dispense even-handed and impartial justice. Thus, David's vengeful order was mitigated by "reasons of state." The portrayal of David as a vindictive seeker of vengeance was neutralized even further by the Bible's inclusion of a second, highly spiritual farewell monologue by the king. There, David reminded Solomon that from God's perspective, man's prowess as a warrior was not a significant and prized talent. Rather, it behooved mortal man to practice humility and to appreciate that omnipotent God was the source of man's blessings.[15]

The stark contrast in the pages of the *Pentateuch* between the degenerate moral standards of the Gentile and the ethical nobility of Jewish life necessitated vindication and exoneration, as far as possible, of biblical descriptions of blatant barbarism and inhumanity. These included: the spoiling of the Egyptians (Exod. 3:21–22; 11:2–3; 12:35–36); the persecution of witches (Exod. 22:17); the trial by ordeal of the *sotah* (Numbers 5); the incident of Jephthah (Judges 11); the law of the incorrigible disobedient son (Deut. 21:18–21); the binding of Isaac (Genesis 22); the injunction to annihilate the seven pagan nations living in Canaan (Deut. 20:10–18); and the mandate to take interest from foreigners (Deut. 15:3, 23:21).

The Torah recorded three passages conveying God's order to Israel, prior to the departure from Egypt, to plunder (*nitzel*) the Egyptians by asking (*sha'al*) them for their jewels. Offended by the literal rendering of the divine command, Rabbi Hertz incorporated Benno Jacob's face-saving interpretation of the root *nitzel* as meaning "rescue" or "save." Thus, the Israelites' taking of the jewels did not constitute an act of plunder. To the contrary, Israel "saved" the Egyptians thereby. The jewels, in effect, became tokens of friendship and repentance. God, in His inscrutable wisdom, had set up conditions allowing the Egyptians to clear their name and vindicate their humanity. In the process, Israel learned a crucial lesson of how to transform memories of hate into feelings of compassion.[16]

In analyzing the Torah's imposition of the death penalty for the practice of witchcraft, the Commentary summarily removed the command to execute witches from any hint of association with the "hideous cruelties" perpetrated by the witch trials in medieval Christian Europe. In the annotator's estimation, the Christian Bible was "a demon-haunted book," unlike the Torah, which never ascribed reality to witchcraft. Scripture's prohibition of sorcery rested solely on its idolatrous denial of God's unity and its clear-cut connection to vice and immorality. The commentator insisted that well before the end of the Second Commonwealth, witchcraft had ceased to have any bearing "as a sinister danger in Jewish social life," despite the "haggadic" (i.e., fictional) incident associated with Simon ben Shetach. Furthermore, rabbinic legislation, in contrast to medieval trial procedure, would never have resorted to torture to extort confession. By drawing attention to the Church's despicable exercise of hunting for witches down to quite modern times, the Commentary was able to reinforce a primary claim: acts of barbarism were organically woven into the history of the Church.[17]

There was, however, one "explicit" case of physical torture of women ordained in Scripture that could not be covered up: the ordeal of jealousy inflicted on a wife suspected of adultery (*sotah*) by her husband. Without denying the reality of this trial in biblical times, the editor rationalized it as a serious attempt to preserve "the foundations of social order . . . and at the same time to afford protection to the innocent wife against unreasonable jealousies." Despite this justification, the Commentary noted that the case of the *sotah* was summarily abolished by Rabbi Johanan ben Zakkai shortly after the Second Exile. This de facto repeal was totally at odds not only with the prevailing practice of contemporary pagan nations, but stood in marked contrast as well to the persistent practice of the trial in medieval Christian Europe. Once again, the Commentary kept squarely before the reader the polar images of Christian cruelty and its pagan antecedents, on the one hand, and Jewish humanism on the other.[18]

Equally disturbing to the ethical sensibilities of the modern reader was the apparent killing of Jephthah's daughter as a sacrificial offering in fulfillment of her father's vow following his victory over the Ammonites:

> And Jephthah vowed a vow unto the lord, and said: "If Thou wilt indeed deliver the children of Ammon into my hand, then it shall be, that whatsoever cometh forth of the doors of my house to meet me, when I return in peace from the children of Ammon, it shall be the lord's, and I will offer it up for a burnt-offering."[19]

Though one contemporary, prestigious Christian scholar had dubbed the interpretation as "nationalistic subterfuge,"[20] the Commentary nevertheless courted David Kimchi's unprecedented

Chapter 5: Aspects of a Jewish Theology

translation of the pivotal verse (Judges 11:31). Doing so effectively guarded the humanitarian impulse of the Bible:

> Kimchi ... maintain[s] that the "and" before *I will offer* it should be rendered "or," and the phrase read: "It shall be the lord's, or I will offer it up as a burnt-offering"; i.e., if it be an object permitted for sacrifice I will offer it; otherwise, it shall be dedicated, in some other way, to the lord. (Support for this rendering is given [by Kimchi] in the verse "He that smiteth his father and mother," Exod. xxi, 15, where the obvious meaning is: "He that smiteth his father or his mother"). ... Jephthah therefore did not offer her up as a burnt-offering, but "he made a house for her and brought her into it, and she was there separated from mankind and from the ways of the world."[21]

Preserving the ethical integrity of the biblical text via a grammatical loophole could not, however, exonerate Jephthah's behavior completely. Rabbinic tradition had correctly perceived that this meanest of persons who had been entrusted with authority, deliberately chose to bypass the available option of annulling his "unhallowed" and "criminal" vow.[22]

A more clear-cut case of child killing that the chief rabbi reckoned with revolved around the disobedient incorrigible son (Deut. 21:18–21). Although the annotator did not confute the literal meaning of the biblical text, he did seek to place the law within the context of biblical parental attitudes: "Israelite parents were particularly affectionate and even indulgent." Thus, the theoretical possibility of inflicting the death penalty on one's child would only have occurred as a last resort after "milder measures to reclaim" the adolescent had failed; and even then, only after due process. The Commentary was making a powerful conceptual claim: carrying out the death penalty against a child had to be fathomed, of necessity, not by a modern universal ethical barometer, but within the specific social context of a community dedicated to the fostering of parental love and impartial legal justice. Thus, it was obvious to the commentator that the Hebrew parent did not possess the power of life and death over his child. If further vindication of this humanitarian spirit were needed, it came directly from rabbinic tradition, which taught "that this law was never once carried out.... Its presence in the Torah was merely to serve as a warning, and bring out with the strongest possible emphasis the heinous crime of disobedience to parents."[23]

In glaring contrast to this compassionate worldview, "in Greece, weak children were *exposed*, i.e., left on a lonely mountain to perish; and in Rome, a father could at will put even a grown-up son to death."²⁴

The Hertz *Pentateuch* had highlighted once more the glaring gap between Israel's distinctive ethical standard and the moral bankruptcy of the classical world. Lamentably, the latter had subsequently contributed much to the shallow moral standards operative in the modern world.

It was precisely this dichotomy between Hebraic-Jewish and gentile modes of behavior that accounted for the inability of many ancients and moderns to fathom the spiritual profundity in Abraham's readiness, at God's behest, to sacrifice Isaac. The binding of Isaac exemplified man's unhesitating preparedness to surrender his moral will to that of God. The *akedah* (binding) was an especially relevant religious category for modern man when interpreted as a concrete expression of martyrdom:

> Many today have no understanding of martyrdom. They fail to see that it represents the highest moral triumph of humanity—unwavering steadfastness to principle, even at the cost of life. They equally fail to see the lasting influence of such martyrdoms upon the life and character of the nation whose history they adorn. Those who are thus blind to unconquerable courage and endurance naturally display hostility to the whole idea of the Akedah and its place and associations in Jewish thought. . . . But in all human history, there is not a single noble cause, movement or achievement that did not call for sacrifice, nay sacrifice of life itself.²⁵

Focusing on another problematic text, the Commentary conceded that the reader was justifiably shocked by the Torahitic command to annihilate ruthlessly the seven heathen nations in Canaan. Yet here, too, the editor dismissed application of an absolute ethical standard. The prescription to ban the Canaanite pagans needed to be evaluated against the particular historical circumstances confronting the Israelites on the eve of their invasion of the Promised Land. What they met was a pagan enclave steeped in foul immorality and crime. Israel's order to wage genocidal warfare was thus linked causally to explicit exhibitions of licentiousness, bestial behavior, and gruesome cults, as practiced by the native heathen populations in violation of Levitical norms (Lev. 18:26–28).²⁶ At the same time, the Canaanite ban most assuredly did not seek to interfere with the explicit biblical notion of religious tolerance and pluralism (Deut. 4:19). It was not paganism's polytheistic worship that

Chapter 5: Aspects of a Jewish Theology

defiled the land but rather, its moral transgressions.[27] In what was tantamount to a restatement of Maimonides' stance in *The Guide for the Perplexed*, the editor posited an ethical justification for the ban: the need to maintain Israel's religious integrity, which would historically benefit all mankind:

> In an organized society, it is essential to institute penalties for the violation of enactments that are vital to its existence.[28]

> The judicial extirpation of the Canaanites is but another instance of the fact that the interests of man's moral progress occasionally demand the employment of stern and relentless methods.[29]

Another irksome regulation bearing on the nature of Jewish-Gentile relations concerned the taking of interest. While Scripture permitted one to charge and receive interest from a foreigner (*nokhri*), it explicitly prohibited such a transaction with one's brother (*ahikha*) (Deut. 23:21). Similarly, while an Israelite creditor was allowed to collect on a debt incurred by a foreigner during the Sabbatical year, he was restricted from doing so with his brother. These verses, at first blush, seemed to contradict the spirit of those biblical passages that called not only for decent treatment of the resident alien (*ger*) (Deut. 24:17; Exod. 22:20), but for actual equality under the law between the alien-stranger and the native Hebrew (Exod. 12:49; Lev. 19:34, 24:22; Num. 15:16; Deut. 10:19). The Commentary waxed eloquent over the civilizing quality of these latter verses and their subsequent impact on the evolution of Jewish life:

> The fact that a man is a stranger should in no way justify treatment other than that enjoyed by brethren in race.[30]

> There was to be one law only, the same for home-born and alien alike.[31]

> In no other code was there one and the same law for native-born and alien alike.[32]

> This demand to *love* the alien is without parallel in the legislation of any ancient people.[33]

> No other system of jurisprudence in any country at any period is marked by such humanity in respect to the unfortunate. . . . The stranger, fatherless, and widow should be treated with a generous perception of the peculiar difficulties of their lot. Care for them is

characteristic of Jewish civilization generally, whether in ancient, medieval, or modern times.[34]

Confronting these self-congratulatory encomiums was the explicit permission or command of Deut. 15:3 and 23:21, which drew a sharp distinction between how the Israelite treated "insiders" and "outsiders." The correct evaluation of these verses was critical to Hertz's thesis, for on them hinged the reader's perception of the biblical and Jewish attitudes toward those who stood outside the framework of God's covenant with Israel. The need for cogent interpretation went far beyond an objective or curious need to define accurately who it was that could be charged interest. At stake was the critical variable of how the two related-faith communities—Israelite and Jewish—chose to understand their relationship and responsibility, or lack thereof, toward the gentile world. There lurked an implicit question: was the controlling feature of Israel's relationship toward outsiders one of exploitation or of caring?

The editor's response was unequivocal: the threatening force posed by the problematic passages in Deuteronomy could not dent the strong, fundamental axiom of brotherhood and neighborly concern so evident in the legal codes of Scripture and rabbinic literature. The legal thrust embodied in Jewish civilization had as its aim the fostering of harmonious relations among men.[35] The apparent moral dilemma posed by the Deuteronomic verses dissipated rapidly once the economic dynamics of biblical society were taken into account. The annotator's resolution rested on the pivotal definition of the word "foreigner" (*nokhri*) and the rationale under which loans were secured in biblical times. Unlike the quasi-citizen status conferred on the resident alien (*ger*), the foreigner was usually a transient gentile merchant-trader who entered the country temporarily in order to conduct business. Hence, the clear-cut distinction drawn in Deut. 15:3 and 23:21 between him and the Hebrew debtor:

> The "foreigner" merely visits Canaan, temporarily, for trade. He is not like the Israelite (Exod. xxiii, 10f), under the obligation of surrendering the produce of his land every seventh year; there is, therefore, no reason in his case for any relaxation of his creditor's claims (Driver).[36]
>
> The caravan trade was very extensive, and the foreign trader enjoyed ample protection in the customs and laws of the land. . . .

The foreigner could not very well be expected, in a year which the Israelites celebrated as a Release Year, to remit the debt of his Israelitish debtor. Nor could he be expected to lend money to his Israelitish customer without taking interest (Guttmann).[37]

Obvious, as well, was the rationale behind loan-giving—the relief of poverty and distress:

[A]n Israelite must lend money to a necessitous brother without expectation of any profit whatsoever. It is otherwise in the case of the alien merchant, who requires money not to relieve his poverty but as a business investment.... One of the great duties of *charity* is ... to assist persons in reduced circumstances with timely loans, so that they may be enabled to maintain themselves.[38]

It is noteworthy that the editor's favorite Christian exegete, Samuel Rolles Driver, had preempted the chief rabbi's position by a quarter century:

In modern times money is commonly lent for *commercial* purposes, to enable the borrower to increase his capital and develop his business; and it is ... natural and proper that a reasonable payment should be made for this accommodation.... But this use of loans is a modern development: in ancient times money was commonly lent for the relief of poverty brought about by misfortune or debt; it partook thus of the nature of a charity.... The interest which ancient feeling condemned was thus not the interest taken on a *commercial* loan, such as is taken habitually in the modern world, but the interest taken on a charitable loan; which only increases the borrower's distress.[39]

The description of the *nokhri* as an alien businessman was a conventional interpretation of the period adopted by a score of gentile and Jewish biblical scholars.[40] The reference from the *Pentateuch* above, to Guttmann, was to Rabbi Michael Guttmann of the Jewish Theological Seminary of Breslau, later head of the Budapest rabbinical seminary and responsible for the 1939 Hungarian translation of the five-volume Hertz *Pentateuch*. The Guttmann quotation cited in the Commentary was extracted from the 1926 edition of the American Reform movement's scholarly journal, *Hebrew Union College Annual*, to which Rabbi Guttmann had contributed the essay "The Term 'Foreigner' (*nakery*) Historically Considered." A year later, this English essay appeared in German as chapter 2 of Guttmann's book *Das Judentum und seine Umwelt*. Its defense of rabbinic Judaism's humanitarian dealings with non-Jews can be appreciated as a polemical response to the rising tide of German anti-Semitism and Germany's assault on the innate moral values embedded in Jewish civilization.[41] Following Guttmann's lead, Hertz, too, used the quotation to confirm to the reader of the Commentary the ethical integrity of biblical society.

By placing the legislative passages of Deut. 15:3 and 23:21 within a historical context, the editor felt he had preserved intact the Torah's humanitarian thrust. He reinforced this claim by maintaining that the precise phraseology of these laws left it entirely to the discretion of the Israelite creditor as to whether he wanted to exercise his right to collect interest from the foreigner: "It should be noted that the Torah does not declare that the creditor must exact payment; he may do so, if he wish."[42] The Commentary pointed with pride to the attitude of both biblical and rabbinic legislation that the

> permission to exact interest from a foreigner applied only to sums borrowed for mercantile purposes. When the Gentile needed the money for his subsistence, there was no longer any difference between Israelite and foreigner. "And if thy brother be waxen poor, and his means fail with thee; then thou shalt uphold him: *as a stranger and a settler* shall he live with thee. . . . Take thou no interest of him or increase; but fear thy God" (Lev. xxv, 35,36). The Talmud maintains the interest prohibition throughout, even in regard to foreigners.[43]

These bold notions meshed with what may be termed a substantive "liberal" trend within rabbinic tradition vis-à-vis non-Jews. The fine point giving the Israelite creditor the option of exacting payment was upheld by several rabbinic decisors: Nachmanides (Ramban), Abraham ben David of Posquieres (Rabad), Solomon ibn Adret (Rashba), and Joseph Karo.[44] A decisively more "conservative" bent on this topic was advanced by two of Nachmanides' illustrious predecessors, Solomon ben Isaac (Rashi) and Maimonides (Rambam), who, incidentally, were among the most cited Jewish commentators in the Hertz *Pentateuch*. Basing themselves on the rabbinic commentary to Deuteronomy, the *Sifrei*, Rashi and Rambam postulated that it was a positive commandment and thus, obligatory to exact a debt with interest from a foreigner. Maimonides taught: "By this injunction we are commanded to exact debts from the heathen, and to press him for payment, just as we are commanded to be merciful with the Israelite, and forbidden to exact payment from him."[45]

Hertz's decision to forgo Maimonides' rulings in favor of a more tolerant viewpoint fit in naturally with his tendentious aim of making sure to depict Judaism's legal tradition as a totally pervasive humanitarian system.[46] Hence, the Commentary stressed the low esteem in which the usurer was held in both rabbinic and contemporary circles.[47] How then, asked the editor, was one to account for the "moral tragedy" of the high-profile Jewish moneylender during the Middle Ages? In reply came the assertion that Jews were not gifted with an innate commercial bent, but acquired it as a consequence of being excluded by feudal Christian law from agricultural pursuits:

> Through no fault of their own, Jews were divorced from agriculture and confined to commerce for over 1,500 years. . . . It helps us to realize the fact that Israel was once an agricultural people and that its commercial character is not, as is commonly thought, inborn, but is the result of the unkindly conditions in later ages.[48]

> "If we prohibit the Jews from following trades and other civil occupations, we compel them to become usurers," said Martin Luther . . . "O nations, if you record the past faults of the Jews, let it be to deplore your own work" (Abbé Gregoire).[49]

The analysis in the Hertz *Pentateuch* of the enumerated problematic issues and episodes reflected a unified conceptual program: the unbiased reader must pass moral judgment on Scripture's mortal heroes and legal code only after 1) evaluating them within their specific historical-social settings; and 2) curbing the temptation to measure moral behavior by applying an absolute and inflexible ethical standard. Considering biblical and rabbinic culture in this way, it was apparent to the editor that mighty and irrefutable ethical considerations were integral. Israel's ethical position shone especially brightly when set against the decadent pagan orientations of Israel's neighbors—ancient, medieval, and modern. When the respective religious scripts of Jewish and gentile-Christian civilizations were laid out side by side, there was no gainsaying—from a global perspective—Israel's unique and superior religious ethos, which bore testimony to the Jews as God's chosen people.

The Chosen People

The *Pentateuch* cast the Jewish people in the role of God's elect, entrusted by divine Providence with the mission of serving as a light to the nations (Isa. 42:6). The concrete symbol of this mission in rabbinic tradition was the lamp that burned continually in the Temple and, later, in the synagogue.[50] It was a trust inherited from the first patriarch, Abraham.[51] The notions of chosenness constituted a natural corollary to the Commentary's sharp critique of the lack of spirituality inherent in Western civilization. The chief rabbi advanced the claim that, despite their proclivity as humans for sinning, the collective lifestyle of the people Israel testified to their being the carriers and implementors of an outstanding, superior religious civilization, one that was at odds with the behavioral modes of other nations and religions: "the Jews remained a chosen race, a peculiar people, faulty enough, but redeemed at least from the grosser vices—a little human islet won from the waters of animalism by the genius of ancient engineers" (I. Zangwill).[52]

Significantly, in quoting Anglo novelist-poet Israel Zangwill, Hertz was careful to censor the former's recognition of the genius of the pagan civilizations of Phoenicia, Egypt, Greece, and Rome, even though Zangwill had relegated their genius to an inferior status in comparison with the Hebrews.[53]

In the Commentary, the legitimacy of the chosen people idea was linked and reinforced by Hertz's devastating critique of Christian life in the West. Historically, Christendom had failed to foster a humanizing ethic among its adherents. This happened because of its heavy borrowing from and reliance on pagan culture in general, and Hellenism in particular. In its institutional life, Christianity perpetuated pagan, not biblical-Judaic values. The editor's probe of Christianity, however, went far deeper than the one performed by Dean Inge.[54] In Hertz's estimate, the Dean of Saint Paul's face-saving gesture indicting the institutions of Christianity for perverting Jesus' message was little more than a cosmetic analysis. The unabashed truth was that Western societies reeked of spiritual toxins transmitted from the pagan-Christian alliance. Paganism was the nemesis of a Christianity that had erred by dismissing the spiritual orientation and pietistic forms of Rabbinism. Hence, the Western Christian world was sorely in need of a spiritual transfusion. Rescue was at hand through the living witness of the Jewish people.

In a 1924 address before a Jewish-gentile audience commemorating several milestones in the life of Anglo-Jewry, Rabbi Hertz set out the general parameters of Israel's mission. His remarks were subsequently incorporated into the text of the *Pentateuch*:

Chapter 5: Aspects of a Jewish Theology

> By its life and history, Israel is to set forth the existence of spiritual values and a Divine purpose in the Universe: without which spiritual values, life would be meaningless; and without which Divine purpose, the material Universe would, morally speaking, be no better than primeval chaos, *tohu va-bohu*.[55]

This theme was reinforced in the *Pentateuch*'s explications of the Jewish people's role as a kingdom of priests: "As it is the duty of the priest to bring man nearer to God, so Israel has been called to play the part of a priest to other nations; i.e., to bring them closer to God and Righteousness. This spiritual Kingdom constitutes the highest mission of Israel."[56]

Admittedly, mankind's moral consciousness had evolved to the point of acknowledging biblical history as a primary source of moral guidance. Missing from humanity's perception, however, was a recognition and respect for the ongoing educational role of Jewish civilization, the natural religious successor to the Hebrew way of life: "The thousand years' martyrdom of the Jewish people, its unbroken pilgrimage, its tragic fate, its teachers of religion, its martyrs, philosophers, champions—this whole epic will in days to come, sink deep into the memory of men. It will speak to the heart and conscience of men, and secure respect for the silvery hair of the Jewish People."[57]

Hertz amplified the chosen people concept by touching on several of its key aspects: its origin as tied to race, the precise categories of the mission, the iron-clad unconditionality of the relationship between Israel and God, and the burden inherent in the election.

Jewish Genius

Israel's uniqueness was not of its own choosing; rather, it was ignited by "a unique impact of the Spirit of God upon the soul of Israel." The editor concurred with the Reform theologian and historian Abraham Geiger's estimate that this act of grace was uniquely tied to Israel's "native endowment" for spiritualization. From the outset of its odyssey, there had been "a predisposition in the nature of the Jewish people to receive the Message of Sinai."[58] The phrases in quotes certainly carried a racial connotation.[59] It was surely apropos, then, that in analyzing the origins of Israel's election, Hertz specifically incorporated a remark by Judah Halevi, who argued that Jews were genetically a *sui generis* nation with a divine inclination toward superior moral conduct. In fact, this was the implication of the citation from The Kuzari selected by the chief rabbi for inclusion in the *Pentateuch*: "Israel's pre-eminence is ... derived from ... the Divine love [which] went out towards the descendants of the Patriarchs."[60] Those sufficiently familiar with Halevi's theological language could appreciate that a critical aspect of God's manifestations of love was the bestowing of divine influence or essence on the collective soul of His chosen people. Consequently, godly qualities flowed, as it were, into Israel's bloodstream; the body of God's people was transformed, via genetic engineering, into an "angelic caste."[61]

Hertz's biological definition of the Jewish people as a superior religious race, penned in 1930, bristled with polemical overtones. It may be understood first as a refutation of Christianity's declaration that it had supplanted the Hebrews as the "new Israel," and second, as a tactical counterpoint to the Nazi premise of the racial inferiority of the Jewish people. Several years later, when the Nazis had risen to full power in Germany, the editor—this time more with tongue-in-cheek—raised the audacious idea that genetic programming was a way of deciphering the Hebraic-Jewish passion for moral virtue. The editor drew the reader's attention to the reasoning of Cardinal Michael Faulhaber, archbishop of Munich, a sworn enemy of Hitlerism. In view of 1) the Nazis' disgust for what to him was the ethical posture of biblical laws governing human conduct and 2) the Nazis' denial of the divine origin of Scripture and its laws, the only logical alternative available—and here, the *Pentateuch* concurred—was to admit that the Good Book was "the product of a people endowed above all other peoples with positive *genius* for ethical and social values.... Those who do not regard these books as the word of God and as Divine revelation [i.e., the Nazis] must admit that Israel is the *super-people* in history of the world."[62]

In light of Faulhaber's diatribe against Nazism, it was apparent that his use of the term "super-people" was intended to counter the Nazi notion of Aryan racial superiority. Faulhaber, of course, believed in divine inspiration and called on the German people to preserve biblical instruction within the German classroom.[63]

Categories of the Mission

The Commentary spelled out the two primary expectations inherent in Israel's functioning as a spiritual beacon to the nations. Conceptually, these may be categorized under the heading: *creed*,

Chapter 5: Aspects of a Jewish Theology

understood as theological reflection; and *deed,* equated with normative action. On the creed side, Israel was entrusted to communicate the existence and knowledge of God to the nations of the world; on the deed side, it was to impart with reverence and a sense of duty the requirement to practice and love righteousness.[64] In essence, knowledge of God implied that the attributes of righteousness, justice, and love emanated from the Almighty Himself.[65] Rabbi Hertz chose not to stress, however, the importance of Jews as articulate theologians or metaphysicians for all mankind. He highlighted, rather, the critical role of the Jewish people in modeling itself after the lofty concept of a just God depicted so boldly in Abraham's ringing plea to God on behalf of the residents of Sodom.[66] In other words, knowledge of God was refracted through human beings created in His image: "Man is made in the 'image' and 'likeness' of God: his character is potentially Divine. . . . Man alone among living creatures is gifted, like his Creator, with moral freedom and will. . . . [H]e can subdue his impulses in the service of moral and religious ideals."[67]

Granted, this was not an easy task. Nevertheless, it certainly meant that righteousness was a hallmark of Jewish behavior.[68] The Jewish mission was to humanize mankind, to point the way of righteousness and salvation to all the children of men, and "to rescue the world from moral degeneracy" by blotting "out from the human heart the cruel Amalek spirit."[69] Jews were mandated to strive after genuine peace, which was synonymous with the drive to "ethical and spiritual ends which men call the Kingdom of God."[70]

Indeed, the Jewish people's profound dream was to see the establishment of "universal justice and peace and brotherhood." These moral aspirations were already embodied and operative in the life of Joseph. Indeed, from the dawn of its peoplehood, "high conceptions of morality were entertained" in Israel. Thus, for example, the patriarch Isaac's passive domestic virtues of patience, meditation, affection, and love subsequently became the spiritual trademark of his descendants. Virtues like these earned the Jewish people the designation "Champions of God, Contenders for the Divine, conquering by strength from Above."[71] The reader was reminded in this connection that the word *Yeshurun* in Deut. 32:15, one of the honored designations for Israel, was derived etymologically from the root "to be righteous."[72] Thus, Israel was, so to speak, a divine experiment in history established upon a firm basis so as to play a great and lasting part in world history.[73] "Whenever mankind seeks to be cured of moral leprosy, it can gain that cure ... only in the rivers of Jewish inspiration and teaching. The waters of India and Greece, of Italy and Germany, may be far greater, stronger, clearer; but they cannot restore moral health to the ailing soul of man."[74]

By making God and the ethical virtues embodied in the Torah beloved in the eyes of humanity, a Jew presented a palpable demonstration of his love for the Almighty.[75] In short, religion was intended to be a continuous active influence in daily life; and the *sine qua non* of that religious life was moral character expressed through deed.[76]

A stunning claim of the Hertz *Pentateuch*, in keeping with its polemical outlook, was that Israel *alone* had cultivated religious teachers who were "dumbfounded at human ferocity . . . and whose cry of indignation at these inhumanities re-echoed the wrath of the Deity." Consequently, she shouldered a profound task of eradicating "causeless enmity."[77] Fulfillment of her universal obligation was facilitated by the combination of her small numbers and willingness to missionize to the young via the synagogue and other educational forums:[78]

> "All the great things have been done by the little nations" (Disraeli). "God has chosen little nations as the vessels by which He carries the choicest wines to the lives of humanity, to rejoice their hearts, to exalt their vision, to stimulate and strengthen their faith" (Lloyd George).[79]

Chosenness was more than a collective concept. It applied equally to the lifestyle of the individual Jew. By the way he freely decided to live out his life, each Jew was witness, for good or ill, to the heroic mission: "Each Jew and each Jewess is making his or her mark, or his or her stain, upon the wonderful unfinished history of the Jews. . . . A witness of some sort every Jew is bound to be."[80]

A premise of Israel's election was noblesse oblige; it did not imply the inferiority of other nations. "The universality of Israel's idea of God is sufficient proof against such an assumption. Every nation requires a certain self-consciousness for the carrying out of its mission. Israel's self-consciousness was tempered by the memory of its slavery in Egypt, and the recognition of its being the servant of the Lord."[81] "There is no thought of favouritism in God's choice."[82]

Chapter 5: Aspects of a Jewish Theology

Chosenness conferred an identity that would be synonymous with righteousness. Israel had no special claim on God's favor. The privileges granted her merely increased her responsibilities proportionately. "Israel is the chosen of God. *Therefore*, God demands higher, not lower, standards of goodness from Israel, and will punish lapses more severely. The higher the privilege, the graver the responsibility. The greater the opportunity, the more inexcusable the failure to use it."[83] "Israel's call has not been to privilege and rulership, but to martyrdom and service."[84]

God's Unconditional Love of His People

In the spirit of the doctrine of God's eternal covenant with his people (Lev. 26:44), the Commentary emphasized that divine punishment for sinning did not mean God's rejection of His people.[85] Indissoluble was the link between God and His people. Separated from the heathen, Israel belonged to God in a more intimate sense than any other ethnic group.[86] Through statements that were remarkably reminiscent of Nachmanides' theology,[87] the editor implied that the momentum of Jewish history operated on a level separate and distinct from those of the gentile nations. Despite the forces of evil arraigned against the Jewish people, its indestructibility, eternality, deathlessness, and "perennial resurrection" was assured.[88] The dreadful experience of exile, of being "flung to the four winds of heaven," of suffering that took the form of being ground, as it were, into dust, could not drain Israel of her vitality;[89] she was not a race like others:[90] "as the dust causes even metals to decay but itself endures, so will all worshippers of idolatry perish, but Israel will continue forever" (Midrash).[91]

These references exalting God's unconditional love[92] of the Jewish people certainly stood in stark contrast to the classical Christian claim that with the advent of Jesus, God had abrogated His covenant with the Jewish people.

From a Hertzian perspective, when the Jewish people suffered adversity and misery in the Diaspora, what was required of them as God's "kingdom of priests" was the cultivation of a proper historical perspective. Scripture served in this regard as an invaluable source of instruction. Biblical history bore positive testimony to the eventual "triumph of moral and spiritual forces amid the vicissitudes of human affairs." God, as Lord of History, realized His purposes "through the complex interaction of human motives."[93] Analyzed from this perspective, "history becomes one continuous

Divine revelation of the gradual growth of freedom and justice on earth."[94] If this were not enough to reassure Jewish anxiety, God's chosen could take comfort in the knowledge that the Almighty, as it were, went into exile with His people. Translated into human terms this bold theological metaphor meant that wherever the Chosen People became the victims of barbarism and tyranny, "the whole cause of the Divine [was] in temporary eclipse from the world."[95]

The Burden of Chosenness

Following in the historiographical tradition nurtured by Reform Judaism, the Hertz *Pentateuch* conceived of the Exile as a positive stimulus that abetted the Jewish people in carrying out its divinely ordained mandate.[96] Both within the land of Israel and outside its borders, Jews and Gentiles were antagonists locked in struggle, competing for the soul of humanity. The Jewish orientation to life stood pitted against the false ideals and neo-paganism that ran rampant in the Western world.[97] It was these latter values that the editor, following the prophet Isaiah's cue, likened to mountains seeking to block Israel's message from seeing the light of day:

> The mountains and the hills represent the powerful, worldly forces that seek to block the spiritual and ethical ideals in Israel's message and work. These shall be reduced to powder and scattered by the whirlwind, and Israel shall rejoice in the vindication of his faith in God.[98]

A theology that justified dispersion permitted Rabbi Hertz to account for the inescapable factor of pain, which shadowed the wandering Jews. Suffering was interpreted following biblical and rabbinic precedent, as an "instrument of Divine love," as "chastisement of love," and, in particular, as a purifying disciplinary and educative agent.[99] Unlike Claude Montefiore, who found this solution to suffering very inadequate,[100] the editor found the biblical and rabbinic responses to suffering both compelling and comforting. Like the wandering patriarch Jacob, who underwent a "genuine reformation" by experiencing misfortune,[101] so was Israel's missionary resolve refined through trial: "the pathway of suffering [is] the necessary road to the beatitudes of the higher life."[102] The spiritual benefit derived from suffering was a motif especially applicable to sorrow and pain experienced by the Jewish people in the Diaspora:

Israel's sufferings would educate him to a higher and holier standard of conduct. He would take to heart the hard lessons taught him by his exile, and would return in sincere repentance (*teshuva*) to God.[103]

Divine discipline is for moral ends, and in truth the Exile proved a purifying furnace unto Israel.[104]

Hertz's rationale for observance of the Law conformed in many respects to the spirit of Maimonides' teaching. In his *Guide for the Perplexed*, Maimonides taught that Jewish law (halakhah) functioned as a catalytic agent spurring the Chosen People on to give full expression to intellectual, social, and moral virtues:

> The Law as a whole aims at two things: the welfare of the soul [*tiqun hanefesh*, consisting of the acquisition of correct beliefs] and the welfare of the body [*tiqun haguf*, attained by the acquisition of a noble ethical character].... As for the welfare of the body, it comes about by the improvement of their ways of living one with another. This is achieved through two things. One of them is the abolition of their wronging each other.... The second thing consists in the acquisition by every human individual of moral qualities that are useful for life in society so that the affairs of the city may be ordered. Know that ... the second aim—I mean the welfare of the body—is prior in nature and time.[105]

The dominant orientation of the Commentary coalesced around the more practical Maimonidean "body welfare" motif, urging concrete action and edification. Hertz's adoption of this approach was reflected in his extensive ethical notations to the civil, criminal, and cultic legislation that occupied so much space in the Torah. The glory of the Law from a Jewish perspective was its intimate involvement with every phase of human and national life— civil as well as religious, physical as well as spiritual.[106] The chief rabbi did appreciate the need to acquaint the Jew with a traditional set of faith principles, corresponding roughly to Maimonides' model.[107] At the same time, the popular nature of the Commentary precluded entering into an intensive theological discussion; besides which, the many explications of basic Jewish terms[108] pointed to readers who were deficient in higher forms of Jewish learning.[109] Hence, priority in terms of allocation of space in the Commentary was given to promoting the causes of social well-being and developing the ethical personality.

The editor maintained that both ritual and moral laws were beneficial catalysts in pursuing these aims. Outward rites aided considerably in the drive to achieve holiness.[110] This outlook had little in common with the Liberal platform enunciated in England by Claude Montefiore. Though willing to grant a measure of respectability to both law and doctrine,[111] Montefiore felt that the most authentic Torahitic instruction came from the unwritten moral law:

> Liberal Judaism tends to exalt the "prophetic" elements in Judaism, and to depreciate, though not to abandon, the purely legal elements. It sets the Prophets above the Law. It desires to make Judaism no longer a predominantly legal religion, though it does not desire to deny or ignore the place of law and of the Law (i.e., the Pentateuch) in the Jewish religion as a whole. . . . To our forefathers, Amos, Hosea and Isaiah were all later than the Law in time, and inferior to the Law in greatness and authority. The difference is far-reaching and profound. . . . We take the prophetic doctrine of the secondary value of outward rites and ceremonies very seriously.[112]

Worlds apart was the chief rabbi's perception: in the final analysis, the prophetic call to spiritual regeneration, though admirable, was inadequate. General ethical pleas like the Decalogue constituted only the foundations of morality;[113] they needed to be actualized in the life of common folk. In the editor's estimation, this requirement was admirably executed under rabbinic supervision: "In modern times, various exponents of Judaism have shown that all the ritual observances prescribed in the Torah are visible embodiments of the general truths enshrined in the Decalogue; and that, in fact, the whole content of Judaism as Creed and Life can be arranged under the ten general headings of the Commandments."[114]

Unlike the prophet, who relied solely on personal charisma and moral persuasion to affect human behavior, the rabbinic-sage, during certain periods of Jewish history, was coercive and decisive. The authority of the sage was derived from his capacity to decipher and apply the sanctions of the law according to the accepted norms of biblical interpretation.[115] Law in his hand was a coefficient of the concept of liberty.[116] Thus, it was hardly happenstance that the editor lavished praise on a founder of rabbinic tradition who was among the foremost leaders responsible for Israel's rebirth following the debacle of the First Commonwealth.[117] With Ezra began the transformation and shift from the miracle-based charisma of the prophet to the knowledge-based authority of the scholar, who ascertained God's will by analyzing the constitutional body of the Bible.[118] The editorial decision to quote consistently from the value-laden treasure trove of rabbinic literature was ample testimony that a Jewish understanding of the Law went well beyond the biblical frame of reference.[119] Implicit in the *Pentateuch*'s praise of the rabbinic sage in general, and of Ezra in particular, was a thwarting of the Wellhausenian reconstruction of the biblical past that (as previously noted in chapter 3), focused so heavily on painting a malevolent portrait of Rabbinism. Rabbi Hertz was unabashed in his praise of Talmudism, under whose aegis ceremonies became object lessons in religion, national history, and morality.[120]

This organic transference of power from prophet to rabbi, however, did not detract one iota from the fundamental principle that ethical shortcomings were infinitely more grave than ritual offenses. There was no retort to the truth that prophetic religion had proclaimed the higher law and that it was man's duty to become "a living embodiment of the Moral law."[121]

According to Hertz, there was no essential conflict between prophetic and rabbinic forms of religion, so there was no fundamental antagonism in the Bible between prophet and priest. The two classes were mutual custodians of the Law. They were compatible:

> The prophets never preached the abrogation of the Law. What they did stress ... was that only the heart which is right with God can find fit and proper expression in the well-ordered Temple-worship, and be brought nearer to the Eternal by ritual and ceremony. Nor did the good and genuine priest ... ever hold that one could shelter himself behind sacrifices from the judgment of Heaven upon his moral turpitude and waywardness of conduct.[122]

The prophets Amos, Isaiah, and Jeremiah, for example, were not per se hostile to ritual and cult. What plagued them was the substitution of ritual and cult for nobility of character and righteous conduct:[123]

> None must have known better than the Prophets that acts of worship both kindle and express true religion. But, it is their immortal merit to have proclaimed that the sacrifices of "judges of Sodom" are an insult to God. ... Throughout this section [of Isaiah, chap. 1], it is not the offerings in themselves that are condemned, but the hypocritical character of those who bring the sacrifices.[124]

The Prophets do not seek to alter or abolish the externals of religion as such. They are not so unreasonable as to demand that men should worship without aid of any outward symbolism. What they protested against was the fatal tendency to make these outward symbols the whole of religion.[125]

Law as Spiritual Therapy

Hertz certainly appreciated that man's reflexive obedience to God's will commanded a hallowed niche within the matrix of biblical and rabbinic theology. Man's great purpose was to subject his will to that of his Father in Heaven:[126] "The phrase *hukkim umishpatim* is a standing one in Deuteronomy, but always *hukkim* comes before *mishpatim*, in order to indicate the basic importance of unquestioning obedience to the Divine Will."[127]

Yet from the many underlying social and moral motives treated by the Law and enumerated with regularity throughout the Commentary, it was equally obvious that man's submission to God's will was not the sole rationale behind observance of tradition. Hertz incorporated two other notations that categorized unthinking obedience to the Law as a sign of religious immaturity. A life guided by the precepts of Jewish tradition was intended to be both intelligible and personally edifying: "[In Lev. 18:4] the two verbs are complementary. *Do* is the mechanical performance; *keep* includes the idea of study and understanding of the principle underlying the command. Only where there is *intelligent* conformity to the letter of the Torah, does its spirit become a transforming power in the lives of men."[128]

The Necessity for Religious Segregation

The Commentary emphasized another primary aspect of Jewish existence: the Jew's retention of his confessional distinctiveness. This editorial posture may be understood as a logical extension of appreciating Jewish law as a moral catalyst. The fostering of a religious segregationist mentality was a most desirable predicate of the Jewish mission. It was this spirit of religious exclusivity that motivated Hertz to extract a maximum lesson from Balaam's prophetic blessing concerning Israel: "Lo, it is a people that shall dwell alone, and shall not be reckoned among the nations" (Num. 23:9): "Israel has always been a people apart, a people isolated and distinguished from other peoples by its religious and moral laws, by the fact that it has been chosen as the instrument of a Divine purpose."[129]

This proposition meshed closely with the Reform movement's plank articulated by Kaufmann Kohler, one of its famed theologians: "The underlying idea is that the mission of Israel to battle for the Most High imperatively demands separation from the heathen peoples."[130] According to the *Pentateuch*, a commitment to nurture a ghetto outlook would effectively shield the Jewish people from neo-pagan values, which had polluted Western life via the conduit of Christian civilization. Hertz clearly had no sympathy for Claude Montefiore's earnest hope that Judaism wed itself to what Montefiore regarded as specific superior values that emanated from Hellenism and Christianity. The editor was adamant in his cry that Israel's battle with heathendom was a perennial and inescapable fact of her destiny. It was an ever-present force with which she had to reckon and contend:

> It was by a sure instinct that Esau or Edom was ever regarded as representative of that heathendom against which Israel had to realise its destiny in the world as God's own nation.[131]

> [T]he same reasons that would not permit the Jews to bend the knee to the gods of pagan Rome, prevented them in later generations from allowing themselves to be absorbed by the two great Religions that issued from Israel's bosom. Here too they found, both in dogma and morality, novelties and concessions that were repugnant to the austere simplicity of their absolute monotheism.[132]

Esau, Edom, and their spiritual descendants collectively made up two-thirds of the hostile army arrayed against Israel. Rounding off the triumvirate was the tribe of Amalek, whose biblical lineage went back to Amalek, a grandson of Esau (Gen. 36:8, 12). Thus, the Hertz *Pentateuch* quite naturally focused on the Jewish people's perpetual confrontation with the belligerent pagan forces of Amalek and pointed to the required armaments necessary to achieve victory: "Amalek has disappeared from under heaven, but his spirit still walks the earth. In the battle of the Lord against the Amalekites in the realm of the Spirit, the only successful weapons are courage and conviction, truth and righteousness."[133]

The dietary laws were a particularly dramatic way of implanting a separatistic feeling in the consciousness of the Jewish people: "Israel is to be 'holy,' i.e., distinct, marked off from the other peoples; and these laws powerfully served to maintain the separateness of Israel."[134] In short, a coherent and logical connection existed between being chosen as a divine instrument and being set apart by a distinctive calendar[135] and a unique set of laws. The editor affirmed that living apart from other peoples had prevented Israel from being "contaminated by foul and cruel worship" and tainted by pagan practices. Her most grievous sins resulted from imitating the morals and idolatries of her allies.[136] While historian Heinrich Graetz labeled as prophylactic the separatistic aspect of the Law, Hertz adopted a traditional metaphor: the Law functioned as a "protective fence" insulating the Chosen People from spiritual contamination and assimilation: "As a matter of fact Israel preserved its identity among the nations, and survived the influences which overwhelmed the religions of its neighbours, by its obedience. The Law was a fence about the people (G. A. Smith)."[137]

Rabbinic Innovations

A significant aspect of the theology of the Hertz *Pentateuch* was the notion that the Law had developed and crystallized into novel forms under the watchful and guiding eyes of the Rabbis. Though the Commentary claimed unequivocally that the details of the Mosaic code, including the Decalogue, were revealed atop Sinai, there was also an appreciation in its pages that the ideas and institutions of Jewish civilization had evolved historically. In this, Hertz's approach was clearly differentiated from Samson Raphael Hirsch's conviction that the Oral Law preceded the giving of the Torah at Sinai. In Hirsch's system, the written Torah was perceived as something like crib notes to the oral tradition.[138]

The Commentary was forthright in distinguishing between the recorded words of the Torah and the later insights discovered by scholars who consciously undertook to interpret and apply the written word. The biblical texts were like diamonds waiting to be discovered, excavated, and mined by competent laborers. It was in this sense that later generations of interpreters did not create laws anew, but merely uncovered nuances in Scripture that had always been there: "Every interpretation of the Law given by a universally recognized authority is *regarded as* given on Sinai; for every shade of meaning which Divinely inspired interpreters discover in the Law merely states *explicitly* what is implicitly and organically contained in it from the beginning."[139]

The Commentary was paraphrasing the following rabbinic passage: "Even that which a distinguished disciple was destined to

Chapter 5: Aspects of a Jewish Theology

teach in the presence of his master was already said to Moses on Sinai."[140] Although this talmudic declaration most certainly lent itself to the interpretation that the oral and written laws were twin codes transmitted simultaneously at Sinai, the Commentary's paraphrase of it left a qualitatively different impression. It was one thing to maintain, following the Talmud, that Moses already knew the content of later rabbinic traditions; it was quite another to affirm, as did the editor, that Moses was regarded as knowing the later rabbinic sources. Whereas the former claim blocked out historical consciousness, the latter supported it.

It would appear that the source of Hertz's subtle, though radical, recasting of the above-mentioned talmudic passage derived from Zacharias Frankel, the founder of European Conservatism. Frankel's *Darkhei ha-Mishnah* (1859), methodologically demonstrating the historical development of the oral law, contained the following eye-catching contention: ancient laws for which there was no basis in the biblical text, described traditionally as *halakhot le-Moshe mi-Sinai*, referred, in fact, either to laws of such remote antiquity that the identity of their authors was forgotten, or to laws that were firmly established as if they had been given orally by God to Moses at Mount Sinai.[141] True to form, Samson Raphael Hirsch condemned Frankel for implying that these laws then were, in fact, only of human origin.[142] Hertz's indebtedness and agreement with Frankel's claim also came through with the publication of the one-volume edition of the *Pentateuch* in 1938. The chief rabbi made sure to strike an explicit reference included in the 1930 edition of the Commentary to Exodus, confirming the Sinaitic revelation of both the prophetic-hagiographic writings and oral traditions.[143]

The editor's daring notion of portraying authorized Torah teachers as intrepid explorers uncovering relevant spiritual treasures by combing through biblical caverns was in keeping with the stance of Abraham Cohen, the most prolific manuscript contributor on Hertz's research team:

> From the nature of the Oral Law, it would necessarily be of gradual development, growing larger in the course of centuries as new conditions demanded fresh enactments or modifications of the written code.... It was not contended that every part of the Oral Law originated then.... What the Talmud ... intends to teach is that the Oral Law is *contained in* the Written Law. As the full-grown oak may be

said to be potentially in the acorn, so the whole corpus of Jewish traditional teaching was considered the natural growth from the seed planted at Sinai.[144]

Acknowledging the evolutionary development of rabbinic law did not prevent Rabbi Hertz from insisting on the validity of the Deuteronomic theorem, "ye shalt not add unto the word which I command you, neither shall ye diminish from it" (Deut. 4:1). He noted that two of Judaism's most celebrated rabbinic codifiers, Maimonides and Joseph Karo, had insisted that modification, enlargement, and even the temporary abrogation of biblical prescriptions were constitutive components of a living legal tradition:

> Constant changes would tend to disturb the whole system of the Torah, and would lead people to believe that it was not of Divine origin. But permission is at the same time given to the wise men, i.e., the Sanhedrin of every generation, to make "fences" round the judgments of the Torah in order to ensure their keeping (Maimonides).
>
> [T]he enactments of the Mosaic Code could . . . be added to or modified as new conditions warranted the change, provided all such modifications were not proclaimed as new revelations from on High (Joseph Karo).[145]

Adopting a historical consciousness served as an excellent conduit for neutralizing discrepancies and contradictions within the biblical text itself. One could legitimately argue for the necessity of law adapting to new social conditions. Thus, the editor was able to contend that the contradictory rulings in Leviticus 17 and Deuteronomy 12—over the designated place of slaughter of animals earmarked as food—made sense once account was taken of the Israelites' having changed their desert wanderings for the more pastoral, sedentary setting of Palestine.[146]

The factor of fluid and changing cultural norms also explained why the chronicler of the Book of Samuel found it necessary to point out that Tamar's wearing a long robe (2 Sam. 13:18) was a symbol of her royal station. Yet in an earlier period, when the significance of this insignia of royalty was perfectly obvious—as in the Joseph narrative (Gen. 37:3)—any editorial explanation would have been dismissed as superfluous by the readers of the story.[147] A sense of historical development accounted for the Commentary's oblique hint that King David was not the sole author of the entire Psalter.[148] The concept of organic change as reflected in the metamorphosis of Mosaic law under the rabbinic mantle became a formidable weapon in Hertz's hand. With it, he sought to demolish the harsh judgment of the Law rendered by scholars with a Wellhausenian bent, including Claude Montefiore. The chief rabbi took the approach that rabbinic reformulations of the biblical code reflected a deep passion for ethical virtue and nobility. Hence, a Jew's commitment to rabbinic legal forms did not reflect slavish, bizarre, or rigid behavior. Hertz mounted several illustrations testifying to Rabbinism's capacity to revere the past while making ample room within its theology for evolving ethical insights.

In matters of divorce, for example, the woman suffered from a technically inferior legal position to her husband. Nevertheless, over the ages rabbinic divorce law reflected a gradual improvement in her status: "The uniform aim of the Rabbis . . . was to develop the law in the direction of greater equality between the man and the woman."[149] The editor could point to one instance, the ordeal of jealousy, which led to the actual abrogation of a biblical law: whereas Scripture stipulated that a woman suspected by her husband of having committed adultery go through a virtual trial by ordeal, the Rabbis of a later age introduced the more humane edict of a husband divorcing his wife if he could furnish proof of infidelity.[150] The developmental character of Judaism was epitomized well in the area of ritual. Not only had the early scribes and the Pharisees modified the biblical laws of purity and impurity, but outright innovation was apparent through the postbiblical creation of the festival of Simchat Torah and by alteration of the archaic Day of Atonement rite surrounding the animal designated as Azazel. Originally the Azazel, symbolically laden with the sins of the community, was driven into the wilderness from where it could not wander back. By the talmudic era, however, the term "Azazel" applied to a specific precipice from which the animal was cast down, in view of the fact that "it was no longer possible to send the goat to a place whence it would not return to inhabited parts."[151]

As a perceptive reader of rabbinics, Hertz realized that just as talmudic exegesis effectively abrogated a biblical law, so could a rabbinic enactment itself gradually become inoperative. This occurred principally when a regulation was disregarded over time by laymen. The case cited in the Commentary was a strict ruling of Ezra the Scribe that a man who had a seminal emission was barred from reading the Torah until he had cleansed himself ritually. In time, Ezra's ordinance fell by the wayside. It was never adopted universally among Jews because, according to Maimonides, the majority of the community were unable to observe it.[152]

The chief rabbi showed development in theology by pointing to the full-blown crystallization and acceptance of immortality from the days of the Maccabees and the "new spiritual conceptions" surrounding the nature of life beyond the grave.[153] In the field of civil law, note was taken of rabbinic Judaism's modification of inheritance law, thereby improving a daughter's position vis-à-vis her brother. Although the sages of the Talmud continued to deny the daughter an equal share of the estate, her maintainence and support were safeguarded as long as she remained unmarried.[154] A fundamental reinterpretation of biblical law that illustrated the developmental mode of Jewish tradition was Hillel's enactment of the *prosbul*. In consonance with the principle of justice, Torahitic legislation declared that all debts were canceled in the seventh year. This law made sense within the confines of an agricultural community, where loans were regarded as a form of charity extended to a brother in distress. However, with the changing complexion of economic life and more complex patterns of commerce and trade in the talmudic era, the flow of credit was effectively blocked by the fear that debts would be canceled by the Sabbatical year. Hence, the biblical law actually hindered the impoverished borrower rather than aided him. The altered economic circumstances persuaded Hillel to introduce the legal fiction of *prosbul*, whereby the creditor in the seventh year was able to circumvent the biblical prohibition that prevented him from demanding payment from the debtor. By merely transferring his debt "to the court (*prosbul*)" the creditor was able to "secure his debt against forfeiture by appearing before the Beth Din, and making the declaration, 'I announce unto you, judges of this Court, that I shall collect any debt which I may have outstanding with N. N., whenever I desire.'"[155]

An illustration from the realm of criminal law strengthened Hertz's conviction that Rabbinism had humanized and tempered the literal severe application of biblical law. The Talmud rendered more humane the stoning process of one found guilty of Molech-worship (Lev. 20:4): in capital offenses, delinquents were drugged in order to deaden the senses before execution.[156] Hertz sought to convey that the Jewish legal system had a built-in capacity for flexibility and development. Rabbinism did not chain the tradition to a fixed, rigid norm, but allowed and, at times, even encouraged the

Chapter 5: Aspects of a Jewish Theology

eternally unfolding life of the spirit. Approached with a sense of joy and responsibility, the Law was capable of rendering a community holy and virtuous. Unlike Christian and Jewish detractors of the Law, who perceived its paths as dark and dreary, Hertz in his *Pentateuch* related to it as an abiding source of normative spirituality. The conviction held by the Cambridge talmudic scholar Israel Abrahams, despite his ardent sympathy with the cause of Liberal Judaism, may be taken as an eloquent summary of Rabbi Hertz's perception of halakhah: "If there be one penetrating 'Jewish' principle of interpretation of the Old Testament it is just this belief in the power of Law to moralize a whole people. . . . Law [is] the means of making simple prophetic ideas work in the complex life of society.[157]

Abrahams legitimized the reaction of scholars like Hertz and his research associates when confronted by the anti-legal Christian bias: "An excessive antinomian proclivity in certain sections of 'Christian' exegesis thus provokes a defensive pronomian excess in a new 'Jewish' exegesis."[158]

Rational Religion: Reason and Revelation

One of the most striking features in the *Pentateuch* was its presentation of Judaism as a rational religion. Editor Hertz made only passing reference to the mystical writings of the Zohar.[159] Similarly, no attention whatsoever was paid to those aspects of Nachmanides' theology that fit into a nonrational mold.[160] The work abounded, on the other hand, with the rational insights of Maimonides.[161] The attraction to Maimonides was natural. Like the medieval philosopher, Hertz and his research associates were committed to constructing a paradigm of Judaism that was both rational and grounded in divine prophecy. In Hertz's estimation, Maimonides' genius lay not only in "the originality of [his] creative synthesis" of Jewish sources, but in his masterful reconciliation of Hellenism and Hebraism. The chief rabbi designated Maimonides as "Israel's most universal mind and its greatest spiritual force since the close of Bible times."[162]

In the spirit of Maimonides, Hertz pronounced as a major theological axiom the intrinsic compatibility of divine revelation with human reason. There was no need to subordinate reason to the authority of Scripture. At the same time, like Maimonides—though unlike the later view of Moses Mendelssohn—the editor placed clear limits on what reason could achieve. From a Hertzian perspective, as a source of truth, revelation was superior to fallible human intellect.[163] At times in man's historical evolution, his capacity to penetrate the deepest moral questions had failed him, necessitating God's revelational intervention in history. In other words, there were times when reason was in need of divine guidance. Such a moment was the giving of the Ten Commandments, which were "so sublime that no man could attain to them by his own power." Similarly, the Commentary highlighted the fact that though the notion of the seventh day seemed a simple one, it required Mosaic prophecy to reveal what no legislator in the world was able to envision on his own initiative.[164]

Rational Religion: Sacrifice

In analyzing the overall religious significance of the sacrificial cult and the related matter of ritual purity, the editor did not perceive the cultic commands through the mystical mode of a Nachmanides as having an "intrinsic identity with the Divine [and as] powerful instruments in the unfolding, creative process of the Divinity in the universe and in the history of mankind."[165] Instead, Hertz relied heavily on a symbolic appreciation of Temple ritual as an educative instrument training man to morality. This idea had received favorable mention by Maimonides, most especially in the *Mishneh Torah*. An outstanding example of this ethicization as articulated by Maimonides was the anthropomorphic notion of the burnt offering being a sweet savor to the Lord:

> The burning of the offering is called "a sweet savour unto the Lord"; and so it undoubtedly is, since it serves to remove sinful thoughts from our hearts. The *effect of the offering upon the man* who sacrificed it, is pleasant upon the Lord (Maimonides).[166]

Sacrifices represented spiritual-ethical truths cloaked in bodily forms; they were external signs of proper attitude of the mind and heart toward God and man: "It is clear that the spiritual and ethical ideals of which the sacrifices are the exponent, must remain for all time the kernel of Religion."[167] Hence, Hertz found totally untenable the view held in certain Jewish circles, including that of Nachmanides, which personified the Azazel, the goat driven away into the wilderness, as a demon or fallen angel. More reasonable were the rational biblical and talmudic interpretations that stressed the symbolic transference of sin and guilt from the body of the community onto the animal.[168] Symbolism aside, the editor gravitated to an alternate Maimonidean explanation of sacrifices that focused on a historical rationale: the gradual weaning of the primitive community of Israel away from ubiquitous pagan practices.[169]

Hertz's frequent references to Maimonides' rational perception of religion in general, and of sacrifices in particular, was part of a conscious decision he took in 1929 as he struggled with the task of editing Leviticus, the book of the Torah regarded as the most problematic for the edification of laymen.[170] The chief rabbi ultimately incorporated more than fifty separate notations in the pages of the *Pentateuch* on the disciplining effect of sacrifices.[171]

Rational Religion: Miracles

Hertz's analysis of miracles did not reflect a unified conceptual model. Nowhere did he present the reader with the claim that there was a single correct way—as well as false ways—to decipher or unravel the meaning of Scripture's reliance on the miraculous. To the contrary, in at least two instances in the Commentary, the editor legitimized two alternative interpretations, juxtaposing one that relied on supernaturalism with another based on a naturalistic explanation. The first case centered on the priestly command (Lev. 6:5–6) to keep a perpetual fire burning on the altar. A question arose in rabbinic tradition over whether this required that a perpetual fire be kept burning during the period of transit through the desert. The editor recorded Rashi's extraordinary observation derived from the Talmud that a lump of coal that fell from heaven continuously fueled the fire of the altar of sacrifice. In the wilderness, this fiery lump used to crouch beneath the wrappings like a figure of a lion at the times of the journeyings, and was rendered innocuous by means of an intervening plate of bronze.[172] Immediately above this supernatural interpretation was a rational one that effectively neutralized any supernatural thrust: "But in all probability the command concerning the perpetual fire did not apply to the period of transit."[173] In similar manner, Hertz classified the "fire of the Lord" that broke out against the people of Israel at Taberah as either "a miraculous outburst of flame" like what consumed Nadab and Abihu, or "an ordinary conflagration," or possibly even "lightning."[174] Hertz's perception of miracles included a critical caveat. Under no circumstances was a miracle proof of the validity of a prophet's mission. Both Judah Halevi and Maimonides had argued cogently that a prophet's authenticity, such as that of Moses, was derived from his personal experience of God's word.[175]

The editor's willingness to incorporate a supernaturalistic understanding side by side with a naturalistic explanation did not preclude the tendency to perceive the miraculous as compatible with the given physical order of the world. Miracles generally did not have to contravene nature's laws. This was in line with the talmudic dictum favored also by Rambam: "Everything in nature follows its natural course."[176] By adopting this posture, Rabbi Hertz placed himself patently at odds with the theological claims of two medieval giants: Judah Halevi and Nachmanides. Halevi argued consistently that miracles were a dramatic deviation from natural law, and Nachmanides made frequent mention of "hidden" miracles that were unmediated by natural forces. Miracles were related directly to God's safeguarding the triumphalist destiny awaiting His people. Solomon Schechter, writing in 1893, summarized Nachmanides' system as leaving hardly any room "for such a thing as nature or 'the order of the world'. . . . 'No man,' he declares, 'can share in the Torah of our Teacher, Moses . . . unless he believes that all our affairs and events, whether they concern the masses or the individual, are all miracles (worked by the direct will of God), attributing nothing to nature or to the order of the world.'"[177]

The talmudic principle of the immutability of the natural order, which played so critical a part in Maimonides' *Guide for the Perplexed,* meant that though a particular event appeared to deviate from an expected causal pattern, it was actually in synchronization with the natural established laws of the universe. A corollary of this notion, documented once again in rabbinic literature and in the writings of Maimonides, held that specific miracles were programmed into creation by God's will at the moment when He brought the universe into existence. Hence, miracles were merely the outcome of special characteristics implanted in nature by God:

> [T]he Rabbis gave expression to their conception of the miraculous in the scheme of things. Miracles, they held, were not interruptions of Nature's laws; for *at Creation, God had provided for them in advance, as part of the cosmic plan.* The Fathers of the Mishna, who taught that Balaam's ass was created on the eve of the Sabbath, in the twilight, were not fantastic fools, but subtle philosophers, discovering the reign of universal law through the exceptions, the miracles that had

to be created specially and were still a part of the order of the world, bound to appear in due time much as apparently erratic comets are.[178]

This theory had an obvious appeal for Hertz's ordered perception of reality. It could be maintained that miracles were produced by the unfolding of nature itself—even what was unique was governed by natural law.

Hertz's preference for a naturalistic miracle model did not, however, preclude his including an alternative viewpoint synonymous with another Maimonidean theory that highlighted the short-term dramatic effect of the supernatural. Maimonides also presented a miracle as an expression of God's independent will, which lay outside the realm of human rational understanding. God did, albeit infrequently, suspend or otherwise interfere in the physical order of nature. At the same time, this interruption did not constitute a permanent alteration in the natural properties of physical objects; it produced only a temporary time-bound change. For example, Rambam placed into this matrix the daily provision of manna for forty years. Hertz followed suit: "unless miracles are prejudged to be impossible, account must be taken of the miraculous provision made for the sustenance of the Israelites till the time that they entered Canaan."[179]

There remained a third Maimonidean classification of miracles, highly rational, to which Hertz gravitated. The medieval sage had designated some miracles as a manifestation of man's imagination as a vision or dream. Into this theological construct, Maimonides placed the episodes of Balaam's talking donkey and Jacob's all-night wrestling match with God's angelic messenger. The controlling variable in both cases was the intervening presence of an angel. From a Maimonidean perspective, the mention of an angel was sufficient cause to interpret the incident as having happened within the recesses of the mind during prophetic fantasy. The editor not only concurred with Maimonides' perception of these episodes;[180] he applied Rambam's paradigm to other problematic Torah texts that contradicted reason. Thus, God's image vouchsafed to Moses, Aaron, Nadab, Abihu, and the seventy elders on top of Mount Sinai (Exod. 24:10) "is, of course, beyond human ken; but it is supposed that they fell into a trance in which this mystic vision was seen by them."[181] Similarly, the chief rabbi was not drawn to the Talmud's supernatural explanation that God constructed for Moses a model in fire of the gold lampstand (Exod.

25:40). He preferred in its place Samuel David Luzzatto's rational interpretation, laden with Maimonidean overtones: "from the text, it is not necessarily to be inferred that an actual model was shown to Moses. . . . [T]he verb 'to see' may signify mental perception as well as ocular vision."[182]

Hertz was extremely comfortable claiming that Scripture interwove the supernatural and the natural. Events that might otherwise be construed as bizarre or even false could be classified as miraculous once a miracle was defined as an extraordinary happening within the bounds of natural law. To wit, the figure of 600,000 emigrants from Egypt: "There are no doubt difficulties in conceiving the departure at one time and in one place of such a large body of men; but the event has its parallels in history. At the close of the 18th century, 400,000 Tartars started in a single night from the confines of Russia towards the Chinese borders."[183] This notion of the miraculous taking place within the bounds of nature explained the sudden off-season summer thunderstorm mentioned in connection with Samuel's farewell address (1 Sam. 12:17).[184]

Continuing the nineteenth-century exegetical spadework of Marcus Kalisch and Samuel David Luzzatto,[185] Hertz maintained that the phenomena of the Egyptian plagues and the Red Sea crossing were to be deciphered not by supernaturalism, but by known laws of physics: "the Plagues are but miraculously intensified forms of the diseases and other natural occurrences to which Egypt is more or less liable."[186] "There was a hurricane raging with tornado force, causing the sea to go back."[187]

The editor showed his naturalistic bent, as well, in veering away from a literal reading of the Song at the Sea (Exodus 15), highlighting instead the song's composition as poetry. Nature's wonders also provided Hertz with an opening, following Ibn Ezra's suggestion, to explain Isaiah's mention of the heavens being clothed in blackness (50:3) as a reference to God's power in nature as manifested in eclipses.[188]

The sharp theological differences between the chief rabbi and Claude Montefiore were reflected in their evaluations of the miraculous in history. The Liberal leader found absolutely unsatisfying and incredible a modern religious model that was flexible in allowing for a natural or supernatural understanding of miracles. Montefiore explained the relevance of miracles using the same historical model Maimonides had used to rationalize the institution of sacrifices:

Very many—probably most—Jews still believe that . . . miracles really took place, and they regard them as instances or even proof of God's omnipotence. Those who think with me do not believe that these miracles ever took place. . . . [T]herefore . . . miracles are among the illusions or temporary beliefs through which God in His wisdom educates the human race. When we need them no longer, our belief in them can fall away.[189]

Rational Religion: Evolution

A significant manifestation of the Hertz *Pentateuch*'s rationalism was its unequivocal high regard for the theory of evolution. The doctrine was premised on the gradual ascent "from inorganic to organic, from lifeless matter to vegetable, animal and man."[190] As mentioned here in chapter 3, biblical scholars gravitated to the theory of evolution as a means of tracing the development of religious institutions and ideas. Just as Darwinism provided seminal information about man's physical evolution from lower to higher forms, so could evolutionary theory testify to the development of ideas from the primitive to the complex. Indeed, the spirit of Darwinism applied to the field of religious anthropology confirmed the Wellhausenian hypothesis that Mosaic religion had but a minimal connection to structural forms of legal behavior. The culture of the ancient Hebrews was grounded in spontaneous worship and was far removed from a fixed, rigid prescriptive code of behavior. Hertz sought to demonstrate that the so-called clash between spontaneity of worship and heartfelt morality, on the one hand, and a burdensome cult and legalism, on the other, was a figment of the modern imagination. This theory, while obviously supportive of a Christian anthropology and propagated by many Bible critics, did not reflect the genuine historical matrix of biblical religion and its evolutionary successor, Judaism.

In similar fashion, Hertz regarded the attempt to apply the organic principles of evolutionary doctrine to the institutional growth of religion as absolutely illegitimate. The Commentary gave no quarter to the sweeping allegation that the growth of life organisms from simple to complex was replicated in the sphere of religion by a progressive advancement from lower to higher forms. The editor specifically denounced such a claim as erroneous: "the whole idea of evolution does not apply to a field of human history like the institution of sacrifice. . . . The same holds true in the development of ritual laws."[191]

Hertz was convinced that the amalgamation of biblical criticism and evolutionary theory constituted a tendentious campaign to support the antinomian claims of Christian theology and hence, "deprive Israel of its halo." From his perspective, evolutionary doctrine was ontologically unequipped to shed any light whatsoever on the institutional forms that gave expression to man's religious yearnings. Conceptually, the editor was apprising readers of an Aristotelian caveat that was *au courant* in English scientific circles: the fallacy of explaining facts of one branch of knowledge in terms and concepts of another.[192]

Despite his restrictions on the application of evolutionary theory to institutional forms of religious life, Hertz did see evidence of evolution in the process of creation. Recasting some of the salient points formulated by the veteran Reform spokesman Emil Hirsch in a 1903 *Jewish Encyclopedia* article, the chief rabbi contended that there was "nothing inherently un-Jewish in the evolutionary conception of the origin and growth of forms of existence from the simple to the complex, and from the lowest to the highest."[193]

There was, however, one critical proviso: it was not chance, but God's purposeful creative will that was responsible for the universe's orderly development, culminating in man's creation. Man's unique qualities of intellect and morality differentiated him in kind and not merely degree from other animal species. Hertz was insistent that man's place in the universe was not explainable by the strict Darwinian notion of natural selection and fortunate coincidence. Rather, man owed his marvelous biological and intellectual ascent to God. Hertz acknowledged the name of naturalist Alfred Russel Wallace, who supported his contention that man's evolution was conceivable only as the activity of a creative Mind: "a superior intelligence has guided the development of man in a definite direction, and for a special purpose, just as man guides the development of many animal and vegetable forms."[194]

By aligning himself with Wallace's claim that *homo sapiens* had escaped the influence of the law of natural selection, Hertz had definitely joined forces with those who regarded evolution as a credible doctrine. At the same time, he in no way relinquished or forfeited his Judaic belief in a God who was directly responsible for man's grandeur and dignity.

Hertz was such a devotee of evolutionary theory that he found its spirit already present in ancient and medieval Jewish sources, namely, in the notion that the present universe was preceded by

Chapter 5: Aspects of a Jewish Theology

earlier, more primitive, cosmic births that were aborted.[195] An interesting variation of this "Jewish" theory, probably unknown to the editor, was put forward by the English astronomer Edmund Halley (1656–1742), whom Hertz held in high regard. In 1725, Halley theorized that the planet earth itself once existed as a former world that underwent a re-creation. According to his hypothesis, Scripture's description of the Flood was a reference to the destruction of this former world from which the planet earth was born in its present form.[196]

Hertz supported his conviction concerning the long periods of time involved in the creation of the world by paraphrasing a midrashic text: "With Him [i.e., God] a thousand years, nay a thousand thousand ages, are but as a day that is past; Psalm xc, 4. . . . The beginning of each period of creation is called morning; its close, evening. . . . [I]n the same way, we speak of the morning and evening of life."[197] This passage, along with one more from Maimonides' *Guide* (II, 29), reflected the editorial conviction that the world was far older than the approximately six thousand years yielded by a literal reading of the Bible. At the same time, there was a hesitancy to read scientific data into the pages of Scripture. A safer route had been mapped out by English churchmen from the early nineteenth century onward. Genesis and geology, religion and science, were not at war; their respective agendas were mutually exclusive. Religion was focused on establishing religious truths respecting God, man, and the universe, and not with the verification of scientific facts. Therefore the decisive move for man was to affirm the fact of creation and not the manner in which the universe was born.[198]

As expected, Claude Montefiore did not feel the slightest need to resort to midrashic sources as a means of harmonizing scientific hypotheses with biblical data. He was forthright in insisting that the creation story was a legend reflecting the thought patterns of the early Hebrews. Consequently, it and the other opening ten chapters in Genesis were not to be construed as historical statements. Creation and man's origin were "veiled in the deepest obscurity, and science is only now beginning to lift the utmost corner of the veil. . . . The world is millions of years, and man is thousands of years older than these Hebrew writers knew of. Indeed, knowledge on those matters they had none. All they had was tradition."[199]

Hertz's willingness to accord respectability to the theory of evolution cannot be understated. Not only did he not enjoy any universe of discourse with Montefiore, but he was patently at odds with two outstanding contemporary religionists who were theologically polar fields apart from each other: Isaac Mayer Wise, president of Hebrew Union College and one of the mentors of American Reform; and Michael Friedlaender, a strict traditionalist who was for many years principal of Jews' College in London. Both men objected strenuously to the findings of evolutionary theory, but for markedly different reasons: Friedlaender, because he saw in it a contradiction of the literal truth of creationism; and Wise, because, as he put it, the notion of man being descended from the apes "is nugatory to morals, robs man of the consciousness of his dignity and preeminence, and brutalizes him."[200] However, the chief rabbi accentuated the spiritual truths that could be extracted from the discoveries of modern science: "[b]elief in the dominion of spirit over matter, of mind over nature, of man over the physical and the animal creation (Lyman Abbot)."[201] In other words, scientific methodology was a useful handmaiden that cast light on the eternal verities of Scripture. Hertz's desire to uncover the religious implications inherent in evolution was eloquent confirmation of his belief—attributable in large measure to Maimonides—that the sources of truth were multiple.[202]

The chief rabbi's courting of the theory of evolution coincided with the aim of defending the integrity and authenticity of Scripture as the word of God. As he used the discipline of archaeology as a prop in the pages of the Commentary for his own specific purpose of building a case for the Mosaic authorship of the Torah,[203] so evolutionary theory became in Hertz's hands a powerful weapon testifying to the harmony of the universe under God's Providence and especially to the unique spot allocated to man in the scheme of creation.[204] Fundamental to the Bible as theology was the portrait of man being created uniquely in God's image. Thus, his probable evolutionary descent from a manlike ape was not to be perceived as a blot on his unique dignity. Man differed from the lower animal kingdom not only in degree, but in kind, because his character was potentially divine. Man alone was a rational animal endowed with the capacity to think, the ability to reach out in prayer toward his Creator, and the power to subdue his impulses in the service of moral and religious ideals: "it is not the resemblance, but the *differences* between man and the ape, that are of infinite importance. It is the differences between them that constitute the humanity of man. ... Man is of God ... and what is far more, he *knows* he is of God."[205]

Chapter 5: Aspects of a Jewish Theology

Included in the Commentary was a most striking manipulation of scientific data in the service of faith. Incorporating the evidence gathered by Marcus Kalisch, the nineteenth-century exegete, Hertz contended that the nebular theory, as postulated by Halley, adequately explained how light penetrated to earth on Day One of the earth's formation in the absence of heat from the sun that was not manufactured until Day Four: "These nebulae reply fully to the difficulty which has been raised against the Mosaic description of creation, in asserting that light could not be generated without the sun."[206]

Unfortunately, this particular citation did not clarify and enlighten the reader, for the quotation presupposed a familiarity first with the concept of nebulae (interstellar gas and dust clouds) and more specifically, with Halley's formulation of the nebular hypothesis. To complicate the matter, in the early years of the twentieth century, the conventional explanation of the nebular theory as to the origin of the planetary system did not follow Halley, but rather, the formulation of Pierre Laplace (1749–1827), which did not fit the biblical account. Hertz's drive to authenticate the Torah's account of creation within scientific parameters required of him to stop short of sharing with his readers the more current explanation of the nebular hypothesis as formulated by Laplace. Moreover, Hertz's tendentiousness came through strikingly in censoring from the Commentary Kalisch's personal doubt about the validity of Halley's observation.[207]

Rational Religion: Allegory

The editor's qualifying statement, mentioned above, that science and religion dealt with mutually exclusive concerns, paved the way for the use of nonscientific methodology in extracting spiritual lessons from the Creation and Garden of Eden stories: "There is nothing in Judaism against the belief that the Bible attempts to convey deep truths of life and conduct by means of allegory. The Rabbis often taught by parable; and such method of instruction is, as is well known, the immemorial way among Oriental peoples."[208]

By comparison, one of Hertz's mentors, Solomon Schechter, was not quite as certain about the wisdom of resorting to allegory. He based his hesitation on two criteria: 1) the fact that allegory was a favorite technique of Christians bent on justifying the nullification of halakhah and 2) the allegorical method became a way of investing anthropomorphic expressions with a semi-independent existence or personifying them as the creatures of God.[209] An even stronger rejection of the allegorical method was pronounced by Israel Zangwill. Reconciling the revelational text of the Bible with reason would not be accomplished by adopting an allegorizing rationalism like that of Maimonides. Only a dispassionate reading of history could distinguish between lower and higher strands of literary worth. Zangwill reechoed Schechter's concern about the application of allegory by the Church: "The same method that softened the Oriental amorousness of 'The Song of Solomon' into an allegory of God's love for Israel became, in the hands of Christianity, an allegory of Christ's love for His Church."[210]

From where Hertz was sitting, however, allegory and parable were not only ideal for edification, but integral to the task of reconciling the empirical data of science with the transmitted testimony of biblical tradition. This latter aim was articulated cogently by the rabbinic scholar Louis Ginzberg, writing in *The Jewish Encyclopedia*:

> [W]henever the literature of a people has become an inseparable part of its intellectual possession, and the ancient and venerated letter of this literature is in the course of time no longer in consonance with more modern views, to enable the people to preserve their allegiance to the tradition it becomes necessary to make that tradition carry and contain the newer thought as well. Allegorism is thus in some sense an *incipient phase of rationalism*.[211]

In Hertzian terms, it was this tension between reason and tradition that had motivated Maimonides to write *The Guide for the Perplexed*. It was there that Maimonides formulated a principle aimed at reconciling rational truth and revelation: all scriptural passages that contradicted rational insight when taken literally were to be interpreted allegorically. Hertz and his research colleagues stood squarely within this Maimonidean tradition. Resorting to parable, allegory, and the frequent assertion that certain biblical verses were to be interpreted as anthropomorphisms, testified to a serious commitment to preserve the integrity of reason while holding on to the doctrine of revelation. It was Hertz's optimistic vision that allegory would serve as a precious tool that would not merely increase a reader's knowledge, but substantially contribute to a deepening of faith in God, the Torah, and Israel.[212] Hertz appreciated that these techniques, so central to Maimonides' exegesis,

Chapter 5: Aspects of a Jewish Theology

applied especially to his unraveling the mystery of the Creation epic: "no less an authority than Maimonides declared: 'The account given in Scripture of the Creation is not, as is generally believed, intended to be in all its parts literal.'"[213]

From a Liberal angle, Claude Montefiore was highly skeptical of the effort to harmonize faith with reason. Standing in the intellectual tradition of Spinoza, rather than Maimonides, he perceived harmonization of the two disciplines as a deft maneuver that effectively sidestepped the crucial issue: was it Scripture or the theory of evolution that had final word on the manner of creation?[214] In similar fashion, he found the resort to anthropomorphisms personally repugnant, though conceding that they were a pragmatic "concession for weaker intelligences, and also for purposes of education."[215] The difference between Montefiore and Hertz on this particular issue was merely symptomatic of the unbridgeable gulf separating their respective perceptions of the religious life. As a Liberal Jew, Montefiore did not claim to speak as a devotee of Rabbinism. In contrast to the Hertz *Pentateuch*'s "medieval" model of religion, which sought to harmonize Scripture and philosophy along Maimonidean lines, Montefiore built his religious house on a firm, Greek foundation, very much in the philosophic spirit of Spinoza: the freedom to reject what one considered as false and to accept what one recognized to be true. It therefore followed that the contents of revelation were not eternal truths. The contents of revelation were not pure and perfect teachings but were subject to the empirical findings of human intelligence. Reason was not in need of a religious model of history (which took account of and legitimized revelations, miracles, and divine intervention in history); reason itself was competent to sit in judgment on the validity of Scripture's teachings—hence, the right to reject, modify, and add innovative insights on the basis of current knowledge.[216]

In his bid to present a rational religious alternative to Liberalism, Hertz erected a triumphalist edifice inspired by several classical theological categories: the superiority of Jewish morality, the historical reality of the Jews as God's Chosen People, the Jewish mission to the world, and the role of the Law as a cementing agent in humanizing and shaping Jewish character. Hertz punctuated this master plan for religious vitality with a keen appreciation that one could lead a spiritual life without abandoning a sense of the reasonable. Hertz claimed, paradoxically, that as a prerequisite for living out its destiny as a missionary people to the world, the Jewish people was required to nurture a separatistic consciousness and thereby protect itself from the spiritual contamination of Western civilization. The insular strain within Judaism aimed at imbuing a Jew with a reverence for justice and righteousness. Hence, acceptance of a religious ghetto mentality was not a convenient way of shutting the door on the world. To the contrary, being rooted in a particular world outlook equipped and fortified the Jewish people for bringing its universal mission to fruition. In short, particularism was not at all to be equated with Jewish isolation from worldly concerns; it was, rather, a *sine qua non* of Judaism's universal thrust. A Jew imbibed the spirit of universal love only after first anchoring himself to the mundane concerns and values of his own community.

Chapter 6:
Achievement and Impact

Hertz was not initially successful in his bid to sell large numbers of the first English-language Torah commentary written by Jews. In view of the anticipated publication of the *Pentateuch* in a one-volume edition, people and congregations were hesitant to buy the five single volumes (Genesis–Deuteronomy) of the first edition, published between 1929 and 1936.[1] When American sales of Genesis amounted to a mere 237 copies out of 5,000 printed in the first six months, the chief rabbi was understandably despondent.[2] His net loss on the American reprint came to the considerable sum of $4,000. Over the next few years, he complained bitterly of having incurred a very large deficit.[3] This forced him to consider seriously halting publication of Exodus or canceling the remaining volumes following the printing of Exodus because of the less than "brilliant" sales record in England.[4]

In an effort to trigger sales, Hertz tried to convince himself that two potential markets had not yet been tapped: the public libraries in the United States and the several thousand registered members of the Jewish Publication Society of America.[5] He also wrote personally to clergy serving under him in England and to others within the British Empire[6] and made an impassioned appeal to Orthodox and Conservative spiritual leaders and educators in America. He was quick to point out to some American colleagues that if he were forced to terminate his undertaking prematurely, "Reformers and Liberals would not be slow to point to the moral."[7]

In one instance, he vented his frustration at a local colleague, Joshua Abelson of Leeds:

> I am rather surprised to have had no reply or even acknowledgment to my letter in regard to the introduction of *Genesis*. . . . Your silence

would by an outsider be interpreted either as indifference to the whole question in stake, or suggest such nullity of personal influence as not to be able to raise the not very alarming sum of 7 Pounds 10 shillings—in your important Congregation. It could not even be accounted for under the score of hostility, as you are one of the Collaborators in the enterprise.[8]

Hertz's pleas did not translate into larger sales. Two years after Genesis appeared, the chief rabbi regarded it as "a thousand pities" that neither the Orthodox nor Conservative rabbinates, particularly in America, had been of the slightest help to him.[9]

New hope surfaced when he was approached in 1936 by the Soncino Press following the issuing of the final volume, Deuteronomy. The director of the publishing house was convinced that tremendous sales throughout the world would ensue by compacting the five volumes into one.[10] A friend's subvention of the new printing enabled the *Pentateuch* to be sold at less than one-third of its former price.[11] The conviction of Soncino's director was indeed prophetic. The chief rabbi's grandson has estimated that in the postwar years, 20,000 to 50,000 copies of the Commentary have been distributed annually, primarily to synagogues throughout the Jewish world.[12] The hope of Hertz's brother, Emanuel, for the *Pentateuch* came to pass: "I have no doubt that when it becomes known, and it ought to become known to the whole world, it will have a greater circulation than the Book of Thoughts."[13]

The complete *Pentateuch* was eventually translated into German (1937–38) and Hungarian (1939–42) editions; a Hebrew version of the Book of Genesis appeared in 1942.

Critical Reviews

The Hertz *Pentateuch* was reviewed worldwide in scores of Jewish and gentile newspapers, journals, and magazines. In almost all the reviews is an appreciation for the Commentary's inspirational tone, commendation for the invaluable contribution rendered by the chief rabbi and his collaborators in using sound scholarship to mine the ethical insights embedded in the Torah, and a recognition of an effort to quiet skepticism in the mind of the layman. The homiletical style adopted by the chief rabbi was dubbed by one reviewer as a sort of extension of the modern Jewish sermon; and there was general agreement that Hertz and his colleagues had argued persuasively for Judaism's legitimacy and glory.[14]

At the same time, several critical reviews, both of a public and

Chapter 6: Achievement and Impact

private nature, crossed Hertz's desk. A few analysts commenting in the early 1930s found it bizarre that Hertz had favored the revised King James version for the English translation over the preferred Jewish translation issued by the Jewish Publication Society of America.[15] This allegation, though understandable, was unfounded. The truth was that Hertz had tried strenuously to gain permission from the Society's board to use the Bible translation but gave up the effort when it became apparent that the rights to the translation would be limited to a period of twenty years.[16] Several recurring complaints surfaced among serious reviewers: his recourse to anthropomorphism as a convenient way of circumventing problematic verses[17] and, especially, his penchant for glossing over puzzling passages. One critic found incredible the chief rabbi's derision of Edom's so-called "causeless hatred" of Israel. In his opinion, Edom's hostility to Israel was based on the Edomites' tenacious memory of the patient massacre of their people over a half-year period by Joab and his troops following the initial loss of 18,000 of their men in battle. Moreover, Israel's persecution of the Edomites placed in serious doubt the Hertzian conviction that Israel was committed to preaching and implementing universal righteousness toward other nations.[18]

Several writers spotted the chief rabbi's affinity for rationalization. For example, Hertz shielded Jacob's pure character by interpreting the Torah's factual statement that Jacob hated Leah (Gen. 29:31) as meaning that he loved her less than he loved Rachel. A similar unnecessary "Victorian" feature was the notation (following Ibn Ezra) that Jacob's kissing of his cousin Rachel (Gen. 29:11) referred to his kissing her hand.[19] An illustration of tendentiousness was the long-winded, yet unconvincing interpretation of Exod. 3:22 in which Hertz—following the German biblical scholar Benno Jacob—interpreted the phrase "ye shall *spoil* the Egyptians" as "ye shall *save* the Egyptians," i.e., clear their name and vindicate the humanity of the enemy.[20] The editor's rationalizing tone was also apparent in his interpretation of the phrase "cut off from Israel" (Exod. 12:15). It was obviously literally meant to indicate the death penalty and not excommunication, as the chief rabbi asserted.[21]

Others found the Commentary's often bombastic dogmatic tone inappropriate. One expositor chided Hertz for claiming with such certainty that the sole purpose behind the creation epic was to explain man's spiritual kinship with God. While such an interpretation might indeed be cogent in the twentieth century, the reviewer implied that the original intention in the story may well have been to offer evidence of the biological origins of the human race.[22] Another writer classified the chief rabbi's categoric disqualification and malevolent portrait of all higher biblical critics as "dangerously like a caricature."[23] Other analysts were perturbed by Hertz's adamant posture that Judaism stood or fell on its belief in the historic actuality of the revelation at Sinai and the Mosaic authorship of the Torah. Was Judaism so poor, queried a reviewer, that it rested on one particular doctrine? To say so was tantamount to confirming the suspicions of those who argued that Judaism maintained adherence not by persuasion but by instilling a policeman-like obedience and fear of God.[24] A Canadian colleague who was generally impressed with the Commentary nevertheless noted his disappointment over the chief rabbi's having avoided the delicate yet relevant issue of whether to restore the sacrificial cult in the future.[25]

Among the many reviews forwarded to Hertz, two in particular seriously sought to invalidate his labors. One was submitted by a layman friend, the geneticist Dr. Redcliffe Nathan Salaman (1874–1955).[26] The other was published by a colleague, Hakham Moses Gaster (1865–1939), who disliked Hertz personally and to whom Hertz felt an equal aversion.[27] Salaman was sorely disappointed that the so-called Commentary was actually an anthology of biblical homiletics; it had taken on the shape of a long-winded sermon. Salaman found most disturbing and unforgivable Hertz's insistence in using the Bible to explain science instead of permitting science to shed light on the Bible:

> I do not suppose that any commentary can be free altogether from bias, but, if I may say so, your commentary reads as thumbnail notes for a series of sermons. . . . You [Dr. Hertz] must realise that your Commentary could be riddled by any young intelligent student armed with modern methods. I am confident you cannot successfully mix two things, science and scholarship on the one hand, and emotional teaching on the other.[28]

In reply, Hertz appreciated that he and Salaman obviously started out from diametrically different positions:

> [O]ur respective conceptions of a Bible Commentary are antipodal. In my opinion . . . the immanent spiritual potentialities of the Text must be brought out, or at any rate indicated. Such likewise, is the

Chapter 6: Achievement and Impact

attitude of a commentator like Coleridge or Bradley to Shakespeare. No greater compliment could be paid me than your statement that my Commentary "reads as thumbnail notes for a series of sermons." In other words it is in line with the Midrash.[29]

This evident spirit of friendship between two intellectual adversaries contrasted sharply with the chief rabbi's reaction to the review of the Genesis volume by Dr. Moses Gaster. Known generally for his intolerance and "combative personality,"[30] Gaster justified his censure of the *Pentateuch* in the pages of the *Jewish Guardian* by relying on a loose paraphrase of a talmudic dictum: "When fundamental principles are at stake there is no room left for paying any special respect, even to a Rav." He asserted that the Commentary was a representative sample of "dilettantism" and "thoughtless sycophantism." Bearing in mind the book's popular audience, Hertz ought to have avoided controversial issues that would tend to confuse or go beyond the comprehension of the general public—issues like theological disquisitions, metaphysical speculation, evaluation of Higher Criticism, and the shifting conclusions of archaeology. Gaster found particularly erroneous the chief rabbi's claim that there existed a Jewish dogma. Lamentably, the chief rabbi had dashed his hope and expectation for a "standard work of consummate value."[31]

Needless to say, Hertz perceived Gaster's review as a personal attack.[32] His consternation was eased somewhat, however, when two colleagues quickly came to his defense, thereby fulfilling, according to him, the command not to stand idly by the blood of one's neighbor (Lev. 19:16). One was the venerable minister emeritus of New York's Spanish-Portuguese Congregation, Dr. Henry Pereira Mendes, whom Hertz regarded as one of his mentors. Mendes believed that the Anglo-Jewish community owed the chief rabbi a debt of gratitude for undertaking the unenviable task of presenting Genesis in a way that would appeal to both layman and scholar.[33] A more detailed rejoinder to Gaster came from Professor Isidore Epstein of Jews' College. After berating Gaster for his insulting and unprofessional language, Epstein called into question Gaster's claim that Jewish theology did not recognize any dogma:

> It may sound a very attractive phrase, but Dr. Gaster will agree that the place of dogma in Judaism is still a moot point. Why, there are many good and learned and pious scholars who maintain that there

are dogmas in our religion. One need not go further than recall the father-in-law of Dr. Gaster, the late Dr. M. Friedlaender, who issued an Appendix of the Revised Version setting forth alterations in the text "where it is opposed to *Jewish traditional interpretation or dogmatic teaching*" [italics mine]. Surely good company enough for the Chief Rabbi to be in when writing of "Jewish dogma" and "Jewish tradition in interpretation."[34]

Judaism's Legitimacy: The Evidence of Archaeology

Archaeology and philology became significant weapons in the chief rabbi's arsenal as he sought to authenticate the historicity of the Torah. With all the evidence he presented in hand, it is fair to say that the Hertz *Pentateuch* contained, at best, confirmation of the feasibility of Mosaic authorship. The archaeological and philological evidence collated and sifted by Hertz merely showed that Scripture mirrored accurately the social, intellectual, and religious milieu of the ancient Near East. While not proving Mosaic authorship, the evidence marshaled by Hertz showed that Mosaic authorship was not impossible. Hence, on the fundamental point of preserving the literary unity of the Torah, Hertz had dented—but most certainly not demolished—Wellhausen's edifice. Nevertheless, Hertz and his research staff may be credited with perceiving how critical a variable archaeology was in sustaining an alternate developmental model of biblical religion. As recently as 1960, the Protestant theologian and Bible scholar Harold Henry Rowley attested—in the spirit of Hertz—that archaeology had modified somewhat the absolute rectitude of Wellhausen's assumptions about Israel's origins: "Archaeology has shown that the pentateuchal narratives of J and E reflect the customs of the age with which they deal, and while it has not proved the accuracy of the history it has disproved the dictum of Wellhausen that they give us little knowledge of the age about which they write but much of the age in which they were written."[35]

Editor Hertz stood on much firmer ground in arguing for the preexilic authenticity of the Mosaic code and its moral divergence from the legislative codes enacted by Israel's pagan neighbors. Archaeological data supported the contention that institutional law forms and religious traditions were prominent features in the life of ancient man. This conclusion served as a strategic linchpin in claiming rabbinic Judaism's integrity in having carried forward both the legal and prophetic teachings of Israelite tradition while adapting them to the multifarious needs of the Jewish people. In short, the prophets held aloft the vision of universal brotherhood and a humanity guided and ultimately perfected by notions of justice and righteousness. However, the task of applying and actualizing these ideals in everyday life, of fashioning them into a practical regimen of observance, fell at first to biblical, and later, to rabbinic lawmakers.

Judaism's Legitimacy: Gentile Testimony

Having the breadth and insight of Jewish humanism corroborated by gentile spokesmen may be considered one of Chief Rabbi Hertz's major tactical maneuvers. His tacit assumption was that "the testimony of the nations" (a chapter title in his *A Book of Jewish Thoughts*) did as much to legitimize Jewish contributions to Western civilization as a score of Jews who might have defended Judaism against slander. This ploy had been specifically recommended in 1919 by the Unitarian minister and defender of Pharisaism, Robert Travers Herford, one year before the chief rabbi officially launched the project of writing a biblical commentary. Addressing a Jewish audience, Herford outlined the psychological benefit of using non-Jewish sources to firm up Jewish credibility: "the words of an outsider may carry weight where those of the home-born might be set down to mere natural desire to exalt his own people."[36]

The chief rabbi broke new ground in choosing to pepper his *Pentateuch* with the supportive testimony of gentile men of letters. For example, he departed from the commentary format adopted in the late nineteenth century by Frankfurt's Samson Raphael Hirsch, who relied exclusively on classical rabbinic sources. The audacity of Hertz's move is vividly highlighted by Hirsch's excoriation of Berliner David Zevi Hoffmann for having committed, in Hirsch's estimation, the unconscionable sin of referring in his doctoral dissertation to non-Orthodox *Wissenschaft* activists like Frankel, Graetz, and Prague rabbi Solomon Judah Leib Rapoport. Hirsch, who was the founder of German neo-Orthodoxy, feared that pupils drawn to these secular Jewish writers might relinquish their commitment to the tenets (as he formulated them) of traditional Judaism.[37]

There was obviously no way of bridging the methodological premises of Hertz and Hirsch. The latter believed that classical internal Jewish sources were adequate to sustain faith and that a student ought to be protected as much as possible from potentially faith-shattering notions from without. The former started with an alternate assumption: the Western Jew educated in a secular environment would not tolerate the censoring of his reading material. In a world where a Jew encountered a marketplace of ideas ready for the taking, his allegiance to the Jewish mission would not be won through intellectual screening and censorship, but through force of reason and persuasive argumentation.

Medieval Triumphalism

Joseph Herman Hertz initiated the writing of his Torah commentary, largely a panegyric on Rabbinism, in response to conditions of religious and intellectual duress. The foremost catalytic agents were Wellhausenian-oriented biblicists "from without" and Montefiorean-type Liberal Jews "from within." Their historical reconstruction of Jewish literary sources validated for them the notion that the dictates of conscience took precedence over outward authority, a premise articulated forcefully at the dawn of the emancipation era by Spinoza in his *Theological Tractate*. With the close of the emancipation debate in the West by the end of the nineteenth century, the principle of private choice in religious affairs was framed in political language and enshrined in statute. Hence, for many modern religionists, personal autonomy had eclipsed obedience to ecclesiastical authority. Philosophically, this meant (to quote Immanuel Kant) "the ability and duty of the individual to use his own reason and experience to determine the nomos or laws governing truth, theoretical and practical."[38]

In the mind of a committed Wellhausenian, the premises of Spinoza and Kant translated to 1) a reaffirmation of the ethical-based authenticity of the prophets and 2) the consigning of rabbinic Judaism's authority-based law system to the trash bin of history. For religionists like Montefiore, the reason-based autonomy of Spinoza and Kant pointed to the progressive and continuous revelation of God's word,[39] the right to abrogate at will rabbinic laws and traditions felt to be at odds with one's personal ethical-aesthetic sensibilities, and an open possibility that Judaism and Christianity might one day effect a religious merger.

Hertz stood far away from this brand of religious expression. Conceptually, he belonged to the camp of traditional conservatives who argued that Jews ought not to be so anxious to reconstruct Judaism but to be reconstructed by the wisdom of rabbinic tradition, which derived its authenticity from a supernatural source. It was this conservative orientation that prompted him to reject the new dictum that "*all* moral laws are man-made; and that *all* can, therefore be unmade by man."[40]

Hertz was deeply troubled by the pressures of secularization, which, besides undermining the authority of Scripture, tended to foster ambivalence to religious tradition. The chief rabbi had taken note of the Jewish world's fundamental ignorance of Scripture, of Hebrew language, and of Israel's history. He was especially agitated by a generation of apathetic and even self-hating Jews, some of whom confessed to belonging to a morally inferior religion and some of whom believed halakhic Judaism to be an anachronism.[41] Hence, the commentary format provided the chief rabbi with an intriguing way of inspiring this Jewish type with an alternate vision of the Jew emancipating himself from the deprecating gentile critique of Judaism and rediscovering the worth and perennial modernity of Jewish civilization:

> I believe some are now prepared to agree with me that the first step to a spiritual rebirth in Jewry is a Jewish Declaration of Independence from the judgment of an unsympathetic world! And the second step toward any resurrection of the Jewish spirit is discovery—the revelation to the Western Jew of the infinite worth and wealth of Jewish thought and ideals enshrined in the Jewish past.[42]
>
> Our greatest need . . . is emancipation from self-contempt from the idea that we are worse than all the world. Otherwise, we may in course of time become in reality what we now imagine ourselves to be.[43]

In Hertz's estimation, contempt for traditional Judaism was featured most prominently in the religious anthropology of Liberal Judaism and in that brand of Christian triumphalism sustained by Wellhausen's reconstruction of Scripture. The intellectual counteroffensive launched in the pages of the *Pentateuch* characterized Christendom and Western civilization as substantively malevolent, decadent, and marred by hideous illustrations of cruelty. The Commentary presented the reader with an array of Christian sins against humanity: persecution, truculence, and intolerance. These were contrasted by the excellence of Jewish life. In short, through the power of Rabbi Hertz's pen, Western civilization and Christianity became foils for the ethical accomplishments of the Jewish people.

Unlike the writings of Claude Montefiore, Kaufmann Kohler, and even Heinrich Graetz, the Hertz *Pentateuch* harbored no trace of an ecumenical spirit.[44] Kohler, for example, had pointed to a fifteenth-century parable in which Esau (i.e., Christendom) and Jacob (i.e., Judaism) were together the recipients of a precious jewel (i.e., religious truths) from their monarchical father (i.e., the Almighty).[45] Graetz was similarly willing to grant a modicum of spirituality to Christianity: "A part, I might say the flower, of this pure ethical system [i.e., Judaism] has become the common property of the world, through the medium of Christianity."[46]

It is of special significance that Hertz's ideological alliance with Breslau, already noted through the teachings of Frankel and Kohut, was also fortified by Heinrich Graetz, professor of Jewish history at Breslau. It turns out that Hertz cast his polemic in terms that were echoed strongly in Graetz's multi-volume *History of the Jews*. The chief rabbi's anti-pagan and anti-Christian outbursts, coupled with his central themes of Jewish impact on general history and Jewish triumphalism, received major play in Graetz's historical outlook. The latter's *oeuvre* was replete with expletives against Roman and Christian oppressors, an unmitigated hatred for Roman Catholicism, a knee-jerk reaction at placing blame for many of the misfortunes of medieval Jewry at the doorstep of the Church, and the redemption of mankind through the dissemination by Jews of their unique ethical and theological systems.[47] It is worth noting that the lesson that Graetz drew from Jewish suffering as a means to intensify attachment to Judaism by appreciating the commitment of countless martyrs also found a sympathetic ear with Hertz.[48]

On the specific theme of religious triumphalism, Hertz also reflected the teaching of Alexander Kohut, one of his major professors, who was himself a Breslau graduate. Several months before his death in 1894, Kohut addressed (in absentia) an international conference of world religions held in Chicago. In triumphalist tones, he argued that it was the Jew, perceived eternally as pariah, who sowed the seeds of monotheism in the often infertile ground of an ungrateful humanity. In fact, the eloquence of Plato, Demosthenes, Cicero, and Aeschylus could not compete on equal footing with the eminence, magnetic power, and sublimity of the masterpieces penned by Israel's prophets and psalmists. "The Hebrews drank of the fountain, the Greeks from the stream, and the Romans from the pool. . . . [T]he poetry as well as the philosophy of Greece

Chapter 6: Achievement and Impact

shrink before the single sentence [of the *Shema* and the Ten Commandments]."[49]

Kohut's claims at the assembly were further substantiated by the Reverend H. Pereira Mendes, whom Hertz had acknowledged as yet another religious influence on his life. Mendes' sharp critique of Christianity and Greek thought and his uncompromising belief that Judaism fostered a religious segregationist spirit were pillars in the chief rabbi's philosophy. At times throughout history, Mendes intoned, the Jewish voice was in harmony with the moral strains of other belief systems. Most often, however, it was discordant as it clashed with what happened to be the dominant notes of immorality and error.

Mendes' stance of superiority led him to the following conjecture: ancient Babylonian Jewry's geographic proximity to the East might have accounted for the initial influence (though later obscured) of Judaic thought on the three great oriental faiths of Zoroastrianism, Buddhism, and Confucianism. If this were indeed true, it would be partial fulfillment of Isaiah's prophecy (27:6) that "Israel shall sprout and blossom, and the face of the world shall be covered with fruit." In the final analysis, however, Judaism's historical disagreement with the world's religions was so acute as to leave her with no other recourse than to retain her distinctiveness and her vigilant spirit of protest.[50]

The chief rabbi's public speeches bristled with the claim that validity and authenticity were found exclusively within Jewish culture. Gentile culture did not embody any serious spiritual and ethical values: "in religious things, Israel has nothing to learn from the Western peoples or from Oxford. Long before Oxford, Israel was; and long after Oxford shall have ceased to be, Israel will endure."[51]

In short, Jewish civilization alone had achieved a recognition of the eternal difference between the holy and the profane, between the sacred and the secular.[52] The Commentary also overflowed with this triumphalist spirit: what was spiritually valid in Christianity was already contained fully in classical Jewish sources:

> It is only the Jew, and those who have adopted Israel's Scriptures as their own, who see all events in nature and history as parts of one all-embracing plan; who behold God's world as a magnificent unity; and who look forward to that sure triumph of justice in humanity on earth which men call the Kingdom of God. And *it is only the Jew,*

and those who have gone to school to the Jew, who can pray . . . "May His kingdom come."⁵³

Consequently, when the chief rabbi incorporated gentile comments into the *Pentateuch*, he did not do so in a Montefiorean sense that wisdom "from without" ought to trigger dramatic upheavals and revolutionary reformulations of Jewish theology. Nor did his use of non-Jewish insights imply a Montefiore-like perception that the sources of religious revelation or inspiration were multiple and that no single book and certainly no one people were the exclusive carriers of human salvation.⁵⁴ Rather, for a Jew like Rabbi Hertz, who asserted that the nuances of spiritual truth were enshrined in the written and oral laws and whose epistemology was heavily indebted to Maimonides, gentile spiritual insights could merely confirm time-honored Jewish norms.

The Ethical Thrust

Whether consciously or not, the chief rabbi was also indebted to the medieval moralist Bachya ibn Paquda, whose ethical classic, *The Duties of the Heart*, had been the subject of Hertz's first foray into the world of Jewish scholarship in 1898. Therefore, it was perhaps more than coincidence that a specific methodological principle used by Bachya found its way into the Hertz *Pentateuch*. While Bachya's work integrated hundreds of quotations from non-Jewish sources, they were incorporated not to dictate the direction of Bachya's thinking, but rather as props to support his already conceived thesis.⁵⁵ The chief rabbi followed suit. The Commentary's reliance on a large number of supportive Christian/gentile citations showed how an early twentieth-century Jewish moralist successfully copied Bachya's technique; and by doing so, he effectively transmitted the case for Judaism's legitimacy and relevance to two generations of English-speaking Jews worldwide.

Hertz was indeed Bachya's disciple. From the outset of his rabbinic career, he was convinced that when all was said and done, it was ethical behavior that marked a person as religious. As his student days at the Seminary drew to a close, his preoccupation with the interplay of ethics and religion found determined expression in his doctoral thesis, entitled *The Ethical System of James Martineau*,⁵⁶ which was a close reading of the writings of James Martineau (1805–1900), an English Unitarian theologian and philosopher. From the perspective of hindsight, it is fair to say that Hertz related to Martineau as an intellectual adversary. His doctoral essay enabled Hertz to clarify for himself Martineau's treatment of the psychological origins of moral behavior.

In seeking an alternative to biblical authority, Martineau began from the premise that morality derived from the intuitive capacity of man's conscience. Listening to the dictates of an unruffled conscience enabled every person to build a moral philosophy; one could trust his own built-in sense of what was right and wrong in human conduct. Through force of free will, a person could, in fact, compel his baser "animal motive" to surrender to his more saintly "rational motive." Hence, Martineau posited that ethics preceded religion![57] Hertz the pugilist entered at this point. He could not abide Martineau's claim that each man's conscience revealed to himself the law of correct duty. Hertz countered that Martineau's edifice, based on common sense, was doomed to fail because of a reliance on the "relativity of conscience." Had not Martineau himself admitted that conscience was a fluctuating and relative variable varying with different stages of human civilization? Moreover, had not Martineau conceded that conscience was not a mirror image of God's absolute ideal, but was rather "dwarfed and stained by the self-incurred perversions of our sight"?[58] Hertz spared Martineau no sympathy: one could not rely on man's conscience to reveal the law of duty because intuitive ethics disclosed both error and uncertainty. "Historians and travelers tell us that there is scarcely a vice which has not in some age or country been approved, scarcely a virtue which has not been condemned; in one country it is right for children to support their aged parents, in another to despatch them."[59]

Precisely because conscience was an unauthoritative and fallible faculty, it was an impractical guide for the mass of humanity. It did not follow at all, as Martineau claimed, that man came face-to-face with a higher than himself in the act of conscience. Ethics did not logically precede religion; the reverse was true—morality depended upon "something else which makes it, calls it forth step by step," and that something was God.[60]

When viewed against the backdrop of his Torah commentary, Hertz's analysis of Martineau—when Hertz was a young man of twenty-one—revealed an interlocking of concepts that would make their full-blown reappearance in the *Pentateuch*. First, was the young scholar's keen appreciation for the discipline of history, illuminated by his ability to place Martineau conceptually among a pantheon of like-minded predecessors.[61] Hertz used this skill as a historian to consummate advantage in the Commentary. His decision to view the text of the Bible against the broader panorama of the ancient Near East, along with his familiarity with comparative religions, allowed him to exploit the fledgling field of archaeology in order to defend Judaism as an evolving and precious religious civilization.

Second, his focus on ethics in his doctorate took on ever more prominence as he matured, highlighted by his monograph on Bachya, his public preaching, and above all, his description of the relationship between law and ethical behavior in the pages of the *Pentateuch*. Finally, it was his own deep personal belief in God and the revelation at Sinai as the universal repository of mankind's duties, which may be said to have fueled his critique of Martineau's epistemology. These two tenets found explicit expression in the Torah commentary:

> No interpretation, however, is valid or in consonance with the Jewish Theistic position, which makes human reason or the human personality the *source* of . . . revelation. . . . No view of God that grew up "of itself" in the human mind, owing nothing to God's self-disclosing action, could have any value.[62]

Chosenness and Mission

The Hertz *Pentateuch* reflected a belief in the duty of the Jewish people to serve collectively as the carriers of a superior religious civilization unparalleled in the annals of history. World Jewry exemplified Maimonides' directive that the function of religion was to induce men to promote one another's welfare. Hence, Jewish thought could offer substantive spiritual therapy to a mankind that was spiritually misguided. By government legislatures heeding the Jewish call to implant justice and righteousness, the Hebraic ethos would strip the Greek of its "pagan sensuality."[63] While engaged in the task of editing the Commentary, Hertz gave expression to this sentiment in a 1926 homily: "As in hoary antiquity, as in the Graeco-Roman world, it is now the glorious privilege of Israel to proclaim the holiness of the moral life in the anarchic world of to-day."[64]

Meanwhile, the Jewish people's own salvation was intrinsically linked to its reverence for halakhah. The mechanism of the Law was a tried and tested pragmatic code for implanting virtue; first, in fashioning communities committed to justice, and then alerting them to manifold ways of caring motivated by love. Only an anti-

Jewish bias equated Judaism with being an irregular product of history that had petrified obedience into a barren formalism. On the other hand, Western civilization with its Christian overlay was, to an appreciable degree, morally bankrupt. For Montefiore, a burning question was whether a Jew could appreciate Christian spirituality.[65] From a Hertzian perspective, the question was not only irrelevant, but preposterous. Christian teaching had been judged and found wanting. Lamentably, its spiritual merger with pagan forces had shattered the precious unity of religion and morality. There was no way to align the antipodal value systems of Hebraism and Hellenism; to try to do so posed a mortal threat to the Jewish mission. Only by remaining a distinct religious entity could the Jewish people effectively shield itself from exposure to immoral pollutants emitted by the Western ethos. Jewish survival was predicated on religious nonconformity.

At the same time, the notion of the Jews as the Chosen People did not imply a parochial tribalism and a turning away from the world. The claim made by one gentile savant that "the religion of the Jews is indeed light . . . but it is as the light of the glow-worm which gives no heat and illumines nothing but itself,"[66] simply did not ring true. To the contrary, the watchwords of the Jewish mission were privilege and *noblesse oblige*.

Judaism's Superiority

It may be argued that the sharp distinction that Hertz drew between the moral standards of Jewish and Western societies was to some degree unfair. Unlike the complete social and political frameworks of power built by gentile nations, Diaspora Jewry had not contended seriously with the uncertainties and moral ambiguities of national life for two millennia. Even within medieval corporate life, the shaping of healthy Jewish character was effected primarily through the important yet limited spheres of family, school, and synagogue. Thus, Hertz's strident denigration of the standards of Western morality and particularly of Christendom would have had considerably more bite and cogency had he been able to point concretely to the living reality of Hebraism's spirit inside a Jewish state that had grappled with and appreciably overcome its susceptibility and vulnerability to the full range of temptations: economic, social, political, and religious.

Instead, he skirted the critical question: had Jewish nationalism done a more credible job of wedding morality to power and implanting moral virtue among its citizens than pagan or Christian nations? Indeed, his frequent reliance on midrash and recourse to rationalization to neutralize the obvious inequalities and inequities of daily life in the First Jewish Commonwealth testify to how difficult it was for flesh-and-blood Jews to promote, let alone approximate, the prophetic dream of nurturing human dignity. The world governments that Hertz so roundly condemned were engaged in the colossal enterprise of fashioning total social and political orders. That they failed, in Hertz's estimate, to moderate the exercise of power by moral sensitivity may be granted, but at least there were sufficient data to render a judgment against them. The same cannot be said of Jewish Diaspora life, which, owing to its political powerlessness and statelessness, never brought complete political, economic, and social concerns to the center of its religious consciousness. To be sure, Hertz would have expected a Jewish state of the future to balance and temper the use of power and coercion with a healthy respect for justice, righteousness, and acts of kindness. He would not, however, have been able to base such an expectation on the past performance of the First and Second Jewish Commonwealths, for both were riddled with internal moral corruption.

Conclusion

For more than half a century, the Hertz *Pentateuch* provided a significant section of world Jewry—predominantly foreign-born and lacking a broad general education—with an overview of Jewish theology, and traditional practice along with a transmission of Jewish pride and the need to refine the ethical impulse. On the threshold of the twenty-first century, Joseph Hertz's magnum opus may be regarded as a historical period piece. The Commentary's blatant polemical style—its denigration of Christianity on moral grounds and its vilification of classical Liberal/Reform Judaism for its anti-halakhic platform—can be evaluated today with greater objectivity and with a measure of sympathy.

The chief rabbi felt the need to inform a lay audience that the brand of Judaism he cherished was beleaguered by hostile forces from without and from within. Clearly, however, his agenda and his critique no longer reflect the existential reality and concerns of many contemporary Jews. The spirit of the *Pentateuch*, in fact, no longer resonates among two very different constituencies. College-educated Jews do not agonize to the same degree, if at all, over

Hertz's angst of having to harmonize the tenets of religion and science. A consensus reigns that each domain deals with different ontological questions. Religion does not presume to convey scientific truths about cosmology; it is at its best responding to eternal questions arising from the predicament of being alive and human.

Nor do most Jews at the close of this century gravitate to Hertz's compelling need to validate Judaism through an unrelenting critique of other faith postures. To the contrary, in a world increasingly perceived as a global village, vast numbers of Diaspora Jews concur with the postures of ecumenicism and religious toleration. Finally, Chief Rabbi Hertz's deep suspicion (emanating from Montefiore) that Judaism might mistakenly absorb basic elements of Christian teaching, hardly reflects the sentiments of Jews seriously committed to an ever-enriching Jewish lifestyle, while equally accepting the evolution of Jewish thought and practice.[67] Indeed, it has been cogently argued by a spate of modern scholars that Jewish civilization avoided the fate of fossilization precisely by being open to fertilization from the dominant culture. For all of his understandable mistrust of this proposition, as applied to Montefiore's theology, Hertz was actually sympathetic to this claim in a serious way. Quite consciously, he drew attention to Maimonides' aphorism (lifted from his *Shemonah Perakim*) in the preface to the *Pentateuch*—"Accept the true from whatever source it come."

There is another distinct audience that must also find the Hertz *Pentateuch* entirely irrelevant to its reading of Jewish history, theology, and halakhah. These are the substantial numbers of Orthodox and ultra-Orthodox Jews who portray the Torah as a fundamentalist document and tolerate secular learning as a necessary evil to earn a livelihood. Unlike Hertz, they view a broad humanistic education as an anathema, standing at loggerheads to the restricted talmudic-based curriculum of the yeshiva world. Validity and authenticity, they believe, are found exclusively or predominantly within the narrow confines of a parochial Judaism sealed hermetically from whatever is different from itself.

It is perfectly understandable how these very perceptions would have rankled Hertz. The content of his public preaching and his multiple eclectic references to world literature in the pages of the Commentary—when set against the backdrop of his earned university degrees—testify to his indefatigable belief in the mastery of general learning wedded to an extensive familiarity with classical Jewish texts. To be more precise, Jewish education for Joseph Hertz went beyond the exclusive confines of Talmud and halakhah. Of necessity, it required an athletic agility to maneuver through the diverse terrains of the Bible and midrash (interpretive opinion). This was coupled with his unswerving conviction of the development of the halakhah as an organic response to concrete life issues. Both of these axioms have clearly fallen out of favor among a discipleship within Orthodoxy's orbit, which venerates the ahistorical sensibilities of Samson Raphael Hirsch. They begin from the premise of rendering the *peshat* with the meaning given to it through midrashic license.[68]

This spirit of intellectual insularity has also led in recent years to the Hertz *Pentateuch* being roundly condemned in some Orthodox circles for its copious references to non-Jewish commentators. It is not only a matter of finding fault with the chief rabbi's polemical strategy to prop up Judaism's legitimacy by engaging sympathetic gentile voices, but rather adhering rigidly to a principle: rejecting the validation of Judaism through non-Jewish spokesmen. The harshness of the criticism has reached such proportions whereby the Commentary has been banned from a growing number of synagogues affiliated with the United Synagogue in Great Britain owing their allegiance to the office of the Chief Rabbi.

There is, however, one conclusion central to Hertz's thinking in the Commentary that warrants faithful scrutiny: his sober claim that Judaism's perception of humanism and its serious quest for ethical nobility stood pitted against a vibrant strain of Christian paganism and barbarism running rampant in Western society. Hertz believed that there was little appreciation for Judaism's alliance with political liberalism, which translated into a passion for equity, the civil rights of the stranger, and the moral unity of mankind. In short, humanity's gravitational pull inclined heavily toward civil and political inequality, favoring Hellenism's legitimization of "might" and evading Hebraism's call to "right." A world dominated by the Hellenistic spirit was intolerant of Jewish notions of justice and equity.

The implication of Hertz's proposition takes on particular relevance for those seeking to discover the ideological roots of the Holocaust. Precisely because it was completed before the beginning of World War II, the Hertz *Pentateuch* reads as a remarkably prescient document pointing to a significant reason for the isolation and ultimate rejection of the Jew within Christian society. In Hertzian terms, Nazism could be explained as the efflorescence and venting of a brand of paganism that despised the sentiments of moral conscience and liberty articulated by Judaism. In 1938, Hertz referred to Nazi Germany as a "persecuting paganism."[69] Such a characterization was, of course, fully consistent with his theory of the latent power of paganism and of barbarism in Western life, a theory he had documented fully in the *Pentateuch*. Though the Jewish people was fortunate in having been redeemed from the "waters of animalism" by "the genius of ancient engineers," Western Christian life was highly prone to being engulfed by these very waters.[70]

In recent years, prominent historians, theologians, and psychologists seeking to discover the roots of modern anti-Semitism have corroborated Hertz's thesis and have reinforced his linking of barbarism and paganism to Christianity and the institution of the Church:

> [A]nti-Semitism also constitutes a Christian protest against the Jewishness of Jesus and against pure monotheism represented by the Jews; it is a revolt of residual paganism which has persisted in Christianity. . . . "Whenever the pagan within the Christian soul rises in revolt against the yoke of the Cross, he vents his fury on the Jew." . . . [A]nti-Semitism functions, among other applications, as a catharsis. It gives release to a repressed paganism, a pre-Christian heritage of the gentile, which remained latent, mostly subconsciously, in Christianity.[71]

> [O]nce the Jew was defined as one of the major symbols of Evil within Christian society, . . . he fulfilled the essential function of a collective counter-ideal, a means of distinguishing between Good and Evil, between Pure and Impure, between what society ought to be and what it was forbidden to be.[72]

Equally damning from this perspective was the censure by post-Holocaust Christian theologian Franklin Littel. He called attention to the "comparatively few Christians who maintained their faith during the Holocaust" while millions of others wittingly or unwittingly accommodated or collaborated with the mass murder of Jews in the heart of Christendom. Thus, he was forced to concede that "it is not the Jewish people that has become incredible, it is Christianity and those who call themselves 'Christians.'"[73]

The Hertz *Pentateuch*, the first English commentary on the Five Books of Moses, testifies above all to its editor's passionate love of

Rabbinism, a love poignantly conveyed in a story told shortly after his death in 1946. The incident recounted took place in Rhodesia during the chief rabbi's pastoral tour of the dominions in 1920:

> On his return journey from Bulawayo just as the train was about to leave the railway station . . . a man of Jewish appearance passed and repassed his window. When Dr. Hertz approached him with the traditional *Shalom Aleichem* the man told him how he and three other Jewish families from Que Que had traveled some ten hours by train on the road from Bulawayo to Salisbury, hoping to see him. But though he was so anxious to hear of the Jewish life of that miniature *Kehillah* Que Que, he did not manage to do so because the train was already beginning to move and he had only time to ask, "Is there a *Shass* [a complete set of Talmud] in Que Que?" "Two sets [*zwei Shassin*]," he answered. "Then you are safe even without the visit of the Chief Rabbi," was his farewell word.[74]

Appendix

A Letter of Complaint from Hertz's Research Associates

July 8th 1929

The Very Rev. Dr. J. H. Hertz,
Chief Rabbi
48 Upper Hamilton Terrace,
London N.W.

Dear Dr. Hertz,

It is with regret that we feel compelled to pen this letter to you. Our object is to express our surprise and disappointment that:

(1) On the title page of the Commentary the names of your collaborators do not appear. In all similar works, proper tribute is paid in this way to those who have collaborated, as for instance in Kittel's "Biblia Hebraica."

Accordingly we feel strongly that following the words: "Edited by the Chief Rabbi" some such phrase as "With the collaboration of the Revs. Dr. A. Cohen, Dr. J. Abelson, the Rev. S. Frampton and the late Rev. G. Friedlander" should certainly follow. We do not consider that our point is covered by the bare reference in the Introduction.

We submit that in the subsequent volumes, and also when a new edition of Genesis appears, we should be favored in the way indicated.

(2) We further consider that the repression of all reference to ourselves in the advertisements is not right; and we hope that all

future advertisements in the Jewish and general press will likewise be on the lines we have above suggested.

We feel it is unnecessary to assure you of the deep respect in which we hold you, and are therefore satisfied that you will understand the spirit in which this letter is written.

We beg to remain,
Yours sincerely,

S. Frampton
J. Abelson
A. Cohen

Chief Rabbi Hertz's Rejoinder

12th July, 1929

Dear Sirs,

I am in receipt of your letter of the 8th inst.

1. I deeply regret that you found it necessary to send it to me, as nothing is further from my nature than to deprive others of the honour which is justly their due. I have throughout my life been meticulously careful to indicate the source of, or my indebtedness to, any literary help received from any person or book.

2. Your complaint, moreover, is quite unjustified. The English usage in regard to any collective enterprise of a literary nature, is that only the editor's name appears. (The example of Kittel's Bible is not an analogous case). An absolute parallel case is Bishop Core's new Commentary on the Old Testament, New Testament and Apocrypha, which has just appeared. Each contribution is signed by the contributor, and yet only the name of the editor appears on the title page. The same applies not only to other commentaries of the Bible, but to such standard works as the Cambridge History of English literature, Ward's English Poets, and others works too numerous to mention. Such is the rule when the contribution of each man is reprinted as it is, without any recasting on the part of the editor. How much the more should it apply in a case where the contributions have been recast and often altogether rewritten by the editor!

Appendix

3. Moreover, the matter in dispute was definitely decided when the idea of a Commentary was first launched. On October 6th 1920, before proceeding on my World Tour, I had a meeting of some 20 ministers whose help I had hoped to enlist for the Commentary. The question was then raised whether the names of the men who would collaborate in the various books would appear on the title page. I then clearly stated that only the names of the editors (Dr. Buechler had at that time promised to cooperate with me) would appear, whereas the share of the other collaborators would be indicated in the Preface.

4. I trust that the above explanation is satisfactory.

Sincerely yours,

[Dr. J. H. Hertz]

cc: Rev. S. Frampton, B.A.,
cc: Rev. Dr. J. Abelson, M.A.,
cc: Rev. Dr. A. Cohen, M.A.

Notes

Abbreviations for Notes to All Chapters

AOJ: Hertz, *Affirmations of Judaism*
B.T.: *Babylonian Talmud*
Guide: Maimonides, *The Guide for the Perplexed*
H.A. The Hertz Archives (references to the Hertz Archives are cited as H.A., followed by the specific box number)
JQR: *Jewish Quarterly Review*
M.T.: Maimonides, *Mishneh Torah*
Pentateuch: Hertz's Commentary on the Pentateuch (when italicized; when not italicized, the term refers to the Five Books of Moses (Torah)
SAS: Hertz, *Sermons, Addresses and Studies*

Chapter 1

1. S. Schechter, "Four Epistles to the Jews of England," pp. 197–99.
2. Ibid., pp. 185–86.
3. Ibid., pp. 200–201.
4. *The Pentateuch and Haftorahs*, ed. J. H. Hertz (London: Soncino Press, 1938). All references are to this edition unless otherwise stated. Hertz is also referred to by the following terms: the editor; the annotator; the commentator.
5. Joseph Hertz, *Early and Late*, p. 141. At the same time, Hertz paid homage to the decisive influence of his own father, Simon, in guiding his intellectual maturation. The elder Hertz, who died before Hertz's induction as chief rabbi, had studied for three years at the Eisenstadt rabbinical seminary, established by the modern Orthodox scholar Esriel Hildesheimer. Although Simon Hertz was an accomplished Hebraist, poet, and talmudist, there is no decisive evidence that he completed his rabbinical studies in the old country. The *Jewish Chronicle* obituary on him of 28 March 1913 refers to him simply as Mr. Hertz.
6. Hertz, *Early and Late*, pp. 124–25.
7. Joseph Hertz, "Bachya: The Jewish Thomas à Kempis," preface; *SAS*, 1:310.
8. By way of illustration, see Julius Wellhausen, *Prolegomena to the History of Ancient Israel*, pp. 509–10.
9. *American Hebrew* 23 (10 July 1885): 136.

10. Alexander Kohut, "Secular and Theological Studies," p. 49.

11. *American Hebrew* 9 (25 November 1881): 15.

12. *American Hebrew* 59 (10 July 1896): 247.

13. *American Hebrew* 29 (7 January 1887): 132.

14. As pointed out by M. Davis, *The Emergence of Conservative Judaism*, pp. 313–19, Hertz's willingness in 1898 (along with other Seminary supporters) to sit on the provisional committee of the newly founded Orthodox Jewish Congregational Union of America did not necessarily constitute proof of his adherence to the tenets of religious Orthodoxy. Rather, with the death of Morais a year earlier, H. Pereira Mendes and Bernard Drachman (active heads of the fledgling Seminary, who did lean toward Orthodoxy), felt "they could save the institution and exert more influence within American Judaism through a union with Orthodoxy and a conversion of the Seminary into the official institution for the training of its rabbis." The scheme, however, came to naught when the Seminary, as the original sponsoring institution of the Union, came under increasingly harsh criticism by Orthodox rabbis of Eastern European extraction.

15. On Morais' religious posture, see below, n. 53.

16. L. Ginzberg, *Students, Scholars and Saints*, p. 205.

17. M. Soloveichik and Z. Rubashov, *Toldot Bikoret ha-Mikra*, pp. 139–41.

18. On Hildesheimer's theology, see D. Ellenson, "A Response by Modern Orthodoxy to Jewish Religious Pluralism: The Case of Esriel Hildesheimer," p. 78; On Hirsch, see his *The Pentateuch: Exodus*, pp. 288–89. On Hirsch's efforts to refute both Frankel and Graetz, see his *The Collected Writings*, vol. 5.

19. S. Morais, "The Talmud," pp. 165–66. One can dismiss as completely false the highly tendentious claim of Max Nussenbaum ("Champion of Orthodox Judaism: A Biography of the Reverend Sabato Morais, LL.D," pp. 3, 85–86, 118) that Morais believed that Moses received the substance of the contents of the Mishnah atop Sinai.

20. For example, see *Pentateuch*, p. 744.

21. For example, see *Pentateuch*, p. 555.

22. For example, see *Pentateuch*, pp. 404–6.

23. C. Adler, ed., *The Jewish Theological Seminary of America: Semi-Centennial Volume*, p. 189; C. Adler, *Selected Letters*, pp. 13–14.

24. *Pentateuch*, p. 555.

25. *American Hebrew* 50 (26 February 1892): 65; Kohut, "Secular and Theological Studies," p. 49.

26. Hertz, *Early and Late*, p. 123.

27. *American Hebrew* 29 (7 January 1887): 132.

28. D. Philipson and L. Grossman, ed., *Selected Writings of Isaac Mayer Wise*, p. 96; Isaac Mayer Wise, *Pronaos to Holy Writ*.

29. M. A. Meyer, *Response to Modernity: A History of the Reform Movement in Judaism*, p. 273; D. Philipson, "History of the Hebrew Union College: 1875–1925," p. 43.

30. I am indebted to my colleague Rabbi Shmuel Avidor Hacohen of Rehovot, Israel, for this illuminating fact.

31. Soloveichik, *Toldot Bikoret*, pp. 136–38.

Notes to Chapter 1

32. Examples abound in the *Pentateuch*; see pp. 322, 459, 486, 505, 554.
33. Davis, *Emergence*, p. 300, and *The Jewish Messenger* 38 (17 December 1875): 4.
34. *American Hebrew* 23 (3 July 1885): 115.
35. *American Hebrew* 23 (26 June 1885): 99, and *American Hebrew* 23 (10 July 1885): 137. On Eisenstein's censure, see his "Between Two Opinions," pp. 123–42. Nussenbaum, "Champion of Orthodox Judaism," conveniently omitted that part of Morais' stance where he openly proclaimed his repugnance at the restoration of the cult in the messianic era. In fact, Nussenbaum intimated (pp. 100–101), quite falsely, that Morais believed God would require sacrifices in the third temple, but in an altered format.
36. A. Kohut, *The Ethics of the Fathers*, p. 25. On the medieval origins of Kohut's legitimate use of the pigmy-giant aphorism, see S. Leiman, "Dwarfs on the Shoulders of Giants," pp. 90–94.
37. Davis, *Emergence*, pp. 139–40.
38. S. Morais, "Can We Change the Ritual?" p. 62; Nussenbaum, "Champion of Orthodox Judaism," pp. 73, 193–94; Kohut, *Ethics*, p. 66.
39. *SAS* 2:131–32, 3:61; *Pentateuch*, p. 933.
40. *Pentateuch*, pp. 475, 589, 692, 756, 805, 811–12.
41. *Pentateuch*, pp. 274, 489.
42. A. Kohut, "Which Is Right? A Talmudic Disputation," pp. 70, 72; I. Schorsch, "Zacharias Frankel and the European Origins of Conservative Judaism," p. 347.
43. Davis, *Emergence*, pp. 298–99; *American Hebrew* 23 (3 July 1885): 115.
44. S. Morais, "Samuel David Luzzatto," p. 88.
45. H. Morais, "Sabato Morais: A Memoir," p. 91. On Morais' relentless opposition to kabbalah, see the *Jewish Messenger* 25 (1 February 1867): 4; *Jewish Exponent* 25 (30 April 1897): 4. Though Morais placed rationalism on a pedestal, believing reason to be the path for securing observance among the masses, he cautioned the need for humility. The human mind could not grasp the essence of God's ways. It was presumptuous for man to think "that all the Creator does should be put into the crucible of human understanding, and tried whether it accords with our faulty standard!" (S. Morais, "Luzzatto's Introduction to the Pentateuch," p. 147).
46. *SAS* 1:307.
47. J. Hertz, "Jewish Mysticism: An Historical Survey," p. 787. This same article, revised with slight modifications under the title "Rise and Development of Cabala," was republished in 1938 in *SAS* 3:297–318.
48. J. Hertz, *Mystic Currents in Ancient Israel*, pp. 9–11; Hertz republished this piece in *SAS* 3:274. See also his lecture "Jewish Religious Education: Its Meaning, Scope, and Aim," in *SAS* 2:26.
49. *Pentateuch*, p. 196; *Jewish Guardian*, 26 July 1929, p. 7.
50. Hertz, "Jewish Mysticism," pp. 789, 793, 796; *SAS* 3:302–3, 309, 314.
51. *Pentateuch*, pp. 42, 406, 929.
52. B. Drachman, *The Unfailing Light*, pp. 261, 446.
53. S. Schechter, "The Charter of the Seminary," pp. 11–13. While there was unanimity about Kohut's ideological identification as a Conservative Jew, Morais was identified as both a Conservative and an Orthodox Jew. Both Hertz and Drachman, for example, called him Orthodox (Drachman, *Unfailing Light*, p. 101; C. Adler, ed., *JTSA Semi-Centennial Volume*, p. 47), as did an editorial in the *American*

Hebrew 50 (26 February 1892): 61. Morais' son, Henry, also recorded that his father was "strictly orthodox in his views being, in fact, the acknowledged leader of the Orthodox wing of Judaism in America" (H. Morais, *The Jews of Philadelphia*, p. 62). A few years later, however, when eulogizing his father, he claimed that his thinking was synonymous with Conservative Judaism (H. Morais, "Sabato Morais: A Memoir," p. 79). Morais referred to himself as an exponent of Conservative Judaism (*American Hebrew* 9 [25 November 1881]: 14; *American Hebrew* 26 [19 February 1886]: 3) and proclaimed that the Seminary was consecrated simultaneously to "cultured conservatism," "intelligent conservatism," and "enlightened orthodoxy" (*American Hebrew* 29 [31 December 1886]: 196–97). Judah David Eisenstein, a prominent spokesman of Orthodoxy in New York, insisted on labeling Morais a Conservative Jew because he "has stated publicly that he would not believe in the sacrificial service after the messianic redemption" ("Between Two Opinions," p. 133). A most intriguing formulation came from the mouth of one of Morais' students, who, in eulogizing him, opined that his mentor was not Orthodox, yet "his orthodoxy was unbending and unshakable" (Congregation Mikveh Israel, *Commemoration of the One-Hundredth Anniversary of the Birth of the Reverend Doctor Sabato Morais*, p. 58).

The most cogent way to decipher Morais' Orthodoxy/Conservatism is to appreciate the multifaceted aspects of his religious posture. The earlier studies by Moshe Davis (*Emergence*, p. 11) and Abraham Karp, "The Origins of Conservative Judaism," pp. 33–48, along with the evidence marshaled in this chapter, place Morais squarely within the circle of the traditionalist wing (as opposed to the progressive wing) of the positive-historical school. Within this context, Morais' Orthodoxy/Conservatism was linked to four unwavering factors: 1) his personal punctilious halakhic observance and preservation of venerable institutions; 2) his valiant, though unsuccessful, struggle to unite all of American Jewry under a single broad religious umbrella (*Emergence*, pp. 203–4); 3) his acceptance of the evolving nature of Jewish tradition; and 4) his commitment to religious tolerance, as evidenced by the broad religious coalition of colleagues he chose to constitute the Advisory Board of the Seminary (Karp, "Origins," p. 45). In this context, particular attention can be drawn to his defending the right of Alexander Kohut to serve as a Seminary teacher, notwithstanding the latter's more liberal religious orientation (*Jewish Exponent* 8 [30 January 1891]: 5).

54. *American Hebrew* 70 (4 April 1902): 599.
55. *SAS* 1:225, 3:361; *Early and Late*, p. 182.
56. *SAS* 2:156.
57. A. Karp, *A History of the United Synagogue of America (1913–1963)*, pp. 7–8.
58. *SAS* 1:84.
59. Hertz, *Early and Late*, p. 182; J. H. Hertz, *Seventieth Birthday Celebration of the Very Reverend J. H. Hertz*, p. 5, and reprinted in *Early and Late*, p. 142.
60. *SAS* 2:129. Hertz generally labeled his religious orientation as "Traditional" (*SAS* 1:289, 293, 328; 2:156) but was not adverse to using the term "Orthodoxy" (*SAS* 2:157; *Affirmations of Judaism*, p. 127).
61. *SAS* 1:99, 2:48; Hertz used the exact same phrase to describe Leopold Zunz's *Die Gottesdienstlichen Vortraege der Juden* (*SAS* 2:176). For an analysis of Frankel's

use of the term "positive historical Judaism," see Schorsch, "Zacharias Frankel," pp. 344–54.

62. *SAS* 1:100, 107. Elsewhere (*SAS* 2:30), he referred to Jews' College as the Jewish Theological Seminary of Great and Greater Britain.

63. D. Ellenson, "A Response by Modern Orthodoxy," pp. 77–79.

64. *SAS* 1:258, 2:117; *Early and Late*, p. 154.

65. *SAS* 1:7.

66. Hertz Student File, 2 April 1919. The correspondence, comprising some forty letters, is on deposit at the archives of the Jewish Theological Seminary of America.

67. Hertz Student File, 16 January 1935.

68. Hertz Student File, 15 October 1938. In declining the latter invitation, he did so with "deep regret."

69. Hertz Student File, 15 February 1938; 10 March 1938.

70. Hertz Student File, 1 August 1939.

71. On Asher, see P. Cowen, *Memories of an American Jew*, pp. 378, 380.

72. Hertz Student File, 27 December 1909. Hertz remained utterly convinced to the end of his life that apologetics was an essential weapon in the rabbi's arsenal: "I have repeatedly asked, where are the books, pamphlets, tracts—where is the religious propaganda, if you so please to call it—by which we spread in our camp a knowledge of what we are and stand for in the world? Our failure in this generation to have such agencies for the promotion of Judaism among Jews, is astounding" (Hertz, *Early and Late*, p. 142; *Seventieth Birthday*, pp. 4–5).

73. *Jewish Chronicle*, 7 February 1913, p. 30 and 14 February 1913, p. 13. Counted among the dozen ministers who objected to Hertz's candidacy was Gerald Friedlander, who, prior to his death in 1923, collaborated with Hertz in the writing of an early draft of the Commentary.

74. I am indebted to Professor Sefton Temkin of Albany, New York, for this story, based on his conversation with Hertz in October 1945. Schechter, in fact, wrote two letters in praise of Hertz in the summer of 1912, one to the editor of the *Jewish Chronicle* dated 5 August, and the other dated 12 August to Albert H. Jessel, who headed the selection committee in charge of appointing the new chief rabbi. In both letters, Schechter delegitimized the candidacy of Bernard Drachman alongside that of Hertz, pointing out that there was a general consensus in America that Drachman lacked the requisite credentials to be chief rabbi: "Dr. Hertz is decidedly the greater scholar, even in rabbinics, the greater gentleman, and the great preacher. . . . The difference between the two candidates is so greatly to the advantage of Dr. Hertz, as to exclude all comparison. . . . I know of no greater calamity which could happen to British Jewry than the election of Dr. Drachman to the chief rabbinate. Even the extending of an invitation to him is humiliating to English Jewry in the eyes of those who know the man and his position here" (Solomon Schechter to Albert H. Jessel, 5 August 1912, Jewish Theological Seminary Library Archives, Solomon Schechter Collection, Correspondence, 101–3, Box 3).

75. *Jewish Chronicle*, 14 February 1913, p. 13. Initially, Schechter indicated that he did not want the letter published, but apparently, he changed his mind after receiving an urgent telegram urging him to do so from Lord Rothschild and Mr. Jessel.

76. *New York Times*, 3 March 1913, p. 9. In expressing his regrets at not being able to attend, Cyrus Adler observed: "We of the Seminary . . . are not much given to boasting, but I think it is a source of pardonable pride to us that our first graduate should be elected to the most important rabbinic post in English-speaking Jewry" (Cyrus Adler, *Selected Letters*, 1:226).

77. Hertz, *Early and Late*, p. 142; *SAS* 2:34, 153–5.

Chapter 2

1. *SAS* 2:31; emphasis is mine.

2. In 1927, he again made reference to "misunderstanding from without and within," which had unduly irritated the Jewish community (*AOJ*, preface). In his 1930 essay "Fundamental Ideals and Proclamations of Judaism," p. 56, Hertz hailed the Rabbis, who "defended the Jewish God-idea whenever its purity was threatened from without or within." This particular statement was incorporated into the *Pentateuch*, p. 923. In a 1925 congratulatory letter to the president of Hebrew Union College on its jubilee anniversary, Hertz was pleased to note how the graduates of the college were beginning to realize the necessity of "common action in defense against dangers from without and within" (*Early and Late*, p. 227, and cited in S. Temkin, "Orthodoxy with Moderation: A Sketch of Joseph Herman Hertz," p. 293). See also the same phrase employed in a 1927 address by Professor Isidore Epstein of Jews' College. He decried the formidable assault against Jewish legalism "from within and from without" (I. Epstein, *Judaism of Tradition*, p. 109). The cliché was repeated once more, a year after Rabbi Hertz's demise by one of his rabbinic admirers who described him as "a spiritual warrior . . . championing Israel against attacks from within or from without" (W. Gottlieb, ed., *Essays and Addresses in Memory of Joseph Herman Hertz*, p. 33).

3. On these charges, see *Pentateuch*, p. 555, and *AOJ*, p. 43.

4. On Montefiore's leadership role, see Hertz's remarks in his *AOJ*, p. 21; on Montefiore's denial of Mosaic authorship of the Torah, see ibid., pp. 40–41.

5. *AOJ*, p. 31.

6. I am grateful to Judith Schonfeld, Hertz's daughter, for this illuminating fact.

7. H.A., A/13.

8. H.A., Scrapbook (1936–42), p. 53. The text of the telegram, which was subsequently published in the *Jewish Chronicle*, 10 June 1938, p. 14 read: "Heartiest best wishes on entering eighty-first year. God grant you good health *ad meah shanah* [to a hundred years]."

9. *AOJ*, pp. 41, 46.

10. In a 1919 sermon, Hertz defined traditional Judaism as "the teachings and practices which have come down to the House of Israel through the ages; the positive, Jewish beliefs concerning God, the Torah, and Israel; the festivals; the historical synagogue service; the holy resolve to maintain Israel's identity; and the life consecrated by Jewish religious observance—all of these in indissoluble union with the best thought and culture of the age and with utmost loyalty to king and country" (*SAS* 1:289, and repeated in J. H. Hertz, *The New Paths: Whither Do They Lead?*, p. 5).

Notes to Chapter 2

11. *SAS* 2:117. In 1931, Hertz defined progressive conservatism as "religious advance without loss of traditional Jewish values and without estrangement from the collective consciousness of the House of Israel."

12. Ibid., 1:309.

13. See, in general, C. G. Montefiore's *The Synoptic Gospels* (1909), and his *Judaism and Saint Paul* (1914).

14. I am grateful to Israel Finestein for analyzing the tension between the religious right and left with which Hertz had to contend.

15. Compare Hertz's early and later evaluation of Liberal Judaism recorded in *SAS* 1:309, with that made in *AOJ*, p. 125.

16. *New Paths*, pp. 8, 16–17, 24, 30–31, 33–34; *AOJ*, pp. 19–20, 63, 93; cf. p. 125.

17. Ibid., pp. 32, 170.

18. *Jewish Chronicle*, 31 August 1928, p. 9; *Jewish Chronicle Supplement*, 26 October 1928, p iii.

19. *AOJ*, pp. 55, 124. Samuel Daiches penned a reply to Montefiore in another issue of *The Nineteenth Century*. He sent a manuscript copy of the article to Hertz (H.A., A/13). A more conciliatory view of Montefiore's position came from academician Herbert Loewe, who had a good relationship with the Liberal leader (H.A., G/6, Herbert Loewe to Hertz, 16 November 1921).

20. C. G. Montefiore, "A Plea for the Old Testament," pp. 831–838.

21. B. L. Q. Henriques, *Sir Robert Waley Cohen*, p. 344; H.A., G/6, Robert Waley Cohen to Hertz, 21 December 1925.

22. H.A., E/6/2, an undated draft of a letter, probably to Aaron Blashki; see also Hertz to Blashki, 2 February 1928.

23. *Jewish Chronicle*, 13 August 1915, p. 6; 20 August 1915, p. 12; 3 September 1915, p. 11; 10 September 1915, p. 7; in general, see J. M. Shaftesley, "Religious Controversies," p. 108.

24. *Jewish Chronicle*, 27 August 1915, p. 18; 10 September 1915, pp. 13–14; 1 October 1915, p. 17.

25. Ibid., 31 (1 August 1928), p. 9.

26. Epstein, *Judaism of Tradition*, prefatory note.

27. *Jewish Chronicle*, 20 January 1922, p. 14.

28. A. Hyamson, *Jews' College, London: 1855–1955*, pp. 64–65.

29. *Jewish Chronicle*, 7 April 1922, p. 9; see also P. Paneth, *Guardian of the Law*, pp. 15–16; J. H. Hertz, *Seventieth Birthday Celebration*, p. 5.

30. *SAS* 2:65.

31. Ibid., 2:35. In this context note Schechter's 1901 observation that for Jews "to acquire a knowledge of [Torah] through the medium of Christian commentaries means to lose by proxy." *Studies in Judaism*, Second Series, p. 200.

32. *SAS*, 2:71–72; on this same theme, see also ibid., 2:35.

33. Ibid., 2:31.

34. Solomon Schechter, "The Study of the Bible," pp. 33–34.

35. Solomon Schechter, "Higher Criticism—Higher Anti-Semitism," pp. 36–39.

36. *SAS* 2:65.

37. *SAS* 2:60.

38. Epstein, I., ed. *J. H. Hertz, In Memoriam*, p. 2.

39. *The Pentateuch and Haftorahs: Genesis*, ed. J. H. Hertz, preface.

40. H.A., E/6/1, Hertz to Sir Phillip Sassoon, dated circa September/October 1920.

41. *Pentateuch*, p. 425; on this same theme, see also ibid., p. 519.

42. H.A., E/6/l, letters by Hertz to the Jewish Publication Society of America, 3 September 1917; 28 October 1917; 17 July 1918; I. George Dobsevage (Jewish Publication Society secretary) to Hertz, 2 May 1918.

43. *Jewish Chronicle,* 22 October 1920, p. 13; deposited in H.A. E/6/1. Letters of invitation to various colleagues are deposited in ibid., E/6/2.

44. Ibid., E/6/1, Hertz to Leo Jung, 28 October 1924.

45. Ibid., E/6/2, Hertz to I. Raffalovich, 25 October 1920.

46. *Jewish Chronicle,* 22 October 1920; H.A., E/6/1; ibid., E/6/2, Hertz to Max Margolis, 7 October 1920.

47. Ibid., E/6/2, Hertz to Salis Daiches, 20 January 1923.

48. These letters are deposited in ibid., E/6/1.

49. Ibid., E/6/2, Gerald Friedlander to Hertz, 29 September 1920; 1 October 1920. Several years later, Hertz acknowledged the correctness of Friedlander's judgment in a letter to his sole financial backer at the time, Aaron Blashki (ibid., E/6/2, undated letter, circa 1928).

50. Ibid., E/6/1, Hertz to Henry Pereira Mendes, May 25, 1922; ibid., E/6/2, Hertz to Salis Daiches, 15 November 1922; Hertz to Daiches, 6 February 1923; payment receipts acknowledged by Gerald Friedlander to Hertz during the years 1921–23; Hertz to Abraham Cohen, 6 June 1923; Cohen to Hertz, 10 April 1924.

51. Ibid., E/6/2, Hertz to Abraham Cohen, 6 June 1923; Salis Daiches to Hertz, 26 February 1923; Hertz to Daiches, 1 March 1923; Daiches to Hertz, 2 March 1923; Daiches to Hertz, 18 July 1923.

52. Ibid., E/6/2, drafts of two letters by Hertz to Salis Daiches, 15 and 16 November 1924; Hertz to Abraham Cohen, 15 November 1924.

53. By mid-April, the chief rabbi had received the final portion of Abraham Cohen's research on Leviticus (ibid., E/6/2, Hertz to Cohen, 14 April 1924). By the fall of that year, he could inform his New York colleague, Leo Jung, that he had received a completed manuscript of the Commentary (ibid., E/6/2, Hertz to Jung, October 1924).

54. Ibid., E/6/1, Hertz to Samuel Frampton, 2 March 1929; in a 26 April 1931 communiqué (ibid., 5/6/1), Hertz acknowledged receiving Frampton's notes on Leviticus.

55. Ibid., E/6/1, Hertz to Leo Jung, 28 October 1924; Hertz to I. Dobsevage, 27 October 1925.

56. This fact can be ascertained by comparing Hertz's letter to Aaron Blashki dated 19 October 1928, in which the chief rabbi still refers to Buechler as a coeditor, with Hertz's letter of 12 July 1929, written jointly to Joshua Abelson, Abraham Cohen, and Samuel Frampton, in which it is clear that Buechler had failed to fulfill his editorial commitment (ibid., E/6/2).

57. Ibid., E/6/2, Salis Daiches to Hertz, 18 June 1923. In a 16 November 1922 letter to Daiches (ibid.), Hertz indicated his intention to call a planning meeting of the contributors, but on the basis of the correspondence between Hertz and his staff, there is no indication that such a meeting was ever held.

58. Ibid., E/6/2, Hertz to Salis Daiches, 1 March 1923; emphasis is mine.

59. Ibid., E/6/2, undated draft letter directed to the attention of one of two men: Aaron Blashki, at the time Hertz's sole financial backer of the Commentary, or to Blashki's son-in-law, Wilfred Samuel, a lawyer who negotiated with Hertz con-

Notes to Chapter 2

cerning Blashki's complaints about the length of time it was taking to publish the Commentary in five volumes.

60. Ibid., E/6/2, Wilfred Samuel to Hertz, 30 January 1928; Hertz to Blashki, 2 February 1928; Hertz incidentally confirmed that Samuel's concerns about the protracted time it was taking to publish the Commentary were "substantially correct."

61. Ibid., E/6/2, Hertz to Jung, 6 February1928.

62. Ibid., E/6/2, Joshua Abelson, Abraham Cohen, and Samuel Frampton to Hertz, 8 July 1929; reply by Hertz 12 July 1929. See appendix for complete transcripts of the two letters.

63. Ibid., E/6/2, Hertz to Frampton, 25 November 1932.

64. Ibid., E/6/2, undated draft letter in the file of Aaron Blashki.

65. Ibid., E/6/2, Samuel to Hertz, 18 January 1928; Blashki to Hertz, 28 November 1928. In a communiqué to Leo Jung, Hertz put the publication figure at an even 4,000 pounds sterling (ibid., E/6/1, Hertz to Jung, 28 April 1924).

66. Ibid., E/6/2, Hertz to Blashki, 19 October 1928.

67. Ibid., E/6/2, Hertz to Blashki, 19 November 1928; Blashki to Hertz, 28 November 1928.

68. Ibid., E/6/2, Hertz to Blashki, 2 February 1928; Hertz to Blashki, 6 December 1928.

69. Ibid., E/6/2, Hertz to Blashki, 6 December 1928.

70. Ibid., E/6/2, Hertz to Blashki, 24 December 1928; Blashki to Hertz, 28 December 1928. For a listing of benefactors who subvented the substantial publication costs of the various books, see the original prefaces to each of the five volumes in the *Pentateuch*.

71. A. Cohen, *The Teachings of Maimonides*, p. viii; Maimonides, *The Eight Chapters of Maimonides on Ethics (Shemonah Perakim)*, p. 36. On Maimonides' use of the principle in the *Mishneh Torah*, see M.T., Hilkhot Kiddush ha-Hodesh, 17:24. A recent study that takes this claim seriously is D. Hartman's *A Living Covenant: The Innovative Spirit of Traditional Judaism*, pp. 8, 11–12.

72. See chap. 4, "Hebraism and Hellenism."

73. J. Abelson, *The Immanence of God in Rabbinical Literature*, pp. 15, 286.

74. Abelson's two works analyzing mysticism were *The Immanence of God in Rabbinical Literature* and *Jewish Mysticism*. On his interest in Maimonides, see "Maimonides on the Jewish Creed," pp. 24–58; "Maimonides as Philosopher," pp. vi–vii; *Encyclopaedia of Religion and Ethics*, 1915, s.v. "Maimonides," J. Abelson.

75. H.A. E/6/2, Cohen to Hertz, 17 September 1924; Hertz to Cohen, 18 September 1924; Cohen to Hertz, 10 April 1924; Hertz to Cohen, 14 April 1924.

76. Ibid., E/6/2, Hertz to Leo Jung, 17 December 1924.

77. Ibid., E/6/2, Cohen to Hertz, 21 September 1923.

78. Ibid., E/6/2, Hertz to Leo Jung, 17 December 1924; ibid., E/6/3, Hertz to Rosenbaum, 27 January 1931.

79. A. Cohen, *Jewish Homiletics*, pp. 18, 38–39.

80. *The Babylonian Talmud: Tractate Berakot*, trans. A. Cohen, p. vi.

81. *Jewish Chronicle*, 13 July 1923, p. 31–33.

82. Ibid., 1 January 1926, p. 21.

83. A. Cohen, "Supplementary Notes to Gorfinkle's Edition of Maimonides' Eight Chapters," pp. 475–79; "Maimonides and Aristotle's Doctrine of the Mean," pp. iii–iv.

84. *Jewish Chronicle*, 7 March 1919; rejoinder by Montefiore, ibid., 14 March 1919, p. 13.

85. G. Friedlander, *The Jewish Sources of the Sermon on the Mount*, pp. xxiii–xxiv, 1, 261; *SAS* 2:143; *Jewish Chronicle*, 24 August 1923, p. 7.

86. Friedlander, *The Jewish Sources*, p. xxvii; see also ibid., pp. 263, 266. Montefiore defined this perception as a distinguishing mark between the Orthodox and Liberal Jew: "For Orthodox Judaism can hardly allow that any aspect of religious truth is contained in any other sacred book, which is not contained, or not so fully or plainly presented, in the Old Testament and the Talmud. But Liberal Judaism does not believe that God has enabled the human race to reach forward to religious truth so exclusively through a single channel" (C. Montefiore, *Liberal Judaism and Hellenism*, p. 78).

87. Friedlander, *The Jewish Sources*, p. 265; Maimonides, M.T., Hilkhot Melakhim, 11:4.

88. Friedlander, *The Jewish Sources*, p. xxvii. In the 1930 preface to the commentary on Exodus, the chief rabbi took credit for writing the notes on chapters 1 through 20. At the same time, he noted that he had embodied some glosses submitted to him by Friedlander. In the preface to the one-volume 1938 edition of the *Pentateuch*, however, Hertz acknowledged that it had been Friedlander who submitted a manuscript to the first twenty chapters of the book. Hertz's correction, in effect, granted Friedlander, who had died several years earlier, more credit than one might have suspected with only the 1930 preface in hand (*The Pentateuch and Haftorahs: Exodus*, preface; *Pentateuch*, preface). In an undated list of work done by the various collaborators (H.A., E/6/3), Hertz clearly indicated that Friedlander had contributed material on Gen. 27–50 and Exod. 1–20. A letter to this effect also made the point (ibid., 176/1, Hertz to I. Dobsevage, 15 September 1925).

89. *Jewish Chronicle*, 5 May 1922, p. 19.

90. A point noted a few years later by the Unitarian minister R. Travers Herford in *What the World Owes to the Pharisees*, p. 29.

91. G. Friedlander, *Hellenism and Christianity*, pp. ix–x, 196; on the Commentary's theological dissection of Christianity, see chap. 4 in this work, "Hebraism and Hellenism."

92. On Frampton's tenure, see D. Hudaly, *Liverpool Old Hebrew Congregation*, pp. 35–37, 56–60.

93. *The Pentateuch and Haftorahs: Genesis*, p. vi; Hertz, *The Pentateuch and Haftorahs: Exodus*, p. v, emphasis is mine; *Pentateuch*, p. vii; *SAS*, preface.

94. *Pentateuch*, p. 202; *SAS* 2:73.

95. *Pentateuch*, p. 399; *AOJ*, p. 48.

96. *Pentateuch*, pp. 401–3; *SAS* 2:67–69; 3:25–35.

97. J. H. Hertz, "Ancient Semitic Codes and the Mosaic Legislation," pp. 207–21; a copy is deposited in H.A., E/6/3.

98. *Pentateuch*, p. 562; *AOJ*, p. 130.

99. *Pentateuch*, p. 563; *SAS* 1:296.

100. *Pentateuch*, p. 923; *AOJ*, p. 15.

101. *Pentateuch*, pp. 402, 920–21, 923, 931, 936; Hertz, "Fundamental Ideals," pp. 55–58, 60, 63.

Notes to Chapter 2

102. *Pentateuch*, pp. 925–26; *SAS* 2:8–17, 20; *Pentateuch*, p. 36; *SAS* 2:16.
103. *Pentateuch*, p. 926; *AOJ*, p. 89.
104. *Pentateuch*, pp. 934–35; *AOJ*, pp. 76, 78–79; this thought was repeated again in part in "Fundamental Ideals," p. 66.
105. *Pentateuch*, pp. 935–38; *SAS* 1:273–74.
106. *Jewish Chronicle Supplement*, 28 June 1929, p. iii–iv.
107. Epstein, *Judaism of Tradition*, pp. 73–74; *Pentateuch*, p. 194.
108. Epstein, *Judaism of Tradition*, p. 217 n. 8; *Pentateuch*, p. 194.
109. Epstein, *Judaism of Tradition*, pp. 78–80; *Pentateuch*, 195.
110. Interview with Nahum Sarna, 27 June 1982.
111. *Pentateuch*, p. 560; I. Epstein, "Introduction to Seder Kodashim," pp. xxi–xxii.
112. *Pentateuch*, p. 562; I. Epstein, "Introduction to Seder Kodashim," p. xxix.
113. *Pentateuch*, p. 562; I. Epstein, "Introduction to Seder Kodashim," p. xxiv.
114. *Pentateuch*, p. 562; I. Epstein, "Introduction to Seder Kodashim," pp. xxix–xxx. On the rabbinic source, see *Midrash Rabbah: Leviticus*, trans. J. J. Slotki, 22:8 (pp. 286–87).
115. *Pentateuch*, p. 562; I. Epstein, "Introduction to Seder Kodashim," pp. xxxi–xxxii.
116. I. Epstein, ed., *Moses Maimonides, 1135–1204*, pp. 61–82.
117. *Jewish Chronicle Supplement*, 26 October 1928, p. vii.
118. Ibid., p. viii.
119. On the term "conservative bloc" and Graetz's positive orientation to a Jewish future, see the illuminating essay by Ismar Schorsch in Heinrich Graetz's *The Structure of Jewish History and Other Essays*, pp. 31, 50.
120. *Pentateuch*, p. 936.
121. *SAS* 2:49–50.
122. *Pentateuch*, p. vii. The phrase quoted was lifted by Hertz from Emil Reich's *The Failure of the 'Higher Criticism'*, preface, and was cited by the chief rabbi in *AOJ*, p. 31.
123. Mattuck was a regular contributor to the *Jewish Guardian*, which often sympathized with policies adopted by the Liberals. Hertz, as well as Waley Cohen, was disturbed over this journalistic bias. Just prior to his public excoriation of the Liberals, which began at the end of 1925, Hertz criticized Mattuck for challenging beliefs that were the foundation of Israel's existence (H.A., G/6, Waley Cohen to Laurie Magnus, 21 December 1925; ibid., A/13, Hertz to the editor of the *Jewish Guardian*, 23 September, 18 and 19 October 1925).
124. *Jewish Chronicle*, 22 October 1920. p. 13.
125. In his own valiant efforts to restore self-respect to the nonscholarly Jewish public, Frankel highlighted the need to distinguish between popular and academic genres of scholarship. The intelligent, though Jewishly uninformed, layman was quite understandably put off by the obsessive scholarly reliance on meticulous, pedantic footnotes. Frankel understood that the push to restore Jewish self-confidence and loyalty was intrinsically linked to replacing dry and unimaginative attention to details with edifying instruction. See Schorsch, "Zacharias Frankel," pp. 349–50. Solomon Schechter also recognized that the canon of history could be used to support or denigrate the legitimacy of Judaism. See his *Studies in Judaism*, 3d ser., pp. 81–82.
126. *SAS* 2:59.

Chapter 3

1. A consensus prevails among philosophers and historians of religion that Spinoza's critique of religion, and of Judaism in particular, constitutes the watershed between medieval and modern thought. See L. Strauss, *Spinoza's Critique of Religion*, pp. 15, 19; H. Wolfson, "Spinoza and Religion," p. 167; A. Hertzberg, "Modernity and Judaism," pp. 125–29. For a more recent statement, see E. Schweid, "Judaism and the Solitary Jew," pp. 38–45.

2. B. de Spinoza, *A Theologico-Political Treatise and a Political Treatise*, pp. 8, 47, 165, 237, 247–50.

3. For a synopsis of the history of biblical criticism, see *Encyclopaedia Judaica*, 1971, s.v. "Bible: Bible Research and Criticism," by H. D. Hummel.

4. *The Anchor Bible: Genesis*, trans. E. A. Speiser, pp. xxx–xxxi; Y. Kaufmann, *The Religion of Israel from Its Beginnings to the Babylonian Exile*, p. 155; J. Wellhausen, *Prolegomena to the History of Ancient Israel*, p. 421.

5. J. Wellhausen, *Prolegomena*, pp. 422–24.

6. Ibid., pp. 421–22; M. Weinfeld, "Julius Wellhausen's Understanding of the Law of Ancient Israel and Its Fallacies," pp. 62–64.

7. This quotation, covering pp. 499–513 in the *Prolegomena*, is supposed to be an exact reprint of his comments evaluating the nature of Judaism and Christianity, which appeared originally in an article in the *Encyclopaedia Britannica*, 9th ed., s.v. "Israel," by J. Wellhausen. In fact, this quotation and the entire section covering pp. 499–513 of the *Prolegomena* do not form part of the original article. The *Encyclopaedia Britannica* article is not only considerably reduced, but there is no effort at all by Wellhausen to distinguish between Judaism and Christianity.

8. H. F. Hahn, *The Old Testament in Modern Research*, pp. 8, 13.

9. W. R. Smith, *Lectures on the Religion of the Semites*, pp. 256, 258.

10. Wellhausen, *Prolegomena*, pp. 112, 421, 424–25, 486. As early as 1818, Zunz noted the bias of gentile scholarship that perceived Judaism to be an inferior expression of spiritual life: "More objectionable than the indifference to the academic study of Judaism, more shocking than the contempt, is the partisanship, not of love but of hatred, with which this study is approached. Anything in it which can be used against the Jews or Judaism has been a welcome find. These scholars have gathered half-understood expressions from every corner in order with their aid to pillory their eternal rival" (L. Zunz, "On Rabbinic Literature," p. 201).

11. S. R. Driver, "The Permanent Moral and Devotional Value of the Old Testament for the Christian Church," pp. xiv–xv; S. R. Driver, "The Voice of God in the Old Testament," p. 140. See also his sermon "Mercy and Not Sacrifice," p. 229, where he refers to "Pharisees in whom the religion of the Old Testament became . . . de-spiritualized."

12. S. Schechter, "The Study of the Bible," pp. 33–34. For further corroboration of Schechter's theory, see E. Schuerer, *A History of the Jewish People in the Time of Jesus Christ*, pt. 2, 2:124–25.

Notes to Chapter 3

13. S. Schechter, "The Law and Recent Criticism," pp. 762–63; reprinted in his *Studies in Judaism*, 1st ser., pp. 243–44, 248. For a recent confirmation of Schechter's evaluation, see A. A. Cohen, *The Myth of the Judeo-Christian Tradition*, p. 199.

14. Though Schechter and W. Robertson Smith were at opposite poles theologically, the latter nevertheless "perceived the value of Schechter's contribution to scholarship and to theology" (N. Bentwich, *Solomon Schechter: A Biography*, p. 81).

15. Wellhausen, *Prolegomena*, pp. vii, ix–x. On Smith's acceptance of the late dating of the Priestly Code, see W. R. Smith, *The Old Testament in the Jewish Church*, pp. 223–53, and W. R. Smith, *Lectures on the Religion of the Semites*, pp. xv, 215, 258. On the personal friendship between the two men, see R. Smend, "Julius Wellhausen and His Prolegomena to the History of Israel," p. 7. Smith himself acknowledged their friendship in his *The Prophets of Israel and Their Place in History*, preface.

16. W. R. Smith, *The Prophets*, p. 73.

17. W. R. Smith, *Lectures on the Religion of the Semites*, pp. 439–40.

18. S. R. Driver, "The Voice of God in the Old Testament," pp. 131–32, 142.

19. S. Schechter, "Higher Criticism—Higher Anti-Semitism," pp. 36–39.

20. B. S. Childs, "Wellhausen in English," p. 85.

21. H. Hahn, *The Old Testament in Modern Research*, p. 46.

22. He had not seen fit to include Babylonian and Assyrian cultures in his research on grounds that neither represented pure Semitism. Besides, they reflected "a relatively late stage of cultural and religious development" (W. R. Smith, *Lectures on the Religion of the Semites*, p. 13).

23. H. Hahn, *The Old Testament in Modern Research*, p. 56.

24. J. Frazer, *Folk-Lore in the Old Testament: Studies in Comparative Religion*, 3 vols., (1918), preface.

25. J. Frazer, *Folk-Lore in the Old Testament*, abridged ed. (1923), pp. viii, 360.

26. H. Hahn, *Old Testament in Modern Research*, pp. 85–89.

27. A. F. Kirkpatrick, "The Claims of Criticism upon the Clergy and Laity," p. 6.

28. T. O. Beidelman, *W. Robertson Smith and the Sociological Study of Religion*, p. 20.

29. H. Wace, "Summary," pp. 610–11.

30. R. Smend, "Julius Wellhausen and His Prolegomena to the History of Israel," p. 3.

31. J. A. Faulkner, "The Miraculous Birth of Our Lord," p. 432.

32. R. T. Herford, *Pharisaism, Its Aim and Its Method*, p. 332.

33. G. F. Moore, "Christian Writers on Judaism," pp. 197–98.

34. G. F. Moore, "The Rise of Normative Judaism," pp. 315–16; G. F. Moore, *Judaism*, 1:13.

35. G. F. Moore, "The Rise of Normative Judaism," p. 323; G. F. Moore, *Judaism*, 1:16.

36. For an evaluation of Moore's historiography, see the penetrating comments of Morton Smith in *The Harvard Library Bulletin* 15 (1967): 176–77. Prior to Moore, in the waning years of the nineteenth century in America, serious attempts to refute Wellhausen were attempted by W. H. Green and E. C. Bissel. See R. J. Thompson, "Moses and the Law in a Century of Criticism since Graf," p. 69.

37. H. Hahn, *Old Testament in Modern Research*, p. 51.

38. G. F. Moore, "The Rise of Normative Judaism," pp. 318–23.

39. A. H. Sayce, "The Archaeological Witness to the Literary Activity of the Mosaic Age," pp. 17–18.

40. L. Abbot, *The Life and Literature of the Ancient Hebrews*, p. 88.

41. On Moore, see *Pentateuch*, pp. 283–87, 485, 489, 491; on Sayce, see ibid., pp. 554, 940; on Abbot, see ibid., p. 5.

42. H. A., E/6/3, Hertz to Sayce, 1 December 1931; ibid., E/6/3, Sayce to Hertz, 18 May 1932.

43. *Pentateuch*, p. 555.

44. I. Abrahams, "Jewish Interpretation of the Old Testament," pp. 406–7, 425.

45. Thompson, "Moses and the Law," p. 59; cf. *Pentateuch*, p. 555.

46. *Pentateuch*, pp. 306, 402.

47. *Pentateuch*, p. 763. Judah Halevi, for example, made this claim. See his *The Kuzari*, I, 86, 88, 91.

48. *Pentateuch*, pp. 521, 758.

49. These points were argued, for example, by W. Oesterley, "Worship and Ritual," pp. 333, 350; and W. F. Lofthouse, "Hebrew Religion from Moses to Saul," pp. 235–37.

50. *Pentateuch*, pp. 406, 557–58.

51. George Rawlinson is not to be confused with his elder brother, Sir Henry Creswicke Rawlinson, acclaimed as the "father of Assyriology." Biographical information is provided in G. Rawlinson, *Ancient History*, p. vii. The reference in the Commentary was drawn from Rawlinson's article "Moses, the Author of the Levitical Code of Laws," pp. 28–29.

52. *Pentateuch*, pp. 277, 283, 792.

53. Ibid., p. 940.

54. Ibid., pp. 588, 801, 849, 940. Although there were places in the Commentary where Hertz made use of different biblical versions to corroborate his interpretation of a given passage (see, for example, on Exod. 3:22 and 23:19; and Lev. 8:31), he held back in this instance. This was understandable; not to have done so would have been tantamount to throwing into doubt the accepted accuracy of transmission of God's Word to Moses. Thus, Hertz avoided use of the Samaritan version, which reads *ba-makom* instead of *bekhol-ha-makom*; the inclusion of this reading, though identical in meaning with the verse in Deut. 12:11, would have marked a departure from the literal meaning of the Exodus passage. Similarly, he avoided the Syriac version (*tazkir* = you will remember), which implied that the final decision of where to worship God was left entirely in man's hands. It would appear that the Syriac rendering was known to the editor. This is evident from the comments to Deut. 12:5: "Not the place that the worshiper chooses, but the place chosen by God" (ibid., p. 801).

55. Ibid., p. 940; G. C. M. Douglas, "The Deuteronomic Code," p. 81; emphasis is mine.

56. By 1905, Wellhausen had come around to appreciating that Israelite antiquity could not be studied in isolation: "One sees too clearly how closely it is bound on all sides with the near and distant environment" (P. D. Miller, Jr., "Wellhausen and the History of Israel's Religion," p. 66).

57. W. R. Smith, *Lectures on the Religion of the Semites*, pp. 20–21.

58. W. R. Smith, *The Old Testament in the Jewish Church*, p. 265.

59. Frazer, *Folk-Lore in the Old Testament*, abridged ed., pp. 350, 352.

Notes to Chapter 3

60. *Pentateuch*, pp. 399, 555, 941. On their respective attitudes to biblical criticism, see Thompson, "Moses and the Law," pp. 53, 60–61.

61. S. R. Driver, *Introduction to the Literature of the Old Testament*, p. 145.

62. G. F. Moore, "The Rise of Normative Judaism," pp. 318–23; *Pentateuch*, p. 554.

63. *Pentateuch*, p. 926; Thompson, "Moses and the Law," p. 78.

64. Schechter, "The Study of the Bible," pp. 40–41, 43.

65. L. Jacobs, *We Have Reason to Believe*, pp. 75–76.

66. Thompson, "Moses and the Law," p. 124.

67. *Pentateuch*, p. 630. Peet argued for the historicity of the Egyptian bondage on exactly the same grounds (ibid., p. 396).

68. Ibid., p. 395.

69. J. Skinner, *A Critical and Exegetical Commentary on Genesis*, International Critical Commentary, vol. 1, pp. 447–48.

70. *Pentateuch*, p. 144. Surprisingly, the Commentary did not incorporate Rashbam's suggestion of equating the Ishmaelites and Midianites as ethnic clansmen, nor Ibn Ezra's prooftext for this contention based on Judg. 8:24.

71. *Pentateuch*, pp. 554, 814. Understandably, Hoffmann's interpretation was corroborated by Samson Raphael Hirsch in *The Pentateuch: Deuteronomy*, p. 281. Moses Mendelssohn, however, accepted the literal rendering of the verse in Deuteronomy. See Naphtali Herz Homberg's "Commentary to Deuteronomy 15:20," published as part of M. Mendelssohn's German translation to the Hebrew Pentateuch, commonly referred to as the *Biur* or *Netivot Shalom*, p. 42a. On Hoffmann's interpretation, see D. Hoffmann, *Das Buch Deuteronomium*, pp. 246–50.

The Commentary did not record Hoffmann's mention of Neh. 10:37 as an additional proof for his case. The possible objection to Hoffmann's otherwise brilliant juxtaposition of verses is that the word *la-kohanim* (in Neh. 10:37) could be translated as "to the priests," instead of "for the priests." Even if one accepts the latter translation, this could, theoretically, reflect the cultic demands of the hierocracy in the postexilic period alone.

72. *Pentateuch*, p. 740.

73. Spinoza, *Treatise*, p. 121; S. R. Driver, *A Critical and Exegetical Commentary on Deuteronomy*, International Critical Commentary, vol. 5, pp. xlii–xliii; emphasis is partly mine.

74. *Pentateuch*, p. 736.

75. Ibid., p. 189.

76. *The Pentateuch and Haftorahs: Exodus*, p. 127. M. Kalisch's interpretation appeared in his *A Historical and Critical Commentary on the Old Testament: Exodus* with a new translation by M. Kalisch, p. 196. His interpretation of the Chronicles passage was acceptable to E. L. Curtis, *A Critical and Exegetical Commentary on Chronicles*, p. 514.

77. I. Grunfeld, "Introduction to the First English Edition of Rabbi Samson Raphael Hirsch's Commentary on the Torah," p. 14.

78. J. E. McFayden, "The Present Position of Old Testament Criticism," p. 190.

79. F. Delitzsch, *Babel and Bible*. On the moral inferiority of Israelite traditions to Babylonian, see ibid., pp. 187–91, 197–202.

80. G. H. Richardson, *Biblical Archaeology: Its Use and Abuse*, p. 25.

81. A. H. Sayce, *Monument, Facts and Higher Critical Fancies*, p. 25; Thompson, "Moses and the Law," pp. 92–93.

82. *Pentateuch,* p. 555.
83. Ibid., p. 941.
84. Ibid., p. 848.
85. Ibid., p. 12.
86. Ibid., p. 940. W. R. Smith, *Kinship and Marriage in Early Arabia,* p. 208.
87. *Pentateuch,* p. 568.
88. Ibid., pp. 55, 58.
89. Ibid., pp. 234–35, 844.
90. Ibid., p. 211; A. S. Yahuda, *The Language of the Pentateuch in Its Relation to Egyptian,* pp. 258–59.
91. *Pentateuch,* p. 265.
92. Ibid., pp. 155, 157–58, 189–90.
93. Ibid., p. 276. The explanation in the Commentary is a slight rewording of that found in F. Brown, ed., with the cooperation of S. R. Driver and C. A. Briggs, *A Hebrew and English Lexicon of the Old Testament,* p. 577.
94. *Pentateuch,* p. 46. Spinoza had incorporated Ibn Ezra's interpretation as a support for the non-Mosaic composition of the Torah (*Treatise,* p. 122).
95. *Pentateuch,* p. 142.
96. Ibid., p. 149. On the midrashic sources, see *Midrash Rabbah: Genesis,* 87:9 (p. 812); *Midrash Lekah Tov: Genesis* (Hebrew), Gen. 39:20 (p. 200); *Midrash ha-Gadol: Genesis* (Hebrew), Gen. 39:20 (p. 770).
97. *Pentateuch,* p. 190.
98. Ibid., pp. 51–52, 151. Adam C. Welch, whose views on the antiquity of Deuteronomy were appreciated by Hertz, concurred with the Commentary's estimate of equating the Habiru with the Hebrews. See his article "The History of Israel," p. 123. Welch thanked the chief rabbi when he received a copy of the Commentary to Leviticus: "Everything which serves to make the Hebrew Scriptures better understood and more widely appreciated is a benefit in a world which has largely lost the sense for spiritual values" (H.A., E/6/3, Welch to Hertz, 7 January 1933).
99. *Pentateuch,* p. 52.
100. *Pentateuch,* p. 395. On the alternative theory of the higher critics, see A. C. Welch, "The History of Israel," pp. 122–23. Hertz's interpretation appears more plausible than that of Yehezkel Kaufmann, who began his serious research into Israel's origins in the 1930s. See the latter's *Toldot ha-Emunah ha-Yisre'elit,* vol. 2, bk. 1, p. 65.
101. *Pentateuch,* pp. 54, 185.
102. Ibid., p. 340.
103. Ibid., pp. 240, 250.
104. Ibid., p. 780.
105. Ibid., p. 862; emphasis is mine.
106. Ibid., p. 736. Robinson was professor of biblical literature at the Union Theological Seminary, New York. A similar reference to geographical accuracy in the Torah was the identification of "the way to the Red Sea" in Num. 14:25 and Deut. 1:40 "with the modern pilgrim-track from Suez to Akabah" (ibid., p. 742).
107. The following references from the *Pentateuch* correlate, respectively, with the pages, enumerated in parentheses, found in G. A. Smith's *The Historical Geography of the Holy Land,* p. 651 (p. 63); p. 660 (p. 377 n. 1); p. 661 (pp. 377–78); p. 744 (p. 377); p. 707 (pp. 335–38, 341); p. 792 (p. 62). The reference to Smith in the *Pen-*

tateuch, p. 745, matches the *The Cambridge Bible for Schools and Colleges: Book of Deuteronomy*, with introduction by George Adam Smith, pp. 37–38. The citations from Smith in the Commentary are either almost verbatim extracts or represent good précis.

108. G. A. Smith, *The Historical Geography*, pp. 20, 89. Though appreciative of Smith's research as a geographer, Hertz reminded the reader that his theological observations were often tainted, reflecting notions akin to "a New Testament apologist" (*Pentateuch*, p. 806). Moreover, like S. R. Driver, his basic orientation as a biblical scholar was to Graf-Wellhausen. See Thompson, "Moses and the Law," p. 70 n. 2.

109. Quoted in G. H. Richardson, *Biblical Archaeology*, p. 54. Richardson himself concurred with Driver's view: "even though archaeology gives the historical setting into which the biblical narrative looks as if it would fit, it is not the same as having proved the biblical account. . . . Archaeology alone can give the historical setting of Scripture. But when it has done this, it has usually gone as far as it can" (ibid., p. 174).

110. S. A. Cook, "The Religious Environment of Israel," p. 54; *Pentateuch*, p. 739; H.A., E/6/3, Hertz to Cook, 1 December 1931; Cook to Hertz, 3 December 1931.

111. Hertz was keenly aware of this risk factor. See *Pentateuch*, pp. 404–5.

112. Frazer was joined in his perception by W. Oesterley, "Worship and Ritual," p. 323.

113. S. R. Driver, "Hebrew Authority," in *Authority and Archaeology, Sacred and Profane*, reprint, pp. 6–7.

114. The editor acknowledged the "considerable influence on the Hebrews" by Hurrian civilization, referred to as Horites in the Torah (*Pentateuch*, p. 744). In retrospect, this admission by the editor was nothing short of daring. Subsequent biblical scholarship has revealed how deeply Hurrian customs penetrated some biblical stories. See *The Anchor Bible: Genesis*, pp. xl–xliii.

115. *Pentateuch*, pp. 116, 406, 846, 941.

116. S. R. Driver, *Modern Research as Illustrating the Bible*, p. 27; emphasis is mine.

117. *Pentateuch*, p. 406; emphasis is mine. Understandably, Hertz categorically rejected the second alternative posed by Driver that "some knowledge of Hammurabi's laws reached the Hebrews indirectly—perhaps through the Canaanites who . . . were for some centuries profoundly influenced by Babylonia—and determined the form and the character of some of the provisions of Hebrew law" (Driver, *Modern Research*, p. 27).

118. *Pentateuch*, pp. 404–6, 555.

119. Ibid., p. 401. The quotation, extracted from the English translation of Renan's *History of the People of Israel*, vol. 2, pp. 337–38, completely falsifies his views on metaphysics. The correct citation reads in full: "The extraordinary good fortune which has made these laws the code of universal morality was not unmerited. . . . The 'ten words' of Iahveh are suitable for every nation, and will be during all succeeding ages the 'Commandments of God.'" By placing quotation marks around the term "Commandments of God," Renan meant to indicate, as he did repeatedly throughout his work, not that biblical precepts emanated in any way from on high, but that they were the penultimate fruits of human genius. Elsewhere in his *History* (p. 388), Renan, in fact, recorded his opinion that the Decalogue was written around the ninth century at the temple in Jerusalem. Moreover,

the idea of deity was superfluous for him. Renan did not in any way subscribe to miracle and revelation, but to "the principle of scientific Atheism." See William Barry, *Ernest Renan*, pp. 40–41. On his notion of God as a pragmatic feature of religious life, see J. M. Robertson, *Ernest Renan*, pp. 110–11, 114–15. Hertz himself, as editor, noted Renan's secular posture of ascribing the rise of monotheism to the geographic influence of the desert (*Pentateuch*, p. 924).

120. *Pentateuch*, pp. 404, 406.

121. The italicized phrase, which neatly summarizes the conceptual argument in the Commentary, was coined by Moshe Greenberg and used by him in a similar context. See his "The Biblical Grounding of Human Value," p. 44.

122. *Pentateuch*, pp. 404–5; see also p. 533; emphasis is mine.

123. Ibid., pp. 308, 851.

124. Ibid., p. 848.

125. Ibid., p. 834. In keeping with this tone, a murderer, unlike a fugitive, could not obtain safety by seizing hold of the altar horns (ibid., p. 334). The explication in the Commentary is remarkably similar to the view expounded, some twenty-five years later, by Moshe Greenberg: "Underlying the differing conceptions of certain crimes in biblical and cuneiform law is a divergence, subtle though crucial, in the ideas concerning the origin and sanction of the law. In Mesopotamia . . . the immediate sanction of the laws is by the authority of the king. Their formulation is his, [as] is the final decision as to their applicability. . . . In the biblical theory the idea of the transcendence of the law receives a more thoroughgoing expression. . . . [T]he law is a statement of his will. . . . The right of pardon in capital cases which Near Eastern law gives to the king is unknown to biblical law. . . . Only the author has the power to waive it; in Mesopotamia he is the king, in Israel, no man. Divergent underlying principles alone can account for the differences between Israelite and Near Eastern laws of homicide" (M. Greenberg, "Some Postulates of Biblical Criminal Laws," pp. 9–11). Chronologically, the Commentary preceded Greenberg's penetrating interpretation on the sanction of the laws in Israel and among her neighbors: "Among all other Oriental peoples, the word 'king' connotes an irresponsible despot, vested with unchallenged authority. All law is the expression of his will. . . . It was otherwise in Israel. There it is God who is the real king and the sole supreme authority; and the monarch is but the agent of the divine king" (*Pentateuch*, p. 927).

126. *Pentateuch*, p. 722.

127. Ibid., p. 829.

128. Ibid., p. 720.

129. H. Hahn, *The Old Testament in Modern Research*, p. 86, and W. R. Smith, *Lectures on the Religion of the Semites*, p. 13.

130. *Pentateuch*, pp. 405–6.

131. S. A. Cook, "The Religious Environment of Israel," pp. 44–45, 49, 54. Cook repeated this theme two years later in his critical introduction to W. R. Smith's *Lectures on the Religion of the Semites*, p. li.

132. A. J. F. Koebben, "Comparativists and Non-Comparativists in Anthropology," p. 584.

133. *Pentateuch*, p. 406; E. Sellin, "Archaeology versus Wellhausenism," pp. 236, 261–62.

134. A. H. Sayce, review of W. R. Smith's *Lectures on the Religion of the Semites*, in *The Academy* 36 (30 November 1889): 357–58.

135. *Pentateuch*, p. 262. Compare, however, the view of James Frazer, who, "based on the analogies of other races" concluded that "the ancient Hebrews . . . had probably passed through a stage of barbarism and even of savagery . . . such as the sacrifice of the firstborn" (*Folk-Lore in the Old Testament*, abridged ed., preface, p. ix). In fairness to Wellhausen, it must be pointed out that by 1905, he was ready to confess to the uniqueness of Israelite religion. However, he cautioned against a process leading to the homogenization of the religions of the Near East. His notion was that Israel was *sui generis*, but in a negative sense: "One may not with regard to the similarities of beginnings and the analogy of the development overlook the difference in end result." Thus, for Wellhausen, archaeological proof of Israelite contact with Mesopotamia did not necessarily mean a more positive interpretation of Israel's religion. It was, thus, not a matter of disinterest (as Hahn suggests in *Old Testament in Modern Research*, p. 88), but conviction, which explains Wellhausen's adamant posture vis-à-vis Israel. See P. D. Miller, Jr., "Wellhausen and the History of Israel's Religion," p. 66. Similarly, W. Robertson Smith reasoned that even during the era of Egyptian bondage, the Hebrews resisted external influences (*The Prophets*, pp. 379–80).

136. *Pentateuch*, p. 759. The reference is to W. R. Smith, *Lectures on the Religion of the Semites*, p. 288. In the same work, Smith admitted to the exceptional sacrificial pattern among the ancient Hebrews: "I am not aware that anything quite parallel to the ordinary Hebrew sin-offering occurs among the other Semites; and indeed no other Semitic religion appears to have developed to the same extent the doctrine of the consuming holiness of God, and the consequent need for priestly intervention between the laity and the most holy things" (W. R. Smith, *Lectures on the Religion of the Semites*, p. 350).

137. *Pentateuch*, p. 711. The quotation, taken from Cornill's *History of the People of Israel*, p. 143, is accurate, but misleading, as it is cited out of context. Cornill indeed spoke of Israel's uniqueness following the destruction of the Judean state. However, he was referring to that minority in Israel's midst who, believing in universal religion, forged a new path of spirituality that was destined "in the fullness of time to illuminate the whole world with its light" (p. 143). In fact, Cornill categorically consigned the Jewish people, as followers of the Law, to oblivion: "Politically and nationally the Babylonian captivity put an end *forever* to the people of Israel" (p. 145, emphasis is mine). This theme was previously mentioned in Cornill's *The Prophets of Israel*, p. 178. Cornill's hypothesis was remarkably similar to that propounded a generation earlier by W. Robertson Smith. In the latter's contribution to the ninth edition of the *Encyclopaedia Britannica*, he claimed that prior to the political debacle of 586 B.C.E., there was present in Israel a more enlightened element that had imbibed the spiritual stress of the preexilic prophets. It was the views of this lay element that underlay the thoughts of many of the Psalms and the popular literature of the nation (*Encyclopaedia Britannica*, 9th ed., s.v. "Bible," W. Robertson Smith).

138. S. R. Driver, "Evolution Compatible with Faith," p. 6. For a repetition of this theme, see his remarks as quoted in *Authority and Archaeology*, p. 7. Compare his somewhat contradictory comment above, n. 113, from the same article. Another who posited the positive particularity of Israel's laws was the German Orientalist

August Dillmann: "It is evident that Mosaism brought the world a new message in the matter of marriage" (*Pentateuch*, p. 490).

139. A rare technique used to suggest the authenticity of the Torah's composition was the literal fulfillment of Scripture's word in history. This came through in the Commentary to Deuteronomy, pp. 865, 868, 870, 872.

Chapter 4

1. M. Arnold, *Culture and Anarchy*, pp. 131–32, 135–36. The first modern exponent of this view was B. de Spinoza, *A Theologico-Political Treatise*, pp. 75, 180–81, 189, 194–95, 198–99, 258–59.

2. D. J. DeLaura, *Hebrew and Hellene in Victorian England*, p. 165; R. W. Livingstone, *Greek Ideals in Modern Life*, p. 26.

3. M. Arnold, *Culture and Anarchy*, pp. 132, 136–38. M. Arnold, *Literature and Dogma*, pp. 84, 86, 96; E. Renan, *History of the People of Israel*, 5:355–56; S. H. Butcher, *Some Aspects of Greek Genius*, pp. 77–78. The German Orientalist and early mentor of Seminary scholars Louis Ginzberg and Israel Friedlaender, Theodore Noeldeke, went so far as to claim that Christianity's most exalted features were absorbed not from Judaism, but from the Greeks (B. Shargel, *Practical Dreamer: Israel Friedlaender and the Shaping of American Judaism*, p. 65).

4. For an early expression of this view, see A. Werner, "Heinrich Heine (1797–1856): On the 100th Anniversary of the Poet's Death," pp. 25–26.

5. M. Margolies, *Samuel David Luzzatto: Traditionalist Scholar*, p. 77; M. Joseph, *The Message of Judaism*, p. 167.

6. H. Heine, *A Biographical Anthology*, p. 370; A. H. Ginsberg [Ahad Ha'am], "The Transvaluation of Values," pp. 229, 234; B. Shargel, *Practical Dreamer: Israel Friedlaender*, p. 61.

7. Joseph, *The Message of Judaism*, p. 169.

8. Moses Maimonides, *The Guide of the Perplexed*, trans. S. Pines (Chicago: University of Chicago Press, 1963), III, 27 (p. 510). All references to the *Guide* in this volume originate from the same edition.

9. Cohen's claim was not revolutionary. It had been advocated, for example, by Samson Raphael Hirsch. On his call for a fusion between Hebraism and Hellenism, see his *The Pentateuch: Genesis*, pp. 191, 193; Abraham Cohen's sermon is unpublished. I am indebted to David Cohen for making available to me his grandfather's manuscript. The sermon was delivered four times in the course of Cohen's ministry, the first time in 1925; emphasis is mine.

10. A. H. Ginsberg [Ahad Ha'am], "Job and Prometheus," p. 281.

11. D. Neumark, "The Beauty of Japhet in the Tents of Shem," pp. 12, 15. This essay was an elaboration and development of thought featured in his 1915 article bearing the title "Hebraism," also published in his *Essays*, p. 86.

12. J. Klausner, "Judah and Greece—Two Opposites?" 1:222–24.

13. C. G. Montefiore, *Liberal Judaism and Hellenism*, p. 185.

14. C. G. Montefiore, *Old Testament and After*, pp. 469–70.

15. V. E. Reichert, "The Contribution of Claude G. Montefiore to the Advancement of Judaism on the Commemoration of His Seventieth Birthday," pp. 509–510; N. Bentwich, *Claude Montefiore and His Tutor in Rabbinics: Founders of Liberal and Conservative Judaism*, pp. 4–5, 11.

16. C. G. Montefiore, *The Synoptic Gospels* (1927), l:xix–xx.
17. Montefiore, *The Synoptic Gospels* (1927), 1:xxv, cxxviii, 305–6.
18. Montefiore, *Liberal Judaism and Hellenism*, p. 90; Montefiore, *Old Testament and After*, pp. 225, 564.
19. Montefiore, *Old Testament and After*, p. 291.
20. Ibid., p. 265.
21. Ibid., pp. 556–57. See also on this theme, Montefiore's "Some Notes on the Effect of Biblical Criticism upon the Jewish Religion," p. 304.
22. Montefiore, *Liberal Judaism and Hellenism*, pp. 83, 85, 88–89; Montefiore, *Old Testament and After*, pp. 3–11, 552.
23. C. G. Montefiore and H. Loewe, *A Rabbinic Anthology*, preface.
24. *AOJ*, pp. 41, 46.
25. Hertz, *The New Paths*, pp. 24, 34. The chief rabbi specifically labeled Montefiore's move to fuse Christianity to Judaism as an "attempt to starve a Jewish Christianity."
26. *Pentateuch*, p. 805.
27. *The Pentateuch and Haftorahs: Exodus*, p. 530. This quotation is a reworking of a Hertz address delivered in 1919 in Birmingham: "And alas, too often liberal Houses of Worship resound with the abuse of 'the Judaism of the Synagogues,' and re-echo with the noise of axe and hammer wielded against ideals and institutions vital to Judaism—and all in the name of spirituality and faith" (*Jewish Chronicle*, 21 February 1919), p. 12.
28. H.A., E/6/2, Daiches to Hertz, 18 June 1923.
29. Ibid., E/6/2, Hertz to Daiches, 1 March 1923.
30. Ibid., E/6/2, Wilfred Samuel to Hertz, 30 January 1928.
31. Interview with Josephine Hertz, 27 June 1985.
32. H.A., E/6/2, Hertz jointly to Abelson, Cohen, and Frampton, 12 July 1929.
33. Ibid., E/6/2, Hertz to Frampton, 6 May 1936.
34. J. H. Hertz, "Ancient Semitic Codes and the Mosaic Legislation," pp. 220–21; *Pentateuch*, p. 406.
35. Hertz, "Ancient Semitic Codes," pp. 210–13; *Pentateuch*, p. 851.
36. The citations from "Fundamental Ideals," pp. 55–58, parallel excerpts recorded in the *Pentateuch*, pp. 920–21, 923, 936.
37. Citations from "Fundamental Ideals," p. 60, correspond to excerpts cited in the *Pentateuch*, pp. 401–2.
38. This notion, recorded in "Fundamental Ideals," p. 71, was incorporated into the *Pentateuch*, p. 363, v. 19, and was first formulated in *AOJ*, pp. 136–37.
39. See "Fundamental Ideals," pp. 62–63, 65–66, 72, and the parallel observations in the *Pentateuch*, p. 314, vv. 20, 25; p. 527, v. 18; p. 299, v. 13; p. 931, sec. a; p. 935.
40. The H.A. contain a typed manuscript submitted to Hertz by Frampton, entitled "Commentary on the Haftorahs of Bamidbar" by Frampton. The manuscript includes notes as well on some of the Haftarot to Leviticus. This title page lends considerable support to the notion that the manuscript in question was in fact an original draft submitted by Frampton to Hertz. Frampton made a point of dispatching typed copies of his research for Hertz's consideration (H.A., E/6/2, Frampton to Hertz, 11 May 1928; 5 March 1929; 11 June 1929).
41. *Pentateuch*, p. 495, v. 6.
42. Ibid., p. 495, v. 10.

43. Ibid., p. 530, vv. 28–31.
44. H.A., E/6/3; *Pentateuch*, p. 649. This point was extracted verbatim from Hertz's article "Ancient Semitic Codes," p. 214.
45. For a confirmation of this part of Hertz's thesis, see K. Kohler, *Jewish Theology*, p. 399.
46. *Pentateuch*, p. 197. On the rabbinic source of this midrash, see *Pirkei de-Rabbi Eliezer*, chap. 24.
47. *Pentateuch*, p. 35.
48. Ibid., p. 65. On the rabbinic source, see *B.T., Sanhedrin*, 109b.
49. *Pentateuch*, p. 208. The Spartans were equally sinful (ibid., p. 209).
50. Ibid., p. 314. The rabbinic source is found in *B.T., Bava Metzia*, 59b.
51. *Pentateuch*, pp. 148, 931. The Persians also came in for condemnation. They had an abominable penchant for marrying their nearest blood-relatives (ibid., p. 865).
52. Ibid., p. 151.
53. Ibid., p. 537. See the corroborating remarks of Kohler, *Jewish Theology*, p. 365.
54. *Pentateuch*, p. 307.
55. Ibid., pp. 397, 927–28.
56. Conversation with Raphael Loewe, 22 June 1985. One reviewer found Hertz's comparison of "the excellency of the moral code promulgated in Deuteronomy with the rottenness of the cultures of Greece and Rome" both refreshing and bold (H.A., E/6/1, review in the *Inquirer*, 24 October 1936, p. 501.)
57. *Pentateuch*, p. 406. Elsewhere, the Commentary referred to the virtues of justice, mercy, and humility—or justice, mercy, and purity where purity was associated with modesty, decency, chastity, and personal holiness (ibid., p. 685).
58. Ibid., p. 772; see also pp. 924–25.
59. D. Hartman, *Maimonides: Torah and Philosophic Quest*, pp. 50, 80.
60. *Pentateuch*, pp. 897, 911. Maimonides concurred; see G. Blidstein, *Political Concepts in Maimonidean Halakha*, pp. 97–101. Hertz proclaimed this thought in a 1933 anti-Nazi sermon: "'In a free land,' pleaded Leopold Zunz, 'it is not the Christian that rules the Jew, neither is it the Jew that rules the Christian; it is justice that rules'" (*SAS* 1:140).
61. *Pentateuch*, p. 32.
62. Ibid., pp. 65, 316, 684, 821.
63. Ibid., p. 739. This story is related in *B.T., Ketubbot* 105b.
64. *Pentateuch*, pp. 65–66, 821.
65. Ibid., p. 500.
66. Ibid., p. 772. On a rabbinic source, see *B.T., Bava Metzia* 35a. On the application of this principle in Maimonidean thought, see D. Hartman, *Maimonides*, pp. 90–101.
67. Arnold, *Literature and Dogma*, p. 86.
68. Montefiore, *Old Testament and After*, pp. 209–10.
69. In one place, the Commentary defined righteousness as "holiness of life in the individual" (*Pentateuch*, p. 43). The editor also noted Hosea's pronouncement, which modified that of Micah, stressing *hesed* as a condition in the exercise of justice (ibid., p. 136). Compare the claim of Kaufmann Kohler that Judaism's highest principle was justice, not mercy and love (*Jewish Theology*, pp. 120, 123, 126, 485); *Jewish Encyclopedia* (1903), s.v. "Christianity," K. Kohler.

Notes to Chapter 4

70. *Pentateuch*, p. 152, 685, 821.
71. Ibid., p. 936.
72. Ibid., p. 315.
73. Ibid., p. 498.
74. Ibid., p. 872.
75. Ibid., pp. 363–65, 497.
76. Ibid., p. 920.
77. Ibid., p. 397.
78. Ibid., p. 865.
79. Ibid., p. 73.
80. Ibid., pp. 759–60. On the rabbinic source, see *Tanna de-vei Eliyahu*, ed. M. Friedmann, 9 (p. 48); *Tanna debe Eliyyahu*, trans. W. G. Braude and I. J. Kapstein, 9 (pp. 152–53); compare in the New Testament, *The Holy Bible*, revised standard version, Gal. 3:28.
81. Montefiore, *Old Testament and After*, pp. 209–11; C. G. Montefiore, *Judaism and Saint Paul*, p. 210; Butcher, *Some Aspects of Greek Genius*, pp. 77–78; Livingstone, *Greek Ideals in Modern Life*, pp. 165–68.
82. *Pentateuch*, p. 152.
83. Ibid., pp. 152, 778, 821; emphasis is mine.
84. Ibid., pp. 402, 920, 834. On the mention of the immoral rites of heathenism, see ibid., p. 878.
85. Ibid., pp. 400–1, 920. Nevertheless, the Commentary (p. 103), in its interpretation of Mal. 1:11, acknowledged that one could not overlook the sincere intent of heathens to worship a supreme being.
86. Ibid., p. 402. For a confirmation of this perception by a Christian scholar of the period, see Livingstone, *Greek Ideals*, p. 157.
87. Montefiore, *Liberal Judaism and Hellenism*, pp. 202–4.
88. *Pentateuch*, p. 497. Hertz had earlier cited this passage in *AOJ*, p. 137. Hertz's reference therein to Abrahams is found in I. Abrahams, *Studies in Pharisaism and the Gospels*, p. 152. The reference to Schechter was from his *Some Aspects of Rabbinic Theology*, p. 204. Schechter's rabbinic source was from his edition of *Midrash ha-Gadol*, p. 549.
89. *Pentateuch*, p. 358.
90. Ibid., p. 295; see also p. 921.
91. Ibid., pp. 6, 18, 22, 29–31, 39, 55, 214, 219, 221, 293, 296, 425, 760–61, 806, 880, 885.
92. Ibid., p. 364. This denial of God's emotional nature was based on the talmudic passage in *B.T.*, *Rosh Hashanah* 17b: "I am He before a man sins and the same after a man sins and repents." The Commentary (ibid.) provided the reader with Rashi's rendering of the talmudic passage: "I am the merciful before a man commits a sin; and I am the same merciful and forgiving God after a man has sinned." The idea that God's nature remains constant, that He is unaffected by man's behavior is an idea found in the Bible (Num. 23:19; 1 Sam. 15:29) and was central to Maimonidean theology. See *Guide*, I, 54 (pp. 124–25); III, 27 (pp. 510–12).
93. *Pentateuch*, pp. 872, 920; emphasis is mine.
94. Montefiore, *Liberal Judaism and Hellenism*, p. 222; *Pentateuch*, pp. 926–27.
95. *Pentateuch*, p. 927.

96. Kohler, *Jewish Theology*, p. 355.
97. *Pentateuch*, pp. 923–24.
98. Ibid., p. 929.
99. Ibid., p. 533.
100. *Pentateuch*, pp. 537, 813, 924; emphasis is mine. See also *The Pentateuch and Haftorahs: Exodus*, p. 246. This humanitarian spirit was captured in the Commentary's notation, citing Nachmanides, that Sarah and Abraham's ill-treatment of Hagar triggered the hatred of Ishmael and his descendants for the people of Israel (ibid., pp. 56–57). The Commentary did acknowledge one instance of mutilation in the Torah (Deut. 25:11–12), but was quick to point out that the severe penalty was commuted to a fine under rabbinic jurisdiction (ibid., p. 856). On the rabbinic source, see *Sifrei on Deuteronomy* [Hebrew], ed. L. Finkelstein, 193 (p. 312).
101. *Pentateuch*, pp. 308–9, 538, 721.
102. Ibid., p. 848.
103. Montefiore, *Liberal Judaism and Hellenism*, p. 218.
104. *Pentateuch*, pp. 308, 721, 829, 834.
105. *The Pentateuch and Haftorahs: Exodus*, p. 530.
106. *Pentateuch*, p. 563.
107. Ibid., pp. 299, 308, 841.
108. Ibid., p. 54, 299, 931.
109. Ibid., pp. 54, 931. The quotation by Tacitus in the previous citation and the quotation that children "are the Messiahs of mankind" were originally presented in a 1926 sermon, "The Holiness of the Home," which was published in *AOJ*, p. 70, and repeated in Hertz's 1930 address "Fundamental Ideals," p. 63. The rabbinic source identifying children as the Messiahs of mankind is found in *B.T., Shabbat* 119b.
110. *Pentateuch*, pp. 42, 78.
111. Ibid., p. 888.
112. Ibid., pp. 804, 924.
113. Ibid., pp. 151, 842. On the talmudic source, see *B.T., Sanhedrin*, 46a.
114. *Pentateuch*, p. 854.
115. Ibid., p. 32.
116. Ibid., p. 487.
117. Ibid, pp. 83, 673, 854–55.
118. Ibid., p. 298.
119. Ibid., p. 854.
120. Ibid., pp. 489–90, 492, 865.
121. Ibid., p. 492. Hertz toned down considerably his denunciation of homosexuality after receiving an evaluation from a well-known geneticist, Redcliffe Nathan Salaman, who advised him to avoid such words as "hideous" and "execrable" in speaking of homosexuals on grounds that "homosexuals are born such. . . . It is true to say that with many of these people they are no more responsible than they would be for being born black" (H.A., E/6/1, Salaman to Hertz, 19 February 1932).
122. Montefiore, "Rabbinic Judaism and the Epistles of Saint Paul," p. 192.
123. Montefiore, *Old Testament and After*, p. 300.
124. Montefiore, *Liberal Judaism and Hellenism*, pp. 205, 231–33.
125. *Pentateuch*, p. 921.

Notes to Chapter 4

126. Ibid., p. 936.
127. Ibid., p. 7. See also p. 102. On the rabbinic source, see *B.T., Sanhedrin* 38a.
128. *Pentateuch*, p. 489. On the rabbinic source, see *B.T., Sanhedrin* 59a.
129. *Pentateuch*, p. 854. On the rabbinic source, see *B.T., Makkot* 3:15.
130. *Pentateuch*, pp. 21, 102–3, 595.
131. Ibid., pp. 103, 759.
132. Ibid., pp. 314, 316, 563. On the decent treatment of the stranger, compare the similarity of thought and expression of Claude Montefiore in *Liberal Judaism and Hellenism*, pp. 44, 563, and in his *The Synoptic Gospels* (1927), 1:80.
133. *Pentateuch*, pp. 313, 504.
134. Ibid., p. 316.
135. Ibid., p. 739. On a similar story in the midrash, see *Midrash Rabbah: Genesis*, 48:3 (p. 406).
136. *Pentateuch*, pp. 316, 502.
137. Ibid., pp. 125, 129, 143, 159.
138. Ibid., pp. 66, 499; emphasis is mine. On the talmudic sources, see, respectively, *B.T., Betzah* 32b and *B.T., Yevamot* 79a. See also on this theme, *Pentateuch*, p. 857.
139. *Pentateuch*, p. 65. Abraham's expression of compassion for his neighbor did not, however, obviate his duty to reprove his fellow man when he felt he was a victim of the latter's wrongdoing (ibid., p. 73).
140. Ibid., p. 122. The midrashic source is found in *Midrash Rabbah: Genesis*, 76:2 (p. 702).
141. *Pentateuch*, p. 821. On the repetition of the idea, see ibid., pp. 7, 89.
142. Ibid., p. 499.
143. Ibid., p. 868. On rabbinic sources, see *B.T., Megillah* 24b and *Yalkut Shimeoni*, pt. 1, p. 663.
144. Hirsch, *The Pentateuch: Genesis*, p. 191.
145. *Pentateuch*, pp. 927–28. In a rare passage, the Commentary (p. 498) echoed the Talmud's praise (*B.T., Kiddushin* 31a) for the reverence shown a parent by his pagan son.
146. *Pentateuch*, pp. 848, 920.
147. Ibid., p. 536.
148. Ibid., p. 929.
149. Ibid., pp. 505, 927. In what must be judged as an understandable, yet sloppy, departure from the conceptual thrust of the *Pentateuch*, the editor asserted that "the Rabbis never regarded the heathens of their own day as on the same moral level with the Canaanites. Their contemporary heathens in the Roman and Persian empires obeyed the laws of conduct that the Rabbis deemed vital to the existence of human society, the so-called seven commandments given to the children of Noah" (ibid., p. 759). In fact, the Commentary's general claim was exactly the opposite! Greco-Roman civilization had failed to sustain the minimal standards prescribed in the Noachide laws. The inclusion of this favorable assessment of Roman and Persian societies stemmed from a desire to see reflected in Deut. 4:19 the consistent attitude of religious toleration adhered to not only by the Torah, but also by rabbinic Judaism.
150. Ibid., p. 820.
151. Ibid., p. 928.

152. Ibid., p. 404; excerpted from "Ancient Semitic Codes," p. 213.
153. *Pentateuch*, p. 306.
154. Ibid., p. 537; emphasis is mine. See also ibid., p. 208.
155. Ibid., p. 824.
156. Ibid., p. 404.
157. Ibid., p. 848. See also p. 538. The Commentary identified Israel existentially with the motifs of *Uncle Tom's Cabin* (ibid., p. 222).
158. Ibid., p. 307.
159. Ibid., p. 929.
160. Ibid., pp. 260, 527, 739; emphasis is mine.
161. Ibid., p. 63; emphasis is mine.
162. Ibid., p. 314; emphasis is mine.
163. Ibid., p. 855.
164. Ibid., p. 854.
165. *The Pentateuch and Haftorahs: Genesis*, pp. 86–87.
166. See p. 88.
167. M.T., *Hilkhot Avodah Zarah*, 9:4.
168. *Encyclopaedia Judaica* (1971), s.v. "Disputation of Barcelona," C. Beinart.
169. M. Harris, "The Theologico-Historical Thinking of Samuel David Luzzatto," p. 227.
170. J. Klausner, "Judah and Greece—Two Opposites?" p. 217; Harris, "The Theologico-Historical," p. 225.
171. I. Husik, "Hellenism and Judaism," p. 12.
172. On Gerald Friedlander's views, see chap. 2; on Kohler's views, see his *Jewish Theology*, pp. 437–38; Graetz wrote of Christianity's indebtedness to paganism in "The Significance of Judaism for the Present and the Future," p. 259: "Christianity was perfectly justified in priding itself on having vanquished the essential corruption of paganism. . . . [However,] it had not itself remained free from some heathen contamination."
173. H.A., E/6/l, Inge to Hertz, 4 July 1936. Hertz was an avid enthusiast and student of the preaching styles of Christian clergymen, hence, his knowledge of Inge's views would have been known to him firsthand. Their respective communal careers coincided roughly with each other. Inge was invited to his post in 1911. Hertz came to London two years later. In addition, both men held office for many years—Inge until his retirement in 1934 and Hertz until his demise in 1946. In 1934, Hertz shared the dais with Inge on the occasion of raising support for the acquisition of the Sinai codes (Hertz, *Early and Late*, p. 187). I am indebted to Nahum Sarna of Boston for noting that Hertz's personal library contained volumes on contemporary Christian sermonic literature.
174. *Pentateuch*, pp. 489, 928, 933.
175. W. R. Inge, "Religion," p. 26.
176. Ibid., pp. 27–29.
177. Ibid., pp. 29–33, 43–44; emphasis is mine. In his criticism, he highlighted Greek civilization's lack of respect for human dignity and gestures of social apathy within the Church (ibid., pp. 39, 44).
178. R. T. Herford, "The Significance of Pharisaism," pp. 154–56. Compare the even gentler reformulation of Herford's criticism in his *The Pharisees*, pp. 230–31. Four years earlier in an address before the Jewish Historical Society of England,

Herford hedged on this point of pagan infiltration, preferring to posit instead that "the Hebrew Scriptures . . . have acted like salt to keep the Christian teaching from corruption; and the witness of Judaism has been a constant reminder that that salt has not lost its savour" (R. T. Herford, *What the World Owes to the Pharisees*, p. 30).

179. Montefiore, *Liberal Judaism and Hellenism*, p. 188.
180. Livingstone, *Greek Ideals*, p. 150.
181. Livingstone, *The Influence of the Greek and Hebrew Traditions on Western Ideals*, p. 20.
182. Livingstone, *Greek Ideals*, p. 26.
183. *Pentateuch*, pp. 310–11.
184. Ibid., p. 536.
185. Ibid., pp. 308, 721.
186. Ibid., pp. 309, 405, 527. In keeping with the thrust of portraying Judaism's ethical impulse in the highest light, the editor conveniently omitted mention of the dissenting opinion of Rabbi Eliezer, who favored taliation (*B.T., Bava Kamma* 84a).
187. *Pentateuch*, p. 316.
188. Ibid., p. 527. The biblical trial by ordeal arising out of a husband's jealousy was resolved by the Commentary. See ahead in this chapter.
189. Compare, however, Maimonides' ruling in the *M.T., Hilkhot Ishut*, 21:10, where he legitimized the beating of a wife who refused to perform her wifely chores.
190. *Pentateuch*, p. 935. Common law, it should be remembered, evolved partially under the combined impact of Roman and Canon law: see *Encyclopaedia Britannica*, 14th. ed., s.v. "Common Law," T. S. Legg and T. F. T. Plucknett.
191. H.A., G/6, Hertz to Herbert Loewe, 10 February 1933.
192. *Pentateuch*, p. 589. By talmudic times, the trial procedure took place within the precincts of the sanctuary and involved the bringing of a meal offering to the priest by the accused woman, as well as the water of bitterness being prepared by mingling it with the dust from the temple floor. Naturally, following the temple's destruction, it was no longer technically possible to continue this procedure. Nevertheless, the rabbinic rationale offered for its abrogation was utterly moral. With an upsurge in adultery among both sexes, the ordeal lost its efficacy, given that it was premised on the chastity of the male partner: "at the time when the man is free from iniquity, the water proves his wife; but when the man is not free from iniquity, the water does not prove his wife" (*B.T., Sotah*, 47a–47b).
193. *Pentateuch*, p. 935.
194. Montefiore and Loewe, *A Rabbinic Anthology*, p. 507. Abraham Cohen, one of the principal scholars associated with the writing of the Hertz *Pentateuch*, offered a more balanced, impartial presentation of the attitude toward women as depicted in biblical and rabbinic sources. See his 1931 anthology, *Everyman's Talmud*, pp. 98, 160–61, 164–65, 267, 280, 295. Cohen took strong exception to those, like Montefiore, who derided the benediction "who has not made me a woman" (p. 159). On the Commentary's concurring with Cohen's interpretation of the benediction, see *Pentateuch*, p. 318.

195. For example, women were not included in the commandment to study Torah; they were exempted from certain time-bound commandments, and they were susceptible to the status of *agunah* (*Pentateuch*, pp. 318, 633–34, 925–26, 933).

196. Ibid., p. 113. See p. 934, where the phrase used was "are almost the equals of their husbands."

197. Ibid., pp. 56, 87, 481, 935.

198. Ibid., p. 935. The respective citations from rabbinic literature are as follows: B.T., *Bava Metzia* 59a. I have been unable to trace the notion that God counts the tears of a woman whose tears were instigated by her husband. Compare B.T., *Shabbat* 105b, where it is said in the name of Bar Kappara that "if one sheds tears for a worthy man, the Holy One, blessed be He, counts them and lays them up in His treasure house"; compare, also, B.T., *Gittin* 90b: "He who divorces his first wife causes the altar to shed tears"; B.T., *Sotah* 11b; *Midrash Zuta on Megillat Ruth*, 4:2 (p. 246). Hertz first cited these quotations in *AOJ*, p. 76.

199. *Pentateuch*, p. 490.

200. Ibid., p. 935.

201. Ibid., pp. 804, 924.

202. Ibid., pp. 804–5; C. Roth, ed., *The Ritual Murder Libel and the Jews: The Report by Cardinal Lorenzo Ganganelli*, pp. 24, 101, 106; J. H. Hertz, ed., *A Book of Jewish Thoughts*, p. 181.

203. *Pentateuch*, p. 808; emphasis is mine.

204. Ibid., pp. 922–23. On the theme of Jewish martyrdom, see also ibid., p. 518.

205. Ibid., pp. 812, 814.

206. Ibid., pp. 933–34.

207. Ibid., p. 401.

208. Ibid., p. 770.

209. Ibid., p. 921.

210. Montefiore, *Old Testament and After*, pp. 28–29.

211. H.A., A/13, Hertz to the editor of the *Jewish Guardian*, 12 April 1926; Montefiore, *Old Testament and After*, p. 561.

212. *Pentateuch*, p. 923. For a reference in the Commentary to the Jewish translation of the verse relating to Christianity's understanding of the virgin birth, see ibid., p. 85.

213. Ibid., p. 757; see also pp. 313, 360, 763.

214. Ibid., p. 401. The connection between pagan idolatry and Christian image worship was obvious, as noted by Joseph Karo, compiler of the *Shulhan Arukh*, *Hilkhot Avodat Kokhavim*, 141:1.

215. *Pentateuch*, p. 196. Hertz's perception was confirmed by Kaufmann Kohler, who viewed the doctrine as depriving "man of both his moral and his intellectual birthright as the child of God" (K. Kohler, "Christianity," in *The Jewish Encyclopedia*).

216. *Pentateuch*, pp. 9–10; see also ibid., p. 930.

217. Ibid., p. 931.

218. *The Jewish Encyclopedia*, Kohler, "Christianity," p. 53.

219. *SAS* 1:297; *Pentateuch*, pp. 501–2.

220. *Pentateuch*, p. 761.

221. Ibid., p. 406; Hertz, "Ancient Semitic Codes," p. 221.

222. *Pentateuch*, p. 936. The italicized phrase in this citation originated in a 1930 Hertz essay contrasting heathen and rabbinic notions of morality (Hertz, "Fundamental Ideals," p. 58).
223. *Pentateuch*, pp. 80–81; references to this concept are peppered throughout the Commentary. See ibid., pp. 324, 419, 505, 713, 992, 1002. Hertz was familiar with the theory submitted to him by Salis Daiches, who translated the term *am ha-aretz* as "landed gentry" or "landed aristocracy." See S. Daiches, "The Meaning of Am Ha'aretz in the Old Testament," p. 245. The article is contained in H.A., E/6/3.
224. *Pentateuch*, pp. 820, 928.
225. Ibid., p. 854.
226. Ibid., pp. 42, 818.
227. Ibid., p. 929.
228. Ibid., p. 536.
229. Ibid., pp. 260, 527.
230. Ibid., p. 848.
231. Ibid., p. 854.
232. Ibid., p. 490, 492, 932, 935.
233. Ibid., pp. 401–3; 936.
234. Ibid., p. 935. The source is found in I. Zangwill, *Children of the Ghetto*, p. 179.
235. *SAS* 2:69; *Pentateuch*, p. 495.
236. *Pentateuch*, p. 209; cited as well in Hertz, *A Book of Jewish Thoughts*, p. 66. The quotation is a translation from Heinrich Heine's *Gesammelte Werke*, VII, 473; see also A. Werner, "Heinrich Heine (1797–1856)," pp. 25–26.
237. *Pentateuch*, p. 45; cited originally in *AOJ*, p. 102.

Chapter 5

1. *Pentateuch*, pp. 47, 70.
2. Ibid., p. 141. Parallel sentiments were expressed by a Catholic divine of the period, Michael Faulhaber: "The biblical characters are not saints ready made. They, like us, felt one law in their mind and 'another law in their members' (Rom. vii, 23). But they had the nobility of soul to acknowledge their faults and to be converted from the evil of their ways, and precisely for this reason they are ethical models for the youth of all time. The power of divine grace is perfected in the weakness of human nature (2 Cor. xii, 9)" (M. Faulhaber, *Judaism, Christianity and Germany*, p. 44).
3. *Pentateuch*, pp. 47–48. On Abraham and Sarah's sinning, see also ibid., p. 56.
4. Ibid., pp. 97–98.
5. Ibid., p. 94.
6. Ibid., p. 180.
7. Ibid., pp. 169, 184.
8. Ibid., pp. 148, 175.
9. Ibid., pp. 82, 97, 101, 774.
10. Ibid., p. 102. See also ibid., pp. 93–94, 100. On Edom being synonymous with Rome, see also *The Pentateuch and Haftorahs: Deuteronomy*, p. 549. On rabbinic sources associating Edom with Rome, see, for example, *Midrash Rabbah: Genesis*, 65:21 (p. 598); 67:7 (p. 611). Compare, however, the willingness of the Commen-

tary to award ethical points to Esau for displaying a forgiving attitude when he and Jacob were reunited after so many years (*Pentateuch*, p. 125).

11. *Pentateuch*, p. 139.

12. Ibid., p. 145.

13. Ibid., p. 114.

14. *The Pentateuch and Haftorahs: Genesis*, pp. 264, 294.

15. *Pentateuch*, p. 192.

16. Ibid., pp. 217, 504.

17. Ibid., pp. 295, 313. The Commentary's labeling as "haggadic" the talmudic incident involving Simon ben Shetach's burning of witches at Ashkelon (*Mishnah Sanhedrin* 6:4) requires correction. In support of his contention, the editor cited as conclusive the supposed verdict of three historians: Joseph Derenbourg, Israel Levi, and Herman Strack. Both Levi and Strack, indeed, concurred with Hertz that the Simon ben Shetach story was historically unfounded. Derenbourg, however, did conclude that witchcraft was an issue during the era of the Second Commonwealth, though not specifically in the days of Simon ben Shetach but rather, earlier, during the rule of Simon Maccabee. Furthermore, conveniently overlooked in the *Pentateuch* were the contemporary assessments of I. H. Weiss and H. Graetz that the Simon ben Shetach episode was factual (I. H. Weiss, *Dor Dor ve-Dorshav*, 1:139; H. Graetz, *History of the Jews*, 2:54). Though this section of Exodus dealing with witchcraft was originally assigned to Abraham Cohen (see preface to the *Pentateuch*), he can hardly have been the author of this interpretation. In his *Everyman's Talmud*, p. 161, Cohen held that witchcraft posed a danger to Jewish life in ancient Judea. As to Simon ben Shetach's burning of witches, Cohen most certainly did not rule out the plausibility of such a trial taking place (ibid., pp. 291, 297). Hence, it would appear that the author of the passage on p. 313 of the *Pentateuch* was the chief rabbi himself, who, as editor, executed his stated right to rewrite at will the manuscripts submitted to him. This allowed him to protect the ethical integrity of biblical legislation.

18. *Pentateuch*, p. 589.

19. Judg. 11:30–31.

20. G. F. Moore, *A Critical and Exegetical Commentary on Judges*, International Critical Commentary, vol. 7, p. 304.

21. *Pentateuch*, p. 667.

22. Ibid., pp. 650, 667. Hertz had occasion to cite Kimchi's exegesis as part of a 1919 lecture focusing on the need to produce a Jewish translation of Scripture to supplant the King James version (*SAS* 2:76–77). However, in his address, the chief rabbi attributed the improved reading of the Judg. 11:31 passage to Selig Newman, who had taught Hebrew at Oxford in the mid-nineteenth century. Interestingly, Newman, in his *Emendations of the Authorized Version of the Old Testament*, pp. v, 13 had appropriated Kimchi's rendering verbatim, but did not give credit to the medieval biblicist.

23. *Pentateuch*, p. 842. For the rabbinic source, see *B.T., Sanhedrin* 71a.

24. *Pentateuch*, p. 841.

25. Ibid., p. 201.

26. Ibid., pp. 747, 759. Compare the rare instance where the editor pleaded ignorance over not being able to justify, not the genocidal fact of Israel's war against

the Midianites (Num. 31), but the ruthlessness with which that campaign was raged (*Pentateuch*, p. 704).

27. Ibid., pp. 493, 527, 759–60.
28. Ibid., p. 505.
29. Ibid., p. 833. On the Commentary's paraphrase of Maimonides, see *The Guide for the Perplexed*, trans. M. Friedlaender, I, 54 (p. 77).
30. *Pentateuch*, p. 313.
31. Ibid., p. 504.
32. Ibid., p. 527.
33. Ibid., p. 790.
34. Ibid., pp. 852–53.
35. For an appropriate prooftext, see *B.T., Gittin* 59b: "The whole of the Law is . . . for the purpose of promoting peace."
36. *Pentateuch*, p. 812. The reference to Driver was to his *A Critical and Exegetical Commentary on Deuteronomy*, p. 175.
37. *Pentateuch*, p. 849. Hertz had occasion during the war years to offer up this interpretation in a letter to *The Times*, 6 February 1943, entitled "The Jews and Usury," written in response to an accusation by the archbishop of Canterbury, who said: "The Mosaic law forbade Israelites to lend at interest to a brother Israelite, but those ethics did not extend beyond the tribal community." The reprint from *The Times* is in H.A., 2/3.
38. *Pentateuch*, pp. 848–49; emphasis is mine.
39. *The Cambridge Bible for Schools and Colleges: The Book of Exodus*, with introduction and notes by S. R. Driver, p. 232. Driver's sentiments were repeated some years later by Semyon Rosenbaum, one of the founders of the Tel Aviv School of Economics, in his article "Taking Interest from a Non-Jew in the Biblical Period," pp. 193–94.
40. Aside from S. R. Driver's posture, see E. Neufeld, "The Prohibition against Loans at Interest," pp. 360, 362; and Salo Baron, in his *A Social and Religious History of the Jews*, 1:156, which is a précis of the posture adopted in the Hertz *Pentateuch*.
41. The citation from Guttmann appeared in *Hebrew Union College Annual* 3 (1926): 5, 7; and in his *Das Judentum und seine Umwelt*, pp. 24–25, 27. A revised Hebrew version of *Das Judentum* was written by Guttmann, of which only a small part survived the carnage wrought by the Nazi occupation of Hungary (*Jewish Studies in Memory of Michael Guttmann*, ed. S. Loewinger, p. vii). On the tendentious nature of *Das Judentum*, see the observation of Loewinger in "Professor Yehiel Michael Guttmann," p. 132.
42. *Pentateuch*, p. 812.
43. Ibid., p. 849. On the problematic phrase "as a stranger and a settler," the Commentary followed Rashi's and Ibn Ezra's rendering: "yea though he be a stranger or a sojourner" (ibid., p. 536).
44. Editor Hertz's liberal posture of allowing an Israelite or Jewish creditor the option of waiving interest payments from a Gentile had substantial backing in Jewish sources: Moses ben Nachman, *Commentary on the Torah: Deuteronomy*, trans. C. B. Chavel (Deut. 15:3), pp. 181–82 (hereafter referred to as Ramban, *Torah Commentary: Deuteronomy*); *M.T., Hilkhot Malveh ve-Loveh*, 5:1. There were talmudic statements that supported the editor's argument (*Pentateuch*, p. 849) that the Talmud maintained the interest prohibition for foreigners who were in need of finan-

cial assistance. The specific rabbinic passages that Hertz probably had in mind were B.T., *Bava Metzia* 70b, and *Makkot* 24a, which were located conveniently in Michael Guttmann's essay, part of which was previously cited (*Hebrew Union College Annual* 3:6 n. 6). Another possible talmudic source was B.T., *Gittin* 61a. "Our Rabbis have taught: 'We support the poor of the heathen along with the poor of Israel . . . in the interest of peace.'" With reference to the universal thrust of the *Makkot* 24a passage as cited by Guttmann, he, as well as Hertz, steered clear of the observation made by Menahem ben Solomon Meiri that the rationale behind such piety by the Jew did not rest fundamentally on feelings of brotherhood that the Jew felt toward the Gentile, but rather was based on a conscious educational motive: by conditioning himself to behave virtuously toward a Gentile, he would be more certain to obey the positive command not to exact interest from his covenantal brother. See on Rashi: *Makkot* 24a, s.v. "And even to a heathen." On the Meiri, see his *Beit ha-Behirah* to the tractate of *Makkot*, p. 116. Maimonides' ruling, M.T., *Hilkhot Zekhiyah u-Matanah*, 3:11 (based on *Avodah Zarah* 20a) that it was forbidden for a Jew to give a free gift to a Gentile was metamorphosed and given a more humanitarian and universal complexion. Asher ben Jehiel (c. 1250–1327; "the Rosh"), basing himself on the *Tosephta*, noted that the *Avodah Zarah* passage applied to a transient heathen or to a heathen stranger, but had no applicability to a heathen whom a Jew admired (*ohavo*) or who was a Jew's neighbor. Giving a gift under these conditions was tantamount to "selling" because (as the *Pilpula Harifta* commented on the ruling of Rabbenu Asher on *Avodah Zarah* 20a (p. 158), the Jew derived a measure of benefit in seeing his heathen friend accept his gift. In a similar spirit, David ben Samuel Halevi (1586–1667; "the Taz"), noted that the giving of a gift to a known heathen could be regarded as a sale because the heathen may already have paid him or in the future would reciprocate in kind (*yeshalem gemulo*); see the commentary of the Taz on *Yoreh De'ah* (Hebrew), *Hilkhot Avodat Kokhavim*, 151:11.

45. Maimonides, *The Commandments*, trans. C. Chavel, Positive Commandment 142 (p. 150) and Positive Commandment 198 (p. 213).

46. This tendentiousness was evident, too, in the Commentary to Deut. 20:10, stipulating that offers of peace be extended to heathen cities at the time of the conquest of the Land of Israel. The annotator asserted that all traditional commentaries concurred that this display of humanitarianism was extended to all enemy cities, which included Canaanite towns. However, as a learned colleague pointed out privately to Hertz, only Ramban adopted the posture of the Commentary, Ibn Ezra was silent, Rashbam explicitly excluded the Canaanites from the ruling, and Rashi insisted that the passage only allowed for the sparing of Canaanites found in far-off cities (H.A., E/6/3, unnamed undated source).

47. *Pentateuch*, p. 849. The reference to the disqualification of a usurer was based on B.T., *Sanhedrin* 24b–25a.

48. *Pentateuch*, pp. 812, 814–15.

49. Ibid., p. 849. The complete and exact quotation of Abbé Gregoire is located in his *An Essay on the Physical, Moral, and Political Reformation of the Jews*, pp. 239–40. It reads as follows: "O! nations, for eighteen centuries ye have been treading under foot the remains of Israel. Divine vengeance hath displayed its severity against them; but have you been commissioned to be the instruments of it? . . . Is it

enough to leave them life, while you deprive them of everything that can render it desirable? Will your hatred form a part of the inheritance which you bequeath to your children? No longer judge of this nation, except from the future; but *if you again review the past crimes, and the present corruption of the Jews, let it be in order to lament your own work.* Being the cause of their vices, become that also of their virtues; discharge your debt, and that of your ancestors" [emphasis is mine].

50. *Pentateuch*, p. 339.
51. Ibid., pp. 58, 60.
52. Ibid., p. 935. On the Israel Zangwill source, see *Children of the Ghetto*, p. 179.
53. Zangwill, *Children of the Ghetto*, p. 179.
54. See previous chapter, pp. 110–111.
55. *Pentateuch*, p. 424; *SAS* 1:254.
56. *Pentateuch*, p. 292.
57. Ibid., p. 936.
58. Ibid., p. 403. The quotation from Geiger is found in his *Judaism and Its History*, p. 61, and cited as well in Hertz's *A Book of Jewish Thoughts*, p. 64. Geiger specifically referred to the Jewish people being endowed with a "religious genius"; genius being defined as "a gift of grace, an impress of consecration stamped upon man, which can never be acquired, if it be not in man" (*Judaism and Its History*, pp. 55, 60).
59. *The Oxford Universal Dictionary*, 3d ed., 1955, p. 1311, defines the adjective "native" to mean "inherent, innate, connected with one's birth." One of Geiger's Reform successors, Kaufmann Kohler, also maintained that Israel's election was "due . . . to hereditary virtues and to tendencies of mind and spirit which equip Israel for his calling" (*Jewish Theology*, p. 328; see also p. 356 and the midrash cited there by Kohler).
60. *Pentateuch*, p. 403. The quotation is found in *The Kuzari*, II, 56 (p. 117) and cited in Hertz's *A Book of Jewish Thoughts*, p. 64.
61. *The Kuzari*, I, 103 (p. 73), 109 (p. 75). Notwithstanding this aspect of genetic manipulation by God, Halevi held firm to the traditional belief in freedom of will. His posture was, indeed, paradoxical, if not outright contradictory, for if man is genetically programmed, in this case to behave in a certain way, it seems to be logically impossible to act otherwise. The case of animals born with certain instincts that they have no choice but to follow proves the case.
62. *Pentateuch*, p. 758; emphasis is mine. Faulhaber, *Judaism, Christianity and Germany*, pp. 23–24, 68–69. The term "genius" was used several times in the pages of the *Pentateuch*. Moses was referred to as "Israel's greatest religious genius" (*Pentateuch*, p. 173); the Jews were "won from the waters of animalism by the genius of ancient engineers" (ibid., p. 935); "the modern monotheistic conception of the universe is largely the product of their genius" (ibid., p. 930); and the Commentary spoke of Ezekiel's "extraordinary genius" in saving those who had been deported to Babylonia (ibid., p. 245). The Nazis would have concurred that the Jews were racially inclined toward fulfilling the values mandated to them by the Torah, but from a Nazi perspective, such values constituted a sickness that had to be extirpated from mankind's consciousness.
63. *Judaism, Christianity and Germany*, p. 69. It is noteworthy that even following the Holocaust, the Hertz *Pentateuch* in subsequent editions had no difficulty subscribing to the linguistic notion that the Jews constituted a "race." However, what

was totally unacceptable by the late 1930s, when the one-volume edition of the Hertz *Pentateuch* appeared, was the positive notion (cited in *The Pentateuch and Haftorahs: Genesis*, p. 392) that Joseph relocated the Egyptian population to "concentration camps" (Gen. 47:21). As a replacement, the word "depot" was inserted (*Pentateuch*, p. 177).

64. *Pentateuch*, pp. 21, 45, 281, 651, 775, 920. On the obligation to inform mankind of God's nature as reflected in rabbinic tradition, see *Midrash Rabbah: Leviticus*, trans. J. Israelstam, 6:5 (pp. 85–86).

65. *Pentateuch*, pp. 7, 66, 152, 199, 244, 255, 399, 735, 789. On God's attributes in general, see ibid., pp. 364–65. On the particular attribute of God's mercy, see ibid., p. 888. On God's ethical perfection, see ibid., p. 896.

66. Ibid., p. 66. On the repetition of the notion of Jews as exemplars to the world of moral behavior, see ibid., p. 857. For an appropriate rabbinic prooftext portraying Israel as the hedge guarding the garden of humanity, see *Midrash Rabbah: Exodus*, trans. S. M. Lehrman, 2:5 (p. 54): "Just as one makes of thorns a fence for a garden, so Israel is a [moral] fence to the world."

67. *Pentateuch*, p. 5.

68. Ibid., pp. 82, 920.

69. Ibid., pp. 21, 231, 713, 995.

70. Ibid., p. 595.

71. Ibid., pp. 124, 127, 132, 186, 190.

72. Ibid., p. 898. It would appear that the specific phrasing of this idea in the Commentary originated with Graetz. See his "The Significance of Judaism for the Present and the Future," p. 261–62.

73. *Pentateuch*, pp. 21, 231, 713, 762, 897.

74. Ibid., p. 468. On the image of Torah as a spiritual medicine in Maimonidean thought, see *M.T., Hilkhot Avodah Zarah* 11:12 and Maimonides, *The Eight Chapters of Maimonides on Ethics*, chap. 4.

75. *Pentateuch*, p. 770.

76. Ibid., pp. 106, 920, and the particular evaluation of Jacob's son Reuben (ibid., p. 184).

77. Ibid., pp. 140, 495.

78. Ibid., pp. 42, 78, 678, 863, 889.

79. Ibid., p. 775.

80. Ibid., p. 25.

81. Ibid., p. 775.

82. Ibid., p. 291.

83. Ibid., p. 153. See also p. 789.

84. Ibid., p. 291.

85. Ibid., p. 880.

86. *The Pentateuch and Haftorahs: Deuteronomy*, p. 400.

87. See Moses ben Nachman's *Commentary on the Torah: Genesis*, trans. C. B. Chavel, Gen. 15:18 (p. 210) (hereafter cited as Ramban, *Torah Commentary: Genesis*); Moses ben Nachman, *Commentary on the Torah: Leviticus*, trans. C. B. Chavel, Lev. 18:25 (pp. 268–69) (hereafter cited as Ramban, *Torah Commentary: Leviticus*); Ramban, *Torah Commentary: Deuteronomy*, 29:25 (p. 338).

88. *Pentateuch*, pp. 43, 102, 137, 213, 264, 890, 896; and *The Pentateuch and Haftorahs: Deuteronomy*, p. 387.

Notes to Chapter 5

89. *Pentateuch*, pp. 547, 881.
90. Ibid., p. 711.
91. *Pentateuch*, p. 49. On the rabbinic source, see *Midrash Rabbah: Genesis*, 41:9 (p. 339).
92. *Pentateuch*, p. 584.
93. Ibid., pp. 141, 882. On God as lord of history, see ibid., pp. 61, 102, 778–79, 936.
94. Ibid., p. 295.
95. Ibid., pp. 880, 886. For a recent survey of the rabbinic theme of God going into exile, see R. Hammer, "The God of Suffering," pp. 34–41. On the specific notion of God suffering with His people in exile, see *Midrash Rabbah: Exodus*, 2:5 (p. 53).
96. *Pentateuch*, p. 545. For a veiled reference to Israel's mission, see ibid., p. 750: "in the life of that tiny land [i.e., Judah, which subsequently went into exile] the moral destinies of the whole world were involved." On Reform Judaism's mission theory in the early years of this century, see K. Kohler, *Jewish Theology*, pp. 364–65.
97. *Pentateuch*, p. 761.
98. Ibid., p. 62.
99. A thorough examination of the issue with emphasis on the Old Testament is found in J. A. Sanders, *Suffering as Divine Discipline in the Old Testament and Post-Biblical Judaism*. See, in particular, Job 23:10, 33:14–28, 36:15; Isa. 48:10; Jer. 5:3, 31:18; Zech. 13:8–9; Ps. 66:10–11. On the theme featured in rabbinic literature, see J. B. Soloveitchik, *Reflections of the Rav*, p. 190; *Sifrei on Deuteronomy*, ed. L. Finkelstein, 32 (pp. 55–56); *Pesikta de-Rab Kahana*, trans. W. G. Braude and I. J. Kapstein, 14:3 (p. 268); 23:2 (p. 354); the last is cited as well in N. Leibowitz, *Studies in the Book of Genesis*, trans. A. Neuman, pp. 303–4. See, as well, *Midrash Rabbah: Genesis*, 41:9 (p. 339); and the observation of Rashi on Deut. 4:20 (*Pentateuch with Targum Onkelos, Haphtaroth and Rabbi's Commentary: Deuteronomy*, trans. M. Rosenbaum and A. M. Silbermann, p. 26). The notion of chastisements of love is adumbrated in Job 5:17 and in the suffering of criminals sentenced for punishment as having a decided moral purpose, i.e., his moral regeneration (*Pentateuch*, p. 854). This was also the primary rationale behind Pharaoh's chastisements (ibid., p. 399).
100. Montefiore, *Outlines of Liberal Judaism*, p. 86.
101. *Pentateuch*, p. 122.
102. Ibid., p. 782; see also on this theme pp. 13, 41, 872.
103. *The Pentateuch and Haftorahs: Deuteronomy*, p. 370.
104. Ibid., p. 546. This theme is repeated several times in the Commentary: pp. 23, 584, 871. Elsewhere, this theme of divine discipline through suffering was also perceived by the Commentary as a consequence of sin (ibid., p. 13). See also the notation to Hos. 2:8–10 (ibid., p. 583), where the aim of Israel's tribulation was intended to teach her to trust in God.
105. *Guide*, III, 27 (p. 510). On a discussion of Maimonides' systemization, see H. Wolfson, *Philo*, 2:312; I. Twersky, *Introduction to the Code of Maimonides (Mishneh Torah)*, pp. 387–88.
106. *Pentateuch*, p. 306.
107. The Commentary was peppered with these faith axioms. On God's existence, see *Pentateuch*, p. 797; on God's unity, see ibid., pp. 735, 770, 920; on God's

incorporeality, see the previously mentioned references to anthropomorphism in Chapter 4, n. 91; on the prohibition against idolatry, see *Pentateuch*, pp. 397, 660, 761, 778, 781, 920; the existence of prophecy is a given axiom throughout the Commentary; on the superiority of Moses' prophecy, see ibid., pp. 359–60, 402, 616, 741–42, 916; on the divine origin of the Law, see ibid., pp. 306, 402; on the eternity of the Law, see ibid., p. 292; on God's foreknowledge of human deeds, see ibid., pp. 148, 603, 742–43, 891; on divine Providence, see pp. 61, 141, 143, 190, 209, 220, 746, 774, 777–79, 782, 936; on the related theme of reward and punishment, see ibid., pp. 542, 865, 924–25; cf., however, the notation (ibid., p. 397) that the Torah ignored the issue of reward and punishment; on free will, see ibid., p. 882; on the messianic era, see ibid., pp. 5, 562, 621; the Commentary ignored the notion of the physical resurrection of the dead in favor of the idea of the soul's immortality. See ibid., pp. 55, 88, 180, 186, 188, 621, 658, 897; cf., however, the notation (ibid., p. 397) that the Torah itself bypassed any direct mention of immortality.

108. For a representative sampling of some of these terms, see, in connection with the structure of the liturgy, *Pentateuch*, pp. 195, 553, 763, 769–71; in connection with the order of the wedding ceremony, ibid., p. 932; on basic Jewish terms, see ibid., p. 7 (*yetzer tov/ra*); 179 (*shekhinah*); 253 (*rosh hodesh*); 256 (*biur hametz/bedikat hametz*); 260 (*pidyon ha-ben*); 294 (*aseret ha-dibrot*); 298 (*mitzvah, zemirot*); 302 (*ha-kadosh barukh hu*); 339 (*ner tamid*); 416 (*lehem*); 483 (*tashlikh*); 485 (*viddui*); 594 (*birkat kohanim*); 762, 880 (*teshuvah*); 919 (*derekh eretz*); 926 (*kiddush/hillul ha-shem*).

109. *Pentateuch*, p. 751.

110. Ibid., p. 448.

111. Montefiore, *Judaism and Saint Paul*, pp. 166, 170.

112. Montefiore, *Old Testament and After*, pp. 558, 583. A similar perception was held by K. Kohler, *Jewish Theology*, pp. 46–47.

113. *Pentateuch*, pp. 401–2. Joining Hertz in this perception was his colleague I. Epstein, *Judaism of Tradition*, p. 102, and the Unitarian scholar R. T. Herford, "The Significance of Pharisaism," pp. 132–33.

114. *Pentateuch*, p. 401.

115. Ibid., pp. 828, 863, 889.

116. Ibid., p. 521.

117. Ibid., p. 621.

118. This claim of superiority of the sage over the prophet was grounded forcefully in rabbinic tradition. See *B.T., Bava Batra* 12a; *Midrash Rabbah: Song of Songs*, trans. M. Simon, I, 2 (pp. 32–33).

119. Examples of rabbinic expansion or modification of biblical phrases abound. By way of illustration, see the notations in the *Pentateuch* to Gen. 32:5 (p. 122); Exod. 25:4 (p. 326); Exod. 25:40 (p. 330); Exod. 27:1 (p. 334); Exod. 34:3 (p. 364); Lev. 13–14 (p. 461); Lev. 17:8 (p. 486); Lev. 18:5 (p. 489); Deut. 10:3 (p. 787). Rabbinic development of civil, moral, and ceremonial biblical laws also appeared frequently in the pages of the Commentary. See, for example, Gen. 50:10 (p. 189); Exod. 12:15 (p. 256); Exod. 13:2 (p. 260); Exod. 16:29 (p. 277); Exod. 20:8, 10 (p. 297); Exod. 21–24 (pp. 306–22); Exod. 27:20 (p. 339); Lev. 16:6 (p. 418); Lev. 19:11–16 (p. 499); Lev. 19:18 (p. 502); Lev. 19:33 (p. 504); Lev. 20:9 (p. 506); Deut. 4:39 (p. 763); Deut. 6:5, 7 (p. 771); Deut. 8:10 (p. 783); Deut. 12:21 (p. 803).

120. Ibid., pp. 757, 773. Equalizing the teaching roles of priests, prophets, sage, rabbi, and teacher was Hertz's own addition to the manuscript submitted by Frampton (H.A., E/6/3).

121. *Pentateuch*, pp. 190, 439, 485, 865. This point was also forcefully stressed by Montefiore in his *Judaism and Saint Paul*, p. 166.

122. *Pentateuch*, p. 828. On this notation, see also ibid., p. 529, v. 23.

123. Ibid., pp. 439, 561.

124. Ibid., p. 752.

125. Ibid., p. 560. Hertz's theory that the prophets made room for legitimate cultic-ritual forms had its detractors and supporters among gentile scholars of the period. On the former, see J. E. McFayden, "The Present Position of Old Testament Criticism," p. 210. On the latter, see B. D. Eerdmans, *Alttestamentliche Studien: Das Buch Exodus*, 3:144; J. M. Powis Smith, *The Moral Life of the Hebrews*, pp. 80–81; see also Smith's identical evaluation of Isaiah (ibid., p. 94). His favorable assessment of the Hebraic allegiance to law contrasted with his completely negative "Wellhausenian" appraisal of the unfortunate passion for law, which arose in the postexilic period under priestly influence (ibid., pp. 290, 319).

126. *Pentateuch*, p. 882.

127. Ibid., p. 756. See also ibid., p. 274. On the talmudic source, see *B.T., Yoma* 67b as well as Maimonides' discussion in *The Eight Chapters*, pp. 76–78. On the Hertzian notion that the divine imperative is its own self-sufficient motive, see *Pentateuch*, p. 489. This view was amplified by a modern theologian, Yeshayahu Leibowitz. See D. Hartman, *A Living Covenant*, pp. 14–15, 109–30.

128. *Pentateuch*, p. 489. See also p. 274, where the Commentary perceives the purpose of the Law to secure the patient's welfare. On the Law's therapeutic value, see, by way of illustration, *B.T., Betzah* 25b: "Why was the Torah given to Israel? Because they are impetuous [i.e., in need of curbing their fierceness] . . . for had not the Law been given to Israel no nation could withstand them. . . . [T]here are three distinguished in strength [i.e., fierceness]: Israel among the nations, the dog among animals, the cock among birds.

129. *Pentateuch*, p. 674. Divine Providence had decreed that Israel be "alone among the nations" (ibid., p. 936). For an appropriate rabbinic metaphor, see *Midrash Rabbah: Exodus*, 36:1 (p. 437). Hertz's posture had historical antecedents. See Maimonides (*Guide* III, 29, pp. 514–22), who was followed in turn by the medieval decisor R. Menahem HaMeiri, cited in Jacob Katz, *Exclusiveness and Tolerance*, p. 122.

130. Kohler, *Jewish Theology*, pp. 328; 445–46.

131. *The Pentateuch and Haftorahs: Genesis*, p. 473.

132. *Pentateuch*, p. 761. On the insidious danger of religious syncretism, see ibid., p. 772.

133. Ibid., p. 281.

134. Ibid., p. 809.

135. Ibid., p. 253.

136. Ibid., pp. 118, 775.

137. Ibid., p. 756; see also ibid., p. 488. On Graetz, see "The Significance of Judaism for the Present and the Future," pp. 263–64. For the Smith quotation, see *The Cambridge Bible for Schools and Colleges: The Book of Deuteronomy*, with introduction by G. A. Smith, p. 58. The quotation, although cited accurately and verbatim, is

misleading. Unlike the Hertzian approach to legalism, Smith interpreted the keeping of the law within "a thoroughly spiritual temper." Quite understandably, therefore, Hertz, as editor, made sure to censor Smith's final sentence, which was a ringing denial of the Jewish commitment to halakhic observance. It read: "But their danger [of the Hebrews and Jews] was to substitute the letter for the spirit, as according to both Jeremiah and Jesus they did." Hertz, however, did not evaluate Jeremiah's prophecy (31:52) as a refutation of Israel's commitment to the Law. Rather, he adopted Nachmanides' posture: the word "heart" was a reference to man's nature, which, in the days of the Messiah, would automatically undergo a transformation. Hence, it would "be no longer closed up, impenetrable, and unreceptive of spiritual teaching. God would help Israel to fulfil his ideal of duty" (*Pentateuch*, p. 881).

138. I. Grunfeld, "Introduction to the First English Edition of Rabbi Samson Raphael Hirsch's Commentary on the Torah," p. xx.

139. *Pentateuch*, p. 322; emphasis is partially mine. For a restatement of this principle by a contemporary scholar, see R. Gordis, "A Modern View of Revelation," p. 67. Gordis writes: "the entire development of Jewish law after Moses is implied in the giving of the Torah on Sinai, as an oak tree is implicit in the acorn, and that the organic unity binding it all together gives to it all divine sanction." For an even more radical alternative claim advanced by a modern traditional Jewish philosopher, see Hartman, *A Living Covenant* (p. 8): "Belief in the giving of the Torah at Sinai does not necessarily imply that the full truth has already been given and that our task is only to unfold what was already present in the fullness of the founding moment of revelation. . . . [T]he Sinai moment of revelation, as mediated by the ongoing discussion and the tradition, invites one and all to acquire the competence to explore the terrain and extend the realm. It does not require passive obedience and submission to the wisdom of the past."

140. *Palestinian Talmud: Pe'ah*, II, 6 (p. 17); *Palestinian Talmud: Hagigah*, I, 8 (p. 76). On a specific statement that Moses learned only the principles of the Torah at Sinai, see *Midrash Rabbah: Exodus*, 41:6 (p. 475). On rabbinic passages confirming that the Oral Law was given simultaneously with the written Torah, see B. Bamberger, "Revelations of Torah after Sinai," p. 97 n. 3.

141. Z. Frankel, *Darkhei ha-Mishnah*, p. 20.

142. S. R. Hirsch, *The Collected Writings*, vol. 5, pp. 229–31.

143. *The Pentateuch and Haftorahs: Exodus*, p. 281. On the midrashic source, see *B.T., Berakhot* 5a.

144. *The Babylonian Talmud: Tractate Berakot*, trans. A. Cohen, pp. xxiv–xxv. See also Cohen's article "Jewish History in the First Century," p. 22.

145. *Pentateuch*, pp. 756, 805. The Maimonidean source was extracted from *Guide*, III, 41 (p. 563). The *Commentary's* paraphrase of Karo's notation was lifted from the *Kesef Mishneh* to Maimonides, *M.T., Hilkhot Mamrim*, 2:4. The editor conveyed accurately Karo's general intent, although in the *Kesef Mishneh* passage, Karo specifically refers 1) to a high court's right to abrogate prohibitive measures that did not have as their purpose the safe-guarding of the Torah, and 2) the condition that the court in question be greater in number and wisdom than its predecessor. Karo cautioned scholars to desist from contending that their enactments had a firmer basis than the original one set down in the Torah. Maimonides came closer to reflecting the *Commentary's* stricture against proclaiming "new revela-

Notes to Chapter 5

tions." In his ruling, he warned against the arrogance of scholars who might impart to their regulations the character and authority of a law that had originated at Sinai. Rambam stipulated that it was incumbent on all decisors to admit that their enactments, which were later additions, constituted a protective fence around the Torah. See *M.T., Hilkhot Mamrim,* 2:9.

146. *Pentateuch,* pp. 486, 735, 803. At the same time, it must be noted that the editor invoked the ahistorical rabbinic proposition that "the events in Scripture are not always in strict chronological order.... Sometimes an inner connection causes events wide apart in time to be mentioned together in one chapter" (ibid., pp. 36, 278, 608). Yet it is significant that there were other times when the editor could have evoked this rabbinic principle but refrained from doing so, preferring instead to either ignore the formula or to seek out a reasonable explanation to account for historical incongruities. For example, see ibid., pp. 361 (v. 7); 483 (v. 23); 665 (intro. to chap. 20); 659 (v. 3).

147. Ibid., p. 142.

148. Ibid., p. 613. Solomon Schechter maintained the same view. See his "The Study of the Bible," p. 39. On Samson Raphael Hirsch's view that all the Psalms were composed by David except for those bearing the superscription of another person, see his commentary *The Psalms,* pp. xvi–xx.

149. *Pentateuch,* p. 933.

150. *Pentateuch,* p. 589.

151. Ibid., pp. 459, 481, 483, 554. On the talmudic source, see *B.T., Yoma* 67a–b.

152. *Pentateuch,* p. 475. On the ruling and its abolition, see Maimonides, *M.T., Hilkhot Keri'at Shema* 4:8. The citation of Maimonides' source in the Commentary is erroneous.

153. Ibid., p. 925.

154. *Pentateuch,* p. 692.

155. Ibid., pp. 811–12. On the talmudic source, see *B.T., Shevi'it* 10:3–4.

156. *Pentateuch,* p. 505. On the rabbinic source, see *B.T., Sanhedrin* 43a.

157. I. Abrahams, "Jewish Interpretation of the Old Testament," pp. 406–7.

158. Ibid., p. 407.

159. *Pentateuch,* pp. 480, 523, 771, 922.

160. On Nachmanides' theology, see C. J. Henoch, "The Religious Thought of Nachmanides—From His Exegesis of the Mitzvot," pp. 64–83; D. Hartman, "Maimonides' Approach to Messianism and Its Contemporary Implications," pp. 10, 28.

161. There were more than sixty direct references to Maimonides as well as several other notations that were traceable directly to his writings. For example, the source for the Commentary's explanation pertaining to the hardening of Pharaoh's heart (*Pentateuch,* p. 220) was found in the *M.T., Hilkhot Teshuvah,* 6:8; the notion that it was important for religion to enlist man's natural fears and hopes of reward as a means of encouraging him to be ethical (*Pentateuch,* pp. 319, 542, 865, 925) was located in the *Guide,* III, 28 (pp. 512–14) as well as in J. Abelson, "Maimonides on the Jewish Creed," pp. 33–34. Abelson's article contained an English translation of Rambam's *Introduction to Helek.*

162. J. H. Hertz, "Moses Maimonides: A General Estimate," pp. 3, 10.

163. *Guide,* II, 24 (p. 327); III, 45 (p. 576) and *M.T., Hilkhot Melakhim,* 8:11; Epstein, *Judaism of Tradition,* p. 139; *Pentateuch,* p. 402.

164. Ibid., pp. 297, 401.
165. Henoch, "The Religious Thought of Nachmanides," p. 73.
166. *Pentateuch*, pp. 346, 412. The Maimonidean reference (*Hilkhot Ma'aseh Hakorbanot*, 4,11) is best understood in conjunction with Rashi's comment (*B.T., Zevahim* 46b, s.v. "hanachat ruah") that the offering was a pleasing savour to the Lord because of the intention of the sacrificer who remarked, "His Will has been done." The dabbing and sprinkling of blood on various parts of the body was also perceived by the Commentary as a means of impressing in a concrete way the priests' consecration to duty and righteousness (ibid., pp. 345–46).
167. *The Pentateuch and Haftorahs: Exodus*, p. 2; see also *Pentateuch*, p. 409.
168. *Pentateuch*, p. 481.
169. Ibid., pp. 486, 562. *Guide*, III, 32 (p. 516–527). For purposes of preciseness, attention is drawn to the Commentary's designation of Maimonides' historical explanation of sacrifices as being rational and the placing of the symbolic explanation of the cult under a separate category (ibid., p. 561).
170. H.A., E/6/2, Hertz to Abraham Cohen, 15 February 1929; Hertz to Leo Jung, 17 December 1924; ibid., E/6/3, Hertz to Morris Rosenbaum, 27 January 1931.
171. A representative sampling can be found in the following pages of the Commentary: Exod. 28:36 (p. 343), 29:4 (p. 344), 30:7 (p. 349); Lev. 1:3 (p. 411), 2:1 (p. 413), 7:30 (p. 434), 9:21 (p. 444), 12:6 (p. 460), 16:8 (p. 481), 16:21–22 (p. 483), 17:34 (p. 485), 26:31 (p. 545); Num. 5:15 (p. 590).
172. *Pentateuch*, p. 580. On the talmudic source, see *B.T., Yoma* 21b.
173. *Pentateuch*, p. 580.
174. Ibid., p. 614. Noteworthy within this stylistic framework was a comparison of the healing remedy—supernatural and natural—used by Elisha to cure his patients (ibid., pp. 79, 468). On a similar juxtaposition of the supernatural to the natural, see the explanation in the Commentary (p. 578) of how the desert population was fed by God in the wilderness.
175. Ibid., p. 806; see *The Kuzari*, I, 13–25; *M.T., Hilkhot Yesodei ha-Torah*, 8:1–3. The reference on p. 806 of the Commentary to the story of R. Joshua is probably that found in *B.T., Bava Metzia* 59b. There, R. Joshua's point was to refute the assertion of relying on a miracle as proof of the correctness of a decision in a matter of law. However, in the story, R. Joshua did not actually use the phrase *ein somekhin al hanes* that was referred to in the Commentary. In fact, the Hebraic wording of this phrase is rare in rabbinic literature. It does appear, for example, in *The Zohar*, 1:352, but within a context outside the framework of rendering a legal decision.
176. *B.T., Avodah Zarah* 54b; *Guide*, II, 29 (p. 345); and *The Eight Chapters*, p. 90.
177. *The Kuzari*, I, 8, 11, 67, 83–87, 89; S. Schechter, "Nachmanides," p. 95; reprinted in his *Studies in Judaism*, pp. 119–20; Moses ben Nachman, *Commentary on the Torah: Exodus*, Exod. 13:16 (p. 174) (hereafter cited as Ramban, *Torah Commentary: Exodus*). On this theme, see also Ramban, *Torah Commentary: Exodus*, 6:2 (p. 65); 8:14 (p. 85); 14:21 (p. 189). On God's shielding of Israel, see also Ramban, *Torah Commentary: Deuteronomy*, 8:18 (p. 105).
178. *Pentateuch*, p. 671. Rabbi Hertz made mention of this view in one of his public Torah lessons (*SAS* 1:170–71); his perception was also appropriated by Samuel Luzzatto (Margolies, *Samuel David Luzzatto*, pp. 69–70); on the rabbinic sources, see *Avot* V, 6; *Midrash Rabbah: Genesis*, 5:5 (p. 36); *Midrash Rabbah: Exodus*, 21:6 (p. 267).

179. *Guide*, II, 29 (p. 345); III, 50 (p. 616); J. Heller, "Maimonides' Theory of Miracle," pp. 120–22. For an attempt at reconciling these two contrasting postures of Maimonides, see Reines, "Maimonides' Concept of Miracles," pp. 243–85; *Pentateuch*, p. 578; see also ibid., p. 276.

180. *Guide*, II, 42 (pp. 389–90); Reines, "Maimonides' Concept of Miracles," p. 273, argued that by adopting this posture, Maimonides effectively neutralized "the reality of the vast majority of miracle stories in Scripture"; *Pentateuch*, pp. 123, 671.

181. *Pentateuch*, p. 322.

182. Ibid., p. 330; on the rabbinic source, see *B.T., Menahot* 29a; on this approach in Maimonides, see *Guide*, I.

183. *Pentateuch*, p. 259.

184. Ibid., p. 651.

185. Ibid., pp. 243, 266.

186. Ibid., p. 400. On the specific natural bases for the Nile turning into blood, the incidents of hail, frogs, locusts, and darkness, see, respectively, ibid., pp. 237–38, 243, 248, 251.

187. Ibid., p. 269. See also p. 266.

188. Ibid., pp. 270–71, 796.

189. Montefiore, *Outlines of Liberal Judaism*, pp. 82–84; *Guide*, III, 32 (pp. 526–27).

190. *Pentateuch*, p. 194.

191. Ibid., pp. 557–558.

192. Ibid., p. 555; the quotation from Aristotle was cited by Epstein, *Judaism of Tradition*, p. 66.

193. *The Jewish Encyclopedia* (1903), s.v. "Evolution," E. G. Hirsch; *Pentateuch*, p. 194.

194. *Pentateuch*, p. 194; A. R. Wallace, *The Action of Natural Selection on Man*, p. 53. On Wallace's refutation of Darwin's theory of natural selection as applied to man, see his *Man's Place in the Universe*, pp. 269–77, esp. p. 274.

195. *Pentateuch*, pp. 193–94; on the rabbinic sources, see, by way of illustration, *Midrash Rabbah: Genesis*, 3:9 (p. 25); *Midrash Rabbah: Ecclesiastes*, trans. A. Cohen, 3:11 (p. 86); *The Midrash on Psalms*, trans. W. G. Braude, 34, (p. 408).

196. E. Halley, "Of the Cause of the Universal Deluge," *The Philosophical Transactions of the Royal Society of London* (1720–32), abridged, vol. 6, pt. 2, 41.

197. *Pentateuch*, p. 3. On the midrashic sources, see *Midrash Rabbah: Genesis*, 8:2 (p. 56); 19:8 (p. 154).

198. *Pentateuch*, pp. 193–95; O. Chadwick, *The Victorian Church*, pt. 1, p. 559. Protestantism's influential neo-orthodox theologian, Karl Barth, adopted an identical posture drawing a distinction between the methods of theology and science. There were no points of contact between them. See I. Barbour, *Issues in Science and Religion*, p. 118.

199. C. Montefiore, *The Bible for Home Reading*, 1:557.

200. C. Montefiore, "Dr. Friedlaender on the Jewish Religion," p. 210; N. Cohen, "The Challenges of Darwinism and Biblical Criticism to American Judaism," *Modern Judaism* 4 (1984): 123–24.

201. *Pentateuch*, p. 5. Lyman Abbot was a prominent American Christian minister of the era, whose support of evolutionary theory mirrored that of the Commentary: "If I could conceive it possible that this universe were governed by a

wisdom no greater than I am able to comprehend, I should not be able to believe in a God of infinite wisdom" (L. Abbot, *The Theology of an Evolutionist*, preface).

202. *Pentateuch*, p. vii. The Maimonidean source is found in *The Eight Chapters*, p. 6 (of Hebrew translation); p. 36 (of English translation). On Maimonides' readiness to accept the learning of Greek wisdom, see, by way of illustration, *M.T., Hilkhot Kiddush ha-Hodesh*, 17:4.

203. The delineation made between the divergent aims of science and religion did not interfere with Hertz holding high hope that continued archaeological discoveries would verify, once and for all, the veracity of the Flood. See *Pentateuch*, pp. 196–97. The reference therein to L. Wooley was to an address delivered by the archaeologist C. Leonard Wooley under the auspices of the Jewish Historical Society of England and published under the title *The Excavations at Ur and the Hebrew Records*, p. 26. In short, Hertz was of the belief that scientific methodology, rather than threatening the biblical record, could become its useful handmaiden.

204. *Pentateuch*, p. 5.

205. Ibid., p. 194.

206. Ibid., p. 2. The reference to Kalisch, though not appearing in the published edition of the *Pentateuch*, was cited in a manuscript of the Commentary to Genesis (H.A., E/6/3).

207. M. Kalisch, *The Book of Genesis*, pp. 64–65.

208. *Pentateuch*, pp. 195–96. See also ibid., p. 9. The definition of allegory had been set down eloquently at the turn of the century in the pages of *The Jewish Encyclopedia*: "That explanation of a scriptural passage which is based upon the supposition that its author, whether God or man, intended something "other" than what is literally expressed." The distinction between allegory and parable was not always clear. A parable could be regarded as a subcategory of allegory. "In the parable, the author himself indicates the analogy by placing interpretation next to image; but in the allegory, judgment is not expressed" (*The Jewish Encyclopedia*, 1903, s.v. "Allegorical Interpretation," L. Ginzberg; s.v. "Allegory in the Old Testament," I. M. Casanowicz).

209. Schechter, *Some Aspects of Rabbinic Theology*, pp. 39–40.

210. I. Zangwill, *Chosen Peoples: The Hebraic Ideal versus the Teutonic*, p. 21.

211. *The Jewish Encyclopedia*, s.v. "Allegorical Interpretation," L. Ginzberg.

212. The Commentary frequently brought to the reader's attention that certain scriptural passages were to be interpreted as anthropomorphisms illustrating the rabbinic dictum that the Bible often resorted to ordinary human language, to "forms of literary expression that would be effective with the hearers to whom they are addressed" in order "to make intelligible to the finite human mind that which relates to the Infinite." On the *Pentateuch*'s references to anthropomorphism, both by direct use of the term and by allusion, see previous chapter, n. 91. On representative rabbinic sources citing the principle of anthropomorphism, see *B.T., Yevamot* 71a; *Bava Metzia* 31b; *Arakhin* 11a; *Berakhot* 31b. On Maimonides' use of anthropomorphism, see, in general, bk. I of his *Guide* and for his resort to allegory, see *Guide*, II, 25 (p. 328).

213. *Pentateuch*, p. 194. On the source in Maimonides, see *Guide*, II, 29 (p. 346). In the *Pentateuch*, pp. 195–96, the editor inclined toward interpreting the paradise story as a parable, and this was in line most definitely with Maimonides, *Guide*, II, 30 (p. 355), and in part with Nachmanides (Ramban, *Torah Commentary: Genesis*,

3:6–8 (pp. 80–81). On the rabbinic perception that accepted the historical reality of the paradise story, see *Midrash Rabbah: Genesis*, 16:5 (p. 130); *B.T., Shabbat* 55b. No less a scholar than I. Epstein, Hertz's collaborator in the writing of the appendices to the Commentary, squared evolutionism with the Torahitic account by relying on Maimonides' interpretation. Shortly after coming to Jews' College, Epstein urged the readers of the *Jewish Chronicle* to adopt Maimonides' way "in dealing with the problems presented to us by modern scientific thought" (*Jewish Chronicle*, 16 November 1928), p. 25. O. Chadwick, in his study *The Secularization of the European Mind in the Nineteenth Century*, p. 166, notes that the use of allegory to decipher the creation and flood epics was commonfare for most of the middle class in northern Europe throughout most of the nineteenth century.

214. C. Montefiore, "Dr. Friedlaender on the Jewish Religion," pp. 210–11.

215. C. Montefiore, *Old Testament and After*, p. 502.

216. C. Montefiore, *Liberal Judaism and Hellenism*, p. 10; C. Montefiore, *Old Testament and After*, pp. 581–82.

Chapter 6

1. H.A., E/6/1, David de Sola Pool to Hertz, 8 June 1930; ibid., E/6/3, Herman Abramowitz to Hertz, 31 July 1930.

2. Ibid., E/6/1, Hertz to Emanuel Hertz, 19 May 1930; ibid., E/6/1, Hertz to E. Noel Burghes, 10 July 1929; ibid., E/6/3, Hertz to Burghes, 4 February 1931.

3. Ibid., E/6/1, Hertz to Samuel Frampton, 26 April 1931; ibid., E/6/2, Hertz to Frampton, 25 November 1932.

4. Ibid., E/6/1, Hertz to Emanuel Hertz, 19 May 1930; ibid., Hertz to Louis Finkelstein, 21 May 1930; ibid., E/6/3, Hertz to E. Noel Burghes, 9 December 1930.

5. Ibid., E/6/1, Hertz to Emanuel Hertz, 27 September 1929; ibid., E/6/1, Hertz to the manager of Oxford University Press, New York, 27 September 1929.

6. Ibid., E/6/3, undated list containing names of colleagues, some of whom had ordered and others who had not yet ordered copies of the *Pentateuch*.

7. Ibid., E/6/1, Hertz to Moses Jung, 11 June 1930; ibid., E/6/1, Max Drob to Hertz, 30 May 1930; Louis Finkelstein to Hertz, 8 June 1930; ibid., E/6/2, Hertz to Julius Rosenwald, 4 September 1931; ibid., E/6/3, Israel Leventhal to Hertz, 3 September 1930; Hertz to Leventhal, 15 September 1930; Herman Abramowitz to Hertz, 31 July 1930; ibid., E/6/1, Hertz to Louis Finkelstein and Julius Greenstone, 21 May 1930; Hertz was appreciative that Stephen Wise of the Free Synagogue in New York had agreed to review the Genesis volume in the *New York Times* (ibid., E/6/1, Hertz to the manager of Oxford University Press, New York, 27 September 1929).

8. Ibid., E/6/3, Hertz to Joshua Abelson, 7 December 1930.

9. Ibid., E/6/1, Hertz to Leo Jung, 24 February 1931. Interestingly, no allusions were made in the correspondence during these years about the Depression as a debilitating economic factor that contributed to the poor sale of the Commentary.

10. Ibid., E/6/1, J. Davidson to Hertz, 3 July 1936.

11. Ibid., E/6/1, Hertz to J. Solis-Cohen, Jr., 23 October 1936; ibid., Maurice Jacob to Hertz, 20 November 1936. The benefactor for the one-volume edition was Joseph Freedman (preface to the one-volume edition).

12. I am indebted to Rabbi Hertz's grandson Jeremy Schonfeld for this information. A second edition of the *Pentateuch* appeared in 1960, containing minor revisions in style undertaken by Hertz's son Samuel Hertz, in collaboration with the editors of the Soncino Press during 1958–59. A file on the recommended revisions is located in H.A., 35/1.

13. Emanuel Hertz to Hertz, 16 July 1936.

14. See, in general, H.A., E/6/1 and E/6/3 for a large number of reviews on deposit.

15. Ibid., E/6/1, review from *JQR* 21 (1931): 92; ibid., E/6/3, review from *Jewish Ledger*, 23 December 1929; ibid., E/6/1, *Jewish Guardian*, 26 July 1929.

16. Hertz informed several colleagues of the "quite impossible conditions" to which he would have had to submit. See H.A., E/6/1, Hertz to H. Abramowitz, 11 September 1931; Hertz to A. Cohen, 16 October 1935; ibid., E/6/3, Hertz to William Rosenau, 8 July 1931. Hertz's authorization to use the JPS translation in the one-volume edition came about under the initiative of the president of the Society, J. Solis-Cohen, Jr. He informed the chief rabbi that an unfortunate misunderstanding was the cause of the Society's refusing Hertz's request to use their translation: "I believe . . . that you have misconstrued the intent of the letter written by a former secretary. . . . [W]hat was meant to be conveyed was that the Society was willing for you to use its authorized version providing the work to be undertaken by you was completed within a period of years, which was originally set at ten and later increased to twenty" (ibid., 33/1, J. Solis-Cohen, Jr., to Hertz, 13 February 1936).

17. See, for example, his explanation of Exod. 4:24 (p. 221) noted by one reviewer (ibid., E/6/3, *Jewish Chronicle*, 13 March 1931), p. 19.

18. H.A., E/6/3, a review from the *Times Literary Supplement*, October 1919. On the reference in the Commentary, see *Pentateuch*, p. 140.

19. H.A., E/6/3, a review from the *Brooklyn Examiner*, 27 December 1929.

20. Ibid., E/6/3, a review from *The Expository Times*, February 1931.

21. Ibid., E/6/3, *Jewish Chronicle*, 13 March 1931, p. 19.

22. Ibid., E/6/3, a review from the *Jewish Guardian*, 11 October 1929.

23. Ibid., E/6/3, *The Zionist Record*, April 1931.

24. Ibid., E/6/3, a review from the *Jewish Chronicle*, 13 March 1931; E/6/1, *Jewish Chronicle*, 3 July 1936.

25. Ibid., E/6/1, a review from *JQR* 25 (1934/35): 324.

26. The friendship between the two men came through in a letter by Salaman to Hertz conveying his concern that his criticisms might have hurt the chief rabbi's feelings. After thanking Hertz for sending him the Commentary to Exodus, he invited the chief rabbi to his home for a weekend (ibid., E/6/2, Salaman to Hertz, 27 February 1932).

27. In a letter to Leo Jung (ibid., E/6/1, Hertz to Jung, 24 February 1931), the chief rabbi was taken aback at Jung's praise of Gaster, which appeared in a note about the contributors at the back of one of Jung's anthologies. Hertz claimed that at least part of Jung's encomiums of Gaster were highly suspect.

28. Ibid., E/6/1, Redcliffe Salaman to Hertz, 19 February 1932. In this vein, see ibid., E/6/3, a review from the *Jewish Chronicle*, 21 June 1929. A similar complaint was voiced by a reviewer who proclaimed that "a preaching, spiritualizing com-

Notes to Chapter 6

mentary does not deserve the appellation of commentary at all" (ibid., E/6/1, *Jewish Chronicle*, 3 July 1936).

29. Ibid., E/6/1, Hertz to Salaman, 26 February 1932.
30. *Encyclopaedia Judaica* (1971), s.v. "Gaster, Moses," C. Roth.
31. H.A., E/6/3, *Jewish Guardian*, 26 July 1929, p. 7. A similar unsympathetic review was written by Gaster on the chief rabbi's Commentary on Exodus (ibid., E/6/3, Scrapbook, excerpt from the *Jewish Guardian*, 6 February 1931). The rabbinic reference Gaster referred to was *B.T., Sanhedrin* 82a: "Whenever the Divine Name is being profaned, honor must not be paid to one's teacher."
32. Ibid., E/6/3, draft of a letter by Hertz to G. R. S. Mead, 5 August 1929.
33. Ibid., E/6/3, letter to the editor of the *Jewish Guardian*, 23 August 1929.
34. Ibid., E/6/3, a review from the *Jewish Guardian*, 2 August 1929, p. 7.
35. Quoted by R. J. Thompson in his "Moses and the Law," p. 159.
36. R. T. Herford, *What the World Owes to the Pharisees*, p. 15. On citations from Herford in the Commentary, see *Pentateuch*, pp. 562, 737, 741, 922.
37. A. Marx, *Essays in Jewish Biography*, pp. 204–5. Though unwilling to grant legitimacy to these Jewish writers, he acknowledged a spiritual dimension in Greek civilization that was a forerunner to the excellence of Jewish morality. See his *Pentateuch: Genesis*, pp. 191, 193.
38. P. R. Mendes-Flohr, "Secular Religiosity: Reflections on Post-Traditional Jewish Spirituality and Community," p. 19.
39. C. Montefiore, "Some Notes on the Effect of Biblical Criticism upon the Jewish Religion," pp. 296, 303, 306.
40. *Pentateuch*, p. 402.
41. Ibid., p. 751; see also ibid., p. 869; *SAS* 1:302; 2:59.
42. *SAS* 2:60.
43. *SAS* 1:339.
44. The one exception in the Commentary was the filial piety shown by a pagan for his father (*Pentateuch*, p. 498). The rabbinic source is located in *B.T., Kiddushin* 31a.
45. Kohler, *Jewish Theology*, p. 431.
46. Graetz, "The Significance of Judaism," p. 259.
47. Graetz, *The Structure of Jewish History*, pp. 52, 54, 56, 59.
48. Ibid., p. 57; Hertz, *SAS* 2:17.
49. A. Kohut, "What the Hebrew Scriptures Have Wrought for Mankind," pp. 308–9.
50. Ibid., pp. 213–15.
51. *AOJ*, pp. 100–101.
52. *SAS* 2:69.
53. *Pentateuch*, p. 921; emphasis is mine.
54. Montefiore, *Liberal Judaism and Hellenism*, p. 78.
55. On Bachya's methodology, see J. Dan, *Jewish Mysticism and Jewish Ethics*, p. 23.
56. Hertz, *The Ethical System of James Martineau*.
57. Ibid., pp. 16–17.
58. Ibid., pp. 43–44.
59. Ibid., p. 46.
60. Ibid., pp. 47–48, 74, 78.

61. Ibid., pp. 13–25.

62. *Pentateuch*, p. 402.

63. The full citation in the *Pentateuch*, p. 376, reads: "When the Hebrew spirit prevails over the Greek, he strips it of its pagan sensuality, so that its beauty stands revealed untarnished by barbaric or ungodly association" (Solomon J. Solomon). The quotation was excerpted from the Jewish Victorian portrait artist Solomon Joseph Solomon's article "Art and Judaism," *JQR* 13 (1901): 553. In the original, the quotation had specific reference not to the cleavage between the Hebrew and Greek spirit, as implied by the editor, but to the specific distinction between Hebrew and Greek forms of art: "When Hebrew prevails over Greek, he strips art of its Pagan sensuality, so that its beauty stands revealed untarnished by barbaric or ungodly assocations; the Greek, in revenge, seduces the Hebrew by force of his Pagan luxuriance from that simplicity of life so essential to his continued existence."

64. *AOJ*, p. 30.

65. Montefiore, *Judaism and Saint Paul*, p. 134.

66. Quoted by Israel Zangwill in his *Chosen Peoples*, p. 72, in the name of Coleridge.

67. It may be presumed that this audience will find particularly attractive the Torah commentary being produced by the Conservative movement's Rabbinical Assembly in collaboration with insights garnered from the five-volume commentary on the Pentateuch (1989–1996) published by the Jewish Publication Society of America.

68. Representative of this approach are the commentaries being written by the ArtScroll publishing house.

69. Hertz, *Early and Late*, pp. 58–59; compare *Pentateuch*, p. 855.

70. *Pentateuch*, p. 935.

71. U. Tal, "Religious and Anti-Religious Roots of Modern Anti-Semitism," pp. 16–17.

72. S. Friedlaender, "The Historical Significance of the Holocaust," p. 44.

73. F. Littel, *The Crucifixion of the Jews*, pp. 3–4, 60. It is, perhaps, not too far afield to surmise that Hertz would have felt an affinity with the absolute censure of Christianity uttered by the modern Orthodox scholar Rabbi Eliezer Berkovits, in a private conversation with the author a few weeks before Berkovits' death in August 1992: "Christianity is the greatest fraud perpetrated on the history of mankind!"

74. W. Gottlieb, ed., *Essays and Addresses in Memory of J. H. Hertz*, p. 40.

Bibliography

The Hertz Archives: A Note of Explanation

Following the death of Chief Rabbi Hertz in 1946, his extensive personal archives went into storage and were effectively closed to researchers, primarily under orders from Samuel Hertz, Rabbi Hertz's son. Following the latter's death, the archives were brought out of storage in the late 1970s. As related to me by Hertz's daughter, Josephine Hertz, the archives—during an interim period of sitting in the family home—were unfortunately rifled by several individuals who took it upon themselves to discard material that, in their judgment, was no longer of historical value. I am convinced that important additional material relating to the composition of the Commentary was destroyed. I base my conclusion on the fact that Hertz went to great lengths to preserve even the most incidental pieces of correspondence that came across his desk.

The Hertz papers were legally transferred to the Anglo-Jewish Archives, which generally houses its archival collections at the Mocatta Library at the University of London. However, because of lack of space, the Hertz papers were transferred to Leo Baeck College (London), where I did my research in June 1985.

At that time, the Hertz papers were not completely cataloged. I opened up several boxes and, upon discovering material relating to the composition of the Commentary, continued the classification process begun by an archivist. The papers were subsequently moved to permanent quarters at the University of Southampton's Hartley Library. An official catalog of the Hertz papers was published in 1993. Thus, future readers will find that my classification system will have been superseded by the final one designed by the archivist at the University of Southampton.

The Hertz Archives

H.A. Scrapbook, 1936–42
H.A. 2/3 (Miscellaneous newspaper reports citing Rabbi Hertz)
H.A. 33/1 (Hertz correspondence with the Jewish Publication Society of America, 1936)
H.A. 35/1 (Proposed revisions to second edition of the Hertz Pentateuch, 1958/59)
H.A. A/13 (Sources relating to Liberal/Reform Judaism)
H.A. E/6/1 (Hertz correspondence relating to the writing of the Commentary with special references to the assignments of Hertz's collaborators)
H.A. E/6/2 (Hertz correspondence with collaborators; with the Jewish Publication Society; with Aaron Blashki and Wilfred Samuel)
H.A. E/6/3 (Extant manuscripts of the Commentary; book reviews of the Commentary; Hertz correspondence relating to the writing of the Commentary; Hertz correspondence with the Jewish Publication Society of America)
H.A. G/6 (Sources relating to Liberal/Reform Judaism)

Oral History Interviews

Nahum Sarna, 27 June 1982
Israel Finestein, 5 December 1982
Josephine Hertz, 27 June 1985
Raphael Loewe, 27 June 1985
Jeremy Schonfeld, 30 June 1985
Judith Schonfeld, 30 June 1985

Primary Hebrew, Aramaic, and Arabic Sources Published in Hebrew, Aramaic, or in English Translation

Abelson, J. "Maimonides on the Jewish Creed." *JQR* 19 (1907): 24–58.
Babylonian Talmud (Hebrew). New York: Shulsinger Bros., 1948.
The Babylonian Talmud: Tractate Berakot. trans. A. Cohen. Cambridge: Cambridge University Press, 1921.
Halevi, David ben Samuel [Taz]. *Turei Zahav* on *Shulhan Arukh: Yoreh De'ah.* New York: Abraham Isaac Freedman, 1958.
Halevi, J. *The Kuzari.* trans. Hartwig Hirschfeld. London: G. Routledge and Sons, 1905.

Heller, Y. T. Lipmann. *Pilpula Harifta.* New York: Shulsinger Bros., 1948.
The Holy Bible. Revised Standard Version. New York: World Publishing, 1952.
Homberg, N. H. Commentary to Deuteronomy (Hebrew). In *Biur = Netivot Shalom.* Fuerth: Zuerndorfer, 1823/24.
Jerusalem [= Palestinian] Talmud (Hebrew). New York: Shulsinger Bros., 1948.
Karo, J. *Shulhan Arukh.* New York: Abraham Isaac Freedman, 1968.
Maimonides [Moses ben Maimon]. *The Commandments.* trans. Charles B. Chavel. London and New York: Soncino Press, 1967.
———. *The Eight Chapters of Maimonides on Ethics (Shemonah Perakim).* ed. and trans. J. I. Gorfinkle. New York: Columbia University Press, 1912; reprint, New York: AMS Press, 1966.
———. *The Guide for the Perplexed.* trans. M. Friedlaender. London: Routledge and Kegan Paul, 1904.
———. *The Guide of the Perplexed.* trans. Shlomo Pines with an introduction by Leo Strauss. Chicago: University of Chicago Press, 1963.
———. *Mishneh Torah.* Jerusalem: Mossad Harav Kook, 1958.
Meiri, Menahem ben Solomon. *Beit ha-Behirah: Makkot.* Jerusalem: Tehiyah, 1965.
Midrash ha-Gadol: Genesis. ed. M. Margaliyot. Jerusalem: Mossad Harav Kook, 1967.
Midrash ha-Gadol. ed. S. Schechter. Cambridge: Cambridge University Press, 1902.
Midrash Lekah Tov: Genesis. ed. S. Buber. Vilna: Romm, 1884.
The Midrash on Psalms. trans. W. G. Braude. New Haven: Yale University Press, 1959.
Midrash Rabbah: Ecclesiastes. trans. A. Cohen. London: Soncino Press, 1939.
Midrash Rabbah: Exodus. trans. S. M. Lehrman. London: Soncino Press, 1939.
Midrash Rabbah: Genesis. trans. H. Freedman. London: Soncino Press, 1939.
Midrash Rabbah: Leviticus. trans. J. Israelstam. London: Soncino Press, 1939.
Midrash Rabbah: Leviticus. trans. J. J. Slotki. London: Soncino Press, 1939.
Midrash Rabbah: Song of Songs. trans. M. Simon. London: Soncino Press, 1939.

Midrash Zuta on Megillat Ruth (Hebrew). ed. S. Buber. Tel Aviv: n.p., 1924.

Nachmanides [Moses ben Nachman]. ———. *Commentary on the Torah: Genesis.* trans. C. B. Chavel. New York: Shilo Publishing House, 1971.

———. *Commentary on the Torah: Exodus.* trans. C. B. Chavel. New York: Shilo Publishing House, 1973.

———. *Commentary on the Torah: Leviticus.* trans. C. B. Chavel. New York: Shilo Publishing House, 1974.

———. *Commentary on the Torah: Deuteronomy.* trans. C. B. Chavel. New York: Shilo Publishing House, 1976.

Pentateuch with Targum Onkelos, Haphtaroth and Rashi's Commentary: Deuteronomy. trans. M. Rosenbaum and A. M. Silbermann. New York: Hebrew Publishing, 1934.

Pesikta de-Rab Kahana. trans. W. G. Braude and I. J. Kapstein. Philadelphia: Jewish Publication Society of America, 1975.

Pirkei de-Rabbi Eliezer. Antwerp: I. Menczer, n.d.

Sifrei on Deuteronomy (Hebrew). ed. L. Finkelstein. New York: Jewish Theological Seminary of America, 1969.

Tanna debe Eliyyahu. trans. W. G. Braude and I. J. Kapstein. Philadelphia: Jewish Publication Society of America, 1981.

Tanna de-vei Eliyahu. ed. M. Friedmann. Vienna: C. Fromme, 1902.

Yalkut Shimeoni. Pt. 1. New York: Pardes, 1944.

The Zohar. Vol. 1. London: Soncino Press, 1935.

Secondary Sources

Abbot, L. *The Life and Literature of the Ancient Hebrews.* Boston: Houghton Mifflin, 1901.

———. *The Theology of an Evolutionist.* Boston: Houghton Mifflin, 1897.

Abelson, J. *The Immanence of God in Rabbinical Literature.* London: Macmillan, 1912.

———. "Maimonides." *Encyclopaedia of Religion and Ethics,* 1915.

———. "Maimonides as Philosopher." *Jewish Chronicle Supplement,* 26 May 1922.

———. *Jewish Mysticism.* London: G. Bell and Sons, 1913. Reprint, New York: Sepher Hermon Press, 1969.

Abrahams, I. "Jewish Interpretation of the Old Testament." In *The People and the Book,* ed. A. S. Peake, pp. 403–31. Oxford: Clarendon Press, 1925.

———. *Studies in Pharisaism and the Gospels.* Cambridge: Cambridge University Press, 1917. Reprint, New York: Ktav, 1967.

Adler, C. *Selected Letters.* ed. I. Robinson. Philadelphia: Jewish Publication Society; New York: Jewish Theological Seminary, 1985.

———, ed. *The Jewish Theological Seminary of America: Semi-Centennial Volume.* New York: Jewish Theological Seminary of America, 1939.

The Anchor Bible: Genesis. trans. E. A. Speiser. Garden City, N.Y.: Doubleday, 1964.

Arnold, M. *Culture and Anarchy.* Cambridge: Cambridge University Press, 1935.

———. *Literature and Dogma.* London: Smith, Elder, 1873.

Bamberger, B. "Revelations of Torah after Sinai." *Hebrew Union College Annual* 16 (1941): 97–113.

Barbour, I. *Issues in Science and Religion.* New York: Harper and Row, 1971.

Baron, S. *A Social and Religious History of the Jews.* Vol. 1. New York: Columbia University Press, 1952.

Barry, W. *Ernest Renan.* London: Hodder and Stoughton, 1905.

Beidelman, T. O. *W. Robertson Smith and the Sociological Study of Religion.* Chicago: University of Chicago Press, 1974.

Bentwich, N. *Claude Montefiore and His Tutor in Rabbinics: Founders of Liberal and Conservative Judaism.* Southampton, England: University of Southampton, 1966.

———. *Solomon Schechter: A Biography.* Philadelphia: Jewish Publication Society of America, 1938.

Blidstein, G. *Political Concepts in Maimonidean Halakha* (Hebrew). Jerusalem: Bar Ilan University, 1983.

Brown, F., ed., with S. R. Driver and C. A. Briggs. *A Hebrew and English Lexicon of the Old Testament.* Oxford: Clarendon Press, 1975.

Butcher, S. H. *Some Aspects of Greek Genius.* London: Macmillan, 1891.

Chadwick, O. *The Secularization of the European Mind in the Nineteenth Century.* Cambridge: Cambridge University Press, 1975.

———. *The Victorian Church.* London: A. and C. Black, 1966.

Childs, B. S. "Wellhausen in English." *Semeia* 25 (1982): 83–88.

Cohen, A. *Everyman's Talmud.* London: J. M. Dent, 1934.

———. "Jewish History in the First Century." In *Judaism and the Beginnings of Christianity.* London: G. Routledge and Sons, 1923, pp. 3–47.

———. *Jewish Homiletics*. London: M. L. Cailingold, 1937.
———. "Maimonides and Aristotle's Doctrine of the Mean." *Jewish Chronicle Supplement*, 3 October 1924.
———. "Shem and Japheth." Sermon, Birmingham, 24 October 1925.
———. "Supplementary Notes to Gorfinkle's Edition of Maimonides' Eight Chapters." *JQR* 4 (1913/14): 475–79.
———. *The Teachings of Maimonides*. London: G. Routledge, 1927.
Cohen, A. A. *The Myth of the Judeo-Christian Tradition*. New York: Schocken, 1971.
Cohen, N. "The Challenges of Darwinism and Biblical Criticism to American Judaism." *Modern Judaism* 4 (1984): 121–57.
Congregation Mikveh Israel. *Commemoration of the One-Hundredth Anniversary of the Birth of the Reverend Doctor Sabato Morais*. Philadelphia, 1924.
Cook, S. A. "The Religious Environment of Israel." In *The People and the Book*, ed. Arthur S. Peake, pp. 41–72. Oxford: Clarendon Press, 1925.
Cornill, K. H. *History of the People of Israel*. trans. W. H. Carruth. Chicago: Open Court Publishing, 1905.
———. *The Prophets of Israel*. Chicago: Open Court Publishing, 1901.
Cowen, P. *Memories of an American Jew*. New York: International Press, 1932.
Curtis, E. L. *A Critical and Exegetical Commentary on Chronicles*. Edinburgh: T. and T. Clark, 1910.
Daiches, S. "The Meaning of *Am Ha'aretz* in the Old Testament." *Journal of Theological Studies* 30 (1929): 245–49.
Dan, J. *Jewish Mysticism and Jewish Ethics*. Seattle: University of Washington Press, 1986.
Davis, M. *The Emergence of Conservative Judaism*. Philadelphia: Jewish Publication Society of America, 1965.
DeLaura, D. J. *Hebrew and Hellene in Victorian England*. Austin: University of Texas Press, 1969.
Delitzsch, F. *Babel and Bible*. trans. T. J. McCormack and W. H. Carruth. Chicago: Open Court Publishing, 1903.
Douglas, G. C. M. "The Deuteronomic Code." In *Lex Mosaica*, ed. R. V. French, pp. 55–96. London: Eyre and Spottiswoode, 1894.
Drachman, B. *The Unfailing Light*. New York: Rabbinical Council of America, 1948.

Driver, S. R. *The Cambridge Bible for Schools and Colleges: The Book of Exodus*. Cambridge: Cambridge University Press, 1911.
———. *A Critical and Exegetical Commentary on Deuteronomy*. Edinburgh: T. and T. Clark, 1895.
———. "Evolution Compatible with Faith." In *Sermons on Subjects Connected with the Old Testament*. London: Methuen, 1892, pp. 1–27.
———. "Hebrew Authority." In *Authority and Archaeology, Sacred and Profane*, ed. D. G. Hogarth. London: J. Murray, 1899; reprint, Freeport, N.Y.: Books for Libraries Press, 1971, pp. 3–152.
———. *Introduction to the Literature of the Old Testament*. New York: C. Scribner's Sons, 1925.
———. "Mercy and Not Sacrifice." In *Sermons on Subjects Connected with the Old Testament*. London: Methuen, 1892, pp. 217–32.
———. *Modern Research as Illustrating the Bible*. London: Frowde, 1909.
———. "The Permanent Moral and Devotional Value of the Old Testament for the Christian Church." In *Sermons on Subjects Connected with the Old Testament*. London: Methuen, 1892, pp. ix–xix.
———. "The Voice of God in the Old Testament." In *Sermons on Subjects Connected with the Old Testament*. London: Methuen, 1892, pp. 119–42.
Eerdmans, B. D. *Alttestamentliche Studien: Das Buch Exodus*. Giessen: A. Toepelmann, 1910.
Eisenstein, J. D. "Between Two Opinions." *American Jewish Archives* 12 (October 1960): 123–42.
Ellenson, D. "A Response by Modern Orthodoxy to Jewish Religious Pluralism: The Case of Esriel Hildesheimer." *Tradition* 17 (1979): 78.
Encyclopaedia Britannica, 9th ed. s.v. "Israel," J. Wellhausen.
———. s.v. "Bible," W. Robertson Smith.
———, 14th ed. s.v. "Common Law," T. S. Legg and T. F. T. Plucknett.
Encyclopaedia Judaica. 1971. s.v. "Bible: Bible Research and Criticism," H. D. Hummel.
———. 1971. s.v. "Disputation of Barcelona," C. Beinart.
———. 1971. s.v. "Gaster, Moses," C. Roth.
Epstein, I. "Introduction to Seder Kodashim." In *The Babylonian Talmud: Seder Kodashim*, trans. and ed. I. Epstein, pp. xvii–xxxviii. London: Soncino Press, 1948.

———. *Judaism of Tradition*. London: E. Goldston, 1931.
———, ed. *Joseph Herman Hertz, 1872–1946: In Memoriam*. London: Soncino Press, 1947.
———, ed. *Moses Maimonides, 1135–1204*. London: Soncino Press, 1935.
Faulhaber, M. *Judaism, Christianity and Germany*. trans. G. D. Smith. New York: Macmillan, 1934.
Faulkner, J. A. "The Miraculous Birth of Our Lord." Aftermath Series, ed. H. M. du Bose. Nashville: Publishing House of the M. E. Church, South, 1924.
Frankel, Z. *Darkhei ha-Mishnah*. Warsaw: M. Cailingold, 1923.
Frazer, J. *Folk-Lore in the Old Testament*. Abridged ed., London: Macmillan, 1923.
———. *Folk-Lore in the Old Testament: Studies in Comparative Religion*. 3 vols. London: Macmillan, 1918.
Friedlaender, S. "The Historical Significance of the Holocaust." *Jerusalem Quarterly* 1 (1976): 36–59.
Friedlander, G. *Hellenism and Christianity*. London: Vallentine and Sons, 1912.
———. *The Jewish Sources of the Sermon on the Mount*. London: G. Routledge and Sons, 1911.
Geiger, A. *Judaism and Its History*. trans. M. Mayer. London: Truebner, 1865.
Ginsberg, A. H. [Ahad Ha'am]. "Job and Prometheus." In *The Complete Writings of Ahad Ha'am* (Hebrew). Jerusalem: Dvir, 1974, pp. 280–81.
———. "The Transvaluation of Values." In *Selected Essays*, trans. L. Simon, pp. 217–41. Philadelphia: Jewish Publication Society of America, 1912.
Ginzberg, L. *Students, Scholars and Saints*. Philadelphia: Jewish Publication Society of America, 1925.
Gordis, R. "A Modern View of Revelation." *Understanding Conservative Judaism*. New York: Rabbinical Assembly, 1978, pp. 62–73.
Gottlieb, W., ed. *Essays and Addresses in Memory of Joseph Herman Hertz*. N.p.: Mizrachi Federation of Great Britain and Ireland, 1948.
Graetz, H. *History of the Jews*. Vol. 2. Philadelphia: Jewish Publication Society of America, 1956.
———. "The Significance of Judaism for the Present and the Future." *JQR* 2 (1890): 257–69.

———. *The Structure of Jewish History and Other Essays*. trans., ed., and intro. I. Schorsch. New York: Jewish Theological Seminary of America, 1975.
Greenberg, M. "The Biblical Grounding of Human Value." *The Samuel Friedland Lectures, 1960–66*. New York: Jewish Theological Seminary of America, 1966.
———. "Some Postulates of Biblical Criminal Laws." In *Yehezkel Kaufmann Jubilee Volume*, ed. M. Haran, pp. 5–28 (English section). Jerusalem: Magnes Press, 1960.
Gregoire, H. B. *An Essay on the Physical, Moral and Political Reformation of the Jews*. trans. London: C. Forster, Poultry, 1791.
Grunfeld, I. "Introduction to the First English Edition of Rabbi Samson Raphael Hirsch's Commentary on the Torah." In *The Pentateuch: Genesis*, trans. S. R. Hirsch and rendered into English by I. Levy. London: I. Levy, 1959.
Guttmann, M. *Das Judentum und seine Umwelt*. Berlin: Philo-Verlag, 1927.
———. "The Term 'Foreigner' (*nakery*) Historically Considered." *Hebrew Union College Annual* 3 (1926): 1–20.
Hahn, H. F. *The Old Testament in Modern Research*. Philadelphia: Fortress Press, 1966.
Halley, E. "Of the Cause of the Universal Deluge." In *Philosophical Transactions of the Royal Society of London* (1720–32), abridged, vol. 6, pt. 2 (London, 1733): 4l.
Hammer, R. "The God of Suffering." *Conservative Judaism* 31 (1976–77): 34–41.
Harris, M. "The Theologico-Historical Thinking of Samuel David Luzzatto." *JQR* 52 (1961–62): 215–44, 309–34.
Hartman, D. *A Living Covenant: The Innovative Spirit of Traditional Judaism*. New York: Macmillan, 1985.
———. "Maimonides' Approach to Messianism and Its Contemporary Implications." *Da'at* 2–3 (1978–79): 5–33.
———. *Maimonides: Torah and Philosophic Quest*. Philadelphia: Jewish Publication Society of America, 1976.
Heine, H. *A Biographical Anthology*. ed. H. Biber. English translation made or selected by M. Hadas. Philadelphia: Jewish Publication Society of America, 1976.
———. *Gesammelte Werke*. Berlin: Grotesche, 1887.
Heller, J. "Maimonides' Theory of Miracle." In *Between East and West: Essays Dedicated to the Memory of Bela Horvitz*, ed. A. Altmann, pp. 112–27. London: East and West Library, 1958.

Henoch, C. J. "The Religious Thought of Nachmanides—From His Exegesis of the Mitzvot." *Tradition* 11 (1970): 64–83.
Henriques, B. L. Q. *Sir Robert Waley Cohen*. London: Secker and Warburg, 1966.
Herford, R. T. *Pharisaism, Its Aim and Its Method*. London: Williams and Norgate, 1912.
———. *The Pharisees*. London: George Allen and Unwin, 1924.
———. "The Significance of Pharisaism." In *Judaism and the Beginnings of Christianity*. London: G. Routledge and Sons, 1923, pp. 125–66.
———. *What the World Owes to the Pharisees*. London: George Allen and Unwin, 1919.
Hertz, J. H., *Affirmations of Judaism*. London: Oxford University Press, 1927.
———. "Ancient Semitic Codes and the Mosaic Legislation." *Journal of Comparative Legislation and International Law* 10 (November 1928): 207–21.
———. "Bachya: The Jewish Thomas à Kempis." Jewish Theological Seminary Association Sixth Biennial Report. New York: Press of Philip Cowen, 1898.
———. *Early and Late*. London: Soncino Press, 1943.
———. *The Ethical System of James Martineau*. New York: n.p., 1894.
———. "Fundamental Ideals and Proclamations of Judaism." Jewish Library, 2d series. ed. L. Jung. New York: Bloch Publishing, 1930, pp. 53–73.
———. "Jewish Mysticism: An Historical Survey." *Hibbert Journal* 14 (July 1916): 784–98.
———. "Moses Maimonides: A General Estimate." In *Moses Maimonides*, ed. I. Epstein, pp. 3–10. London: Soncino Press, 1935.
———. *Mystic Currents in Ancient Israel*. Liverpool: University Press, 1926.
———. *The New Paths: Whither Do They Lead?* London: Oxford University Press, 1926.
———. *Sermons, Addresses and Studies*. 3 vols. London: Soncino Press, 1938.
———. *Seventieth Birthday Celebration of the Very Reverend J. H. Hertz*. London: Austin and Sons, 1942.
———, ed. *A Book of Jewish Thoughts*. London: Oxford University Press, 1935.
———, ed. *The Pentateuch and Haftorahs*. 5 vols. London and New York: Oxford University Press, 1929–36.

———, ed. *The Pentateuch and Haftorahs*. London: Soncino Press, 1938.
Hertzberg, A. "Modernity and Judaism." In *Great Confrontations in Jewish History*, ed. S. M. Wagner and A. P. Breck, pp. 123–35. Denver: University of Denver, 1977.
Hirsch, S. R. *The Collected Writings*. New York: Philipp Feldheim, 1988, from the German ed. of 1910.
———. *The Pentateuch: Deuteronomy*. trans. S. R. Hirsch and rendered into English by I. Levy. London: I. Levy, 1959.
———. *The Pentateuch: Exodus*. trans. S. R. Hirsch and rendered into English by Isaac Levy. London: I. Levy, 1959.
———. *The Pentateuch: Genesis*. trans. S. R. Hirsch and rendered into English by I. Levy. London: I. Levy, 1959.
———. *The Psalms*. New York: Philipp Feldheim, 1960.
Hoffmann, D. *Das Buch Deuteronomium*. Berlin: M. Poppelauer, 1913.
Hudaly, D. *Liverpool Old Hebrew Congregation: 1780–1974*. Liverpool: David Rume, 1974.
Husik, I. "Hellenism and Judaism." In *Philosophical Essays: Ancient, Medieval and Modern by Isaac Husik*, ed. M. C. Nahm and L. Strauss, pp. 3–14. Oxford: Basil Blackwell, 1952.
Hyamson, A. *Jews' College, London: 1855–1955*. London: R. H. Johns, 1955.
Inge, W. R. "The Indictment against Christianity." In *Outspoken Essays*. London: Longmans, Green, 1919, pp. 243–65.
———. "Religion." In *The Legacy of Greece*, ed. R. W. Livingstone, pp. 25–56. Oxford: Clarendon Press, 1921.
Jacobs, L. *We Have Reason to Believe*. London: Vallentine, 1957.
Jakobovits, I. *'If Only My People . . .'*. London: Weidenfeld and Nicolson, 1984.
The Jewish Chronicle. London: 1915, 1919, 1920, 1922, 1923, 1926, 1928, 1938.
The Jewish Chronicle Supplement. London: 1922, 1924, 1928, 1929.
The Jewish Encyclopedia. 1903. s.v. "Allegorical Interpretation," L. Ginzberg.
———. 1903. s.v. "Allegory in the Old Testament," I. M. Casanowicz.
———. 1903. s.v. "Christianity," K. Kohler.
———. 1903. s.v. "Evolution," E. G. Hirsch.

Joseph, M. *The Message of Judaism*. New York: Bloch Publishing, 1907.
Kalisch, M. *The Book of Genesis*. London: Longman, Brown, Green, Longman's and Roberts, 1858.
———. *A Historical and Critical Commentary on the Old Testament: Exodus*. London: Longman, Brown, Green, Longman's and Roberts, 1855.
Karp, A. *A History of the United Synagogue of America (1913–1963)*. New York: United Synagogue of America, 1964.
———. "The Origins of Conservative Judaism." *Conservative Judaism* 19 (Summer 1965): 33–48.
Katz, J. *Exclusiveness and Intolerance*. New York: Oxford University Press, 1961.
Kaufmann, Y. *The Religion of Israel from Its Beginnings to the Babylonian Exile*. trans. M. Greenberg. Chicago: University of Chicago Press, 1960.
———. *Toldot ha-Emunah ha-Yisre'elit*. Vol. 2, bk. 1. Tel Aviv: Dvir, 1976.
Kirkpatrick, A. F. "The Claims of Criticism upon the Clergy and Laity." In *The Higher Criticism*, S. R. Driver and A. F. Kirkpatrick, pp. 3–14. London: Hodder and Stoughton, 1905.
Klausner, J. "Judah and Greece—Two Opposites?" In *Judaism and Humanism*. Vol. 1 (Hebrew). Jerusalem: Mada, 1955, pp. 214–30.
Koebben, A. J. F. "Comparativists and Non-Comparativists in Anthropology." In *Handbook of Method in Cultural Anthropology*, ed. R. Naroll and R. Cohen, pp. 581–96. New York: Natural History Press, 1970.
Kohler, K. *Jewish Theology*. New York: Macmillan, 1918.
Kohut, A. *The Ethics of the Fathers*. trans. M. Cohen. New York: American Hebrew, 1885.
———. "Secular and Theological Studies." *The Menorah* 13 (July 1892): 49.
———. "What the Hebrew Scriptures Have Wrought for Mankind." In *Neely's History of the Parliament of Religions and Religious Congresses at the World's Columbian Exposition*, ed. W. R. Houghton. Chicago: F. T. Neely, 1893.
———. "Which Is Right? A Talmudic Disputation." In *Tradition and Change: The Development of Conservative Judaism*, ed. M. Waxman. New York: Burning Bush Press, 1958.
Leibowitz, N. *Studies in the Book of Genesis*. trans. A. Neuman. Jerusalem: World Zionist Organization, 1972.

Leiman, S. "Dwarfs on the Shoulders of Giants." *Tradition* 27 (1993): 90–94.
Littel, F. *The Crucifixion of the Jews.* New York: Harper and Row, 1975.
Livingstone, R. W. *Greek Ideals in Modern Life.* London: Oxford University Press, 1935.
———. *The Influence of the Greek and Hebrew Traditions on Western Ideals.* London: The Liberal Jewish Synagogue, 1959.
Loewinger, S., ed. *Jewish Studies in Memory of Michael Guttmann.* Budapest: n.p., 1946.
Loewinger, S. "Professor Yehiel Michael Guttmann" [Hebrew]. In *Hokhmat Yisrael be-Ma'arav Eropah,* ed. S. Federbush, pp. 131–47. Jerusalem: Neuman, 1958.
Lofthouse, W. F. "Hebrew Religion from Moses to Saul." In *The People and the Book,* ed. A. S. Peake, pp. 221–53. Oxford: Clarendon Press, 1925.
Margolies, M. *Samuel David Luzzatto: Traditionalist Scholar.* New York: Ktav, 1979.
Marx, A. *Essays in Jewish Biography.* Philadelphia: Jewish Publication Society of America, 1947.
McFayden, J. E. "The Present Position of Old Testament Criticism." In *The People and the Book,* ed. A. S. Peake, pp. 183–219. Oxford: Clarendon Press, 1925.
Mendes-Flohr, P. R. "Secular Religiosity: Reflections on Post-Traditional Jewish Spirituality and Community." In *Approaches to Modern Judaism,* ed. M. L. Raphael, pp. 19–30. Chico, Calif.: Scholars Press, 1983.
Meyer, M. A. *Response to Modernity: A History of the Reform Movement in Judaism.* New York: Oxford University Press, 1988.
Miller, P. D., Jr. "Wellhausen and the History of Israel's Religion." *Semeia* 25 (1982): 61–73.
Montefiore, C. G. *The Bible for Home Reading.* Vol. 1. London: Macmillan, 1897.
———. "Dr. Friedlaender on the Jewish Religion." *JQR* 4 (1892): 204–44.
———. *Judaism and Saint Paul.* London: Max Goschen, 1914.
———. *Liberal Judaism and Hellenism.* London: Macmillan, 1918.
———. *Old Testament and After.* London: Macmillan, 1923.
———. *Outlines of Liberal Judaism.* London: Macmillan, 1923.
———. "A Plea for the Old Testament." *The Nineteenth Century* 90 (1921): 831–38.

———. "Rabbinic Judaism and the Epistle of Saint Paul." *JQR* 13 (1901): 161–217.

———. "Some Notes on the Effect of Biblical Criticism upon the Jewish Religion." *JQR* 4 (1892): 293–306.

———. *The Synoptic Gospels*. London: Macmillan, 1909 and 1927.

———, and H. Loewe. *A Rabbinic Anthology*. London: Macmillan, 1938.

Moore, G. F. "Christian Writers on Judaism." *Harvard Theological Review* 14 (1921): 197–254.

———. *A Critical and Exegetical Commentary on Judges*. Edinburgh: T. and T. Clark, 1895.

———. *Judaism*. Vol. 1. Cambridge, Mass.: Harvard University Press, 1927.

———. "The Rise of Normative Judaism." *Harvard Theological Review* 17 (1924): 307–73.

Morais, H. *The Jews of Philadelphia*. Philadelphia: Levytype, 1894.

———. "Sabato Morais: A Memoir." Jewish Theological Seminary Association Sixth Biennial Report. New York: Press of Philip Cowen, 1898.

Morais, S. "Can We Change the Ritual?" In *Tradition and Change: The Development of Conservative Judaism*, ed. M. Waxman. New York: Burning Bush Press, 1958.

———. "Luzzatto's Introduction to the Pentateuch." In *Italian Jewish Literature*, ed. J. Greenstone. New York: Jewish Theological Seminary of America, 1926.

———. "Samuel David Luzzatto." In *Italian Jewish Literature*, ed. J. Greenstone. New York: Jewish Theological Seminary of America, 1926.

———. "The Talmud." *The Occident* 26 (26 July 1868): 165–66.

Neufeld, E. "The Prohibition against Loans at Interest." *Hebrew Union College Annual* 26 (1955): 355–412.

Neumark, D. "The Beauty of Japhet in the Tents of Shem." In *Essays in Jewish Philosophy*. Vienna: Central Conference of American Rabbis, 1929, pp. 10–22.

Newman, S. *Emendations of the Authorized Version of the Old Testament*. London: Wertheim, Paternoster-Row, 1839.

Nussenbaum, M. "Champion of Orthodox Judaism: A Biography of the Reverend Sabato Morais, LL.D." D.H.L. diss., Yeshiva University, 1964.

Oesterley, W. "Worship and Ritual." In *The People and the Book*, ed. A. S. Peake, pp. 323–51. Oxford: Clarendon Press, 1925.

The Oxford Universal Dictionary. 3d ed. Revised, 1955.
Paneth, P. *Guardian of the Law.* London: Allied Book Club, 1943.
Philipson, D. "History of the Hebrew Union College: 1875–1925." *Hebrew Union College Jubilee Volume (1875–1925).* Cincinnati, n.p., 1925.
Philipson, D., and L. Grossman, ed. *Selected Writings of Isaac Mayer Wise.* Cincinnati: Robert Clarke, 1900.
Rawlinson, G. *Ancient History.* New York: Colonial Press, 1900.
———. "Moses, the Author of the Levitical Code of Laws." In *Lex Mosaica*, ed. R. V. French, pp. 21–52. London: Eyre and Spottiswoode, 1894.
Reich, E. *The Failure of 'Higher Criticism'.* London: James Nisbet, 1905.
Reichert, V. E. "The Contribution of Claude G. Montefiore to the Advancement of Judaism on the Commemoration of His Seventieth Birthday." *Central Conference of American Rabbis Yearbook* 38 (1928): 499–520.
Reines, A. J. "Maimonides' Concept of Miracles." *Hebrew Union College Annual* 45 (1974): 243–85.
Renan, E. *History of the People of Israel.* Vol. 2. Boston: Little, Brown, 1912; vol. 5, Boston: Little, Brown, 1907.
Richardson, G. H. *Biblical Archaeology: Its Use and Abuse.* London: J. Clarke, 1935.
Robertson, J. M. *Ernest Renan.* London: Watts, 1924.
Rosenbaum, S. "Taking Interest from a Non-Jew in the Biblical Period" [Hebrew]. *Ha-Mishpat ha-Ivri* 2 (1926): 191–94.
Roth, C., ed. *The Ritual Murder Libel and the Jews: The Report by Cardinal Lorenzo Ganganelli.* London: Woburn Press, 1935.
Sanders, J. A. *Suffering as Divine Discipline in the Old Testament and Post-Biblical Judaism.* Rochester: Colgate Rochester Divinity School, 1955.
Sayce, A. H. "The Archaeological Witness to the Literary Activity of the Mosaic Age." In *Lex Mosaica*, ed. R. V. French, pp. 3–18. London: Eyre and Spottiswoode, 1894.
———. *Monument, Facts and Higher Critical Fancies.* London: Religious Tract Society, 1904.
———. Review of *Lectures on the Religion of the Semites*, by W. R. Smith. *The Academy* 36 (30 November 1889): 357–58.
Schechter, S. "The Charter of the Seminary." *Seminary Addresses and Other Papers.* Cincinnati: Ark Publishing, 1915, pp. 11–13.

———."Four Epistles to the Jews of England." Studies in Judaism, 2d ser. Philadelphia: Jewish Publication Society of America, 1908, pp. 182–201.

———. "Higher Criticism—Higher Anti-Semitism." In *Seminary Addresses and Other Papers*. Cincinnati: Ark Publishing, 1915, pp. 35–39.

———. "The Law and Recent Criticism." *JQR* 3 (1891): 754–66. Reprinted in S. Schechter, Studies in Judaism, 1st ser. Philadelphia: Jewish Publication Society of America, 1896, pp. 283–305.

———. "Nachmanides." *JQR* 5 (1893): 78–121. Reprint, S. Schechter, Studies in Judaism, 1st ser. Philadelphia: Jewish Publication Society of America, 1896, pp. 99–141.

———. *Some Aspects of Rabbinic Theology*. London: A. and C. Black, 1909.

———. "The Study of the Bible." Studies in Judaism, 2d ser. Philadelphia: Jewish Publication Society of America, 1908, pp. 31–54.

Schorsch, I. "Zacharias Frankel and the European Origins of Conservative Judaism." *Judaism* 30 (1981): 344–54.

Schuerer, E. *A History of the Jewish People in the Time of Jesus Christ*. Vol. 2, pt. 2. New York: Scribner and Sons, 1891.

Schweid, E. "Judaism and the Solitary Jew." *Shefa* 2 (1981): 38–45.

Sellin, E. "Archaeology versus Wellhausenism." The Aftermath Series. ed. H. M. du Bose. Nashville: Publishing House of the M. E. Church, South, 1924.

Shaftesley, J. M. "Religious Controversies." In *A Century of Anglo-Jewish Life: 1870–1970*, ed. S. Levin, pp. 93–113. London: United Synagogue, 1973?.

Shargel, B. *Practical Dreamer: Israel Friedlaender and the Shaping of American Judaism*. New York: Jewish Theological Seminary of America, 1985.

Skinner, J. *A Critical and Exegetical Commentary on Genesis*. Edinburgh: T. and T. Clark, 1910.

Smend, R. "Julius Wellhausen and His Prolegomena to the History of Israel." *Semeia* 25 (1982): 1–20.

Smith, G. A. *The Cambridge Bible for Schools and Colleges: The Book of Deuteronomy*. Cambridge: Cambridge University Press, 1919.

———. *The Historical Geography of the Holy Land*. London: Collins, 1966.

Smith, J. M. Powis. *The Moral Life of the Hebrews*. Chicago: University of Chicago Press, 1923.

Smith, M. "The Work of George Foot Moore." *Harvard Library Bulletin* 15 (1967): 169–79.
Smith, W. R. *Kinship and Marriage in Early Arabia.* Cambridge: Cambridge University Press, 1885.
———. *Lectures on the Religion of the Semites.* London: A. and C. Black, 1937. Introduction by S. A. Cook. Reprint, New York: Ktav, 1969, with a prolegomenon by James Muilenberg.
———. *The Old Testament in the Jewish Church.* London: A. and C. Black, 1902.
———. *The Prophets of Israel and Their Place in History.* London: A. and C. Black, 1902.
Solomon, S. J. "Art and Judaism." *JQR* 13 (1901): 553–66.
Soloveichik, M., and Z. Rubashov. *Toledot Bikoret ha-Mikra.* Berlin: Dwir-Mikra, 1925.
Soloveitchik, J. B. *Reflections of the Rav.* ed. A. R. Besdin. Jerusalem: Jewish Agency, 1979.
Spinoza, B. de. *A Theologico-Political Treatise and a Political Treatise.* trans. R. H. M. Elwes. New York: Dover Publications, 1951.
Strauss, L. *Spinoza's Critique of Religion.* New York: Schocken Books, 1982.
Tal, U."Religious and Anti-Religious Roots of Modern Anti-Semitism." *The Leo Baeck Memorial Lecture* 14 (1971): 3–28.
Temkin, S. "Orthodoxy with Moderation: A Sketch of Joseph Herman Hertz." *Judaism* 24 (1975): 278–95.
Thompson, R. J. "Moses and the Law in a Century of Criticism since Graf." Supplements to *Vetus Testamentum* 19 (1970): 1–173.
Twersky, I. *Introduction to the Code of Maimonides (Mishneh Torah).* New Haven: Yale University Press, 1980.
Velikovsky, I. *Worlds in Collision.* New York: Doubleday, 1950.
Wace, H. "Summary." In *Lex Mosaica,* ed. R. V. French, pp. 609–18. London: Eyre and Spottiswoode, 1894.
Wallace, A. R. *The Action of Natural Selection upon Man.* New Haven, Conn.: Charles C. Chatfield, 1871.
———. *Man's Place in the Universe.* London: Chapman and Hall, 1914.
Weinfeld, M. "Julius Wellhausen's Understanding of the Law of Ancient Israel and Its Fallacies" (Hebrew). *Shenaton* 4 (1980): 62–93.
Weiss, I. H. *Dor Dor ve-Dorshav.* Vol. 1. Vilna: Romm, 1904.
Welch, A. "The History of Israel." In *The People and the Book,* ed. Arthur S. Peake, pp. 121–50. Oxford: Clarendon Press, 1925.

Wellhausen, J. *Prolegomena to the History of Ancient Israel.* trans. J. S. Black and A. Menzies, with preface by W. R. Smith. Edinburgh: A. and C. Black, 1885.

Werner, A. "Heinrich Heine (1797–1856): On the 100th Anniversary of the Poet's Death." *Jewish Quarterly* 3 (winter 1956): 24–26.

Wise, I. M. *Pronaos to Holy Writ.* Cincinnati: Robert Clarke, 1891.

Wolfson, H. *Philo.* Vol. 2. Cambridge, Mass.: Harvard University Press, 1947.

———. "Spinoza and Religion." *Menorah Journal* 38 (1950): 146–67.

Wooley, C. L. *The Excavations at Ur and the Hebrew Records.* London: Allen and Unwin, 1929.

Yahuda, A. S. *The Language of the Pentateuch in Its Relation to Egyptian.* London: Oxford University Press, 1933.

Zangwill, I. *Children of the Ghetto.* London: W. Heinemann, 1902.

———. *Chosen Peoples: The Hebraic Ideal versus the Teutonic.* London: George Allen and Unwin, 1918.

Zunz, L. "On Rabbinic Literature." In *The Jew in the Modern World: A Documentary History,* ed. P. R. Mendes-Flohr and J. Reinharz, pp. 196–204. New York: Oxford University Press, 1980.

Index of Biblical and Rabbinic Citations

Compiled by Gerard Weinberg, M.D.
Edited by Bella Hass Weinberg, D.L.S.

Scope
This index covers primary texts and codes that are referenced by chapter and verse or volume and section number. It does not cover notes containing only page references to the Hertz *Pentateuch*. Commentaries not included here are listed in the Index of Names and Subjects, as are entries for cited modern authors and topical discussions of texts.

Arrangement
The cited works are arranged in the following sequence:

BIBLE	MIDRESHEI AGGADAH
HALEVI, JUDAH	MIDRESHEI HALAKHAH
The Kuzari	MISHNAH
KARO, JOSEPH	NEW TESTAMENT
Shulhan Arukh	TALMUD, BABYLONIAN
MAIMONIDES	TALMUD, PALESTINIAN
The Eight Chapters	ZOHAR
The Commandments	
Mishneh Torah	
Guide of the Perplexed	

Indexer's Note: In consultation with Dr. Menahem Schmelzer, former Provost of the Jewish Theological Seminary, the cited works were originally arranged chronologically, as is traditional in Hebrew citation indexes. Under the direction of the current Provost, Dr. Jack Wertheimer, and with the consent of the author, the cited works were rearranged alphabetically. —B.H.W.

BIBLE

Genesis

1:10	161
3:6-8	232n213
3:20	68
5:1	102
8:1	101
12:6	69
14:18-20	70
15:16	68
15:18	224n87
22	127
29:11	169
29:31	169
32:5	226n119
35:2	126
36:8, 12	147
37:3	150
37:36	64
38:2	126
47:21	224n63
49:10	71
50:10	226n119

Exodus

3:21-22	127
3:22	169, 204n54
4:24	234n17
6:2	230n177
8:14	230n177
11:2-3	127
12:8f.	65
12:15	169, 226n119
12:35-36	127
12:49	131
13:2	226n119
13:16	230n177
14:21	230n177
15	158
16:15	69
16:29	226n119
20:8, 10	226n119
20:21	60, 61
21:15	129
21-24	226n119
22:17	127
22:20	131
23:10f.	132
23:19	204n54
24:10	157
25:4	226n119
25:40	157-158, 226n119
27:1	226n119
27:20	226n119
28:11-12	71
28:36	230n171
29:4	230n171
30:7	230n171
34:3	226n119

Leviticus

1:3	230n171
2:1	230n171
6:5-6	155
7:30	230n171
8:31	204n54
9:21	230n171
12:6	230n171
13:14	226n119
16:6	226n119
16:8	230n171
16:21-22	230n171
17	150
17:7	44
17:8	226n119
17:10-14	101
17:34	230n171
18:4	146
18:5	226n119
18:25	224n87

Index of Biblical and Rabbinic Citations 257

18:26-28	130	12	150
19:11-16	226n119	12:5	204n54
19:16	171	12:11	204n54
19:18	103, 119, 226n119	12:21	226n119
		13:1	88
19:33	226n119	13:13-19	116
19:34	103, 131	14:21	65
20:4	152	15:3	127, 132, 134, 221n44
20:9	226n119		
24:22	108, 131	15:19-23	64
25:10, 13	99	15:20	64, 205n71
25:35, 36	134	16:7	65
26	67	20:10	222n46
26:31	230n171	20:10-18	127
26:44	141	21:18-21	127, 129
		21:23	93
Numbers		22:11	68
5	114, 127	23:19	68
5:15	230n171	23:21	127, 131, 132, 134, 135
14:25	206n106		
15:16	131	24:16	67
18:17-19	64	24:17	131
23:9	146	25:11-12	214n100
23:19	213n92	27:2	72
31	221n26	28:29	104
		29:25	224n87
Deuteronomy		32:15	139
1:1	64	*Joshua*	
1:40	206n106	5:1	65
3:20, 25	65	9:1	65
4:1	150	12:7	65
4:17	78	*Judges*	
4:19	130, 215n149	8:24	205n70
4:20	225n99	11	127
4:39	226n119	11:30-31	220n19
6:5,7	226n119	11:31	129, 220n22
7:20	71		
8:10	226n119	*1 Samuel*	
8:18	230n177	2:13, 15	65
10:3	226n119	12:17	158
10:19	108, 131	15:29	213n92
11:30	65		

2 Samuel
  13:18   69, 150

2 Kings
  14:6   68

Isaiah
  1   145
  27:6   177
  42:6   136
  48:10   225n99
  50:3   158

Jeremiah
  5:3   225n99
  21:6   101
  31:18   225n99
  31:52   228n137

Hosea
  2:8-10   225n104
  13:2   108

Zechariah
  13:8-9   225n99
  14:21   126

Malachi
  1:11   213n85

Psalms
  8:3   100
  36:6   101
  66:10-11   225n99
  89:15   94
  90:4   161

Job
  5:17   225n99
  23:10   225n99
  33:14-28   225n99
  36:15   225n99

Nehemiah
  10:37   205n71

2 Chronicles
  35:13   65

HALEVI, JUDAH
The Kuzari
  I, 8,11   230n177
  I, 13-25   230n175
  I, 67   230n177
  I, 83-87, 89   230n177
  I, 86, 88, 91   204n47
  I, 103, 109   223n61
  II, 56   223n60

KARO, JOSEPH
Shulhan Arukh—Yoreh De'ah
  Hilkhot Avodat Kokhavim
  141:1   218n214
  151:11   222n44

MAIMONIDES
The Eight Chapters
  36   199n71, 232n202
  76–78   227n127
  90   230n126

The Commandments (Positive)
  142   222n45
  198   222n45

Mishneh Torah
  Hilkhot Yesodei ha-Torah
  8:1-3   230n175
  Hilkhot Avodah Zarah
  9:4   216n167
  11:12   224n74
  Hilkhot Teshuvah
  6:8   229n161
  Hilkhot Keri'at Shema
  4:8   229n152

Index of Biblical and Rabbinic Citations

Hilkhot Kiddush ha-Hodesh
17:4   232n202
17:24 199n71

Hilkhot Ishut
21:10 217n189

Hilkhot Ma'aseh Hakorbanot
4:11   230n166

Hilkhot Zekhiyah u-Matanah
3:11   222n44

Hilkhot Malveh ve-Loveh
5:1   221n44

Hilkhot Mamrim
2:4   228n145
2:9   229n145

Hilkhot Melakhim
8:11   229n163
11:4   200n87

Guide of the Perplexed
I   231n182, 232n212
I, 54   213n92, 221n29
II, 24   229n163
II, 25   232n212
II, 29   161, 230n176, 231n179, 232n213
II, 30   232n213
II, 42   231n180
III, 27   210n8, 213n92, 225n105
III, 28   229n161
III, 29   227n129
III, 32   230n169, 231n189
III, 41   228n145
III, 45   229n163
III, 50   231n179

MIDRESHEI AGGADAH

Midrash ha-Gadol
Genesis
39:20   206n96

Midrash Lekakh Tov
Genesis
39:20   206n96

Midrash on Psalms
34   231n195

Midrash Rabbah
Genesis
3:9   231n195
5:5   230n178
7:7   42
8:2   231n197
16:5   233n213
19:8   231n197
41:9   225n91, n99
48:3   215n135
65:21   219n10
67:7   219n10
76:2   215n140
87:9   206n96

Exodus
2:5   224n66, 225n95
21:6   230n178
36:1   227n129
41:6   228n140

Leviticus
6:5   224n64
22:8   201n114

Song of Songs
1:2   226n118

Ecclesiastes
3:11   231n195

Midrash Zuta on Megillat Ruth
4:2   218n198

Pesikta de-Rab Kahana
- 14:3 — 225n99
- 23:2 — 225n99

Pirkei de-Rabbi Eliezer
- 24 — 212n46

Tanna de-vei Eliyahu
- 9 — 213n80

Yalkut Shimeoni
- I, 663 — 215n143

MIDRESHEI HALAKHAH

Sifrei: Deuteronomy
- 32 — 225n99
- 193 — 214n100

MISHNAH

Shevi'it
- 10:3–4 — 229n155

Sanhedrin
- 6:4 — 220n17

Makkot
- 3:15 — 215n129

Avot
- 5:6 — 230n178

NEW TESTAMENT

Matthew
- 5:43 — 113

Romans
- 7:23 — 219n2

2 Corinthians
- 12:9 — 219n2

Galatians
- 3:28 — 213n80

TALMUD, BABYLONIAN

Berakhot
- 5a — 228n143
- 31b — 232n212

Shabbat
- 55b — 233n213
- 105b — 218n198
- 119b — 214n109

Rosh Hashanah
- 17b — 213n92

Yoma
- 21b — 230n172
- 67a-b — 229n151
- 67b — 227n127

Betzah
- 25b — 227n128
- 32b — 215n138

Megillah
- 24b — 215n143

Yevamot
- 71a — 232n212
- 79a — 215n138

Ketubbot
- 105b — 212n63

Sotah
- 11b — 218n198
- 47a-b — 217n192

Gittin
- 59b — 221n35
- 61a — 222n44
- 90b — 218n198

Kiddushin
- 31a — 215n145, 235n44

Bava Kamma
- 84a — 217n186

Bava Metzia
- 31b — 232n212
- 35a — 212n66
- 59a — 218n198
- 59b — 212n50, 230n175
- 70b — 222n44

Index of Biblical and Rabbinic Citations

Bava Batra
12a	226n118
111b	5

Sanhedrin
24b–25a	222n47
38a	215n127
43a	229n156
46a	214n113
59a	215n128
71a	220n23
82a	235n31
109b	212n48

Makkot
24a	222n44

Avodah Zarah
20a	222n44
54b	230n176

Zevahim
46b	230n166

Menahot
29a	231n182

Arakhin
11a	232n212

TALMUD, PALESTINIAN

Peah
II, 6	228n140

Hagigah
I, 8	228n140

ZOHAR

1:352	230n175

Index of Names and Subjects

Compiled by Bella H. Weinberg, D.L.S.

Scope

The index includes significant terms and names, including all cited authors, as well as editors and translators of anonymous classics. Modern works entered under author are not indexed under title, except for the works of Rabbi Hertz. References to passages of the classic works of Judaism are covered by the Index of Biblical and Rabbinic Citations; general discussions of these works are indexed here.

Arrangement

The index entries are arranged in the word-by-word method. A space precedes a letter; a hyphen is treated as a space. Filing stops at parenthetical qualifiers. Thus *de Sola Pool* precedes *death*; *Mendes-Flohr* precedes *Mendes, Henry*; and *David (King)* precedes *David ben Samuel*.

Abbreviations

A = Arabic
Ar. = Aramaic
H = Hebrew
L = Latin
mss. = manuscripts
n = note

Aaron 157
Abarbanel x, 44–45
abbeys, medieval 92
Abbot, Lyman 57, 162, 204n40–41, 231n201–232n201, 240
Abelson, Joshua: on biblical criticism 62–63; career 36–37; correspondence 233n8; on Maimonides 37, 229n161; on rabbinic Judaism 37, 199n73; research associate xv, 3, 30, 33, 34, 35, 187–189, 198n56, 199n62, 211n32; sales of Commentary 167; works cited 199n74, 238, 240
Abihu 12, 155, 157
abolition *see* abrogation
Abraham (patriarch): chosenness 136; compassion 215n139; covenant with God 71; name change 68; plea for Sodom 104, 139; sacrifice of son 118, 130; sin of 124, 219n3; treatment of Hagar 214n100
Abraham ben David of Posquieres 134
Abrahams, Israel 34–35, 58, 153, 204n44, 213n88, 229n157–158, 240–241
Abram 68
Abramowitz, Herman 233n1, n7; 234n16
Abravanel x, 44–45
abrogation (repeal) of: biblical laws 114, 128, 150–151, 217n192, 228n145; rabbinic laws 151–152, 174, 229n152
academic study *see* scientific study
Academy of Jewish Learning 25–26
acknowledgment of associates 31, 33, 36, 89, 187–189, 200n88
action *see* deed
Adam: creation 42, 102; fall of 118
additions to halakhah 229n145
Adler, Cyrus 7, 14, 16, 192n23, 193n53, 196n76, 241
Adler, Hermann 21, 40
Adler, Marcus 21
adolescents *see* children; youth
adultery: divorce and 116, 117; Potiphar's wife 69, 93; suspected 114, 128, 151; upsurge in 217n192
advertisements for Commentary 187–188
aesthetics: Hellenism 81, 82, 83, 91, 97; personal religion 174
affection (virtue) 91, 115, 129, 139. *See also* love

Affirmations of Judaism (Hertz) 22, 23, 25, 246; Notes to Ch. 1: 194n60; Notes to Ch. 2: 196n2–5, n9; 197n15–17, n19; 200n95, n98, n100; 201n103–104, n122; Notes to Ch. 4: 211n24, n38; 213n88, 214n109, 218n198, 219n237; Notes to Ch. 6: 235n51, 236n64
aged parents 179
aggadah: in Commentary 29, 48, 128; Simon ben Shetach story 220n17
agnosticism 8
agriculture 99, 116, 135, 152
agunah (H) 11, 117, 218n195
Ahad Ha'am 82–83, 210n6, n10; 244
Aharei Mot: Haftarah 91
Ahaz 78
ahikha (H) 131
ahistorical readings 7, 149, 184, 229n146
Akabah 206n106
akedah (H) 118, 127, 130
Akiba 85
Alexandria 98
aliens *see* strangers
allegory 163–165, 232n208, n211, n212; 233n213
"alone among the nations" 227n129. *See also* separatism
alphabet, Hebrew 12
altar: asylum for murderers 99, 208n125; construction of 100; location 61; perpetual fire 155; sheds tears 218n198
alteration of laws *see* halakhah: change
altruism 95
am ha-aretz (H) 120, 219n223
Amalek: spirit of 139; tribe of 147
Amaziah 68
America *see* United States
American Hebrew 191n9, 192n11–13, n25, n27; 193n34–35, n43; 193n53–194n54
American Reform *see* Reform Judaism
Ammonites 128
Amos 95, 144, 145
amulets 12
anachronism: halakhah as xv, 175
analogy: parable and 232n208
anarchism: Liberal Judaism 38; morality and 180. *See also* chaos
Anaxagoras 98
ancestors, righteous 119
Anchor Bible 202n4, 207n114, 241

Index of Names and Subjects

ancient history 98. *See also* biblical history
ancient Judaism *see* Israelite religion
ancient languages *see* philology
ancient law *see* Greco-Roman law
ancient Near East *see* Near East, ancient
ancient religion 51, 52, 60, 61, 79, 172. *See also* paganism; Semitic religion
"Ancient Semitic Codes" (Hertz) 200n97, 211n34–35, 212n44, 216n152, 218n221, 246
ancient world *see* Greco-Roman civilization
angels 138, 154, 157
Anglican Church 116
"Anglican" rabbinate 21
Anglo Jewish Archives 237
Anglo-Jewish Preachers' Conference 32, 38
Anglo-Jewry *see* British Jewry
Anglo-Saxons 119
animalism 122, 136, 179, 185, 223n62
animals: Azazel 151, 154; cruelty to 100–101, 108; dead, meat of 44, 45; firstlings 64; forms of God 78; instincts 223n61; kindness to 101, 108, 121; man vs. 160, 162; place of slaughter 150; roasting 65; *shehitah* 108; slaves as 99; strength of 227n128. *See also* sacrifices, animal
annihilation of nations *see* genocide
annulling vows 129
anthropology, Christian 159
anthropology, cultural: and archaeology 78; on behavior 75, 76–77; biblical criticism and 5, 57; and Israelite religion 50, 52–54, 58, 73; on mercy 104
anthropology, religious 77, 79, 122, 159, 175
anthropomorphism 96, 97, 154, 164–165, 169, 226n107, 232n212
anti-Christian polemics 3, 90, 91, 120, 121, 176
anti-Nazism 212n60
anti-Semitism: of Apion 98; of Bible critics 21, 53, 87; Christian 113, 116, 185, 223n49, 236n71; German 134. *See also* bias: against Judaism; self-hating Jews
anti-Zionism 40
antinomianism 9, 13, 22, 58, 153, 160
Antiochus Epiphanes 98

antiquity of: Deuteronomy 60, 62, 67, 68, 206n98; Israelite ritual 61; Jewish mysticism 12; Joseph narrative 69; Leviticus 67; Mosaic Law 149; sacrifices 43; the Torah 58, 68, 73. *See also* dating
apartness *see* separatism
apathy, Jewish 8, 175
apes, descent from 162
Apion 98
apologetics 17, 39, 56, 102, 114, 195n72, 207n108
Arab: religion 54; tribesmen 76
Arabic language 37, 67, 68
archaeology: on ancient religion 60; Driver on 73; Gaster on 171; Hertz use of xv, 7, 29, 66–67, 69–73, 79, 162, 180; Israelite religion and 54–55; Mosaism and 78; proof of Bible 172, 207n109; proof of Flood 232n203; Wellhausen and 62, 209n135
archbishop of Canterbury 55, 221n37
archives: Egyptian 70; Hertz xiii, 237–238; Near Eastern 63
Aria College 36, 40
aristocracy 75, 108, 219n223
Aristotle 36, 38, 99, 102, 160, 200n83, 231n192
armies: against Israel 147; of Israel 63, 169
Arnold, Matthew 81, 94, 112, 210n1, n3; 212n67, 241
art: Egyptian 69, 71; Hebrew vs. Greek 236n63
ArtScroll commentaries 236n68
Aryan racial superiority 138
asceticism 12, 111, 119
aseret ha-dibrot (H) 226n108. *See also* Decalogue
Asher ben Jehiel 222n44
Asher, Joseph Mayor 16, 195n71
Ashkelon 220n17
assimilation, religious 1, 86, 148
Assyrian: culture 203n22; kings 71; laws 68
Assyriology 204n51
astronomy 161
asylum: to murderers 99, 113
Athanasius 102
atheism (godlessness) 39, 92; scientific 208n119
Athenian society *see* Greek civilization

atonement: Christianity 56; Hebraism 52; marriage and 119
atrocities *see* cruelty
Atticism 110
Augustine 110, 113
authenticity of: the Bible (*see* historicity of: the Torah); Israelite religion 59, 66; Judaism 13, 28, 49, 177, 183, 184; Mosaic Code 172; mysticism 12; prophets 155, 174; rabbinic Judaism 19, 87, 175; revelation 55. *See also* legitimacy
author of: Pentateuch (*see* human composition; Mosaic authorship); Prophets and Hagiographa 6, 8; Psalter 150, 229n148
authority: of God 55, 208n125; for halakhic change 11, 148; in Hellenism 111; of Jephthah 129; of law 57, 208n125; of oral law 228n139; of prophets 144; of rabbinic Judaism 25, 174; religious 174; of sages 144; of scholars 229n145; of Scripture 25, 44, 153, 175, 179; of *Shulhan Arukh* 10. *See also* power
autonomy: Kant on 96, 174
axioms: brotherhood 132; Christian 55, 118; Darwinism 4; of faith 225n107–226n107; Hertz's 13, 153, 184; Hirsch's 6; talmudic 7
Azazel 151, 154

ba-makom (H) 204n54
Babylonia 54, 66, 207n117, 223n62
Babylonian captivity 61, 67, 78, 209n137, 225n96. *See also* postexilic period
Babylonian code *see* Hammurabi, Code of
Babylonian culture 66, 91, 203n22, 205n79
Babylonian exile *see* Babylonian captivity
Babylonian Jewry 177
Babylonian society 75, 90, 92
Babylonian Talmud: editions cited 238. *See also* Talmud
"Bachya" (Hertz) 191n7, 246
Bachya ibn Paquda 178, 180, 235n55
Balaam's: ass 156, 157; blessing 146
balance (moderation) 117, 119
Balfour Declaration 40
Bamberger, B. 228n140, 241
Bar Kappara 218n198

barbarian (term) 103
barbarism: of ancient Hebrews 209n135; in the Bible 54, 127; Christianity and 40, 117, 123, 125, 128; in Egypt 93; in Greece 88, 92, 97–99, 236n63; in Hellenism 125; against Jews 142; of primitive races 101; in Western society 106, 184, 185. *See also* cruelty
Barbour, I. 231n198, 241
Barcelona, Disputation of 109, 216n168
Baron, Salo 221n40, 241
Barry, William 208n119, 241
Barth, Karl 231n198
beacon to the nations *see* light: unto the nations
beatitude 142
beauty: of art 236n63; in Hellenism 81, 82, 83, 91, 97; of Judaism 29, 37
bedikat hametz (H) 226n108
Bedouin law 76
Beecher, Henry Ward 38
beetles: plague 71
behavior: allegory and 163; change in 97; Christian 113; code of 159; evaluation of 135; genetic programming 223n61; God and 213n92; halakhah and 151; Hebraic vs. gentile 130; intellect vs. 82; of Jacob 124; of Jephthah 129; Jewish 139, 143; Jews as models of 224n66; law and 138, 180; of nations 136; Noachide laws 215n149; prophets and 144–145; psychology of 179; righteousness 88; social 61, 75, 77
Beidelman, T. O. 203n28, 241
Beinart, Chaim 216n168, 243
Beit ha-Behirah 222n44, 239
bekhol-ha-makom (H) 61, 204n54
belief *see* faith
Ben Azzai 102
Bene Hassein, Egypt 69
benediction *see* blessing
benefactors of *Pentateuch* 168, 199n70, 233n11. *See also* Blashki, Aaron
beneficence *see* charity
Benjamin 125
Bentwich, N. 203n14, 210n15, 241
Berkovits, Eliezer 236n73
Berlin Rabbinerseminar 15, 29
Besdin, A. R. 253
Beth Din 152

Index of Names and Subjects

bias: against Christianity 85, 90, 91; of Commentary 170, 222n46; against Jewish mysticism 12–13; against Judaism 2, 26, 56–57, 123, 153, 180–181, 202n10 (*see also* anti-Semitism); journalistic 201n123
Biber, Hugo 245
Bible: and Christian teaching 217n178; fulfillment in history 210n139; Jewish education 184; miracle stories in 231n180; Orthodox Judaism and 200n86; sequence of events 229n146; suffering in 225n99. *See also* Pentateuch; Torah
Bible, Christian *see* New Testament
Bible commentaries: Christian 2, 26, 46, 59, 133, 153, 184, 197n31; conceptions of 170; English language xv, 2, 26, 28, 35, 65, 167, 185; format 29; Jewish x, 28, 134, 153, 167, 173, 236n67–68; title pages 188. *See also* biblical interpretation
Bible translations: English 26, 34, 68, 169, 172, 239, 241, 247; —King James version 169, 220n22; German 205n71; Jewish 41, 129, 169, 218n212, 220n22, 234n16; Septuagint 102
Bible versions 204n54
Biblia Hebraica 187, 188
biblical archaeology *see* archaeology
biblical criticism, higher: anti-Semitism and 53, 87; archaeology and 67, 69–70; Christians against 55–56; contradictions in Pentateuch 63; evolutionary theory and 159–160; Gaster on 171; Hebrew language and 61; Hertz against 4, 9, 46–47, 55, 59–60, 62, 170, 174; history of 202n3; Jewish Theological Seminary against x, 5–6, 8; Kohut on 5, 6; on rabbinic Judaism 19–20, 50, 51, 52, 58, 78, 81, 87, 145; on uniqueness of Israelites 73. *See also* Documentary Hypothesis; Graf-Wellhausen school; Wellhausen, Julius
biblical criticism, lower 62
biblical exegesis *see* Bible commentaries; biblical interpretation
biblical Hebrew *see under* Hebrew language
biblical history 4, 9, 54, 60, 141–142, 145, 232n203. *See also* historicity

biblical instruction: Germany 138
biblical interpretation: allegory 232n208; anthropomorphisms 164; archaeology and 69; Christian 74; dogma and 172; ethics and 132–133; evolution and 233n213; German-Jewish scholars 205n71; Graf-Wellhausen school 50; halakhic change 152; Hertz criticized for 169–170; Hertz's method 204n54; on interest 221n37; Jewish 26–27, 128, 148; miracles 155; Mosaic authorship and 206n94; nuances of Hebrew 61; parable 232n213; principle of 153; of prophets 213n85; rabbinic 7; rationalism in 154; resolving contradictions 64–65; revelation and 180; sages and 144; on witchcraft 220n17. *See also peshat*
biblical law *see* Mosaic code
biblical personalities 123–125, 135, 219n2. *See also names*
biblical religion *see* Israelite religion
biblical society 132, 133
biblical theology 23, 113, 162
bigamy 118, 119
binding of Isaac 118, 127, 130
biology *see* evolution; race
birkat kohanim (H) 226n108
Birmingham: Hertz address 211n27
birthright 124
bishul (H) 65
Bissel, E. C. 203n36
Biur 205n71, 239
biur hametz (H) 226n108
blackness: eclipses 158
Blashki, Aaron: correspondence with Hertz 197n22, 198n56, 199n60, n64–70; 238; criticizes Hertz 35, 199n59; financial backer 30–31, 32, 198n49, n59; removes financial backing 33–34
blessing: of Balaam 146; *birkat kohanim* (H) 226n108; of Jacob 124; of Judah 125; marriage as 119; of woman 115, 217n194
Blidstein, G. 212n60, 241
blind men 104
blood: drawing 113, 115, 125; eating 101; libel 115; Nile river 231n186; relatives 212n51; revenge 52, 90; sprinkling of 230n166
bloodshed *see* killing; murder

bloodthirstiness 116
body welfare motif 143
boiling vs. roasting 65
Book of Jewish Thoughts (Hertz) 168, 173, 218n202, 219n236, 223n58, n60; 246
book reviews *see* reviews
borrowing: cultural 136, 196n10; linguistic 67, 68; money (*see* loans)
Braude, William G. 213n80, 225n99, 231n195, 239, 240
"breaking of the vessels" 12
Breslau seminary xi, 13, 15, 133, 176
bribery 106
Briggs, Charles A. 206n93, 241
British Empire: chief rabbi (*see* Chief Rabbi); sales of Commentary 167
British Jewry: Commentary for x, 2, 26, 171; Hertz address on 136; Liberal vs. Orthodox 22; Montefiore and 86; publications of 39; scholars 114; selection of chief rabbi 195n74; teachers of 46; youth of 1; Zionism and 40
Brooklyn Examiner 234n19
brotherhood of man 91, 93, 102, 103, 132, 139, 173, 222n44
Brown, Francis 206n93, 241
brutality *see* cruelty
Buber, S. 239, 240
Budapest rabbinical seminary 133
Buddhism 177
Buechler, Adolph: coeditor 29, 30, 32, 33, 89, 189, 198n56; Jews' College principal 26
burden of election 137, 141
Burghes, E. Noel 233n2, n4
burning of witches 220n17
burnt offerings 128–129, 154, 230n166. *See also* sacrifices
business 116, 132–135, 152
businessmen 132–133
Butcher, S. H. 210n3, 213n81, 241

Cabala 12, 13, 193n45, n47
calendar, Jewish 148
calling *see* mission
Cambridge Bible for Schools and Colleges 34, 46, 207n107, 221n39, 227n137, 243, 253
Cambridge University 1, 16, 50, 52, 53, 93, 153
Canaan (Palestine): animal forms of God 78; archaeology and 70; conquest of 68, 222n46; foreigners in 132; geography of 72; Israelites in 150; names of 69; paganism in 142; seven pagan nations 127, 130–131. *See also* Judah (kingdom)
Canaanite(s): Babylonian influence 207n117; genocide 130–131; hornets and 71; morality of 215n149; sparing of 222n46; translation of 126
cancellation of debts 131, 132, 133, 152
canon, biblical 62
Canon law 107, 109, 113, 116, 135, 217n190
capital offenses *see* death penalty
Caro, Joseph *see* Karo, Joseph
Casanowicz, I. M. 232n208, 247
caste system 75, 98
catalog of Hertz archives 237
catastrophes, national 63
catharsis: anti-Semitism as 185
"Catholic Israel" 15
Catholicism 109, 110, 111, 116, 176. *See also* Church
celibacy 118, 119
censorship: by Hertz 119, 126, 163, 217n186, 220n17, 228n137; in Western society 174
Centenary Bible 46
centralization of worship 60–61
ceremony *see* ritual
Chadwick, O. 231n198, 233n213, 241
Chajes, Zevi Perez 9
change: in halakhah (*see* halakhah: change); in religious truth 85. *See also* evolution, religious
chaos: moral 41, 91, 121; mysticism and 12; primeval 137
character: of biblical personalities 123–126; Divine 139; of Gaster 171; halakhah and 143, 165; Hellenism and 82; of Jewish people xvi, 135, 181; martyrdom and 130; of men 97, 162; morality and 140; preaching and 38; of rabbis 18; ritual and 145
charisma of prophets 144
charity 76, 94, 104, 133, 152
chastisement *see* punishment
chastity 115, 124, 125, 212n57, 217n192
chattel 94, 99, 107
Chavel, Charles B. 221n44, 222n45, 224n87, 239, 240
Chief Rabbi: office of 184; selection of 195n74
Chief Rabbi Adler 40

Index of Names and Subjects

Chief Rabbi Hertz: candidacy 195n73–74; Jewish Theological Seminary and 14–18; length of term 2; on Liberal Judaism 21, 23; pastoral tours 186; religious uniformity 24; secures visas for rabbis ix; on state of Judaism 19; workload 3, 28–33
children: affection for parents 91; crimes of parents 67; disobedient 127, 129; killing 76, 98, 100, 129–130 (*see also* sacrifices, human); as Messiahs 41, 100, 214n109; support of parents by 179. *See also* daughters; son; youth
Childs, B. S. 203n20, 241
chivalry 114, 115
Chosen People 135–138, 140–143; biblical critics on 53; Christians on 181; historical reality 165; humanitarianism xvi; Kohler on 223n59; laws of 148; morality and 122, 135, 147
Christ *see* Jesus
Christian bias 2, 26, 56–57, 123, 153, 181, 202n10
Christian scholars: allegory and 163; on archaeology 67; cited by Hertz 72, 207n108; on Hebraism 81; on Hebrew Bible (*see* biblical criticism, higher); Hertz rebuts 87; on Israelite religion 48, 61; on Jephthah 128; on Judaism 1–2, 6, 13, 26, 181, 202n10; on morality 86; on prophets 227n125; on revelation 213n86; on science vs. theology 231n198; on Talmud 38
Christian sects 113
Christian sources *see under* source analysis of Commentary
Christian triumphalism 56, 84, 175
Christianity: allegory and 164; barbarism and 123, 125; Berkovits on 236n73; bloodthirstiness 116; Commentary on 200n91; cruelty to animals 108; Edom and 126; Esau and 176; ethics (*see* ethics, Christian); Graetz on 176; Hebraism and 81–82, 84, 112; Hebrew Scriptures and 217n178; Hellenism and (*see under* Hellenism); Hertz on 36, 87, 92, 118–119, 136, 175, 181–182; Holocaust and 185; image worship 118, 218n214; inwardness 36, 94; Jewish ethics in 176; Judaism and 81, 84–85, 87, 117, 138, 141, 174, 177, 183, 211n25; vs. Judaism xv, 1, 18, 39, 49, 52, 88, 89, 91, 112, 115, 120; Kohler on 119, 176; Liberal Judaism and 22–23, 47; Mendes on 177; Montefiore on 21, 84, 123; morality (*see* ethics, Christian); Noeldeke on 210n3; paganism and (*see under* paganism); prophetic religion and 57; Rabbinism and 51, 56; rejection of Jews 184; virgin birth 218n212; Wellhausen on 5, 9, 202n7; Western civilization and 181; wife-beating 114. *See also* Church; Jesus; New Testament
Christology 26, 41
chronological order of Bible 229n146
Church: allegory used 164; cruelty of 99, 126, 128, 176, 185; early 20, 49; Hellenism and 111; image worship 118; immorality 109, 123; law (*see* Canon law); on marriage 115; medieval 84, 92, 112–114, 116; paganism and 120; ritual murder 116; social apathy 216n177; successor of Judaism 56
circumcision 22
citation analysis of Commentary: Aristotle 231n192; Christian sources 178; Cornill 209n137; Driver 72; earlier Hertz works 41, 90, 114, 211n36–39, 213n88, 214n109, 218n198, 219n222; Geiger 223n58; Graetz 224n72; Guttmann 221n41; Herford 235n36; Jewish commentators 134; Kalisch 232n206; Karo 228n145; Kimchi 220n22; Kuzari 138, 223n60; Maimonides 155, 228n145, 229n152, n161; mystical writings 153; non-Jewish commentators 184; rabbinic literature 145; Rawlinson 204n51; Renan 207n119; Smith, G.A. 207n107, 227n137–228n137; Wellhausen critics 57; world literature 183. *See also* source analysis
cities, heathen 222n46
City College, New York 2
city-states 98
civil law: Babylonian 90; Mosaic 41, 59, 73, 75, 143; rabbinic 152, 226n119; Roman 108
civil rights 99, 121, 184
civility: mercy and 104

civilization, human 179
civilization, Israelite 59
civilization, Jewish: achievements of 122; anti-Semitism and 134; care for needy 131–132; vs. Christian 91; educational role 137; evolution of 148; fertilization 183 (*see also* cultural contact); Hebraism and 81; Hertz glorifies xv, 3, 18, 28, 47, 48–49, 123, 177, 180; insularity 21 (*see also* separatism); modernity of 175; Schechter on 27; superiority of 136, 180; treatment of strangers 131
civilized nations 83, 91, 101, 121
class struggle 98
classical world *see* Greco-Roman civilization
classification of: Hertz archives 237; miracles 157, 158
cleansing, ritual 151, 154
clergy: Christian 216n173; on evolution 231n201; Jewish (*see* rabbis); subject to law 100
coal: perpetual fire 155
coat of many colors 69
Code of Hammurabi *see* Hammurabi, Code of
codes of law 57, 121, 172; Jewish 10, 113
codifiers, rabbinic 150. *See also* decisors, rabbinic; Karo, Joseph; Maimonides
Cohen, Abraham: career 38; correspondence with Hertz 198n50–52, n56; 199n75, n77; 211n32, 230n170, 234n16; edited by Hertz 91; edits Commentary 89; on Hellenism 82, 210n9; on Maimonides 36, 38, 199n71, 200n83; on Midrash 231n195; on Oral Law 149–150, 228n144; on preaching 37, 199n79; research associate xv, 3, 30, 33, 35–36, 37, 187–189, 198n53, 199n62; revises manuscripts 32; on Talmud 38, 199n80, 238; on witchcraft 220n17; on women 217n194; works cited 238, 239, 241–242
Cohen, Arthur Allen 203n13, 242
Cohen, David 210n9
Cohen, N. 231n200, 242
Cohen, Robert Waley 23, 25, 26, 197n21, 201n123
Coleridge, Samuel Taylor 236n66
collaborators: of Hertz (*see* research associates); Nazi 185

Columbia University 2
comets: miracles 157
commandments: benefits of 11; cultic (*see* ritual: laws); diminishing 88, 150; doing vs. keeping 146; engraved on stones 72; on interest 222n44; marriage and 115; priestly 155; separatism and 147; on strangers 93, 134; women and 218n195. *See also* halakhah
Commandments, Ten *see* Decalogue
commentaries, biblical *see* Bible commentaries
Commentary (Hertz) *see* Pentateuch (Hertz)
commerce 116, 132–135, 152
commitment, religious 1, 56, 63, 173, 176, 201n125, 228n137. *See also* observance
common folk *see* laymen
common law 74, 109, 113, 114, 217n190
common sense: ethics 179
communal unity 24
communion with God 37, 102
communism 121
community: Jews' concern for 166; sin of 154; unity of 24
comparative: law 131, 172, 208n125; philology 66, 68; religion 20, 53–55, 73, 77–78, 172, 180, 209n136
compassion (= pity; sympathy) xvi, 92, 104, 105, 121, 127, 129, 215n139; lack of (*see* cruelty)
complexity: of religion 4, 60, 66, 159. *See also* simplicity
comprehension *see* understanding
concentration camps, Egyptian 224n63
conduct *see* behavior
confession: extortion of 128; of sins 219n2; *viddui* (H) 226n108
confiscation of property 105
conflagration *see* fire
conformity, religious 61, 146
Confucianism 177
Congregation Mikveh Israel 194n53, 242
congregations *see* synagogues
conscience 124, 137, 174, 179, 185
consciousness: Jewish xvi, 22, 140, 147, 166, 182, 197n11; of Jewish values 223n62
consecration *see* holiness
conservative biblical scholarship 63
"conservative bloc" 46, 201n119

Index of Names and Subjects

conservative Christians 55–56, 60
Conservative Jews: Hertz 13, 87, 174–175; Morais 10, 193n53–194n53
Conservative Judaism: Bible commentary of 236n67; Chief Rabbi Hertz and 16, 17; in England 14, 23; in Europe 6, 149; Frankel and 15, 48; and Hertz Commentary x, 167; works about 241, 242, 244, 248, 249, 250, 252. *See also* positive historical Judaism; traditional Judaism
conservative rabbinic decisors 134
Conservative rabbis 168
Constantine 112
constitutional monarchy 98
contamination: of Christianity 216n172; spiritual xvi, 148, 166, 181
contemporary Jews 182–183
contradictions: allegory and 164; biblical 63–65, 150; creation story 162; free will 223n61; miracles 157
contributors *see* research associates
controversies in Judaism 171
conversion 22
conviction *see* faith
Cook, Stanley Arthur 73, 77, 207n110, 208n131, 242, 253
Core, Bishop 188
Cornill, Karl Heinrich 78, 209n137, 242
corporal punishment 103
corpses 93, 100
corruption: of Christianity 111, 217n178; in Jewish Commonwealths 182; of Jews 223n49; judicial 106; in paganism 216n172
cosmic: births 161; plan 156
cosmology 183
counter-ideal: Jew as 185
countries *see* nations
courts of law 93, 94, 100, 106, 152, 228n145
courts of love 115
covenant with: Abraham 71; Israel 132, 141
Cowen, Philip 195n71, 242
creation: allegory and 233n213; evolution and 43, 160–165; Greeks on 120; language of 66; marriage and 119; miracles and 156; reviews of Commentary 169–170
creditors 105, 131–134, 152, 221n44
creed vs. deed 94, 95, 138–139, 144

crimes: in Canaan 130; disobedience to parents 129; against humanity 175; of Jews 223n49; of Joab 126; of parents 67–68. *See also* murder; punishment; sin
criminal law 73, 143, 152
criminals 93, 99, 100, 103, 106, 225n99
critical reviews of Commentary 168–170
cruelty: of Amalek 139; to animals 100–101, 108; in the Bible 123; as cardinal sin 95; of Christians 92, 113, 117, 128, 175, 176; to criminals 106; to Diaspora Jewry 116; divorce and 90; of Edomites 126; Greco-Roman 91; Judaism abhors 122, 140; *lex talionis* 113; of Potiphar 69–70; of Simeon and Levi 104; to slaves 93, 98–99, 105, 107; to witches 127; in worship 148. *See also* barbarism; persecution; torture
Crusades 116
cult *see* worship
cultic ritual *see* ritual
cultic sacrifices *see* sacrifices
cults: Hellenistic 39–40; pagan 130
cultural contact: ancient Near East 7, 59, 66, 73, 79; Israel and Mesopotamia 209n135; Jewish civilization 183; loan words and 68
cultural evolution 13, 54, 77, 203n22
cultural norms 150
culture, Jewish *see* civilization, Jewish
"cultured conservatism" 194n53
cultured nations 83, 91, 101, 121
cuneiform law 208n125. *See also* Hammurabi, Code of
cuneiform materials 61
cure *see* medicine
curse of Shimei 126
Curtis, E.L. 205n76, 242
custodians of the Law 145
"cut off from Israel" 169

dabr (A) 68
Daiches, Salis: on Am Ha'aretz 219n223; correspondence with Hertz 198n47, n50–52, n57, n58; research associate 29, 30, 32, 34, 89, 211n28–29; resignation 31, 37; work cited 242
Daiches, Samuel 197n19
Dan, Joseph 235n55, 242
Dante Alighieri: Inferno 102

darkness (plague) 71, 231n186
Darwinism *see* evolution
dating the Pentateuch: archaeology and 67; biblical critics on 60; Decalogue 207n119; Deuteronomy 60, 62, 67, 68, 206n98; Genesis 57, 69; geography and 64; Graetz on 6; philology and 27, 51, 61, 68; Priestly Code 203n15; Wellhausen on 5; Zunz on 62. *See also* antiquity; postexilic period; preexilic age
daughters: inheritance law 152
David (King) 69, 126–127, 150, 229n148
David ben Samuel Halevi 222n44, 238
Davidson, J. 233n10
Davis, Moshe 192n14, 193n33, n37, n43; 194n53, 242
Day of Atonement 151
de Sola Pool, David 233n1
dead: bodies 93, 100; resurrection of the 226n107
death penalty: in biblical law 99; for children 129; in Code of Hammurabi 76, 90, 93, 107; for debtors 105; excommunication vs. 169; in Greece 98; ordered by kings 105; for property offenses 106, 112; rabbinic law 152; right of pardon 208n125; for witchcraft 127
death, spiritual 76
deathlessness *see* eternality
debtors *see* creditors
Decalogue: basic Jewish term 226n108; civil law and 59; eloquence of 177; Hertz address on 41; morality and 96, 144; Renan on 75, 207n119; revelation 148, 154
decency 92, 93, 103, 131, 212n57, 215n132
decentralization of worship 60
decisions, legal 230n175
decisors, rabbinic 134, 227n129, 229n145
deed: character and 140, 143; vs. creed 94, 95, 138–139, 144; God's foreknowledge 226n107
defeat of Israelites 63
deification of: man 96; monarchs 41, 91, 93
deity *see* God
DeLaura, D. J. 210n2, 242
Delitzsch, Franz 55, 62
Delitzsch, Friedrich 21, 66, 205n79, 242
Deluge *see* Flood

democracy 98, 120
demons: Azazel 154; in Christian Bible 127; mysticism 13; sacrifices to 45
Depression 233n9
derekh eretz (H) 226n108
Derenbourg, Joseph 220n17
desert: manna in 157, 230n174; rise of monotheism 208n119; theocracy 50; wandering in 4, 11, 69, 150, 155
desertion of husbands 90
designations *see* names
destiny: Israel's 147, 156, 165; moral 225n96
Deuteronomy (Book): contradictions in 64; dating 60, 62, 67, 68, 206n98; laws in 68, 72, 146; on strangers 132, 134
Deuteronomy (Commentary): contributors 37; Inge receives 110; on Liberalism 88; on paganism 92; proof of Bible 210n139; publication 2, 33, 168; review of 212n56; on women 114
development *see* evolution
deviant groups 12
devotional insights 29
Diaspora: changes in law 128; God in 225n95; Jewry 116, 141–143, 181–183. *See also names of countries*
dibrah torah kilshon bene adam (H) 7
dietary laws 23, 147
dignity (honor): of firstborn 124; human 94, 100, 160, 162, 182, 216n177; of Jews (*see* pride); of labor 107; of Potiphar 70
dilettantism: Commentary 171
Dillmann, August 2, 62, 210n138
Diocletian 105
discipline *see* edification; punishment
discrepancies *see* contradictions
disobedient son 127, 129
dispersion *see* Diaspora
Disputation of Barcelona 109, 216n168
Disraeli, [Benjamin] 140
distinctness *see* separatism
Divine *see* God
divine right of kings 105
divorce 90, 116–117, 121, 151, 218n198
Dobsevage, I. George 198n42, n55; 200n88
Documentary Hypothesis 4, 50, 55, 62, 63, 67, 172, 175
dogma: Christian 120; Jewish 147, 171–172

Index of Names and Subjects

dogmatic tone of Commentary 169
dor revi'i (H) 68
Douglas, G. C. M. 204n55, 242
dowry 90
Drachman, Bernard 13–14, 192n14, 193n52, n53; 195n74, 242
dreams: miracles 157; mysticism 13
dress (fashion) 69, 150
Drew Theological Seminary 56
Driver, Samuel Rolles: anti-Semitism 53; on archaeology 72–73, 207n109; on child-sacrifice 78; on creditors 132, 221n36; on dating of Torah 62, 205n61; on desert wanderings 206n93; on *ever ha-yarden* 64–65, 205n73; on Hebrews 73, 207n113, 209n138; on interest 133, 221n39–40; on Mosaic code 74, 207n116, n117; Pan-Babylonian theory 54; on religions 52–53; on sacrifices 53, 203n18; Wellhausenian 51, 78, 202n11, 207n108; works cited 241, 243, 248
Drob, Max 233n7
due process: child killing 129
Duhm, B. 53
Durkheim, Emile 77
dust: clouds 163; of the earth 42, 102; water of bitterness 217n192
duty, Jewish *see* mission, Jewish

ear: drilling of 107
Early and Late (Hertz) 191n5–6, 192n26, 194n55, n59; 195n64, n72; 196n2, 196n77, 216n173, 236n69, 246
earth (planet) 161, 163
Eastern European: Jews 1, 11; rabbis 21, 192n14
eating *see* food
eclipse of the Divine 142
eclipses: God's power 158
economic factors: biblical law 132; ethics 181–182; halakhah xvi, 152; sales of *Pentateuch* 233n9
economic struggle: Greece 98
ecumenicism 176, 183
edification: allegory and 164; commandments and 11, 146; goal of Commentary 2–3, 28, 29, 48; of laymen 201n125; sacrifices and 155. *See also* education
Edom 125, 126, 147, 169, 219n10

education: allegory and 163; anthropomorphism and 165; character and 181; classical 108; Commentary and 170; in Germany 138; humanistic 183; Jewish 12, 41, 140, 183–184; laws of interest 222n44; miracles and 159; right to 121; ritual and 154; suffering as 142–143; training of rabbis 192n14; of Western Jews 174, 182. *See also* edification; ignorance
educators *see* teachers
Eerdmans, B. D. 227n125, 243
Egypt: Abraham in 124; barbarism in 93; civilization of 136; emigrants from 70, 158; Exodus from 127; idolatry in 44, 45; immorality in 93, 101; Ishmaelite caravan to 63–64; Joseph in 69–70, 125; Judah in 125; plagues in 158; women in 115
Egyptian: bondage 68, 70, 140, 205n67, 209n135; language 68–69; literature 69–70; religion 71
Egyptians: concentration camps 224n63; spoiling of 127, 169
ein somekhin al ha-nes (H) 230n175
Eisenstadt rabbinical seminary 191n5
Eisenstein, Judah David 10, 193n35, 194n53, 243
El Amarna tablets 70
election of Israel *see* Chosen People
Eliezer, Rabbi 217n186
Elijah 105
Elisha 230n174
Ellenson, David 192n18, 195n63, 243
emancipation: of Christians 56; of Jews 28, 86; religious 174; of slaves 99, 107
Emor 92
emotions: in Commentary 170; of God 97
emperors *see* kings
empirical methods 75, 164, 165
Encyclopaedia Britannica 202n7, 209n137, 217n190, 243
Encyclopaedia Judaica 202n3, 216n168, 235n30, 243
Encyclopaedia of Religion and Ethics 37, 199n74
endurance *see* eternality
enemies: cities of 222n46; Egyptians 169; hatred of 113; treatment of 52, 102, 104, 106. *See also* strangers

England: Jews in (*see* British Jewry); juridical system 120–121; Liberal Judaism 5, 9, 20–21, 58, 144; sales of Commentary 167; wife-selling 114
English commentaries *see* Bible commentaries: English
English language: in worship 23
English-speaking Jewry: chief rabbi and 196n76; Commentary and 2, 35, 47, 178; Holocaust and x; literature for 27; Rabbinism and 58. *See also* British Jewry; United States: Jewry
English translations of: Bible (*see under* Bible translations); Maimonides 229n161; rabbinic literature 38; Talmud 43
Englishmen 119
engraving 71
enlightened: Israelites 209n137; nations 83, 91, 101, 121; orthodoxy 194n53
enmity *see* hatred
ephod 71
epistemology 75, 178, 180. *See also* knowledge
Epstein, Isidore: career 45; cited 201n107–109, n111–116; cites Aristotle 231n192; on evolution 233n213; on Gaster 171; on Hertz 197n38; *Judaism of Tradition* 25, 197n26; on morality 226n113; quotes Hertz 196n2; research associate xv, 40–41, 42–43; on revelation 229n163; works cited 243–244
equality of: humans 91, 121; strangers 131; women 23, 115, 151, 152, 218n196
equity *see* impartiality; justice
error *see* fallibility
errors in Commentary 229n152
Esau 104, 124, 125–126, 147, 176, 220n10
Essenes 12
eternal lamp *see* lamp, eternal
eternal questions: religion and 183
eternality of the: Jewish people 141, 177; Law 226n107
ethical insights: Judaism xvi, 3, 35, 48, 151, 168
ethical models xvi, 219n2, 224n66
ethical monotheism 91
ethical nobility xv, 82, 88, 118, 127, 143, 145, 151, 184
ethical perfection: God 224n65
ethical superiority *see under* superiority

Ethical System of James Martineau (Hertz) 178, 235n56–236n61, 246
ethical values *see* values
ethical virtues *see* virtues: ethical
ethics (morality): deeds and 95; evolutionary theory and 162; Hertz study of 178–180; human capability 139, 160, 162; as law 91; Martineau on 179; personal 96, 174, 179; power and 181–182; questions of 154; religion and 178–179, 181; reward and 229n161; ritual and 52; of work 107; worship vs. 159
ethics, Babylonian 90
ethics, biblical 22, 50, 75–76, 124, 127–131, 135, 137–138, 140
ethics, Christian: vs. biblical 127; compatible with Jewish 85, 177; hatred 113, 119; Hertz on xvi, 86, 90, 123, 136, 181–182; kindness to animals 108; paganism and 88, 120; vs. rabbinic 20; Wellhausen on xv, 5
ethics, Greek xvi, 83, 93, 96–99, 111, 180
ethics, Hebraic 95
ethics, Hellenistic 81, 83, 86, 91, 96, 109, 120
ethics, Jewish: vs. Babylonian 90, 205n79; Bachya on 178; children and 100; vs. Christian 52; compatible with Christian 85, 177; conveyed by Christianity 176; Decalogue and 144; Germans on 134; God and 97; vs. Greek 83, 91, 96, 109–110; Greek sources 235n37; Hebraism and 82, 93; Hertz praises 48, 217n186; higher critics on 20; holiness and 144; inferiority of 175; integrity of 3, 9; interest on loans 221n37; Israel's message 142; justice 106; kindness to animals 101; Law and 146, 153; model to the world 224n66; nobility of (*see* ethical nobility); vs. pagan 92, 147, 172, 219n222; of Patriarchs 139; Pharisaism and 50, 54; prophets and 174; rabbinic 85, 104; sacrifices and 154; statelessness and 181–182; suffering and 143; superiority of 123, 137–138, 165, 175, 181; Talmud on 145; Temple ritual and 154; vs. totalitarianism 121; trial by ordeal 217n192; usury and 135; Western critique of xvi, 1
ethics, pagan *see* paganism: morality

ethics, universal 91, 129, 137, 184, 225n96
ethics, Western 41, 106, 177, 181
ethnicity: Hebrews 58; Ishmaelites 205n70
etymology 68–69, 139. *See also* philology
eunechism: Christianity 119
Europe: biblical scholars 8; Conservative Judaism 6, 149; Hellenism in 112; Jewish scholars 53; rabbinic authority 11, 21; secularization 233n213; trial by ordeal in 128; witch trials in 127; women in 114; work ethic 107–108. *See also country names*
Eve 13, 68
even-handedness *see* impartiality
ever ha-yarden (H) 64–65
evil: forces of 141; Jew as 185, 223n49; relativity of 179. *See also* sin
evolution (Darwinism): Christians on 231n201; Epstein on 42, 233n213; Hertz on ix; rationalism and xvi, 159–163, 165; Wallace on 231n194; Wellhausen and 4
evolution, cultural 13, 54, 77, 203n22
evolution, moral xvi, 81, 131, 137
evolution, religious: biblical critics on 4, 52–54, 58–60, 159, 172; biblical interpretation and 50; Christianity 109–110; Israelite law 76; Judaism xv, 3, 18, 148, 180, 183; Morais on 194n53; Semitic cultures 203n22. *See also* halakhah: change
Ewald, Heinrich 2
exclusivity, religious 146, 178
excommunication 169
execution *see* death penalty
exegesis, biblical *see* Bible commentaries
Exile *see* Babylonian captivity; Diaspora
existentialism 182, 216n157
Exodus (Commentary): on Code of Hammurabi 90; Cohen contributes 37, 220n17; Cook receives 73; Epstein contributes 41, 200n93; Gaster review 235n31; publication of 33, 167; on Reform Judaism 88; research associates 200n88; on revelation 149; Salaman receives 234n26; Sayce on 58
Exodus (event) 68, 115, 127, 158

experiment, divine 139
explanation *see* interpretation
Expository Times 234n20
external influences 209n135
externals of religion *see* ritual
extirpation *see* genocide
extramarital affairs *see* adultery
Ezekiel 51, 62, 223n62
Ezra 4, 8, 51, 62, 144–145, 151

factuality *see* historicity
faith: allegory and 164; authorship of Pentateuch 8; axioms 225n107; biblical criticism and 63; Christian xv, 5, 55, 56, 185; Commentary and x; evolution and 160, 232n201; halakhah and 10, 143; history and 7; of Israel 142; Liberal Judaism 211n27; miracles and 156, 159; modern religion 61; principles 88, 143; rationalism and 165; revelation and 170, 228n139; science and 163; sources and 173–174; spiritual weapon 147; strengthening 140; suffering and 225n104; traditional Judaism 196n10
fallacies 160
fallibility of: conscience 179; human intellect 154
family life 110, 113, 119, 181
family members: incest 101; marriage laws 92; and murderers 76, 96, 100. *See also* children; parents
fanaticism 98
fantasy: miracles 157
fascism 121
fathers *see* parents
Faulhaber, Michael 138, 219n2, 223n62, n63; 244
Faulkner, J. A. 203n31, 244
favoritism, God's 140–141
fear of God 94, 170
fears of man 229n161
feeding the hungry 92, 105
fence: around the Torah 150, 228n145–229n145; Israel as 224n66; Law as 148
ferocity *see* cruelty; fierceness
festivals: postbiblical 151; second day of 23; sermons 26; traditional Judaism 196n10. *See also names of festivals*
feudalism 107, 135

fiction: aggadah 128; biblical narrative 72; legal 152
fierceness of Israel 227n128
filial piety 215n145, 235n44
financial backer *see* Blashki, Aaron
fines *see* monetary fines
Finestein, Israel 197n14, 238
finiteness of man 124
Finkelstein, Louis 14, 16, 214n100, 225n99, 233n4, n7; 240
fire: from heaven 122; model of lampstand 157; of Nadab and Abihu 12; perpetual 155; at Taberah 155
First Commonwealth 144, 182; destruction of 209n137
firstborn: Esau 124; sacrifice of 78, 209n135
firstlings, animal 64
Five Books of Moses *see* Pentateuch
flame *see* fire
Flood 161, 231n196, 232n203, 233n213
foes *see* enemies
folk customs 114
food: dietary laws 23, 147; manna 157, 230n174; meat 44, 45, 101, 150
footnotes 201n125. *See also* references
foreigners *see* strangers
forgiveness 95, 213n92, 220n10
formalism, cultic *see* ritual
Frampton, Samuel: annotates Haftarot 31, 89, 91–92, 211n40; career 40, 200n92; correspondence with Hertz 199n62, n63; 211n32–33, 233n3; on Leviticus 198n54; research associate xv, 3, 33, 36, 187–189, 198n56, 227n120; on Zionism 40
France, grand rabbi of 11
Frankel, Zacharias: Breslau school 176; *Darkhei ha-Mishnah* 149, 228n141, 244; on halakhah 11; on historical Judaism 15, 48, 194n61–195n61; on Mosaic authorship 6; non-Orthodox 173, 192n18, 193n42; on scholarship 201n125; on Talmudic tradition 7
Frazer, James: on antiquity of Judaism 61, 204n59; on barbarism 54, 203n24–25, 209n135; on uniqueness of Judaism 73; Wellhausenism 53, 58, 76; works cited 244
Free Church of Scotland 55
free will 139, 179, 223n61, 226n107
Freedman, H. 239

Freedman, Joseph 233n11
freedom (liberty): Greek idea 98; Jewish value 185; justice and 212n60; law and 59, 144; revelation and 142; slavery and 76. *See also* emancipation; free will
freethinkers 75
Friedeberg, Samuel *see* Frampton, Samuel
Friedlaender, Israel 210n3, n6
Friedlaender, Michael 162, 172, 221n29, 231n200, 233n214, 239
Friedlaender, S. 236n72, 244
Friedlander, Gerald: career 38–40; on chief rabbi 195n73; on Christianity 110, 216n172; cited 200n85–88, n91; on Exodus 200n88; on Montefiore 38, 200n84; on payment 30, 198n49–50; research associate xv, 3, 30, 33, 34, 35, 36, 187; works cited 244
Friedmann, M. 213n80, 240
friends, heathen 222n44
frogs (plague) 231n186
fugitive slaves 76, 93, 107, 121
fulfillment: of Bible in history 210n139; marriage and 119
"Fundamental Ideals..." (Hertz) 41, 90, 196n2, 200n101, 201n104, 211n36–39, 214n109, 219n222, 246
fundamentalism, Jewish 183
future, Jewish 46, 100, 182, 201n119. *See also* messianic era

Ganganelli, Lorenzo 218n202, 251
Garden of Eden (paradise) 163, 232n213–233n213
garden of humanity 224n66
Gaster Mahzor 29
Gaster, Moses 21, 170, 171–172, 234n27, 235n30–31
Gehenna 102
Geiger, Abraham 137, 223n58, 244
gematria 12, 13
Genesis (Book): archaeology and 70, 73; dating 57, 69; Mosaic authorship 65; science and 161
Genesis (Commentary): Abelson contributes 37; Cook receives 73; Epstein contributes 41, 200n93; first edition 126; Friedlander contributes 200n88; Haftarot 31; manuscript 32, 232n206; preface 28, 197n39; publication 2, 23, 32, 33,

Index of Names and Subjects 277

168; reviews 13, 171, 233n7; sales 167; Sayce on 58; title page 187; translation 168
genetics: free will and 223n61; homosexuality and 214n121; Jewish 137, 138
genius: author of Decalogue 207n119; author of Pentateuch 58, 122; of Jesus 39; Jewish 82, 122, 136, 137, 185; Maimonides 153; Morais 4; moral 88, 91, 138; pagan 136; religious 73, 223n58, n62; term in Commentary 223n62
genocide 127, 130–131, 185, 220n26, 223n62
gentile *see* Christian . . .; non-Jews . . .
gentleman: English concept 119; Hertz as 195n74
gentry 75, 108, 219n223
geography: Azazel and 151; Babylonia 177; Israel 72; Jordan 64–65; Red Sea 206n106; Smith on 207n108
geology 161
ger (H) 131, 132
German-American scholars 3
German Bible commentaries 29, 36
German Bible scholars 4, 6, 41, 54, 66, 169
German theologians 49, 61–62
German translation of: Bible 29, 205n71; Commentary 168
Germany: anti-Semitism 134 (*see also* Nazism); neo-Orthodoxy 6, 36, 64, 66, 173, 191n5
ghetto: intellectual 82, 184; mentality xvi, 147, 166. *See also* separatism
giant-pigmy aphorism 10, 193n36
gifts: to non-Jews 222n44
Ginsberg, Asher Hirsch 82–83, 210n6, n10; 244
Ginzberg, Louis 164, 192n16, 210n3, 232n208, n211; 244, 247
global village: ecumenicism 183
God: Abraham and 71, 130; attributes 95, 104, 139, 224n65 (*see also subhead* nature of); authority of 208n125; biblical law and 75; Christianity and 40, 85; closeness to 137, 145; conscience and 179; counts tears 115, 218n198; dictates Torah 59, 78, 149; evolution and 160; in exile 142, 225n95; existence 139, 225n107; as father 176; foreknowledge 226n107; genetic manipulation 223n61;

Hebrew language and 66; Hertz's belief in 180; holiness of 209n135; image of, in man 42, 76, 94, 96, 139, 162; images of 78, 157; incorporeality 226n107; infinite wisdom 232n201; intervention in history 120, 141, 154, 165, 225n93; Israel and 132, 137, 138, 141, 142, 164; judgment of 104, 145; kingdom of 41, 120, 139, 177–178; knowledge of 55; knowledge of, by man 139, 193n45; law of 102; Liberal Judaism 200n86; love of 95, 138, 139; love of, by man 94, 95, 140; miracles and 156, 230n174; moral law and 91, 179; names of 68, 226n108; nature of 23, 42, 96–97, 213n92, 224n64 (*see also subhead* attributes); omnipotence 127, 159; partiality to Jews 102; plan of 156, 177; power 158; Rabbis on 196n2; Renan on 208n119; return to 143; sacrifices and 43, 44, 53, 145, 154, 193n35; serving 124; shield of Israel 230n177; sins against 76; son of (*see under* Jesus); spirit of 137; time and 161; traditional Judaism and 196n10; unity of 41, 88, 91, 117–118, 128, 177, 225n107; universality of 140; will of 11, 94, 130, 145–146, 156–157, 160, 230n166; word of 55–56, 138, 156, 162, 204n54; wrath of 140. *See also* man: relationship with God; revelation
godlessness *see* atheism
God's elect *see* Chosen People
goldsmithing: ephod and 71
Gordis, R. 228n139, 244
Gorfinkle, J. I. 200n83, 239, 242
Gospels: biblical criticism and 56; on divorce 117; on hatred 113; Judaism vs. 86; Liberal Judaism and 22; morality 52; Old Testament and 39, 84
Gottlieb, W. 196n2, 236n74, 244
governing classes 108. *See also* kings
government (political structures): Bible and 98, 120; ethics and 182; Hellenism and 81; Jewish state 181, 209n137; justice and 106, 126–127, 180; law and 90; Roman 105. *See also* monarchy; theocracy
grace: of God 95–97, 137, 219n2; of Jews 223n58

Graetz, Heinrich: on Christianity 110, 216n172; ecumenism 176; on Jewish future 46, 201n119; on Jewish history 46, 235n47–48; on Jewish separatism 148; on Judaism 224n72, 227n137, 235n46; on Mosaic authorship 6; non-Orthodox 173, 192n18; on Simon ben Shetach 220n17; works cited 244–245
Graf, Karl Heinrich 4, 49, 62
Graf-Wellhausen school 8, 50, 56–58, 63, 66, 87, 207n108. *See also* Wellhausen, Julius
grammar, Hebrew 129
Greco-Roman civilization: Christianity and 89, 109–110; Hellenism and 81; Hertz on 180; Montefiore on 84; morality xvi, 83, 130, 212n56; Noachide laws 215n149; value of life 99; Western civilization and 106–108; Zangwill on 136. *See also* Greek civilization; Rome
Greco-Roman cults 39–40
Greco-Roman law 90, 92, 95, 99, 107, 113
Greek civilization: child killing in 100, 129–130; Hertz on 41; humanism in 83; lack of ethics 91, 97, 101, 216n177; spirituality 235n37; treatment of strangers 103; Western civilization and 112
Greek culture 98, 105, 109, 176, 236n63
Greek literature 82, 114
Greek morality *see* ethics, Greek
Greek philosophers 83, 96, 110, 111, 165, 176
Greek political models 98
Greek religion 88, 96, 97, 120
Greek wisdom 232n202
Green, W. H. 203n36
Greenberg, Moshe 208n121, n125; 245, 248
Greenstone, Julius 233n7, 250
Gregoire, H. B. 135, 222n49–223n49, 245
Grossman, Louis 192n28, 251
Grunfeld, I. 205n77, 228n138, 245
Guide for the Perplexed see under Maimonides *and citation index*
guilt 44, 50, 51, 118, 124, 154
Gunkel, Herman 54
Guttmann, Yehiel Michael 133–134, 221n41, 222n44, 245, 249

Habiri; Habiru 70, 206n98
Hacohen, Shmuel Avidor 192n30
Haftarot: delays in annotating 31; Frampton annotates 40, 89, 211n40; Hertz edits 3, 91–92; scope of Commentary 27, 29, 30
Hagar 214n100
Hagiographa 6, 149
Hahn, H. F. 202n8, 203n21, n23, n26, n37; 208n129, 209n135, 245
hai (H) 68
hail (plague) 231n186
halakhah (Jewish law): Abrahams on 153; anachronism xv, 175; biblical critics on xv, 52; change xvi, 9–12, 148–152, 165, 173–174, 184, 222n44, 228n145; Chosen People and 143; Christians on 56, 164; confession in 128; divine origin 226n107; on divorce 117, 151; ethics and 146; Friedlander on 39; Hertz Commentary on 3, 8, 9, 11, 29, 48, 59; humanitarianism 135; interpretation of 10, 44, 144–145, 148; Jewish education 184; Liberal Judaism and 144, 182; observance (*see* observance, Jewish); Orthodox Jews and 183; peace and 221n35; penalties 214n100; salvation and 180; separatism and 148; spiritual therapy 227n128; women in 115. *See also* commandments; Oral Law
halakhot le-Moshe mi-Sinai (H) 149. *See also* Sinai, Mount: revelation
halav (H) 65
Halevi, Judah *see* Judah Halevi
Halley, Edmund 161, 163, 231n196, 245
HaMeiri, Menahem 222n44, 227n129, 239
hametz (H) 226n108
Hammer, R. 225n95, 245
Hammurabi, Code of: Deuteronomy and 68; length 72; Leviticus and 67; moral aspects 90; Mosaic law vs. 41, 74, 75–76, 90, 207n117; on slaves 76, 93, 107; value of life 106
hamushim (H) 68
hanachat ruah (H) 230n166
Hanukkah 93
harmony 75, 79, 83, 95–96, 132, 162, 177. *See also* peace
Harris, M. 216n169–170, 245
Hartley Library 237

Index of Names and Subjects

Hartman, David xiii, 199n71, 212n59, n66; 227n127, 228n139, 229n160, 245
Hasidic parables 17, 103
hatred: of Edom 126, 169; of Egyptians 127; of enemies 113; Englishmen and 119; of Ishmaelites 214n100; Israel eradicates 140; of Israel's enemies 102; of Jews (*see* anti-Semitism); of Joseph 125; of Judaism 202n10; of Leah 169; into love 104; of Roman Catholicism 176; in Sodom 92
health *see* medicine
heart: man's nature 228n137; of Pharaoh 229n161
heat and light: creation 163
heathenism *see* paganism
Hebraism: Christianity and 81–82, 84, 112; defined 81, 82, 84, 86, 108; ethical values 93, 95, 102–103, 109, 121, 123, 138, 181; Hellenism vs. (*see under* Hellenism); Hirsch on 210n9; legalism 227n125; Maimonides on 153; Montefiore on 84
Hebrew alphabet 12
Hebrew language: Abelson knowledge 37; and Bible versions 26; biblical 61, 129; etymology 139; Hirsch on 66; ignorance of 175; Judaism and 88; loan words 68; Luzzatto on x; translation of Commentary 168; in worship service 23
Hebrew law *see* Mosaic code
Hebrew Union College 8, 162, 192n29, 196n2
Hebrew Union College Annual 133
Hebrew University xiii, 9, 83
Hebrews: = Habiru 70, 206n98; religion of (*see* Israelite religion)
hedge *see* fence
Heilsgeschichte 55, 120
Heine, Heinrich 210n6, 219n236, 245
Hellenism: barbarism (*see under* barbarism); brotherhood of man 102; Christianity and 40, 86, 88, 109–111, 113, 136; defined 108; Friedlander on 39; Hebraism vs. 81–83, 88, 89, 93, 98, 180–181, 184; Hertz critique xvi, 86–88, 92, 96, 98, 109, 184; Hirsch on 210n9; impact on West 81, 106–107, 110–111, 119; imperfection of 85; Maimonides on 153; Mendes on 177; Montefiore on xv, 47, 147; slavery and 106; virtues in 86, 112
Hellenistic cults 39–40
Heller, J. 231n179, 245
Heller, Yom Tov Lipmann: *Pilpula Harifta* 222n44, 239
Henoch, C. J. 229n160, 230n165, 246
henotheism 4
Henriques, Basil L.Q. 24, 197n21, 246
hereditary virtues 119, 223n59
heresy cases 55
heretics: Frankel 15; persecution of 116
Herford, Robert Travers: on Christian triumphalism 56, 203n32; on Christology 200n80; cited by Hertz 41, 235n36; on Judaism 58; on morality 226n113; on non-Jewish sources 173; on paganism 111, 216n178–217n178; works cited 246
heroes, biblical *see* biblical personalities
Hertz, Emanuel (brother) 168, 233n2, n4, n5; 234n13
Hertz, Joseph Herman: archives xiii, 237–238; biography 2; career 216n173; chief rabbi (*see* Chief Rabbi Hertz); death 186, 237; doctoral thesis 178–180; education 2, 183; works about 244, 246, 253; works cited 246–247 (*see also* individual titles)
Hertz, Josephine (daughter) 89, 211n31, 237, 238
Hertz, Judith (later Schonfeld) (daughter) 196n6, 238
Hertz, Samuel (son) 234n12, 237
Hertz, Simon (father) 191n5
Hertzberg, A. 202n1, 247
Herxheimer, Salomon 29
Herzog, Isaac 21
hesed (H) 212n69
hidden miracles 156
hierocracy 51, 205n71. *See also* priests
higher criticism *see* biblical criticism, higher
Hildesheimer, Esriel 6, 15, 191n5, 192n18
Hildesheimer seminary 15, 29
Hillel 85, 152
hillul ha-shem (H) 226n108, 235n31
Hirsch, Emil G. 160, 231n193, 247
Hirsch, Samson Raphael: on Hebrew language 66, 205n77; on Hellenism 210n9; *cont.*

Hirsch, Samson Raphael *cont.*
  interpretations cited 205n71; on
  Oral Law 6, 148, 149, 192n18,
  228n138, n142; on Psalms 229n148;
  religious position 21, 47, 184; on
  Romans 105, 215n144; sources of
  Commentary 36, 173–174; works
  cited 247
Hirschfeld, Hartwig 238
historians: on anti-Semitism 185; Jewish 6, 137; on Simon ben Shetach 220n17; on Spinoza 202n1
historical: consciousness 149, 150; context 7, 134, 135; literary criticism 8–9, 49, 57–59, 61, 67, 174; models (paradigms) 126, 158, 165; positivism 6, 75; setting of Bible 207n109
historicity of: creation story 161–163; Egyptian bondage 205n67; the Flood 232n203; Jesus 56; miracles 158–159, 231n180; New Testament 55; paradise story 233n213; Simon ben Shetach story 220n17; Sinai revelation 6, 59, 170; the Torah ix, 58, 63, 67–72, 162, 165, 172, 210n139
historiography of: Jewish Theological Seminary 8; Moore 203n36; Reform Judaism 142; Wellhausen xv, 4–5, 9; *Wissenschaft* 12
history (discipline): and biblical criticism 60; evolution and 159; Hertz and 179–180; legitimacy of Judaism and 201n125; religious truth and 85; source of Commentary 29
history, Jewish: attacks on 1; authority of sages 144; Bible critics on 5, 51; black pages in 112; changes in law 11, 150, 151; Divine purpose 137, 139; European scholars 53; Graetz on 46; ignorance of 175; indestructibility 141, 177; individual's role in 140; Jewish Theological Seminary 4; martyrdom and 130; and Midrash 28; and Oral Law 6, 149; Orthodoxy and 183; ritual and 145; super-people 138; and textual interpretation 7; *Wissenschaft* and 63
history, world: creation and 161; fulfillment of Bible 210n139; God in 177; Jews in 140, 165, 176–177, 180–181; parallels to Exodus 158; relativity of ethics 179; sacrifices 155
Hitler, Adolf 93, 108

Hitlerism *see* Nazism
Hittite laws 67–68
Hockman, Joseph 23–24
Hoffmann, David Zevi 64, 173, 205n71, 247
holidays *see* festivals
holiness: Christian 119; of Israel 143, 147, 180, 223n58; Jewish ethics 91, 94, 95, 109; Law and 153; Moses and 122; observance and 196n10; of man 121; of priests 230n166; vs. the profane 177; righteousness and 212n69; ritual and 11, 144; sacrifices and 43; suffering and 143
Holocaust ix, x, 184–185, 223n63. *See also* Nazism
Holy Land *see* Canaan; Palestine
Homberg, Naphtali Herz 205n71, 239
home life *see* family life
homicide *see* murder
homiletics: Cohen on 38; in Commentary 13, 28, 29, 47, 126, 168, 170; Hertz and 16–17
homilies *see* sermons
homo sapiens see man
homosexuality 101, 214n121
honor *see* chastity; dignity; respect
Horites 207n114
Hormah 63
hornet: badge of Pharaoh 71
horses: slaves vs. 99; traffic in 107
Hosea 144, 212n69
hostis (L) 106
Hovevei Zion 40
HUC *see* Hebrew Union College
Hudaly, David 200n92, 247
hukkim (H) 146
human composition of: Decalogue 207n119; Oral Law 149; Pentateuch 7–8, 22, 58, 138, 206n94
human life: after death (*see* immortality; resurrection); length of 70; Mosaic code and 143; prolonging 105; value of 75–76, 99–101, 106, 112
human mind *see* intellect
human nature 219n2, 228n137
human reason *see* rationalism
human sacrifice *see* sacrifices, human
humaneness: of the Bible 129; of Christianity 136; of Egyptians 127, 169; Hebraism and 81; Hellenism 83; Israelite law 75, 113, 121, 131; of Israelite religion 79, 95, 101, 103,

Index of Names and Subjects

162; Jewish 82, 88, 105, 117, 125, 128, 173, 184; of paganism 92; of rabbinic law 151, 152
humanitarianism xvi, 21, 92, 107, 121–122, 133–135, 222n44, n46
humanity: attitude to Jews 176; Christians sins against 175; justice and 177; rights of 94, 99; of slaves 76, 93, 99, 107
humanization of: Biblical law 152; Jewish character xvi, 165; mankind 139
humiliation *see* insults
humility 95, 127, 193n45, 212n57
Hummel, H. D. 202n3, 243
Hungarian translation of Commentary 133, 168
Hungary 221n41
hunting 125; for witches 128
Hurrian civilization 207n114
hurricane: Red Sea 158
husbands: chastity of 217n192; desertion by 90; disappearance of 117; equality of wives 218n196; jealousy of 128, 217n188; legal position 151; murder of 124; recalcitrant 117; tears of wives 218n198
Husik, Isaac 110, 216n171, 247
Hyamson, A. 197n28, 247
"hypercritics" 5, 8. *See also* biblical criticism, higher
hypocrites 15, 145

Ibn Ezra, Abraham: cited by Spinoza 206n94; on God in nature 158; on Jacob 169; on Midianites 205n70; on Mosaic authorship 64, 72; on sacrifice 44; on strangers 221n43, 222n46; style 29, 47
identity, Jewish 141, 148, 196n10
idleness: nobility 108
idolatry: biblical law vs. 75; in Christianity 118; Commentary on 226n107; Crusades and 116; death of worshipers 141; Inquisition and °ź; among Israelites 148; pagan 218n214; Rachel and 126; sacrifices and 44–45; witchcraft and 128
ignorance of: Hebrew 54; Hertz 220n26; Jewish literature 175; Judaism 1, 19, 27, 143, 182, 201n125. *See also* knowledge
illegitimacy of Judaism 1, 49
illusions: miracles 159

image: of God (*see under* God); parable and 232n208; -worship 118, 218n214. *See also* idolatry
imagination: miracles 157
imitatio Dei 91, 97
immigrants 27, 47, 86, 182
immorality, sexual *see* sexual immorality
immortality 152, 226n107. *See also* eternality
impartiality 94, 106, 121, 127, 129
impetuousness of Israel 227n128
impulses, subduing 162
impurity *see* purity
incarnation: Christianity 118
incest: cultured nations 101
incorporeality of God 226n107
incorrigible son 127, 129
indestructibility *see* eternality
indifference, Jewish 8, 175
individual *see* personal . . .
inequality of men 75, 93, 96, 98, 108, 182, 184
inferential reasoning 112, 120
inferiority of: Israelite morality 205n79; Judaism 1, 175, 202n10; pagan civilizations 136; prophets to Law 144; women 151. *See also* superiority
Inferno: Gehenna 102
infidelity *see* adultery
Infinite: anthropomorphism 232n212
Inge, William Ralph 110, 111, 123, 136, 216n173, n175–177; 247
inheritance: anti-Semitism as 223n49; law 152
inhumanity *see* cruelty
iniquity *see* sin
injustice 109
innocence: *sotah* 128
innovations, halakhic *see* halakhah: change
Inquirer 212n56
Inquisition 92
Inscription of Merneptah 70
inspiration: religious 178; tone of Commentary 168, 175
instinct: animal 223n61; bloodshed 125; paganism 91; sacrificial 43; violence 101
institutionalized religion 19–20, 50, 59, 60, 136, 159–160, 172. *See also* Church
instruction *see* education

instruments: divine 146, 148, 222n49; educative 154, 164
insularity *see* separatism
insults to: British Jewry 195n74; Hertz 23, 171
integrity: of the Bible 162; of biblical law xv; moral xvi, 90, 92, 119, 124–125, 129, 134–135, 220n17; of rabbinic Judaism 3, 172; of rationalism 164; religious 86, 87, 131; spiritual 117
intellect: finiteness 232n212; halakhah and 143; Hellenism 81, 82, 97; of Maimonides 153; man vs. animal 160; Morais on 193n45; vs. nature 162; revelation and 154, 165, 180. *See also* genius; knowledge; understanding
intellectual history xiii
intellectual insularity 82, 184
intelligent conformity 146
"intelligent conservatism" 194n53
intelligibility *see* understanding
intercessor with God 118
interest: Code of Hammurabi 90; from foreigners 127, 131–134, 221n39, n44–222n44; from Israelites 133, 221n37
intermarriage 125, 126
intermediaries in: Christianity 118; Israelite religion 209n136
International Critical Commentary 46, 205n69, n73; 220n20
interpretation (of): the Bible (*see* biblical interpretation); blessing of woman 217n194; halakhah 10, 44, 144–145, 148; history and 7; inscriptions 70, 206n100; Israelite religion 209n135; Jewish theology 87; Judaism 51; miracles 158. *See also* midrash
interviews 238
intolerance 98, 102, 113, 171, 175. *See also* tolerance
intuitive ethics 179
inwardness: Christianity 36, 94
iron tools 88, 100
Isaac (patriarch) 118, 124, 127, 139
Isaiah (prophet) 142, 144, 145, 158, 177, 227n125
Ishmaelites 63, 64, 205n70, 214n100
isolation *see* separatism
Israel (Jacob) *see* Jacob (patriarch)

Israel (land) *see* Canaan; Judah (kingdom); Judea; Palestine
Israel (nation): agriculture and 135; in Canaan 70, 130; Cornill on 209n137; designations of 139; Edom and 169; in Egypt (*see* Egyptian bondage); election of (*see* Chosen people); . excommunication from 169; in exile (*see* Diaspora: Jewry); God and (*see under* God); guilt of 51; hatred by Ishmael 214n100; Hertz champions 196n2; history (*see* history, Jewish); mission of (*see* mission, Jewish); origins of 70, 172, 206n100; rebirth 144; religious genius 223n58; separatism 146–148; shortcomings 63, 136; strength of 227n128; traditional Judaism 196n10, 197n11; *Uncle Tom's Cabin* and 216n157; war against Midianites 220n26
Israelite kings 63, 93, 98
Israelite law *see* Mosaic code
Israelite religion: archaeology and 54–55, 79, 172; Bible critics on 4, 48, 49–50, 57, 59, 78, 87, 204n56; Christianity supplants 138; creation story 161; cultural contact 7; Hertz explains xv, 17, 59; law in 66, 159; Montefiore on 87; vs. paganism 74; Pharisees and 53, 202n11; prayer 60; ritual 61, 86; sacrifices 155; spontaneous worship 20, 159; strangers and 132; uniqueness of 73; values of 95, 100. *See also* Judaism
Israelstam, J. 224n64, 239
Italian scholars x–xi, 12

Jacob (patriarch): character of 169; Esau and 104, 124–126, 220n10; family in Egypt 70; Joseph and 69; Rachel and 126; suffering 142; symbol of Judaism 176; wrestling with angel 157
Jacob, Benno 127, 169
Jacob, Maurice 233n11
Jacobs, Joseph 41
Jacobs, Louis xiii, 205n65, 247
Jakobovits, I. 247
Japheth 82, 210n11, 242
Jastrow, Marcus 10
jealousy: of Joseph 69, 104; ordeal of 114, 127, 128, 151, 217n188, n192

Index of Names and Subjects 283

Jephthah 127, 128, 129
Jeremiah 145, 228n137
Jerusalem rabbinate 11
Jerusalem Talmud 239
Jessel, Albert H. 195n74–75
Jesus (Christ): covenant and 141; on divorce 117; ethics of 85; on feelings 94; as God 111; Jewishness of 185; Liberal Judaism and 22; love of Church 164; message of 136; Montefiore on 38, 39, 84; morality of 20; Plato and 110; Rabbinism and 51; revelation and 55, 56; son of God 118; Spinoza on 49; on spirit of law 228n137; teachings of 53, 112; on Torah 109
jewel: religion as 176
jewelry: of Egyptians 127; in Ur 71
"Jewish Christianity" 211n25
Jewish Chronicle: Abelson article 37; on Academy of Jewish Learning 197n27, n29; Cohen in 199n81–82; on Commentary project 29, 198n43, n46; 201n124; Epstein articles 42, 201n106, 233n213; Friedlander in 38–39, 200n84–85, n89; Hertz sermons 21, 211n27; on Hertz, Simon 191n5; on higher criticism 201n117–118; on Hockman 23, 197n23–24; Montefiore in 22, 196n8, 197n18, n25; reviews of Commentary 234n17, n21, n24, n28–235n28; Schechter letters 1, 17, 195n73–75; volumes cited 247
Jewish Encyclopedia 160, 164, 212n69, 218n215, n218; 231n193, 232n208, n211; 247
Jewish Exponent 193n45, 194n53
Jewish Guardian: Hertz correspondence 117, 201n123, 218n211; Liberal Judaism 23, 201n123; review of Commentary in 171, 193n49, 234n15, n22, 235n31, n33, n34
Jewish Historical Society of England 216n178, 232n203
Jewish Ledger 234n15
Jewish Messenger 193n33, n45
"Jewish Mysticism" (Hertz) 193n47, n50; 246
Jewish Publication Society of America (JPS) 34, 167, 169,198n42, 234n16, 236n67, 238
Jewish Quarterly Review (*JQR*) 234n15, n25

"Jewish Religious Education" (Hertz) 193n48
Jewish Theological Seminary of America: acknowledged xiii–xiv; archives 195n66, n74; faculty 7, 192n23, 210n3; founders x; Hertz and ix, 2, 3, 14–18, 48, 178, 192n14, 196n76; higher criticism and 6, 8; Italian heritage x–xi; library 16; opening day 5; religious ideology 14, 194n53; Schechter and 1; work about 241
Jewish Theological Seminary of Breslau xi, 13, 15, 133, 176
Jewish Theological Seminary of the British Empire 15, 195n62
"Jewish Translations of the Bible" (Hertz) 41
Jews' College: alumni 36, 37, 38, 45; appellations 14–15, 195n62; faculty 25, 40, 171, 233n213; Hertz address 46; Hertz presidency 111; Liberal Judaism and 26; location 25; principals 26, 29, 162; religious philosophy 15; work about 247
Jezebel 105
Jezreel 70
Joab 126, 169
Johanan ben Zakkai 128
Johannesburg: Hertz in 2, 16
Jordan 64–65
Jose, Rabbi 104
Joseph: narrative 68–70; Potiphar's wife and 69–70, 93, 125; relocates Egyptians 224n63; royalty 69, 150; sold as slave 63–64; virtues 104, 139
Joseph, Morris 82, 210n5, n7; 248
Joshua, Book of 40
Joshua, R. 230n175
journals, Jewish 9. *See also* press
joy in: Law 153; marriage 119; worship 4, 50, 91
JPS *see* Jewish Publication Society of America
JQR 234n15, n25
Jubilee 99
Judah 71, 125, 126
Judah (kingdom) 78, 83, 225n96. *See also* Judea
Judah Halevi 137–138, 155, 156, 204n47, 223n61, 238
Judaism: allegory and 163; attacks on 19, 39, 47, 53, 56–58, 87, 170, 173–175, 181–182, 196n2; *cont.*

Judaism *cont.*
  basic beliefs 170, 211n27; Christianity and (*see under* Christianity); commitment to 1, 63, 173, 176, 201n125, 228n137; early period (*see* Israelite religion); enduring qualities 86; as ethical system 176; Hebraism and 82, 112; Hertz explains 2–4, 7, 26–28, 89–90, 112, 114, 168, 180; highest principle 212n69; organic growth 4, 9–10, 151, 184, 228n139; originality of 39 (*see also* uniqueness); rebellion against 29; return to 9; separatism and 166; Spinoza on 202n1; successor of Israelite religion 159; symbol of 176; and Wellhausenism xv, 8, 202n7; vs. world religions 177, 183. *See also* civilization, Jewish; ethics, Jewish; Liberal Judaism; Orthodox Judaism; rabbinic Judaism; theology, Jewish
Judea 209n137, 220n17
Judeo-Christian heritage 117
judges of Sodom 145
judgment, God's 104, 145
judicial corruption 106
judicial systems 113. *See also* courts of law
Judische Wissenschaft see *Wissenschaft des Judentums*
Judith, Book of 72
Jung, Leo: colleague of Hertz 37, 198n53; on Gaster 234n27; Hertz correspondence with 32, 198n44, n55; 199n61, n65, n76, n78; 230n170, 233n9; work edited 246
Jung, Moses 233n7
juridical system: England 120–121
jurisprudence *see* law
justice: cancellation of debts 152; death penalty 129; in England 121; God's attribute 95, 139; government and 127; halakhah and 180; Hebraism and 82, 94; Hellenism and 83, 91, 92, 184; *hesed* and 212n69; Jewish call for 121, 139, 180, 184; Jewish morality 106; in Jewish state 182; prophetic vision 95, 173; *rahmanut* and 104; revelation and 142; rule of 177, 212n60; separatism and 166; taliation 113; virtue 94, 212n57
Justinian, code of 112

kabbalah 12, 13, 193n45, n47
Kadesh-Barnea 72
ha-kadosh barukh hu (H) 226n108
Kalisch, Marcus 65, 158, 163, 205n76, 232n206, n207; 248
Kant, Immanuel 96, 174
Kaplan, Mordecai 17
Kapstein, I. J. 213n80, 225n99, 240
Karaites 12, 13
Karo, Joseph 134, 150, 228n145; *Shulhan Arukh* 10, 113, 218n214, 239
Karp, Abraham 194n53, n57; 248
Katz, Jacob 227n129, 248
Kaufmann, Yehezkel 202n4, 206n100, 248
keeping of the law *see* observance
kelev (H) 68
Kesef Mishneh 228n145
Khnumhotep III (Prince) 69
kiddush hashem (H) 226n108
kidnapping 76
killing: for adultery 69–70; in Christianity 109; Jewish aversion to 101; by Joab 126; of parents 129; of slaves 99. *See also* children: killing; death penalty; murder; sacrifices, human
Kimchi, David 128–129, 220n22
kindness to: animals 101, 108, 121; fellowman 104, 182 (*see also* charity; decency)
King James version 169, 220n22
kingdom of: God 41, 120, 139, 177–178; priests 137, 141
kings: authority of 208n125; divine right of 105; Israelite 69, 93, 98; loyalty to 196n10; privileges of 106, 107; symbols of 71
Kirkpatrick, A. F. 55, 203n27, 248
kissing of Rachel 169
Kittel, Rudolf 62, 187, 188
Klausner, Joseph 83, 210n12, 216n170, 248
knowledge: allegory increases 164; Bible and 42–43; of Bible 197n31; of biblical era 172; biblical interpretation and 165; branches of 160; creation and 161; of God, by man 139, 193n45; God's 55; Hellenism 82; Jewish 18, 27, 100, 195n72; Maimonides on 36; of Moses 149; preaching and 38; of research associates 3; of sages 144. *See also* intellect
Koebben, A. J. F. 208n132, 248

Index of Names and Subjects 285

Kohler, Kaufmann: on celibacy 119, 218n218; on Christianity 110, 119, 216n172, 218n215; ecumenism 176, 235n45; on Greek culture 98, 214n96; on Israel's election 223n59, 225n96; on justice 212n69; on paganism 212n45; on prophets 226n112; on separatism 147, 227n130; on slaves 212n53; Wellhausenian 5; on *Wissenschaft* 8; works cited 247, 248

Kohut, Alexander: on biblical criticism 5; Breslau seminary 13, 176; Conservative Judaism 16, 193n53–194n53; on halakhah 9–11, 15, 193n38, n42; Hertz's teacher 3–4, 5, 192n10; on Mosaic authorship 6, 8, 192n25; pigmy-giant aphorism 10, 193n36; on Talmud 7; triumphalism 176–177, 235n49–50; works cited 248

Korah: Haftarah 92

Kuenen, Abraham 2, 4, 5

Kuzari see Judah Halevi *and citation index*

la-kohanim (H) 205n71

Laban 126

labor: attitude to 107–108; laws 121

laity *see* laymen

lamp, eternal 136; *ner tamid* (H) 226n108

lampstand: fire model 157

landowners 90, 92, 93, 105, 219n223

language: anthropomorphism and 232n212; of Commentary 223n63–224n63; complexity of 60; political 174; study of (*see* philology); theological 138

Laplace, Pierre 163

law: behavior and 180; Christianity and 57; complexity 60; freedom and 59; in Israelite religion 66 (*see also* legalism, Jewish); natural 57; Near Eastern 208n125; *nomos* 174; origin of 208n125, 226n107; vs. prophecy 58. *See also* Canon law; common law; halakhah; Hammurabi, Code of; moral laws; Mosaic code; Roman law

laymen: Commentary for 2, 29, 143, 168, 171, 182; difficulty with Leviticus 155; disregard of halakhah 151 Jewish literature for 25, 27, 87, 201n125; Montefiore writes for 24; observance by 193; priestly intervention 209n136; reviews of Commentary 170; ritual and 144; spirituality of 209n137

leaders, Jewish 144. *See also* prophets; rabbinic sages

Leah 169

learning *see* education; scholarship; study

left-wing Judaism *see* Liberal Judaism; Reform Judaism

legal flexibility *see* halakhah: change

legalism, Jewish: Christian scholars on 8, 153, 159, 227n125; Epstein defends 196n2; Ezra and 4, 8; prophets vs. 50, 59; Rabbinism and 20, 78; Smith on 228n137

legends: biblical narrative 72; creation story 161. *See also* aggadah; midrash

Legg, T.S. 217n190, 243

legitimacy of: biblical criticism 4, 62; Chosen People 136; Jewish law 56; Judaism 18, 28, 53, 168, 172, 173, 178, 184, 201n125; *lex talionis* 113; Liberal Judaism 21, 25; rabbinic Judaism xv, 8, 19, 27, 48, 81; revelation 165; ritual 61; secular Jewish writers 235n37. *See also* authenticity

lehem (H) 226n108

Lehrman, S. M. 239

Leibowitz, N. 225n99, 248

Leibowitz, Yeshayahu 227n127

Leiman, Shnayer 193n36, 249

Leo Baeck College (London) xiii, 237

letter of the law 146, 152, 228n137

letters, Hebrew 12, 13

Leventhal, Israel 233n7

Levi 104

Levi (Rabbi) 44, 45

Levi, Israel 220n17

Leviticus (Book) 57, 60, 62, 67

Leviticus (Commentary) 33, 37, 43, 155, 198n53–54, 206n98, 211n40

Levy, Isaac 247

Lex Mosaica 60, 242, 251, 253

lex talionis 76, 113

Liberal Judaism: Abrahams and 58, 153; Cohen on 38; Commentary on 88; in England 5, 9, 20–21, 58, 144; Epstein on 25; Friedlander on 39; halakhah and 144; *cont.*

Liberal Judaism *cont.*
  Hertz and xv, 12, 21–23, 26, 33, 47, 165, 174, 182, 197n15, 211n27; Hertz archives on 238; *Jewish Guardian* and 201n123; Kohut and 194n53; Montefiore and 24, 87, 165, 197n19; Orthodoxy vs. 197n14, 200n86; and sales of Commentary 167; vs. traditional Judaism 175; on women 114. *See also* Reform Judaism
liberal trends: rabbinic Judaism 134
liberalism, political 184
liberty *see* emancipation; freedom
libraries xiii, 167
library, Hertz's 216n173; archives xiii, 237–238
licentiousness *see* sexual: immorality
life: meaning of 137. *See also* animals; human life
lifestyle, Jewish 140, 183
light: creation story 163; unto the nations 122, 136, 138, 181, 209n137
lightning: fire and 155
linguistics *see* language; philology
liquids and roasting 65
literal: application of law 146, 152, 228n137; meaning, see *peshat* (H); reading of the Bible 158, 161–162, 164–165, 204n54, 205n71, 232n208
literary: evidence 63–66; parallels 69; source analysis 8–9, 49, 57–59, 61, 67, 174; unity 6, 62, 65, 172
literature: Jewish 27, 39, 53, 56 (*see also* rabbinic literature); tradition and 164
Littel, Franklin 185, 236n73, 249
liturgy 226n108
Liverpool Old Hebrew Congregation 3, 40, 200n92
Liverpool University 40
Livingstone, R.W. 111, 112, 210n2, 213n81, n86; 217n180–182, 247, 249
Lloyd George, David 140
loan words 67, 68
loans: charity 133, 152; at interest (*see* interest)
locusts (plague) 231n186
Loewe, Herbert 114, 197n19, 211n23, 217n191, n194; 250
Loewe, Raphael 212n56, 238
Loewinger, S. 221n41, 249
Lofthouse, W. F. 204n49, 249
logic 63–64, 84, 223n61. *See also* rationalism

London: Hertz in 216n173
love: allegory and 164; chastisements of 225n99; Christian 94, 95, 113, 212n69; of enemies 103–104; of God 94, 95, 140; God's 95, 138, 139; medieval 115; of neighbor 105, 180; parental 129; of Rachel 169; of righteousness 139; of stranger 108, 131; universal 166
Lower East Side 2
loyalty: of Jews 22, 40, 196n10. *See also* commitment
Luther, Martin 135
Luzzatto, Samuel David: Bible commentary x; on Christianity 109–110, 216n169; on mysticism 12, 193n44, n45; rationalism 158, 210n5, 230n178
lying: by Abraham 124

Maccabees 152
Macmillan (publisher) 24
magic: in Christianity 111; mysticism 13
Magnus, Laurie 201n123
maid servants 93, 103, 126
Maimonides (Rambam): Abelson on 37, 199n74, 240; anthropomorphism 232n212; on Catholic Church 109; cited in Commentary 229n161; Cohen on 38, 199n71, 200n83, 242; on creation 161, 165, 232n213, 233n213; on divine will 227n127; *Eight Chapters* (*Shemonah Perakim*) 38, 183, 200n83, 239; epistemology 178; Epstein on 45; on ethics 82; on evolution of law 150; on function of religion 180; on Gentiles 222n44; on Greek wisdom 232n202; *Guide for the Perplexed* 143, 156, 164, 239; on halakhah 143, 150, 225n105, 228n145–229n145; influence on Commentary xvi, 36; on interest 134–135; on Jesus 39; on justice 212n60, n66; on miracles 156–158, 231n179–180, n182; *Mishneh Torah* 154, 239; on non-Jewish teachings 162, 183; on paganism 131, 221n29; praised by Hertz 153, 229n162; on prophets 155; rationalism 3, 153, 164–165; on ritual cleanliness 152, 229n152; on sacrifices 44–45, 154, 155, 158, 230n166, n169; on serving God 94; *Shemonah*

Index of Names and Subjects

Perakim (see subhead *Eight Chapters*); on spiritual medicine 224n74; on Temple ritual 154; theology 213n92; on wife-beating 217n189; works cited 239. *See also* citation index
man (H) 69; manna 157, 230n174
man: conscience of (*see* conscience); fall of 118, 124; fears of 229n161; image of God (*see under* God); monogamy 119; nature of 219n2, 228n137; origin 161, 170 (*see also* evolution); original language 66; relationship with God 118, 127, 130, 137, 146, 154, 169
man-made laws 175
Manasseh 51, 78
mankind *see* humanity
manna 157, 230n174; *man* (H) 69
manumission 90
Margaliyot, M. 239
Margolies, M. 210n5, 230n178, 249
Margolis, Max 198n46
marriage: ceremony 226n108; Christian vs. Jewish ideas 115, 119; Dillmann on 210n138; humanization and 121; Inge on 110; inheritance law and 152; of relatives 92, 212n51. *See also* adultery; *agunah*; bigamy; divorce; husbands; intermarriage
married women: rape laws 68
Martineau, James 178–180, 235n56–236n61
Martyr, Justin 110
martyrdom 130; Jewish 116, 137, 141, 176, 218n204
Marx, A. 235n37, 249
massacres of: Edomites 169; Jews 116, 185. *See also* genocide
masses *see* laymen
materialism 52–53, 92
matriarchs 126. *See also* names
Mattuck, Israel 47, 201n123
mayim (H) 65
McFayden, J. E. 205n78, 227n125, 249
Mead, G. R. S. 235n32
meaning: of life 137; midrash and 28, 184; of miracles 155; shades of, in Law 148. *See also* interpretation; *peshat* (H)
meat: eating of 44, 45, 101
medicine: compassion and xiv; spiritual 140, 180, 224n74, 227n128; supernatural 230n174

medieval: biblicists 64, 220n22 (*see also* Ibn Ezra, Abraham); Church 84, 92, 112–114, 116; courts of love 115; decisors 227n129; feudalism 107; Jewish thought xvi, 49, 59, 156, 160, 202n1 (*see also* Judah Halevi; Maimonides; Nachmanides); Jewry 116, 135, 176, 181; Karaites 12; model of religion 165; moralists 178; paganism 93; witch trials 127–128
meditation 139
Megillot 29, 30
Meir, Rabbi 102
Meiri, Menahem ben Solomon 222n44, 227n129, 239
Melchizedek 70
memory of: Edom 169; slavery in Egypt 140
Mendelssohn, Moses 153; *Biur* 205n71, 239
Mendes-Flohr, P. R. 235n38, 249, 254
Mendes, Henry Pereira 171, 177, 192n14, 198n50
mental cruelty: Christianity 116, 117
mental perception: miracles 158
mentors, Hertz's 3–4
mercenaries 107
merchants 132–133
mercy: civility and 104; God's 96–97, 213n92, 224n65; and interest 134; lack of (*see* cruelty); virtue 95, 212n57, n69. *See also* compassion
merger of: Christianity and Judaism 174; Christianity and paganism 181. *See also* synthesis
merit: justice and 94
Merneptah (Pharaoh) 70
Mesopotamia 61, 77, 208n125, 209n135. *See also* Babylonia
message of Israel 142, 210n138
Messiahs: children as 41, 100, 214n109
messianic era 10, 45, 170, 193n35, 194n53, 226n107, 228n137
messianic goals 95, 120
metamorphosis of law *see* halakhah: change
metaphysics 139, 171, 207n119
methodology: Bachya's 178, 235n55; empirical 75, 164, 165; Hertz's 173; nonscientific 163; scientific 8, 162, 231n198, 232n203; of theology 231n198
Meyer, Michael A. 192n29, 249

Micah (prophet) 95, 212n69
Middle Ages *see* medieval . . .
middle class: allegory and 233n213
Midianites 63–64, 205n70, 221n26
midrash: in Bible commentaries 28; on creation 42, 102, 161; on eternal Israel 141; Jewish education 184; on Potiphar 69–70, 206n96; on sacrifices 44–45; style of Commentary 48, 171, 182; on *teraphim* 126; on Tower of Babel 212n46; works cited 239–240. *See also citation index*
Midrash ha-Gadol 213n88, 239
Midrash Rabbah 38, 239
midwives, Egyptian 93
might vs. right 184
Mill, John Stuart 41
Miller, P. D., Jr. 204n56, 209n135, 249
mind *see* intellect
Minean language 67
ministers *see* clergy
miracles: Christianity 56; definition 158; legal decisions and 230n175; Maimonides on 156–158, 231n179–180, n182; prophets and 144; rationalism and xvi, 36, 155–159, 165; Renan on 208n119
misfortune *see* suffering
Mishnah: Moses receives 192n19; on miracles 156. *See also* Oral Law *and citation index*
Mishneh Torah see under Maimonides and *citation index*
mishpatim (H) 146
mission, Jewish: allegiance to 174 (*see also* commitment, religious); of Chosen People 135–142, 165; Hellenism and 181; Hertz on 18; Kohler on 223n59, 225n96; separatism and 146; spirituality 180, 228n137
mission, prophet's 155
missionary activity: of Chosen People 142, 165; to Jewish youth 140; to Jews, by Jews 195n72; of Liberal Jews 22
mitzvah (H) 226n108. *See also* commandments
mixed seating 23
Moab 65
Mocatta Library 237
moderation 117, 119
modern (neo-) Orthodoxy 6, 64, 66, 173, 191n5

modern scholarship 170. *See also* secular: learning
modern world *see* Western civilization
modernity of Judaism 175
modesty: purity and 212n57
modifications to Jewish law *see* halakhah: change
Molech-worship 152
monarchs *see* kings
monarchy 92, 98, 106, 120; Jewish 57
monetary fines 76, 99, 113, 214n100
moneylenders 90, 135, 222n47. *See also* interest
monks: holiness and 95
monogamy: Judaism 119
monolatry: primitive belief 51
monotheism: Christianity and 111–112, 120, 185; early Israelites 4; ethical 51; geography and 208n119; Hebrew 102; Jewish genius 223n62; Judaism and 176; sacrifices and 43; simplicity of 147; Trinity and 117–118
Montefiore, Claude Goldsmid: Abelson cites 37; on anthropomorphism 165; *Bible for Home Reading* 5, 249; on Christian love 94, 212n68; on Christianity 84, 112, 113, 123, 147, 174, 181, 210n15, 211n16–20; on creation 161–162, 165; on democracy 98, 213n94; on divorce 116; ecumenism 176; "The English Jew . . ." 24; on Friedlaender (Michael) 231n200; Friedlander (Gerald) on 38–39, 200n84, n86; on God 95, 96, 213n81, n87; on Greeks 97; on Hellenism 83–84, 86, 109, 111–112, 210n13–14; Hertz and 20, 87, 122, 183, 196n4, 211n25; on Judaism 85–87, 211n21–22; Liberal Judaism xv, 20–22, 24–25, 47, 87, 174; *Liberal Judaism and Hellenism* 24, 38, 39, 249; on miracles 158, 231n189; on moral law 144, 227n121; on Mosaic authorship 196n4; *Nineteenth Century* essay 22, 197n19, 249; on non-Jewish sources 178; *Old Testament and After* 24, 39, 249; on Old Testament theology 22–23; *Outlines of Liberal Judaism* 24, 249; on pity 104; *Rabbinic Literature and Gospel Teachings* 20; on rationalism 165; on Stoicism 99, 101; on strangers 215n132; on suffering 142; *Synoptic Gospels*

Index of Names and Subjects

24, 35, 38, 250; talmudist 86; on Trinity 117; on universalism 102; Wellhausenian 5, 9, 87, 151; on women 114, 217n194; works cited 24, 249–250 (*see also subentries for titles, above*)
Montefiore, Moses 86
Moore, George Foot: on anti-Jewish bias 56–58, 203n33–35; cited by Hertz 57, 204n41; on Jephthah 220n20; on Pentateuch 62, 205n62; on sacrifices 44; Smith on 203n36; works cited 250
Morais, Henry 193n45, 194n53, 250
Morais, Sabato: on biblical criticism x, 8; on change in halakhah 9–11, 15, 193n38; Conservative Judaism 16, 192n14, n15; 193n53–194n53; Hertz's teacher 3, 4, 14, 16; Jewish Theological Seminary 7; on Mosaic authorship 6; rationalism 12, 193n44–45; on sacrifices 193n35; on Talmud 7, 192n19; on Wellhausen 5–6; works cited 250
moral autonomy 96
moral laws: barbarism and 88; freedom and 59; God and 91; man-made 175; Martineau on 179; prophetic religion 145; rabbinic changes to 226n119; reviews of Commentary 212n56; unwritten 144
moral progress xvi, 81, 131, 137
moral regeneration 225n99
moral theology 7, 74
moral truth 36
moral unity *see* ethics, universal
moralists, Jewish 178
morality *see* ethics
Mosaic authorship: archaeological evidence 67, 162; biblical critics on 8, 50, 55, 58, 59, 78; Cohen on 38; evidence for xv, 162, 172; historical evidence 210n139; literary evidence 63–66; Montefiore denies 196n4; reviews of Commentary 170; Seminary faculty on 4; *Wissenschaft* and 6, 9
Mosaic code (Hebrew law): on adultery 128; on animals 101; authenticity 172; Babylonian code vs. 74, 76, 208n125; biblical criticism and 8, 19, 20, 46, 52, 59, 78; child-killing 129; Christianity vs. 56; dating 61–62; Dillman on 209n138–210n138; ethics of 135, 143, 220n17; impact on West 121; on incest 101; integrity of xv; on interest 131–134, 221n37; justice in 106; on marriage 115; oral law and 6; vs. pagan law 7, 75; property offenses 112; rabbinic changes to 11, 150–152, 226n119, 228n145 (*see also* halakhah: change); revelation at Sinai 59, 148; Semitic codes and 67; on slaves 99, 107; uniqueness of 73, 77, 148; on witchcraft 127
Mosaism *see* Israelite religion
Moses: dating of Pentateuch 5; desert leader 4; Egyptian word 68; engraves Torah 72; evidence for life of 67; forty-day retreat 59; genius 122, 223n62; God's revelation to 55, 149, 157–158, 204n54; as historian 64; in Moab 65; and Oral Law 6, 149, 192n19, 228n140; as prophet 154, 156, 226n107; rabbinic Judaism and 86; Wellhausen on 20, 50. *See also* Mosaic . . .
Moses ben Maimon *see* Maimonides
Moses ben Nachman *see* Nachmanides
mothers *see* parents; women
Mount Sinai *see* Sinai, Mount
mountains: metaphor of 142
murder (homicide) 76, 96, 99–101, 113, 124, 208n125
mutilation 99, 113, 214n100
Mystic Currents in Ancient Israel (Hertz) 193n48, 246
mysticism, Jewish: Abelson on 36, 37, 199n74; Hertz on 12–13, 193n47, n50; miracles and 157; sacrifices and 154. *See also* Zohar

Naboth 105
Nachmanides (Ramban): on Azazel 154; Bible commentary x; on Canaanites 222n46; on Christianity 109; cited by Hertz 214n100, 228n137; on interest 134, 221n44; on Jewish history 224n87; on miracles 156, 230n177; on paradise story 232n213; on sacrifices 44, 154, 230n165; theology 141, 153, 229n160; works cited 240
Nadab 12, 155, 157
names: of countries 126; of God 68, 226n108; of Israel 139; Semitic sources 68

National Council 120
nationalism: in Commentary 128; Jewish 181; Zionism 40
nations: character of 126, 130, 143; ethics and 181–182; loyalty to 196n10; seven pagan 127, 130; small vs. large 140; strength of 227n128. *See also* Israel (nation)
native spirituality 137, 223n59
natural disasters: interest and 90
natural forces: Greek religion 120
natural law: codes vs. 57
natural order: miracles and 155–158, 230n174; plagues 231n186
natural selection: Hebrews 54; man 160, 231n194. *See also* evolution
nature: God as 97; God in 177; religions 51
nature of man 219n2, 228n137
Nazism x, 108, 138, 184–185, 212n60, 221n41, 223n62. *See also* Holocaust
Near East, ancient 7, 54, 66, 67, 71, 172, 180. *See also* Canaan
Near Eastern: law 208n125 (*see also* Hammurabi, Code of); religions 73, 209n135 (*see also* Semitic: religion)
nebular theory: creation 163
negligence: laws of 76
neighbors, non-Jewish 222n44. *See also* strangers
neo-Babylonian language 67
neo-Orthodoxy 6, 36, 64, 66, 173, 191n5
neo-paganism 142, 147
ner tamid (H) 226n108
Netivot Shalom 205n71, 239
Neufeld, E. 221n40, 250
Neumark, David 83, 210n11, 250
"new Israel" 138
New Paths (Hertz) 21–22, 23, 25, 196n10, 197n16, 211n25, 246
New Testament: demons in 127; on divorce 116; Friedlander on 39; Judaism and 85; on love 94; revelation and 55; Smith on 207n108; spirituality 51, 53. *See also* Gospels
New York City: Hertz in 1, 2
New York Times 196n76, 233n7
Newman, John Henry 119
Newman, Selig 220n22, 250
newspapers *see* press
Nietzsche, Friedrich 98
nihilism, religious 9, 22
Nile 231n182
Nineteenth Century 22, 197n19

nitzel (H) 127, 169
Noachide laws 215n149
nobility 75, 108, 219n223
noblesse oblige 140, 181
Noeldeke, Theodore 210n3
nokhri (H) 131–133
nomadic: Habiri 70; religion 54, 61
nomos 174
non-Jewish scholars *see* scholars, non-Jewish
non-Jewish sources *see under* source analysis of Commentary
non-Jews: audience of Commentary 28; praise Judaism 173; rabbinic Judaism and 133, 134, 222n44. *See also* Christian . . . ; strangers
nonconformity, religious 181
nondenominational Jewish academy 26
nonkosher food 23
nonscholarly Jews *see* laymen
notarikon 13
Numbers [= Bamidbar] (Commentary) 31, 33, 37, 211n40
numerical value of letters 12, 13
Nussenbaum, Max 192n19, 193n35, n38; 250

Obadiah 126
obedience: to commandments 222n44; formalism 181; to God 146, 148, 170; liberty of 98; to older authorities 228n139; to religious authority 174; spirituality and 102
oblivion: Jewish people 209n137
observance, Jewish: by children of immigrants 27; fear of God 170; fences and 150; God's will 146; law and 173; Maimonides on 143; by Morais 194n53; rationalism and 193n45; Smith on 227n125, 228n137; traditional Judaism and 196n10. *See also* deed vs. creed
occupations, Jewish 135
Odyssey 114
Oesterley, W. 204n49, 207n112, 250
offenses *see* crimes; sin
offerings *see* sacrifices
ohavo (H) 222n44
Old Testament *see* Bible
ontology 160, 183
oppression *see* cruelty; persecution
oral history interviews 238
Oral Law 6, 148–150, 178, 228n139–140. *See also* Talmud

Index of Names and Subjects 291

oral tradition *see* Oral Law
orator: Hertz as 17; Moses as 64. *See also* preacher(s)
ordeal of jealousy 114, 127, 128, 151, 217n188, n192
order of the world *see* natural order
orderliness: Greek society 96
organic unity of Jewish law 4, 9–10, 151, 184, 228n139
Oriental: amorousness 164; chronicles 63; kings 208n125; languages 66; people 163; religions 111, 177
origin of: Israel (nation) 70, 172, 206n100; the Law 208n125, 226n107; man (*see under* man). *See also* dating
original sin 118
Orthodox Jewish Congregational Union of America 192n14
Orthodox Jews 10, 15, 22, 167, 183–184, 193n53–194n53
Orthodox Judaism: in Eastern Europe 11; in Germany 15; Hertz and 6, 9, 17, 47, 192n14, 194n60; Jewish Theological Seminary and 14, 192n14; vs. Liberalism 22, 24, 25, 197n14, 200n86; in United States 194n53; *Wissenschaft* and 173; women in 115. *See also* neo-Orthodoxy; rabbinic Judaism; traditional Judaism
Orthodox rabbis 168, 192n14, 236n73
outsiders *see* strangers
Oxford Universal Dictionary 223n59, 251
Oxford University 25, 51, 57, 60, 73, 111, 177, 220n22
Oxford University Press 29, 233n5, n7

pagan civilization *see* paganism
pagan law 7, 74–76, 172. *See also* Greco-Roman law; Hammurabi, Code of
pagan nations *see* Canaan; Egypt; Greco-Roman civilization; Phoenicia
paganism (heathenism): Christianity and 88, 109–112, 119–120, 136, 147, 181, 184, 185, 216n172, 217n178; critique of 41, 89–90, 92–93, 99–100, 109, 121, 176; harmony and 75; idol worship 126, 218n214; impact on West 106, 123; inhumanity 92, 95, 115; Israelite religion vs. 7, 52, 66, 74, 78, 141; Jewish separatism and 147–148; morality xvi, 76, 88, 90–92, 96, 108, 130–131, 135, 213n84, 215n149, 219n222; Nazism and 108, 185; respect for parents 215n145, 235n44; ritual in 57; sacrifices and 155; sensuality 180, 236n63; spirituality 102; trial by ordeal 128; view of God 96; worship 60, 103, 213n85
pain: Christianity 113; paganism 115; psychic 116, 117; Stoicism 99. *See also* cruelty; suffering
Palestine 40, 51, 54, 64, 66, 69. *See also* Canaan
Palestinian Talmud 239
palimpsest 3
pan-Babylonian theory 54, 66
Paneth, P. 197n29, 251
pantheon, Greek 96
parables 44, 163–164, 176, 232n208, n213
paradise (Garden of Eden) 163, 232n213–233n213
paradox *see* contradictions
parallel passages 64–66
pardon, right of 208n125
parents: affection for 91; Israelite 129; respect for 215n145, 235n44; sins of 67; support by children 179. *See also* children
pariah, Jew as 176
parliamentary system 120
particularism, Jewish 166
paschal lamb 65
Passover seder 22
pastoral: theology 17; tours 29, 30, 186
patience 95, 139
Patriarchal Age 69–70
Patriarchs 67, 115, 138. *See also* Abraham; Isaac; Jacob
patriotism: and aliens 108
Paul, St. 85, 110
peace 88, 100, 126, 139, 221n35, 222n44, n46. *See also* harmony
Peake, Arthur S. 240, 242, 249, 250, 253
Peet, T. Eric 205n67
penal codes 121
penalties *see* punishment
Pentateuch: author (*see* human composition of: Pentateuch; Mosaic authorship); commentaries (*see* Bible commentaries); date of (*see* dating the Pentateuch); historiography 4–5; Liberal Judaism and 144. *See also* Torah

Pentateuch (Hertz): 1938 edition 41, 247; advertisements for 187–188; American edition ix, 167; banned in Great Britain 184; contributors (*see* research associates); critical reviews 168–170; financial backer (*see* Blashki, Aaron); first draft 31, 91, 198n53; first edition 167, 246; impact 2; manuscripts 232n206, 238; one-volume edition 167, 168, 224n63, 233n11, 234n16; period piece 182–183; pricing 33, 168; print run 167, 168; project begins 29; publication costs 199n65; publication dates xv, 2, 19, 89; publication delays 33–34, 199n59–60, 234n16; reviews (*see* reviews); sales 34, 167–168, 233n6, n9; second edition 234n12, 238; title page 33, 187–189; translations 133; variations in editions 65, 126, 149, 200n88, 224n63. *See also specific topics and names of individual books*
pentateuchal documents 4, 50, 55, 62, 63, 67, 172, 175
pentateuchal laws *see* Mosaic code
Pereira Mendes, Henry 171, 177, 192n14, 198n50
perfection: in Christianity 52; God's 224n65; human 81, 173; in religious truth 85
perjury 90
perpetual fire 155
persecution: by Christians 175; of Edomites 169; by Nazis 185; religious 111, 116, 126; of witches 127. *See also* cruelty
Persian: kings 71; language 67
Persians 101, 212n51, 215n149
personal: autonomy 174; charisma 144; holiness 76, 212n57; interpretation 10; theology 23
personality *see* character
personification 154, 164
peshat (H) 7, 47, 129, 169, 184
Pesikta de-Rab Kahana 83, 240
Pharaohs 70, 71, 93, 124, 225n99, 229n161
Pharisaic scribes 8, 50
Pharisaism 54, 57, 173. *See also* rabbinic Judaism
Pharisees 53, 151, 202n11
philanthropy 86, 94. *See also* charity
Philipson, David 192n28–29, 251

Philo 39
philology: in Commentary xv, 29, 66, 67–69, 74; dating of Bible 27, 51; methodology 71, 77–78; Moore on 57; proof of Bible 7, 172; *Wissenschaft* 48
philosopher(s): Fathers of the Mishna 156; Hertz as 17; Hertz cites 41, 165, 178; Jewish 137, 228n139. *See also* Greek philosophers; Maimonides; Spinoza
philosophy: moral 179 (*see also* ethics); religious 24, 25, 87, 174; Western x
Phinehas 68
Phinehas (Rabbi) 45
Phoenicia 136; customs 78
physical order *see* natural order
physical welfare 143
physics, laws of 158
pidyon ha-ben (H) 226n108
pietism 136
pigmy-giant aphorism 10, 193n36
pilgrim-track 206n106
Pilpula Harifta 222n44, 239
Pines, Shlomo 210n8, 239
Pirkei de-Rabbi Eliezer 240
pity *see* compassion; mercy
plagues 71, 158, 231n186
planetary system 163
Plato 36, 96, 110, 176
Plautus 105
Plucknett, T.F.T. 217n190, 243
plunder 127, 169
pluralism: ideational 85; religious 25, 130
pocket-picking: death penalty 106
poetry: in the Bible 176–177; Song at the Sea 158; writing 60
polemics: Christian 56, 85; on Christianity xvi, 3, 89, 90, 176, 182; on cruelty 140; Guttmann's 134; on Judaism's legitimacy 184; Montefiore's 5; racial superiority 138; on Wellhausen 8
police: Jewish observance 170
political exchange: Near East 59
political liberalism 184
political structures *see* government
political Zionism 40
pollution *see* contamination
polygamy 52

Index of Names and Subjects

polytheism: brotherhood and 102; in Canaan 130; Christianity 111, 112; Greek 83; inhumanity of 92; Judaism vs. 39, 91; tolerance and 98. *See also* paganism

poor: debtors 105; loans to 133, 134, 152; in modern law 121; non-Jewish 222n44; treatment of 76, 92, 112; wife-selling by 114

popular . . . *see* laymen

popularizations: biblical criticism 54–55

positive historical Judaism 15, 18, 48, 194n53, 195n61. *See also* Conservative Judaism

postexilic period: dating the Pentateuch 5, 50; legalism 8, 227n125; ritual 57, 59, 60, 205n71. *See also* Second Commonwealth

postpentateuchal tracts 6, 8, 149

Potiphar 64, 70; wife of 69–70, 93, 125

poverty *see* poor

power: of the Bible 176; of commandments 11; ethics and 181–182; God and 97; of kings (*see under* kings); of Law 153; of parents 129; over slaves 107; of Torah 146. *See also* authority

powerlessness: Diaspora 181–182

practice *see* observance

pragmatism 75, 96, 121, 124, 208n119

prayer 10, 60, 118, 162; book 115

preacher(s): contribute to Commentary 3, 35, 38; Hertz as 16, 17, 180, 195n74

Preachers' Conference 32, 38

preaching 38, 169, 183, 216n173, 234n28. *See also* homiletics

precepts *see* commandments

preexilic age: dating of Pentateuch 5, 6; J, E, and D documents 50; Mosaic code 7, 62, 67, 172; Priestly Code 61, 67; ritual 58. *See also* prophetic religion

prejudice *see* bias

premeditated murder 99

press: ads for Commentary 188; in Hertz archives 238; Liberal Judaism in 23–24; reviews of Commentary 168; rumors about Hertz 26. *See also titles of newspapers*

pride: in Judaism ix, 8, 27, 46, 48, 182, 201n125; of Seminary in chief rabbi 196n76

Priestly Code (P document) 50–51, 61–62, 67, 203n15

priests: Babylonian 92; *birkat kohanim* (H) 226n108; commandments of 155; hierocracy 51, 205n71; interests of 60–61; intervention of 209n136; kingdom of 137, 141; legalism and 227n125; and Pentateuch 5; prophets vs. 145; right to firstlings 64; sacrifices and 230n166; spirituality 102–103; teaching role 227n120; trial by ordeal and 217n192

primeval chaos 137

primitive: man 43, 44, 113; races 101, 209n135 religion (*see* ancient religion)

prison: debtors in 105; Joseph in 69–70

private choice in: morality 96; religion 174

privileges of Chosen People 141, 181

profane *see under* holiness

profit: interest as 133

progress: moral xvi, 81, 131, 137; religious (*see* evolution, religious)

progressive: conservatism 15, 21, 194n53, 197n11; Judaism (*see* Reform Judaism); revelation 174

promiscuity 101

Promised Land *see* Canaan

propaganda, religious 195n72

property: confiscated by kings 105; vs. humanity 76, 90, 92, 98–99, 112

prophecy 58, 124, 153, 154, 226n107, 228n137

prophetic passages 26

prophetic readings *see* Haftarot

prophetic religion: Christianity and 20, 57; Liberal/Reform Judaism and 98, 144; rabbinic Judaism and 56, 59, 172; ritual 4, 87, 145

prophetic theology 103

prophetic writings 149

prophets: eloquence of 176; on equality 93; ethical monotheism 51; Graetz on 6; humanism of 82; Jesus and 39, 109; miracles and 155, 157; morality 5, 50, 92, 174; on righteousness 95; on ritual 145–146, 227n125; sages vs. 144–145, 226n118; spirituality and 209n137; on spread of Judaism 177; successors of Moses 86; teaching role 227n120; teachings of 112, 120; vision of 1, 173, 182

prophylactic separatism 148

prosbul 152
prosperity: and idolatry 126
prostitutes: maid servants 93; male 68
Protagoras 98
protective fence 148, 229n145
Protestant *see* Christian . . .
proto-: Pharisaism 50; Rabbinism 51, 59
Providence, divine 75, 135, 162, 226n107, 227n129
Psalms: author 150, 229n148; Midrash on 239; poetry 176; spirituality 209n137
psychic pain: Church causes 116, 117
psychology 7, 44, 54, 77, 173, 179, 185
publishers of Commentary 29, 168
pulpit teachers *see* preachers
punishment: brotherhood and 103; of idolators 92; for injuring slaves 93; of Israel by God 141–143, 225n99, n104; mutilation 214n100; reward and 226n107, 229n161; in Semitic codes 67–68; of slaves 105; talionic 113, 217n186
punitive codes 121
purification: Hebraism 52; of Israel 142–143
purity: Christian vs. Jew 185; of God 96, 196n2; of Jacob's character 169; of Jewish descent 104; laws of 151; martyrdom and 116; virtue 212n57
purpose, Divine 146

Que Que, Rhodesia 186

Ra (sun-god) 71
Rabad 134
rabbinate: halakhic change 11. *See also* rabbis
rabbinic college, Liberal 25
rabbinic interpretation 7
rabbinic Judaism: biblical critics on 19–20, 50, 51, 52, 58, 78, 81, 87, 145; and biblical law xv, 11, 129, 150–152, 226n119; Christian attitudes to 1, 56, 58, 136; Christianity vs. 36–37, 123, 136; ethics 85–86, 100, 104, 124, 151, 219n222; Friedlander on 39; function of xvi; Hertz's love of x, 47, 144, 174, 186; impact on West 120–121; integrity 172; on Israel's mission 136; legitimacy of 8, 19, 48, 49, 81; on marriage 115; Montefiore on xv, 39, 87, 165; Moore on 62; mysticism and 13; organic growth 4, 10, 184; religious tolerance 215n149; ritual laws 86, 145; on sacrifices 43, 44, 45; Schechter on 27; on strangers 133, 134; on suffering 142; universalism 102; on usury 135; Wise against 8; on women 114–115
rabbinic law *see* halakhah; Oral Law
rabbinic literature: on authority of sages 226n118; Bible and 59; Cohen translates 38; on Edom 126; Friedlander on 39; on God 97, 224n64; Hertz use of 145; humanism of 82, 88; on miracles 156, 230n175; Moses' knowledge of 149; parables in 163; on paradise story 233n213; on strangers 132; suffering in 225n99; universalism 102. *See also* midrash; Talmud
rabbinic ordination: Hertz 2, 3
rabbinic sages: authority of 144–145, 226n118; on God 196n2; halakhic change 148, 150; on inheritance law 152; Jesus vs. 39; on miracles 156; teaching role 227n120
rabbinic sources *see* sources, Jewish
Rabbinical Assembly 236n67
rabbinics: Hertz scholar of 17, 151, 195n74; Schechter chair 1
Rabbinism *see* rabbinic Judaism
rabbis: apologetics and 195n72; Eastern European 21, 192n14; halakhic interpretation 10; Orthodox 168, 192n14, 236n73; prerequisites 18; respect for 171; sales of Commentary 167–168; teaching role 227n120; training 192n14; Victorian 21. *See also* Chief Rabbi; rabbinic sages
race, Jewish: endurance of 141; God and 102; inferiority 138; superiority 137–138; usage in *Pentateuch* 223n63; values of 223n62
races, primitive 101, 209n135
Rachel (matriarch) 126, 169
radical biblical criticism 78, 87, 149. *See also* biblical criticism, higher
Radicalism 17, 21. *See also* Liberal Judaism
Raffalovich, I. 198n45
raham (A) 68
rahmanut (H) 104
Rambam *see* Maimonides
Ramban *see* Nachmanides

Index of Names and Subjects

rape laws 68
Rapoport, Solomon Judah Leib 173
Rashba 134
Rashbam 205n70, 222n46
Rashi: Bible commentary x; on burnt offerings 230n166; on Canaanites 222n46; on chastisement 225n99; on Gentiles 221n43, 222n24; on God 213n92; homiletics 47; on interest 134; on perpetual fire 155; source of Commentary 29; style 29; translation of 225n99, 240
rationalism: allegory and 163–166; biblical law and 75; ethics and 179; evolution and 159–163; Hellenism and 82; in Judaism 4, 153–154; of Maimonides xvi, 3, 36, 153; miracles and 155–159; Morais on 12, 193n45; mysticism vs. 13; personal autonomy and 174; revelation and 180; sacrifices and 44, 154–155, 230n169; Western Jews and 174
rationalization 128, 169, 182
Rawlinson, George 60, 204n51, 251
Rawlinson, Henry Creswicke 204n51
reality: historical (*see* historicity); miracles and 157, 231n180
reason *see* rationalism
Rebekah 124
rebellion against Judaism 29
Rebrin, Slovakia 2
reciprocation: for gifts 222n44
Red Sea 158, 206n106
redemption: from Egypt 68, 115, 127, 158; Hebraic idea 52; of mankind 176; messianic (*see* messianic era)
references, rabbinic: minimized in Commentary 29, 48. *See also* citation analysis
Reform Judaism: on evolution 160, 162; on exile 142; and halakhic change 10, 11; Hertz against xv, 21, 88, 182; Hirsch against 36; Kohler and 98; mission theory 147, 225n96; Montefiore on 24; and mysticism 13; and sales of Commentary 167; scholarly journal 133; theologians 5, 8; *Wissenschaft* and 48. *See also* Liberal Judaism
Reformation 118
reformation: of Jacob 142
Reich, Emil 201n122, 251
Reichert, V. E. 210n15, 251
Reines, A. J. 231n179–180, 251

relativity of: conscience 179; truth 85
Release Year 131, 132, 133, 152
religion: complexity of 60, 66, 159; man's fears and 229n161; mysticism and 12; personal autonomy in 174; purpose of 161, 180; sacrifices and 44, 154; Spinoza on 202n1; symbols and 146; worship and 145. *See also* faith; theology
religious . . . *see inverted form, e. g.,* anthropology, religious
remedy *see* medicine
Renan, Ernest 75, 112, 207n119–208n119, 210n3
repeal *see* abrogation
repentance of: biblical personalities 219n2; Egyptians 127; God 97; Israel 143; sinners 213n92
reproof of fellow man 215n139
research associates xv, 3; acknowledgment of contributions 31, 33, 36, 89, 200n88; Hertz correspondence with 238; Hertz need for 28; Hertz revises mss. 89, 91, 220n17, 227n120; honoraria 31, 34, 198n50; initial meeting 29, 31, 36, 189, 198n57; letter of complaint 33, 187–189, 199n62; Maimonidean tradition 3, 36, 164; paradigm of Judaism 153; prolific contributor 149; qualifications of 35–36; resignations 31, 32; sales of Commentary 168; unpaid 30. *See also names*
resident alien (*ger*) 131, 132
resistance to external influences 209n135
respect for: human dignity 216n177; Jewish values 182; Jews 137; parents 215n145, 235n44; rabbis 171; teachers 235n31; women 115. *See also* dignity
responsibilities: of Chosen People 137, 141; upholding Law 153
resurrection of: the dead 152, 226n107; Jesus 56; Jewish people 141; Jewish spirit 175
return to Judaism 9
Reuben 224n76
revelation: allegory and 164–165; and altar-building 61; Christianity 56; of God's word 55, 138, 174; in history 142; and Israelite religion 73; natural 96; new 228n145; rationalism and 36, 153; *cont.*

revelation *cont.*
  religious 178; Renan on 208n119; truth and 154, 164. *See also* Sinai, Mount: revelation
revenge *see* vengeance
reverence *see* respect
reviews of the Commentary 13, 168–171, 212n56, 233n7, 234n14–15, n17–25, n28; 235n31, n34; 238
revisionist historiography 5, 48, 62
reward and punishment 226n107, 229n161
Rhodesia: Hertz tour 186
Richardson, G. H. 205n80, 207n109, 251
riding to synagogue 23
Riehm, Eduard August 62
right: vs. might 184; and wrong (*see* ethics)
right to life 100
right-wing Judaism *see* Orthodox Judaism
righteousness: chosenness and 141; defined 212n69; God's attribute 41, 95, 139; Hebraism 94–95, 109, 180; Hellenism 83; hereditary 119; in human society 121; Israel's mission 136, 169; in Jewish state 182; morality and 88; of priests 230n166; prophets on 120, 145, 173; sacrifices and 43; separatism and 166; as weapon 147
ritual: Abelson on 37; biblical critics on 19, 50–52, 54, 58–61, 159; blood libel 115; educational value 145; and halakhic change 11–12, 151; holiness and 91; laws 10, 27, 86, 143, 154, 159, 226n119; Liberal Judaism on 22, 144; murder 116; in paganism 57; pan-Babylonian theory 66; in prophetic era 4; prophets on 145–146, 277n125; purity 151, 154; Semitic life 61; systems xvi, 52
roasting vs. boiling 65
Robertson, J. M. 208n119, 251
Robinson, Edward 72, 206n106
Robinson, Ira 241
Roman Catholicism *see* Catholicism
Roman law 100, 105, 108, 115, 217n190
Rome: child killing in 130; cruelty to animals 101; Edom and 125–126, 219n10; Graetz on 176; Greek culture in 105; human sacrifice in 100; immorality in 91, 101; Noachide laws 215n149; paganism in 147
Rosenau, William 234n16

Rosenbaum, Morris 30, 31, 37, 199n78, 225n99, 230n170, 240
Rosenbaum, Semyon 221n39, 251
Rosenwald, Julius 233n7
Rosh (Asher ben Jehiel) 222n44
rosh hodesh (H) 226n108
Roth, C. 218n202, 235n30, 243, 251
Rothschild, Lord 195n75
Rowley, Henry 172
royalty 69, 150. *See also* kings
Rubashov, Zalman 192n17, n31; 253
rulers *see* kings
runaway slaves 76, 93, 107, 121
Ryle, Bishop 34

Saadyah 72
Sabbath 23, 26, 60, 88, 154, 156
Sabbatical year 131, 132, 133, 152
sacramental magic 111
sacredness *see* holiness
sacrifices, animal: biblical critics on 53; Commentary on 43–45; to emperors 105; in messianic era 10, 170, 193n35, 194n53; prophets on 145; rationalism and xvi, 36, 154–155, 158, 230n169; and religious evolution 60, 159; Smith on 209n136; terminology 67
sacrifices, human: in ancient world 100; in Christianity 115–116; of the firstborn 78, 209n135; Isaac 118, 130; Jephthah's daughter 128–129
safe-guarding the Torah *see* fence
sages *see* rabbinic sages
saintliness 179
saints: biblical 219n2; Jewish 119
sakina harifa (Ar.) 5
Salaman, Redcliffe Nathan 170, 214n121, 234n26, n28; 235n29
sale vs. gift 222n44
sales of the Commentary 34, 167–168, 233n6, n9
salt: Bible as 217n178
salvation xvi, 86, 121, 139, 178, 180
Samaritan Bible 204n54
Samuel (prophet) 158
Samuel (teacher) 94
Samuel, Wilfred 32, 33, 198n59–199n60, 199n65, 211n30, 238
sanction *see* authority
sanctity *see* holiness
sanctuary *see* Temple
Sanders, J. A. 225n99, 251
Sanhedrin 150

Index of Names and Subjects

Sarah 214n100, 219n3; Sarai 124
Sarna, Nahum 43, 201n110, 216n173, 238
Sassoon, Phillip 197n40
savagery 54, 209n135. *See also* barbarism
Sayce, Archibald Henry: on archaeology 67, 204n39, 205n81; on Canaan 69; correspondence with Hertz 58, 204n42; on Genesis 57; on W.R. Smith 77, 209n134; works cited 251
scarab: sun-god emblem 71
Schechter, Solomon: Abelson cites 37; on allegory 163–164, 232n209; on biblical criticism 27, 51, 55, 62, 87, 197n34, 202n12, 205n64; on British Jewry 1, 191n1–3; Conservative Judaism 15, 16; death 26, 28; on defamation of Judaism 19, 53, 58, 203n19; Drachman and 14, 195n74; on God 97, 213n88; on Hertz 17–18, 195n74–n75; on history 201n125; on Jewish law 52, 203n13; on mission of Seminary 14, 193n53; Montefiore and 22; on Nachmanides 156, 230n177; on need for Commentary x, 2, 27–28, 47, 197n31, n35; on Psalms 229n148; Smith and 52, 203n14; on Talmud 38; works cited 239, 251–252
schismatic groups 12, 21
scholar(s): Commentary for 171; Hertz as 4, 16–17, 178–179, 195n74; Montefiore as 24; Schechter as 203n14
scholars, Jewish: biblical interpretation 148; on Christianity 109; on dogma 171–172; in England 25, 87; on evolution 233n213; on Hebraism 81; on Hellenism 82, 87; Hertz and 46, 62; Karo on 228n145–229n145; on mysticism 12; on revelation 228n139. *See also* rabbinic sages
scholars, non-Jewish. *See* Christian scholars
scholarship: biblical 207n114; of Commentary 29, 168, 170; genres 201n125; gentile 28, 202n10; Jewish 3, 62 (see also *Wissenschaft des Judentums*); secular x, 56, 82, 174, 182, 183
Schonfeld, Jeremy 168, 234n12, 238
Schonfeld, Judith 196n6, 238
schoolchildren 100

schools: yeshivas 183. *See also* education
Schorsch, Ismar: acknowledged xiii; cited 193n42, 195n61, 201n119, n125; 245, 252; Foreword ix–xi
Schuerer, E. 202n12, 252
Schweid, E. 202n1, 252
science: and religion x, 161–164, 170, 183, 232n203, 233n213 (*see also* evolution); theology vs. 231n198
scientific atheism 208n119
scientific study of Judaism 8, 48, 202n10. *See also Wissenschaft des Judentums*
scribe, Moses as 59
scribes 8, 50, 151. *See also* Ezra
Scripture *see* Bible; biblical . . .
Second Commonwealth 5, 50, 51, 105, 128, 182, 220n17. *See also* postexilic period
second day of festivals 23
Second Exile *see* Diaspora
secular: Jewish writers 173, 235n37; learning 56, 82, 174, 182, 183; vs. sacred 177; scholars 208n119; society (*see* Western civilization)
secularization 175, 233n213
seder 22
seeing: meanings of 158
segregation *see* separatism
self-consciousness, national 140. *See also* consciousness
self-esteem, Jewish 8, 27, 46, 48, 182
self-hating Jews 1, 28, 175
self-sacrifice 94
Sellin, Ernest 41, 77, 208n133, 252
selling vs. gift 222n44
seminal emission 151–152, 229n152
Semitic: codes 67, 68, 74; culture 54, 203n22; philology (*see* philology); religion 53–55, 61, 77–79, 209n136; rulers 69
Seneca 105
sensuality 125, 180, 236n63
separatism, Jewish xvi, 146–148, 166, 177, 181, 183, 184
Sephardic scholarship 3
Septuagint 102
Sermon on the Mount 38
sermonic literature 216n173

sermons: ephemerality of 26; Hertz's 21, 23, 27, 41, 180, 196n10, 212n60, 214n109; Moses' 64; style of Commentary 168, 170–171. *See also* homiletics; preaching

Sermons, Addresses and Studies (Hertz) 41, 246; Notes to Ch. 1: 191n7, 193n39, n46–48, n50; 194n55–56, n58, n60–61; 195n62, n64–65; 196n77; Notes to Ch. 2: 196n1, n10; 197n11–12, n15, n30–33, n36–37; 200n85, n93–94, n96, n99; 201n102, n105, n121, n126; Notes to Ch. 4: 218n219, 219n235; Notes to Ch. 5: 220n22, 223n55, 230n178; Notes to Ch. 6: 235n41–43, n48, n52

serpent: Eve and 13

servants: of God 140, 141. *See also* maid servants; slaves

seven commandments 215n149

seven heathen nations 127, 130

seventh day *see* Sabbath

seventh year 131, 132, 133, 152

Seventieth Birthday Celebration (Hertz) 194n59, 195n72, 197n29, 246

seventy elders 157

sexual: immorality 93, 101, 119, 130 (*see also* adultery); mores, Christian 118; perversion 121

sha'al (H) 127

shaatnez 68

Shaddai 68

Shaftesley, J. M. 197n23, 252

Shargel, B. 210n3, n6, 252

Shechem 104

shehitah (H) 108

shekhinah (H) 226n108

Shelley, Percy Bysshe 112

Shem and Japheth 82, 210n11, 242

Shema 41, 116, 117, 177

shemitah see Sabbatical year

shield of Israel 230n177

Shimei 126

shofar 22

Shulhan Arukh see under Karo, Joseph and citation index

Sifrei 134, 240

Silbermann, A. M. 225n99, 240

Simchat Torah 151

Simeon 104

Simon ben Shetach 128, 220n17

Simon Maccabee 220n17

Simon, Maurice 226n118, 239

simplicity of: Jewish life 236n63; monotheism 4, 147. *See also* complexity

sin: of Abraham and Sarah 219n3; Azazel rite 151, 154; of biblical personalities 124, 219n2; cardinal 95; ethics vs. ritual 145; gloomy worship and 51; God and 76, 96, 97, 213n92; among Israelites 136, 141, 148; -offering 50, 209n136; original 118; sacrifices and 44, 50; suffering and 225n104. *See also* adultery; crimes

Sinai codes 216n173

Sinai desert *see* desert

Sinai, Mount: camel journey from 72; God's image 157; halakhic change 229n145; message of 137; revelation 6, 59, 75, 148, 178, 180, 228n139; talmudic tradition 6–7, 148–150, 192n19, 228n139

Singer, Simeon 23

sinners 44, 123–125, 212n49

skepticism, religious 8, 9, 39, 168

Skinner, J. 205n69, 252

slander against: Joseph 125; Judaism (*see* Judaism: attacks on)

slaughter of animals: place 150; *shehitah* 108

slaughter of humans *see* massacres

slavery: in Egypt (*see* Egyptian bondage); Greek 98, 107; Israelite 52; Joseph sold into 63–64, 104

slaves: Babylonian 90; kidnapping victims 76; runaway 76, 93, 107, 121; treatment 93, 99, 105, 106–107

Slotki, J. J. 201n114, 239

Smend, Rudolph 203n15, n30; 252

Smith, George Adam 72, 148, 206n107–207n108, 227n137–228n137, 252

Smith, J. M. Powis 227n125, 252

Smith, Morton 203n36, 253

Smith, W. Robertson: on animal forms 78, 209n136; on Christianity 52, 112; comparative anthropology 58; on cultic-ritual rites 57; heresy case 55; Hertz on 87; on Israelite law 52, 76, 203n16, 208n129; on Israelite religion 204n58, 209n135; *Lectures on the Religion of the Semites* 52, 77, 203n17, 208n131, 209n134; on Pentateuch 5, 68, 206n86; on prophets 209n137; Schechter and 53, 203n14; on Semitic religion 51, 53–54, 61,

Index of Names and Subjects 299

202n9, 203n22, 204n57; Wellhausenism 50–52, 68, 203n15; works cited 243, 253, 254
social apathy 216n177
social behavior 61, 75, 77
social context 129, 135
social factors: ethics 181; halakhah xvi, 10, 11, 143, 146, 150; Israelite religion 66, 73, 172; truth and 85
social history 75
social inequality *see* inequality of men
social order 75, 96, 98, 128, 182
Society for Jewish Jurisprudence 41, 90
Socrates 98
Sodom 92, 104, 139, 145
Solis-Cohen, J. 233n11, 234n16
Solomon 126, 127
Solomon ben Isaac *see* Rashi
Solomon ibn Adret 134
Solomon, Solomon Joseph 236n63, 253
Soloveichik, Menahem 192n17, n31; 253
Soloveitchik, J.B. 225n99, 253
son: disobedient 127, 129; respect for parents 215n145, 235n44
son of God *see under* Jesus
Soncino Press 43, 168, 234n12
Song at the Sea 158
Song of Solomon 164
sorcery 127–128, 220n17
sotah (H) 114, 127, 128, 151, 217n188, n192
soul: of biblical personalities 219n2; Christian 185; immortality 226n107; of Israel 137, 138; of mankind 140, 142; welfare of the 143. *See also* spirituality
source analysis of Bible *see* literary: source analysis
source analysis of Commentary: Greek sources 97; Jewish sources 114; modern scholarship 29; non-Jewish sources 36, 173–174, 178. *See also* citation analysis
source criticism *see* literary: source analysis
sources, Hertz's: acknowledgment 188
sources, Jewish: of Christianity 177; in Commentary 35; on evolution 160; vs. Gospels 39; on Greeks 83; Hirsch on 173; on interest 221n44; of Maimonides 153; of Sermon on the Mount 38; Wellhausen and 47
Spartans 212n49

Speiser, E. A. 202n4, 241
Spinoza, Baruch de: on Judaism 49; Montefiore and 165; on Mosaic authorship 64, 206n94; on Pentateuch 50; on religion 202n1; *Theological Tractate* 174; *Theologico-Political Treatise* 202n2, 205n73, 210n1, 253
spirit: of Amalek 147; Christian 113; divine 95; Hebraic 75, 181; human 12, 162; humanitarian 129, 214n100; Jewish 113, 116, 121, 175, 177, 223n59, 236n63; of law 228n137; of Torah 146
spiritual: crises x, 174; leaders (*see* rabbis); rebirth 175; therapy (*see* medicine: spiritual); warrior 196n2
spirituality: ancestors and 119; of children 100; Christian 20, 49, 53, 81, 85, 176–178, 181; Commentary and 29, 170, 206n98, 234n28; creation story 163, 169; Greek 83–84, 86, 235n37; of heathens 102; of Hebraism 82, 86; immortality and 152; of Jacob 124–125; of Judaism 82, 122, 137–139, 142, 202n10; law and 51, 143, 153, 228n137; laws of 59; Liberal Judaism 22, 211n27; Maimonides and 153; of mankind xvi; in messianic era 228n137; Pharisees and 202n11; prophets and 144; of rabbinic Judaism 87, 136; rationalism and 165; ritual and 52, 61; sacrifices and 44, 154; of Stoicism 99; suffering and 142; universal 209n137; war on Amalek 147; in Western civilization 111, 136, 177. *See also* soul
spoiling of the Egyptians 127, 169
spontaneous worship 4, 20, 50, 59, 60, 159
Stade, Bernhard 53
standards, ethical 135, 141, 143, 181, 215n149
state *see* government
statelessness, Jewish 181–182
stealing (theft) 106, 126; plunder 127, 169
Stoicism 99, 101, 102
stoning: Rabbinism and 152
Strack, Herman 220n17
strangers (aliens), treatment of: in the Bible 103, 108, 123, 132; in Egypt 93; interest from 127, *cont.*

strangers (aliens) *cont.*
  131–134, 221n39, n44–222n44; by Israelites/Jews 73, 91, 184; in modern law 121; Montefiore on 215n132; in Rome 106, 108; in Sodom 92. *See also* non-Jews
Strauss, Leo 202n1, 239, 247, 253
strength: of Israel 227n129
study of: Judaism (*see* scientific study of Judaism); Torah 2, 146, 218n195
style of: Commentary ix, x, 3, 29, 32, 47–48, 234n12; Friedlander 39; Montefiore 24
Suez 206n106
suffering: of criminals 103, 225n99; God of 225n95; Graetz on 176; holiness and 95; *rahmanut* and 104; of Roman slaves 105; sin and 225n104; of wandering Jews 116, 141–143; of women 151
Sulzberger, Mayer 120
sun: creation 163; -god 71
super-human: Jesus 55, 56
super-people: Israel 138
superiority of: Christian ethics 117, 147; Greek ethics 109; Jewish ethics 123, 135, 137, 165, 181; Jewish race 138; Judaism 48, 86, 136, 177, 180; Moses' prophecy 226n107; sage over prophet 226n118
supernaturalism 155–158, 230n174; revelation 59. *See also* miracles
supreme being: heathenism 213n85
survival, Jewish 148, 181
suspension of natural order 157
sycophantism: Commentary 171
syllogism, Hertz's 88, 109, 120
symbolism: of Azazel 151, 154; Jew as Evil 185; Jewish mission 136; Liberal Judaism and 22; of sacrifices 44, 154, 230n169; worship and 146
sympathy *see* compassion
synagogues: British youth 1, 23; Christianity and 85; Conservative practices 23; educational forum 140; eternal lamp in 136; Liberal/Reform Judaism 88, 211n27; shape character 181; traditional Judaism 196n10; use of Commentary 26, 27, 167–168, 184
syncretism, religious 227n132
synthesis: Hebraism and Hellenism 84, 153. *See also* merger
Syracuse, New York: Hertz in 2

Syriac Bible 204n54
Szold, Benjamin 10

Taberah: fire at 155
Tacitus 100, 214n109
Tal, U. 236n71, 253
taliation, law of 113, 217n186
Talmud: biblical critics on 47; biblical laws in 6–7, 59, 86, 151, 152; Christian attitude to 20, 38, 56; editions cited 238, 239; on God 97; Hertz praise of 145; on inheritance law 152; on interest 134, 221n44–222n44; in Jewish education 183, 184; on miracles 155–157; Montefiore on 39, 86; mysticism and 13; on pity 104; religious truth 85, 200n86; on respect for rabbis 171; revelation at Sinai 6–7, 148–149; in Rhodesia 186; on sacrifices 43; on sin 154; on universalism 102–103. *See also* Oral Law *and citation index*
Talmudic era 101, 151, 152
Tamar 150
Tanna de-vei Eliyahu 240
Tartars 158
tashlikh (H) 226n108
Taz 222n44, 238
tazkir (Syriac) 204n54
teachers: Hertz's 3–4; honoring 235n31; Jewish 122, 137, 140, 149; preachers vs. 38; rabbinic 35; role of 227n120; use of Commentary 167
tears: of woman 115, 218n198
Tel Aviv School of Economics 221n39
Tel El Amarna 70
Temkin, Sefton 195n74, 196n2, 253
Temple: Decalogue written in 207n119; lamp in 136; nonviolence 88, 100; ritual 145, 154; trial by ordeal 217n192
Temple, first *see* First Commonwealth
Temple, second *see* Second Commonwealth
Temple, third *see* messianic era
temples *see* synagogues
Ten Commandments *see* Decalogue
tendentiousness *see* bias
teraphim (H) 126
terms, Jewish 143, 226n108
teshuvah (H) 143, 226n108. *See also* repentance
"testimony of the nations" 173

Index of Names and Subjects

texts, Jewish: study of 183. *See also* sources, Jewish
textual interpretation *see* interpretation
thanksgiving: worship 50
theft *see* stealing
theism, Jewish 96, 180
theocracy: Catholicism 110; desert 50; rabbinic 50
theologians: on anti-Semitism 185; Catholic 219n2; Christian 55–57, 60, 98, 118, 172, 178, 185, 231n198; German 49, 61–62; Jewish 6, 86, 141, 227n127; Reform 137, 162. *See also* clergy; rabbis
theology: methods 231n198; pluralism 85. *See also* truth: religious
theology, biblical 23, 113, 162
theology, Christian: biblical criticism and 51–53; Commentry on 200n91; evolution and 160, 231n201; Hellenism and 40; on Jewish law 56; Liberal Judaism and 47; Montefiore on 84, 87; of Smith 207n108; Trinity 117–118
theology, comparative 38
theology, Greek 96, 97
theology, Jewish: on Chosen People 165; in Commentary 143, 171, 182; deed vs. creed 139; dissemination of 176; on Divine Will 146, 227n127; on evolution 162; on exile 142; on God 97, 138, 213n92; on halakhic change 148, 151; Hertz's teachers 3; on Hildesheimer 192n18; on immortality 152; on Jacob and Esau 124; Maimonides and 36; on miracles 156–158; Montefiore on 20–22, 84, 178, 183; mysticism and 13; non-Jewish teachers 26, 53; original virtue 118–119; Orthodoxy and 183; on rationalism 153; of Schechter 203n14
therapy *see* medicine
third temple *see* messianic era
Thompson, R. J. 203n36, 204n45, 205n60, n63, n66, n81; 207n108, 235n35, 253
Thothmes III (Pharaoh) 71
thought *see* intellect
thoughts, sinful 154
Tiberius 99
tikun see *tiqun*
time *see* dating; history
time-bound: commandments 218n195; miracles 157
Times, The 114, 115, 221n37; *Literary Supplement* 234n18
tiqun haguf / hanefesh (H) 143
title page of Commentary 33, 187–189
tohu va-bohu (H) 137
Tolemachus 114
tolerance, religious 98, 102, 130, 183, 194n53, 215n149
Tolstoy, Leo 122
tombs, Egyptian 69, 71
topography, biblical 72. *See also* geography
Torah: author (*see* Mosaic authorship); commentaries (*see* Bible commentaries); divine document 6, 150; engraved on stones 72; fundamentalist document 183; given to Israel 227n128; on immortality 226n107; Jesus and 109; laws (*see* Mosaic code); lessons by Hertz 230n177; reading 23, 27, 151; revelation of (*see under* Sinai, Mount); on reward and punishment 226n107; spiritual medicine 224n74; study 2, 146, 218n195; traditional Judaism 196n10; unwritten laws 144; values 223n62
tornado: Red Sea 158
torture 113, 114, 128
Tosephta 222n44
totalitarianism 106, 121
Tower of Babel 92
trade 116, 132–135, 152
traders (merchants) 132–133
trades (occupations) 135
tradition: and change 9, 15; reason vs. 164
traditional Judaism: Commentary defends 45; contempt for 175; definition 21, 196n10; Epstein on 25; Friedlander and 162; Hertz and 17, 55, 58, 86, 87, 174, 194n60, 197n11; Hirsch and 173; *Jewish Guardian* on 23; Liberal Judaism vs. 26, 33; Montefiore on 24; Morais and 194n53; and mysticism 13
trance: miracles 157
transcendence of law 208n125
transference of sin 154
transient heathens 222n44
transit through desert 4, 11, 69, 150, 155
Transjordania 64–65

translations of: Bible (*see* Bible translations); Commentary 133, 168
trial by ordeal 114, 127, 128, 151, 217n188, n192
trials of witches 127–128, 220n17
tribulation *see* suffering
trickery: Rebekah's 124
triennial cycle 23
Trinity 22, 117, 118
tritheism 117
triumphalism: Christian 56, 84, 175; Jewish 39, 48, 84, 156, 165, 176–177
trust *see* faith
truth: of the Bible (*see* historicity); Decalogue and 144; eternal 165; in Hellenism 82; of Judaism 29; multiple sources of 162, 183; of Potiphar's wife 70; private choice 174; religious 9, 43, 85, 161, 163, 176, 200n86; revelation and 55, 154, 164, 228n139; scientific 183; spiritual 52, 162, 178; as weapon 147
Turei Zahav (Taz) 222n44, 238
Tutankhamen 71
Twersky, I. 225n105, 253
tzeli (H) 65

Ukraine 116
ultra-Orthodox Jews 183
uncertainty: intuitive ethics 179; national life 181
Uncle Tom's Cabin 107, 216n157
understanding of: the Bible 232n212; commandments 146; Commentary by laymen 171; God 193n45; halakhah 145; miracles 157–158; virgin birth 218n212. *See also* interpretation
uniformity: of group experience 77; religious 24
Union of Jewish Literary Societies 26
Union of Orthodox Jewish Congregations of America 192n14
uniqueness of: Israel 137, 209n137; Israelite religion 58, 59, 66, 118, 209n135; Jewish ethics 123, 135, 176; miracles 157; Mosaic law 73, 77, 148
United Hebrew Congregations of the British Empire 2, 19
United States: Jewry x, 167, 194n53; Judaism 10, 192n14; Orthodox Judaism 194n53; sales of Commentary 167–168; slavery in 107; views on British chief rabbi 195n74

United Synagogue (America) 14, 194n57
United Synagogue (Great Britain) 23, 24, 39, 184
unity of: God (*see under* God); the Torah 6, 62, 65, 172
universal brotherhood 91, 93, 102, 103, 132, 139, 173, 222n44
universality of: Decalogue 207n119; God 140; interest laws 222n44; Judaism 166, 209n137; Maimonides 153; morality 91, 129, 137, 184, 225n96; righteousness 169; sacrifices 43, 155
universe: age of 161 (*see also* creation); Divine purpose 137; evolution and 231n201; laws of (*see* natural order); monotheism and 223n62
University College, London 27, 51
University of London 41, 237
University of Southampton 237
Ur 61, 71, 232n203
usurers *see* moneylenders
usury 221n37. *See also* interest

validity *see* authenticity
values: Christian 109, 136, 147; Commentary and 206n98; of Edom 126; Greek 105, 147, 181; Hebraic 95, 181; Jewish xvi, 15, 75, 82, 134, 137, 138, 166, 197n11; rabbinic 120, 145; race and 223n62; religious 85; Torah 28; Western 142, 147, 177
Velikovsky, I. 253
vengeance 76, 104, 119, 126–127, 222n49
veracity *see* historicity; truth
vice *see* evil
Victorian: features of Commentary 169; rabbis 21
viddui (H) 226n108
vindictiveness *see* vengeance
violence 88, 100, 101, 109
Virgil 105
virgin birth 56, 218n212
virginity 119
virtues: Christian 86, 95; of Esau 104; ethical 94, 123, 140, 151, 212n57; halakhah and 143, 180; of Hebraism 109, 138; of Hellenism 112; hereditary 223n59; of Isaac 139; in Jewish nation 182, 223n49; relativity of 85, 179; of women 115
visions: miracles 157
vow of Jephthah 128–129

Index of Names and Subjects

Wace, H. 203n29, 253
Waley Cohen, Robert 23, 25, 26, 197n21, 201n123
Wallace, Alfred Russel 160, 231n194, 253
wandering Jews 142
war, genocidal 220n26
warnings: biblical law 129
warriors: God and 127; spiritual 196n2
water of bitterness 217n192. *See also sotah*
Waxman, Mordecai 248, 250
weakness, human 219n2
weaning from sacrifices 155
weapons, spiritual 147
wedding ceremony 226n108
Weinfeld, M. 202n6, 253
Weiss, I. H. 220n17, 253
Welch, Adam C. 206n98, n100; 253
welfare: of body and soul 143 (*see also* medicine); religion and 180
Wellhausen, Julius: on biblical history 60, 62, 145, 172; on Christianity 5, 112, 191n8; critics 8; defamation of Judaism xv, 19, 21, 46, 53, 57–58, 174; Hertz rebuts xv, 5, 7, 9, 47, 76, 87, 151, 172; hypotheses 4–6 (*see also* Documentary Hypothesis); on Israelite religion 50–51, 61, 78, 159, 202n4–7, n10; 204n56, 209n135; on legalism 227n125; on Mosaic authorship 20, 55, 78, 203n30; refutation of 203n36; Sayce on 57; on Sinai revelation 59; Smith and 52, 61, 203n15; Spinoza and 49; works cited 49, 243, 254. *See also* Graf-Wellhausen school
Werner, A. 210n4, 219n236, 254
Western civilization: Christian impact 81, 86, 88, 112–113, 117; Esau and 125; Hellenism and 81, 106–107, 110–111, 119; Jewish impact 13, 90, 120–122, 173; lack of spirituality xvi, 136, 177; moral bankruptcy 106–109, 112, 123, 130, 166, 175, 181; paganism and 121, 142, 147, 185; romance in 115; scholarship (*see* scholarship: secular)
Western Jews 1, 174–175
widows: Jewish law 131
Wiener, Harold M. 63
wife-beating 113–114, 217n189
wife-selling 113, 114
will of God *see under* God
William of Malmesbury 93
Wilson, Woodrow 90, 120
Winckler, Hugo 54, 58, 66, 77
wisdom: in Christianity 85; of God 127, 232n201; Greek 232n202; of Jewish courts 228n145; in Judaism 86; non-Jewish sources 178; of the past 228n139; of rabbinic Judaism 174
Wisdom literature 69
Wise, Isaac Mayer 8, 162, 192n28, 251, 254
wise men *see* rabbinic sages
Wise, Stephen 233n7
Wissenschaft des Judentums: and biblical criticism 9; conservative bloc 46; in England xiii; Hirsch against 173; and Jewish history 7, 63; Jewish Theological Seminary and 48; and Mosaic authorship 6; on mysticism 12
witchcraft 127–128, 220n17
witness: Jew as 136, 140; Judaism as 217n178
wives *see* women
Wolfson, H. 202n1, 225n105, 254
women: in Judaism 41, 114–115; in rabbinic sources 151, 217n194; respect for 91; Semitic laws 68; in synagogue 23; Torah study 218n195; torture of 128. *See also agunah*; daughters; marriage; wife-beating
Wooley, C. Leonard 232n203, 254
word and flesh 20
word of God *see under* God
work *see* labor
world *see* earth (planet); universe
world history *see* history, world
world literature 183
world religions 176, 177
World War II 16. *See also* Holocaust
worlds, former 161
worship: centralized 60–61, 204n54; direct vs. mediated 118; houses of (*see* synagogues); joy of 50; language of 23; pagan 148; Roman Catholic 111; sacrifices and 43; sin and 51; spontaneous 4, 20, 50, 59, 60, 159. *See also* idolatry; prayer; ritual
Wright, A.R. 114
written law *see* Torah

xenophobia 106, 108. *See also* strangers

Yahuda, Abraham Solomon 68, 206n90, 254
Yalkut Shimeoni 240
yeshalem gemulo (H) 222n44
yeshivas 183
Yeshurun (Israel) 139
yetzer tov/ra (H) 226n108
youth: Anglo-Jewish 1, 23, 82; ethical models for 219n2; Jewish 140
Ysiraal 70

Zangwill, Israel 136, 164, 219n234, 223n52–53, 232n210, 236n66, 254
zekhut avot (H) 119
zemirot (H) 226n108
Zemplinska Siroka 2
Zion, love of 88
Zionism 40
Zionist Record 234n23
Zohar 83, 153, 230n175, 240
Zoroastrianism 177
Zunz, Leopold 9, 41, 62, 194n61, 202n10, 212n60, 254